A
DICKENS
GLOSSARY

GARLAND REFERENCE LIBRARY
OF THE HUMANITIES
(Vol. 1210)

A
DICKENS
GLOSSARY

by
Fred Levit

GARLAND PUBLISHING, INC. • NEW YORK & LONDON
1990

Library of Congress Cataloging-in-Publication Data

Levit, Fred.
   A Dickens glossary / by Fred Levit.
      p. cm. — (Garland reference library of the humanities; vol.
   1210)
      ISBN 0-8240-5542-X (alk. paper)
      1. Dickens, Charles, 1812–1870—Language—Glossaries, etc.
   2. Dickens, Charles, 1812–1870—Quotations. 3. English
   language—19th century—Glossaries, vocabularies, etc. I. Title.
   II. Series.
   PR4595.L4 1990
   823'.8—dc20   89-36390
                                                                        CIP

Printed on acid-free, 250-year-life paper
Manufactured in the United States of America

CONTENTS

ACKNOWLEDGMENTS

It would be impossible to list all the people who provided help, in many different ways, to me in completing this project. They range from friends who were simply encouraging to the many anonymous librarians in half a dozen different libraries who suffered in dragging innumerable dusty volumes up from the stacks. Thanks must go, however, to Dr. David Parker of the *Dickens House Museum* in London who ferreted out meanings of some of the most arcane words and who lowered my anxiety level by being able to find some that I had been unable to find. And special thanks to Joan Spiegler who did a professional job that consisted of far more than proofreading.

INTRODUCTION

It is more than one hundred and fifty years since Charles Dickens wrote his first novel. In that time the English language has changed, both for Britons and for Americans. Some of the words and phrases that Dickens wrote are gone from the daily language, others were used by him with meanings that are no longer used, and some are Briticisms and not recognizable by a reader in the United States. Changing technology, which has left behind the candles, oil lamps, stagecoaches, coal fireplaces, and gas light of the nineteenth century has also left behind the large vocabulary associated with those things. To simply disregard those words and phrases leaves the reader with a lesser understanding, appreciation, and enjoyment of Dickens' works.

This glossary was designed to be used in two different ways. It can be used as a dictionary, looking up words and phrases as they are encountered. The advantage of having them in a compact source, as compared to having to seek them out in a large dictionary, is obvious. Many of them are not to be found in easily available sources and the ordinary reader would not be likely to undertake the task of discovering them.

The glossary can also be read for enjoyment. Many of the quotations are long enough to give the flavor of Dickens' writing, as well as showing the way that the words were used. The variety of meanings, and the often surprising difference between the current meanings and the nineteenth-century meanings can be a source of interest and pleasure. Puns and jokes otherwise not apparent can be discovered when the older meanings of the words used are explained.

Most of the entries in the glossary are from the novels, which are probably the most frequently read of Dickens' writings. Others come from the sketches and Christmas novels and stories. The source of each quotation is given. The selection of what to include is of necessity personal. I tried to include those words and phrases that I thought a United States college freshman might not be expected to know, but that criterion does not provide anything near a clear-cut and simple method of selection. I also tried to include anything that I thought a general reader might find interesting; an equally vague criterion. They had to serve.

Johnson wrote, in 1784, "Dictionaries are like watches, the worst is better than none, and the best cannot be expected to go quite true." Since that time watches have certainly improved, and I hope that dictionaries have too.

A
DICKENS
GLOSSARY

abate *[He] hurried away to tell Mrs. Crummles that he had quite settled the only terms that could be accepted, and had resolved not to abate one single farthing.* {Nicholas Nickleby 30}
Diminish, reduce.

abear *And all's fish that comes to my net. And I can't abear to part with anything I once lay hold of . . .* {Bleak House 5}
Endure, suffer (archaic).

a-bed *Early as it was . . . the room in which he lay a-bed was already scrubbed throughout . . .* {Tale of Two Cities 2-1}
In bed.

Abernethy biscuit *. . . a cold collation of an Abernethy biscuit and a saveloy.* {Pickwick Papers 55}
A thin, hard, dry bread.

abroad *"Here!" cried Nicholas, staggering to his feet, "I'm ready. I'm only a little abroad, that's all."* {Nicholas Nickleby 6}
Out or astray, in the sense of being confused.

absence, on absence *He was on absence from India, where he had a post that was soon to grow into a very good one.* {Little Dorrit 2-21}
Away from, absent from. The implication is a permitted absence from a job, a leave of absence.

acceptance, stamped acceptances *The mention of this latter justly celebrated clown reminds us of his last piece of humour, the fraudulently obtaining of certain stamped acceptances from a young gentleman in the army.* {The Pantomime of Life}
A bill or note which a person has formally accepted the responsibility to

pay. The tax on such transactions was paid by affixing a tax-stamp to the document.

accordant *All correct there. Everything accordant there.* {Hard Times 1-12}
Agreeing, conforming.

accoucheur *As to me, I think my sister must have had some general idea that I was a young offender whom an accoucheur policeman had taken up (on my birthday) and delivered over to her, to be dealt with according to the outraged majesty of the law.* {Great Expectations 4}
One who assists a woman in childbirth.

acidulated drop *No, I can't kiss you, because I've got an acidulated drop in my mouth.* {Edwin Drood 3}
A sour drop, a kind of sour-tasting hard candy.

acquirements ... *to any person who had ever been in Mr. Pecksniff's neighborhood, Mr. Thomas Pinch and his acquirements were as well known as the Church steeple* ... {Martin Chuzzlewit 39}
Personal attainments of body or mind, as distinguished from material things.

action for Doe *If he attempted [to remain here] there would be an eject-ment, an action for Doe, and all sorts of things; and then he* must go. {Dombey & Son 59}
A legal proceeding using the fictitious name of Doe because the name of the person involved is not known.

adamant *More obdurate than gate of adamant or brass, this gate of Miss Monflather's frowned on all mankind.* {Old Curiosity Shop 31}
A mythical stone of surpassing hardness.

Adamite, pre-Adamite ... *like rotten pre-Adamite cheeses cut into fantas-tic shapes and full of mites* ... {Little Dorrit 2-6}
Adamite refers to the time when Adam lived, hence pre-Adamite refers to the time before the time of Adam.

adder . . . *Ralph was deaf as an adder.* {Nicholas Nickleby 47}
In classical writings one kind of poisonous snake was referred to as
the deaf adder. There is no evidence that such snakes were really deaf.

addle-pated *He gets more addle-pated every day he lives, I do believe . . .*
{Martin Chuzzlewit 18}
Mentally muddled or confused. The word 'addle' first referred to
liquid filth, then to something decomposed, especially a rotten egg, and
finally came to mean 'muddled'. 'Pate' means head or skull.

address *The Marchioness . . . began to work away at the concoction of*
some cooling drink, with the address of a score of chemists. {Old
Curiosity Shop 64}
He is a mere boor, a log, a brute, with no address in life. {Barnaby
Rudge 15}
To direct one's skills or energies to some work or object.

administer . . . *the creditors have administered, you tell me, and there's*
nothing left for you? {Nicholas Nickleby 3}
To manage and dispose of the estate of a deceased person.

admit . . . *short black hair, shaved off nearly to the crown of his head--to*
admit . . . of his more easily wearing character wigs of any shape or
pattern. {Nicholas Nickleby 22}
To allow.

advert *In freedom's name, sir, I advert with indignation and disgust to that*
accursed animal, with gore-stained whiskers . . . {Martin Chuzzlewit 21}
To pay attention to, take notice of.

advise with . . . *I really don't see what is to be done, or what good crea-*
ture I can advise with. {Dombey & Son 26}
To consult with.

affect . . . *it was Squeer's custom to drive over to the market town every*
evening, on pretence of urgent business, and stop till ten or eleven
o'clock at a tavern he much affected. {Nicholas Nickleby 9}
1. Have a liking for, be fond of.
She affects not to know that his eyes are fastened on her . . . {Our Mutual

Friend 1-10}
2. To pretend, to counterfeit.

affidavit *"With respect to bodily fear," said Mr. Perch, "I'm so timid myself, by nature, sir, and my nerves is so unstrung by Mrs. Perch's state, that I could take my affidavit easy."* {Dombey & Son 22}
... the darling has lived with me, and paid me for it; which she certainly should never have done, you may take your affidavit, if I could have afforded to keep either myself or her for nothing... {Tale of Two Cities 2-6}
A statement in writing sworn to by the maker. In the first example it refers to swearing an affidavit to have young Mr. Biler arrested. In the second, it is used in the sense of 'you can bet your bottom dollar' or 'you can bet your life'.

advocate *... to be an advocate and wear a wig...* {David Copperfield 17}
A kind of lawyer, one who pleads in a court. The title is still used in some parts of the United Kingdom.

after-life *He will make what powerful friends he pleases in after-life, when he is actively maintaining ... the dignity and credit of the firm.* {Dombey & Son 5}
Later in life. It does not mean after death.

ague *"Perhaps a little damp and ague-ish?" said Quilp. "Just damp enough to be cheerful, sir," rejoined Brass.* {Old Curiosity Shop 51}
An acute fever, or the chills of an illness that produces chills and fever.

air *... an air with variations on the guitar, by Miss Tippin...* {Sketches, The Tuggs's at Ramsgate}
A tune or melody.

airy bell *... and in the left-hand corner were the words 'airy bell,' as an instruction to the bearer...* {Pickwick Papers 37}
Area bell (see **area**). Because Sam Weller's letter was addressed to a servant he specified that the area bell, which rang in the kitchen, should be used when delivering the letter, rather than the front doorbell.

ait *Fog up the river, where it flows among green aits and meadows; fog down the river, where it rolls defiled among the tiers of shipping and the waterside pollution of a great (and dirty) city.* {Bleak House 1}
An islet, or small island, especially one in a river.

a-kimbo *... he stood with one arm a-kimbo ...* {David Copperfield 5}
Hands on hips, elbows out.

alamode *... a famous alamode beef-house ...* {David Copperfield 11}
Fashionable.

alarum *He had been running down by jerks, during his last speech, like a sort of ill-adjusted alarum.* {Little Dorrit 2-5}
An alarm clock.

Alderney *She didn't give any milk, ma'am; she gave bruises. She was a regular Alderney at that.* {Hard Times 2-10}
A variety of milk cow which includes both Jersey and Guernsey cows. The breeds are named after the Channel islands, in the English Channel off the coast of France, from which they come.

alehouse *... Mr. Anthony Chuzzlewit and his son Jonas were economically quartered at the Half Moon and Seven Stars, which was an obscure alehouse ...* {Martin Chuzzlewit 4}
Ale and beer were the least expensive alcoholic beverages commonly drunk and they were served in an alehouse, or tavern. A country tavern would also provide meals and lodging.

all along of *"I never had such luck, really," exclaimed coquettish Miss Price, after another hand or two. "It's all along of you, Mr. Nickleby, I think."* {Nicholas Nickleby 9}
Owing to, on account of.

All England *... he always fought All England ...* {Hard Times 1-2}
English uniform rules for boxing. The implication is also that of fighting fairly.

all-fours *Chegg's wife plays cribbage; all-fours likewise.* {Old Curiosity Shop 58}
A card game for two, dealt six cards each with one card turned up as trump. So-called because there are four ways to win.

all on you *That's right--now pull all on you!* {Sketches, The River}
All of you.

all-overs *But we're out of sorts for want of a smoke. We've got the all-overs, haven't us, deary?* {Edwin Drood 23}
Sick all over the entire body.

allowanced ... *you have had as much as you can eat, you're asked if you want any more, and you answer, "no!" Then don't you ever go and say you were allowanced, mind that.* {Old Curiosity Shop 36}
One meaning of allowance is 'a limited portion of food.' Hence the sense of allowanced here is 'allowed an insufficient amount of food'.

allow for keep *She eats a deal. It would be better to allow her for her keep.* {Bleak House 21}
Give an allowance in money instead of providing meals.

ally tor ... *his infant sports are disregarded when his mother weeps; his 'ally tors' and his 'commoneys' are alike neglected, he forgets the long-familiar cry of 'knuckle down'* ...
Ally, a marble, used in the game of marbles but probably originally made of alabaster (ally-baster). Taw, a special or choice marble. An ally taw is a choice marble made of real marble or of alabaster.

almac's, Almacks *One might suppose I was moving in the fashionable circles and getting myself up for almac's* ... {Bleak House 56}
Being located in the immediate neighborhood of your Parks, your Drives, your Triumphant Arches, your Opera, and your Royal Almacks ... {Martin Chuzzlewit 21}
A well-known Assembly Room in London, patronized by fashionable London society.

alms-house ... *we came to the poor person's house, which was part of some alms-houses, as I knew by their look, and by an inscription on a*

stone over the gate . . . {David Copperfield 5}
A privately funded poorhouse, as opposed to the publicly funded workhouse.

along of (see **all along of**)

amain . . . *the major part of the company inclined to the belief that virtue went out with hair-powder, and that old England's greatness had decayed amain with barbers.* {Martin Chuzzlewit 9}
At full speed, without delay.

ambuscade . . . *I shall have the sense to keep the household brigade in ambuscade and not to manoeuvre it on your ground.* {Bleak House 43}
Ambush, concealed and waiting.

anatomise . . *give me the name of any man, American born and bred, who has anatomised our follies as a people* . . . {Martin Chuzzlewit 16}
To dissect.

anatomy *Do you know that it's a hanging matter--and I an't quite certain whether it an't an anatomy one besides* . . . {Nicholas Nickleby 38}
The body of an executed criminal could be used for dissection and the preparation of anatomical specimens, called anatomies. This was considered a worse punishment than simple hanging.

anchorite . . . *notwithstanding her anchorite turn of mind* . . . *she resigned herself with noble fortitude to lodging, as one may say, in clover, and feeding on the fat of the land.* {Hard Times 2-10}
A hermit or recluse.

ancle . . . *and wore little white trousers with frills round the ancles* . . .
{Nicholas Nickleby 14}
Ankle.

aniseed . . . *the stock of wine smelt much stronger than it ever tasted, and so did the stock of rum and brandy and aniseed.* {Tale of Two Cities 2-16}
Seeds of the anise plant, used as a medication and as a flavoring.

ankle-jacks . . . *he changed shoes and put on an unparalleled pair of ankle-jacks, which he only wore on extraordinary occasions.* {Dombey & Son 15}
A kind of boot reaching just above the ankles.

annual *Mr. Blank exhibited a model of a fashionable annual, composed of copper-plates, gold leaf, and silk boards, and worked entirely by milk and water.* {Sketches, Full Report of the Second Meeting of the Mudfog Association}
At the time of the *Mudfog Papers* a number of annuals (books published only once in the year) were brought out. Many had little content and depended for their sales on copper-plate illustrations, gold-leaf edges on the pages, and silk-covered bindings. In the phrase 'worked by milk and water' Dickens both alludes to the insipid contents of these annuals and also imagines them to be a scientific gadget powered by milk and water.

anon . . . *and ever and anon the captain's voice was heard above the crowd--"There's more below; there's more below."* {Martin Chuzzlewit 22}
Anon by itself means immediately, quickly. The phrase 'ever and anon' means continually at intervals.

answer . . . *attired in a suit of thread-bare black, with darned cotton stockings of the same colour, and shoes to answer.* {Oliver Twist 4}
To suit a purpose, to suit.

ante-room . . . *the old gentleman walked . . . into a back ante-room opening from the yard . . .* {Oliver Twist 11}
A room forming the entrance to another room.

antimonial *"Oh, it's sickening," replied the beadle. "Antimonial, Mr. Sowerberry!"* {Oliver Twist 5}
A medication containing antimony, used as an emetic to cause vomiting. The meaning here is 'nauseating'.

apace *Morning drew on apace.* {Oliver Twist 28}
Quickly, swiftly.

apoplexy, apoplectic ... *listen attentively for symptoms of an apoplectic nature, with which the patient might be troubled...* {Martin Chuzzlewit 10}
Apoplexy is a stroke (the illness).

apostrophize *"Oh!" said the old lady, apostrophizing him with infinite vehemence. "I could bite you!"* {Bleak House 14}
To stop suddenly in speaking and turn to address some person in an exclamatory way.

apothecary *There was a certain calm apothecary, who attended at the establishment when any of the young gentlemen were ill...* {Dombey & Son 14}
Druggist or pharmacist.

appanage ... *on the other side of the gateway the Verger's hole in the wall was an appanage or subsidiary part.* {Edwin Drood 18}
Originally a property set aside to support the sons of royalty, a dependent property. Hence something dependent or secondary in worth.

appearance *I judged him about my own age, but he was much taller, and he had a way of spinning himself about that was full of appearance.* {Great Expectations 11}
The action of appearing conspicuously, making a show or parade.

appoint *"... Where's my sister?" "Gone, Miss Pecksniff," Mrs. Todgers answered. "She had appointed to be home."* {Martin Chuzzlewit 37}
To determine or resolve or make up one's mind.

approver *Mr. Noah Claypole: receiving a free pardon from the Crown in consequence of being admitted approver against the Jew...* {Oliver Twist 53}
Someone who turns state's evidence, confesses his crime, and testifies against his confederates.

apron ... *Bently Drummle, at that time floundering about town in a cab of his own, and doing a great deal of damage to the posts at street corners.... Occasionally, he shot himself out of his equipage head-foremost over the apron, and I saw him on one occasion deliver himself at the*

door of the Grove in this unintentional way--like coals. {Great Expectations 34}
A leather or canvas cover placed over the legs and lap of the passenger. In some one-horse vehicles it could be a part of the carriage front, with a half-door in it for passengers to enter or leave.

arbour ... *each [cabin] in its little patch of ground had a rude seat or arbour.* {Barnaby Rudge 44}
A seat surrounded and covered by trees and shrubs or by plants growing on a trellis.

Arcadian *You know I am a sordid piece of human nature, ready to sell myself at any time for any reasonable sum, and altogether incapable of any Arcadian proceeding whatever.* {Hard Times 2-7}
Ideally rural or rustic, simple, unaffected.

arcana ... *you might have some difficulty in penetrating the arcana of the Modern Babylon* ... {David Copperfield 11}
Things hidden, concealed, or secret.

ardent spirits *"... My spirits is ready for 'em." "Do you mean animal spirits, or ardent?"* {Edwin Drood 12}
Volatile, inflammable fluids like alcohol.

area *The Dodger had a vicious propensity, too, of pulling the caps from the heads of small boys and tossing them down areas* ... {Oliver Twist 10}
A small court, several steps below street level, into which opens the kitchen or basement door of a dwelling.

area cellar *This cell was in shape and size, something like an area cellar, only not so light.* {Oliver Twist 11}
A cellar, usually alongside the area (see **area**) but extending below it, with one or more half-windows opening into the area.

area-door ... *a piece of fat black water-pipe which trailed itself over the area-door into a damp stone passage* ... {Our Mutual Friend 1-5}
The basement door, or kitchen door, leading in from the area (see **area**).

area-gate ... *and Protestants are very fond of spoons, I find, and silver-plate in general, whenever area-gates is left open accidentally.* {Barnaby Rudge 35}
The gate in an area-railing (see **area** and **area-railing**).

area-head ... *and lighting the fire below the little copper, prepared ... for his daily occupation; which was to retail at the area-head above penny-worths of broth and soup, and savoury puddings* ... {Barnaby Rudge 8}
The part of the area (see **area**) next to the area gate.

area-railing *One of the young Jellybys been and got his head through the area railings!* {Bleak House 4}
The railing fence surrounding the area (see **area**).

area-steps ... *the kitchen had a separate entrance down the area steps.* {Nicholas Nickleby 36}
The steps leading down into the area (see **area**).

arm-chest ... *the guard of the Dover mail ... keeping an eye and a hand on the arm-chest before him, where a loaded blunderbuss lay at the top of six or eight loaded horse-pistols, deposited on a substratum of cutlass.* {Tale of Two Cities 1-2}
Weapons chest.

arrow-root ... *and calves'-foot jelly, and arrow-root, and sago, and other delicate restoratives* ... {Old Curiosity Shop 66}
A starchy food made from tubers of the arrowroot plant.

articled time ... *when your articled time is over, you'll be a regular lawyer.* {David Copperfield 16}
The duration of an apprenticeship contract.

articles ... *he improved himself, for three or five years, according to his articles, in making elevations of Salisbury Cathedral from every possible point of sight* ... {Martin Chuzzlewit 2}
Apprenticeship agreement or contract.

askant *. . . the Cloisterham police meanwhile looking askant from their beats with suspicion ; . . .* {Edwin Drood 19}
Askance, sideways, with a side glance.

asperse *. . . he asperses his father's memory to his mother!* {Little Dorrit 1-5}
To make false and injurious charges.

assembly *The appearance of Mr. Horatio Sparkins at the assembly had excited no small degree of surprise and curiosity among its regular frequenters.* {Sketches, Horatio Sparkins}
Away from the cities, where social visits were difficult, it was the custom for groups of polite people to meet at a centrally located hall to eat, play cards, dance, and socialize.

assign *Scrooge was his sole executor, his sole administrator, his sole assign, his sole residuary legatee, his sole friend and sole mourner.* {A Christmas Carol 1}
Assignee, one to whom property is transferred. Scrooge inherited all that Marley left when he died.

assizes *A most extraordinary case . . . was tried at the last Maryborough assizes in Ireland.* {Our Mutual Friend 3-6}
The sessions of county courts, held periodically.

assize time *. . . that was generally at assize time, when much business had made them sentimental . . .* {The Battle of Life 2}
The time when the criminal and civil court was in session in the county.

assort *Never can there come fog too thick, never can there come mud and mire too deep, to assort with the groping and floundering condition which this High Court of Chancery, most pestilent of hoary sinners, holds this day in the sight of heaven and earth.* {Bleak House 1}
To place in the same group or class.

assume *She should be an upper servant by her attire, yet in her air and step, though both are hurried and assumed--as far as she can assume*

in the muddy streets, which she treads with an unaccustomed foot--she is a lady. {Bleak House 16}
Take in pretense, pretend. Here the sense is that of a disguise.

Astley's (see **circle at Astley's**)

astrand *There were some boats and barges astrand in the mud . . .* {David Copperfield 47}
Stranded, beached, aground.

astray *Light of head with want of sleep and want of food . . . he had been two or three times conscious, in the night, of going astray.* {Little Dorrit 2-29}
Wandering, in the sense of wandering mentally, being out of one's head.

a-tauto (see **tauto**)

Athol brose *. . . the Highland Inns, with the oatmeal bannocks, the honey, the venison steaks, the trout from the loch, the whiskey, and perhaps (having the materials so temptingly at hand) the Athol brose.* {The Holly-Tree 1}
A mixture of whiskey and honey. Brose by itself is a dish made by pouring boiling water or milk on oatmeal.

atomies *Hunger was shred into atomies in every farthing porringer of husky chips of potato, fried with some reluctant drops of oil.* {Tale of Two Cities 1-5}
1. Tiny fragments, atoms.
. . . the contents of his plate chest, consisting of two withered atomies of teaspoons, and an obsolete pair of knock-kneed sugar tongs . . . {Dombey & Son 9}
2. Emaciated persons, walking skeletons.

a-top *. . . he was covered in a-top, like an old building . . .* {David Copperfield 23}
On top.

attend *"Look here," said Fledgeby.--"Are you attending?"* {Our Mutual Friend 4-8}
Paying attention, paying heed.

attraction *As a mark of respect for the lightening, Mrs. Lupin had removed her candle to the chimney-piece. . . . her supper, spread on a round table not far off, was untasted; and the knives had been removed for fear of attraction.* {Martin Chuzzlewit 43}
Referring here to the superstition that metal knives attract lightning.

auditory *A portion of Scripture was being read when I went in. It was followed by a discourse, to which the congregation listened with most exemplary attention . . . . My own attention comprehended both the auditory and the speaker . . .* {The Uncommercial Traveller, Two Views of a Cheap Theatre}
Audience.

automaton *. . . Mrs. Podsnap . . . looked in at the music-shop to bespeak a well conducted automaton to come and play quadrilles for a carpet dance.* {Our Mutual Friend 1-11}
A person who acts automatically in a monotonous routine.

awfully *There was no change upon his face; and as she watched it, awfully, its motionless repose recalled the faces that were gone.* {Dombey & Son 43}
With reverential fear, reverently and timidly.

axle-tree *. . . sitting himself quietly down on an old axle-tree, began to contemplate the mail-coaches with a deal of gravity.* {Pickwick Papers 49}
The axle of a wheeled vehicle.

Baboo . . . *according to a wild legend in our family, he was once seen riding on an elephant, in company with a baboon; but I think it must have been a Baboo--or a Begum.* {David Copperfield 1}
A Hindu title meaning Mister.

baby-house *She was quite satisfied that a good deal was effected by this make-belief of housekeeping; and was as merry as if we had been keeping a baby-house, for a joke.*
Baby is used here as a diminutive, hence a small house or toy house.

Babylonian . . . *a cocked hat and a Babylonian collar.* {Dombey & Son 5}
Huge, gigantic.

back-attic *The back-attic . . . is coming down-stairs fast, and will be below the basement very soon* {The Chimes 4}
The room in the back of an attic. Here it refers to the person renting that room.

back-comb . . . *ladies would be seen flocking from all quarters universally twisting their back-hair as they came along, and . . . carrying their back-combs in their mouths.* {Our Mutual Friend 2-12}
Small decorative combs worn in the hair at the back of the head.

backer *"Thank'ee mum," said Mr. Toodle. "Yes, I'll take my bit of backer."* {Dombey & Son 38}
Dialect for tobacco.

back-fall . . . *he will throw him an argumentative back-fall presently if he be not already down.* {Bleak House 25}
A throw or fall in wrestling.

back-parlour ... *people will flatten their noses against the front windows of a chemist's shop when a drunken man who has been run over by a dog-cart in the street is undergoing a surgical inspection in the back-parlour.* {Pickwick Papers 25}
Homes often had two living rooms called parlors. The larger and usually fancier one at the front was used to entertain guests, while the smaller one at the back of the house or apartment was used by the family. A place of business was also often a home, with the family living in the back rooms while the place of business replaced the front parlor.

back-shop ... *and the lads were left to their beds; which were under a counter in the back-shop.* {A Christmas Carol 2}
Rooms in the back part of a shop or business which the public did not usually enter. These served as storerooms, offices, and homes for apprentices.

badged ... *his son... [was] huffed and cuffed, and flogged and badged, and taught as parrots are, by a brute jobbed into his place of schoolmaster with as much fitness for it as a hound...* {Dombey & Son 20}
Required to wear a badge, as was done to the poor, beggars, and charity-school children, so that they could be readily identified.

badger-drawing ... *a good many young lords went to see cockfighting, and badger-drawing...* {Oliver Twist 31}
A cruel sport in which a badger was put into a barrel and then dogs were set on it to drag it out and kill it.

badinage ... *in the course of a little lively* badinage *on the subject of ladies' dresses, he had evinced as much knowledge as if he had been born and bred a milliner.* {Sketches, The Young Ladies Young Gentleman}
Humorous banter, amusing small talk.

bagatelle-board ... *such amusements as the Peacock afforded, which were limited to a bagatelle-board in the first floor...* {Pickwick Papers 14}
A table with a rounded end containing nine holes, into which balls were sent using a billiard cue. The game is called bagatelle.

bagman *Comprising a brief description of the company at the Peacock assembled, and a tale told by a bagman.* {Pickwick Papers 14}
A traveling salesman or commercial traveler so-called because he carried his samples in very large saddlebags.

bag wig ... *it was the chief part of his duty to wear silk stockings, and a bag wig like a black watch-pocket* ... {Nicholas Nickleby 33}
A wig with a silk bag covering the back hair (one of many styles which came and went as fashions changed).

bail ... *a neighboring magistrate was readily induced to take the joint bail of Mrs. Maylie and Mr. Losberne for Oliver's appearance* ... {Oliver Twist 31}
Guarantee, not necessarily money, for the appearance of a prisoner in court.

bait ... *they stopped to bait the horse, and ate and drank.* {David Copperfield 9}
To cause an animal to bite for its own refreshment, to feed.

baiting-place *Little clusters of such vehicles were gathered round the stable-yard or baiting-place of every wayside tavern* ... {Martin Chuzzlewit 42}
A place where horses were fed.

baize ... *baize of whitened-green mouldering from the pew sides and leaving the naked wood to view.* {Old Curiosity Shop 17}
A coarse woolen material. When made finer, it was once also used for clothing.

baked jemmy (see **jemmy**)

baked-potato man ... *the principal specimens of animated nature, the pot-boy, the muffin youth, and the baked-potato man.* {Pickwick Papers 32}
Street vendor of baked potatoes.

ball ... *and a case of satisfactory pistols, with the satisfactory accompaniments of powder, ball, and caps* ... {Pickwick Papers 2}
Originally a spherical lead bullet, then a firearm projectile of any shape.

ballast-heaver . . . *among labourers and hammerers and ballast-heavers* . . . {Our Mutual Friend 1-3}
A workman who shoveled ballast, the crushed stone used as ballast in ships and also used between the ties and rails of a railroad bed.

ball-cartridge *But--but--suppose some of the men should happen to have ball-cartridges by mistake* . . . {Pickwick Papers 4}
A cartridge containing both powder and a ball or bullet. When used for demonstrations, firearms would be loaded with powder only, for safety's sake.

ball of St. Paul's *I wonder whether she ever insisted on people's retiring into the ball of St. Paul's* . . . {Our Mutual Friend 3-16}
St. Paul's Cathedral in London has a lantern on top of the dome and above that there is a ball. Above the ball there is a cross. It is actually possible to climb into the ball from inside the cathedral.

ball practice *If a train of heavy artillery could have come up and commenced ball practice outside the window, it would have been all the same to him.* {Barnaby Rudge 55}
Practice firing of the weapons, using cannon balls instead of only a powder charge.

balmy . . . *who, during the short remainder of my existence, will murder the balmy.* {Old Curiosity Shop 56}
Slang for sleep, from balmy sleep.

balsam . . . *bringing her thoughts as well as her sight to bear upon the candle-grease, and becoming abruptly reminiscent of its healing qualities as a balsam, she anointed her left elbow with a plentiful application of that remedy.* {The Battle of Life 2}
An aromatic medication for external use, originally made from plant resins.

Banbury cake *I must make myself flaky and sick with Banbury cake* . . . {The Uncommercial Traveller, Refreshments for Travellers}
A kind of cake named after the town of Banbury in Oxfordshire, England.

band ... *appearing to stab herself in the band with a pin* ...   {Edwin Drood 9}
A strip of material which could be at the waist, wrists, or neck of a dress.

band-box or **bandbox** *With these magnificent portraits, unworthily confined to a band-box during his seclusion among the market-gardens, he decorates his apartment* ... {Bleak House 20}
A light cardboard box for collars, caps, and hats. Originally made for the 'bands', or ruffs, worn in the seventeenth century.

Bandoline ... *it's the room where Our Missis and our young ladies Bandolines their hair.* {Mugby Junction 3}
A gummy material made from boiled quince seeds, used as a hair dressing.

bands *The litter of rags* ... *might have been counsellors' bands and gowns torn up.* {Bleak House 5}
A pair of strips, extending down from the collar and forming part of conventional legal dress.

bankers-book ... *and having read all the newspapers, and beguiled the rest of the evening with his bankers-book, went home to bed.* {A Christmas Carol 1}
Bankbook.

bank-note *Your bank-notes had a musty odour, as if they were fast decomposing into rags again.* {Tale of Two Cities 2-1}
Paper money issued by a bank. Technically, a promissory note issued by a bank and payable to the bearer on demand.

bannocks ... *Highland Inns, with the oatmeal bannocks, the honey, the venison steaks* ... {The Holly Tree}
A kind of homemade bread.

banns *I conceived the idea that the time when the banns were read and when the clergyman said, "Ye are now to declare it!" would be the time*

for me to rise and propose a private conference in the vestry. {Great
Expectations 4}
The proclamation of an intended marriage announced in church.

banshee ... *rattling his feet upon the glass like a Banshee upside down.*
{Old Curiosity Shop 67}
An Irish ghost, said to wail under the window of a house in which some-
one will die.

bar (of a carriage) ... *and taking his seat upon the bar, contented himself
with tapping at the front windows of the carriage, and trying to steal a
glance inside* ... {Barnaby Rudge 59}
This probably refers to the pole to which the horses are attached and
which projects forward from the front axle.

Bard of A 1 ... *Inquiry of Miss Martin yielded (in the language of the
Bard of A 1) "confirmation strong."* {Somebody's Luggage 1}
In the dialect of the speaker, the word 'one' was pronounced 'vun',
hence the Bard of Avon, or Shakespeare.

bargeman *He informed me that his father was a bargeman, and
walked, in a black velvet head-dress, in the Lord Mayor's Show.*
{David Copperfield 11}
Man in charge of a barge, or one of the rowers of a barge. A barge
could be anything from an ornamented and luxurious boat for royalty to
a boat with or without sails for carrying freight, or even a rowboat.

bark *I have been prescribed bark, but I don't take it for I don't wish to
have any tone whatever given to my constitution.* {Dombey & Son 48}
1. The pulverized bark of the Cinchona tree taken as a medication. It
contains quinine, used to treat malaria and other febrile illnesses.
[Dora] was the stay and anchor of my tempest-driven bark. {David
Copperfield 38}
2. A kind of large sailing ship.

barker ... *Barney, opening a cupboard, brought forth several articles,
which he hastily crammed into the pockets. "Barkers for me,
Barney," said Toby Crackit.* {Oliver Twist 22}
Slang for pistol.

barley-sugar temple *Fowls, tongues, preserves, fruits, confectioneries, jellies, neguses, barley-sugar temples, trifles, crackers--eat all you can and pocket what you like* ... {The Schoolboy's Story}
Barley-sugar is a candy made from sugar boiled in barley-water. It was formed into twisted sticks which resembled the columns of a Greek temple.

barley-water *In gruel, barley-water, apple-tea, mutton-broth, and that, it don't signify.* {Martin Chuzzlewit 49}
A drink made by boiling barley in water and often served to invalids.

barouche ... *and all the other children got up behind the barouche and fell off, and we saw them, with great concern, scattered over the surface of Thavies Inn as we rolled out of its precincts.* {Bleak House 5}
A four-wheeled carriage with a half-top which could be raised or lowered, and with seats inside for two couples facing one another and a seat in front for the driver.

barrel-organ ... *my children may be reduced to seek a livelihood by personal contortion, while Mrs. Micawber abets their unnatural feats, by playing the barrel-organ.* {David Copperfield 49}
A kind of mechanical organ in which the keys are activated by pins sticking out of a revolving cylinder (the barrel). It was played by revolving the barrel with a crank. Of boxlike construction, it had two wheels and a pair of handles by which it was pushed from place to place. Most often used by street entertainers it could accompany other performers or be played solo.

barring-out ... *how the old gentleman chuckles over boyish feats and roguish tricks, and tells long stories of a "barring out" achieved at the school he went to* ... {Sketches, The Old Couple}
Shutting the door against a schoolmaster so that he could not get into the classroom.

barrow *A barrow, good people, a mere barrow; nothing to what we could do, if we chose!* {Martin Chuzzlewit 27}
1. A low mound or heap.
He found that the total number of small carts and barrows engaged in dispensing provision to the cats and dogs of the metropolis was one

thousand seven hundred and forty-three. {Sketches, The Full Report of
the First Meeting of the Mudfog Association}
2. The London barrow was a small two-wheeled cart pushed by one person.

bars *Mr. Tulkinghorn warms before the bars, alternately, the palms
and knuckles of his hands* ... {Bleak House 27}
Metal rods placed across the front of the grate of a fireplace to prevent
the burning wood or coal from falling out.

baseness *Besides that I should know it to be hopeless, I should know it to
be a baseness.* {Tale of Two Cities 2-10}
Lowness of condition or rank. Here it refers to an act which might be
expected of a low person.

Bashaw ... *I began to be afraid, my dearest Dombey, you were quite a
Bashaw.* {Dombey & Son 30}
A haughty or imperious person. From the old form of the title Pasha.

basilisk *But to be quiet with such a basilisk before him was impossible.*
{Barnaby Rudge 51}
A mythical reptile whose mere glance could kill.

basket button ... *in a brown coat and bright basket buttons* ... {Pickwick
Papers 14}
A metal button with a basket pattern on it instead of a coat of arms.

basket-hilt ... *he espied, standing in the chimney-corner, an old basket-
hilted rapier in a rusty scabbard.* {Pickwick Papers 49}
A sword hilt made with a kind of bowl shape so that it completely covers
the hand.

basket-trifle *She had a little basket-trifle hanging at her side, with keys in
it* ... {David Copperfield 15}
A trifle is any small thing. This phrase probably means a very small
wicker basket just large enough to hold a few keys.

bason *He has ordered a glass of cold brandy and water, with a hard
biscuit and a bason, and has gone straight to bed.* {Sketches, Full

Report of the Second Meeting of the Mudfog Association}
A form of the word basin. A basin usually means a basin of soup.

bate *Bate some expected gain, for the risk you save, and say what is your price.* {Nicholas Nickleby 53}
Abate, reduce.

bath-chair *After this they walked out, or drove out, or were pushed out in bath-chairs, and met one another again.* {Pickwick Papers 36}
A large wheelchair for invalids, much used in the town of Bath.

bathing-machine ... *even in his Buoyant Boyhood Bathed from a Bathing-machine at Bognor, Bangor, Bournemouth* ... {The Haunted House 3}
A device used in the eighteenth and nineteenth centuries. It looked like a shed on wheels and was rolled down the beach to the water's edge by old horses that could no longer do heavy work. It was used by both ladies and gentlemen to change into their bathing costumes, and then they needed to take only a few steps to conceal themselves modestly in the water.

batter-pudding *"Pudding!" he exclaimed. "Why, bless me, so it is! What!" looking at it nearer. "You don't mean to say it's a batter-pudding!"* {David Copperfield 5}
A pudding made from batter and baked in a hot oven.

battery ... *crept, at last, upon a sort of grass-grown battery overhanging a lane, where a sentry was walking to and fro.* {David Copperfield 13}
A group of cannon, also the platform or fortification on which they stand.

battledore *A tender young cork ... would have no more chance against a pair of corkscrews ... or a little shuttlecock against two battledores, than I had against Uriah and Mrs. Heep.* {David Copperfield 17}
The racket used in the game of battledore or badminton to hit the shuttlecock back and forth.

bay ... *including a neat chariot and a pair of bays* ... {Dombey & Son 30}
Bay is a reddish brown color. Here the word refers to bay-colored horses.

beadle ... *I passed a church or two where the congregation were inside* ... *while the beadle sat and cooled himself in the shade of the porch* ... {David Copperfield 13}
A lower-ranking parish officer meant to keep order in church and act as messenger of the parish. A parish constable.

beak *Why, a beak's a madgst'rate* ... {Oliver Twist 8}
Slang for magistrate.

Bear fat (see **bear's-grease**)

bear-garden ... *[The bar] changed all at once into a bear-garden, a mad-house, an infernal temple: men darting in and out, by door and window, smashing the glass, turning the taps* ... {Barnaby Rudge 54}
A place set aside for setting dogs to fight with bears and for other rough sports.

bearing-rein *Then there was a great to-do to make the pony hold up his head that the bearing-rein might be fastened* ... {Old Curiosity Shop 14}
A short rein that held up the horse's head and kept his neck arched. This gave a fashionable appearance but, carried to an extreme, was cruel to the horse.

bear-leader *A bear-leader, a popular street character of the time* ... {Tale of Two Cities 2-14}
A man who had a more-or-less tame or trained bear which he led from place to place and displayed for money.

bear's-grease *Besides which, he quite scented the dining-room with bear's-grease and other perfumery.* {Bleak House 9}
The fat of the bear, used in medical and cosmetic preparations.

bear up tight *I'll put him in harness, and I'll bear him up tight, and I'll break him and drive him.* {Our Mutual Friend 3-14}

A bearing rein is used to pull up a horse's head; hence, the phrase means 'rein him in tight' (see **bearing-rein**).

beat up *Sunday coming round, he set off, therefore, after breakfast, once more to beat up Captain Cuttle's quarters.* {Dombey & Son 15}
To beat up someone's quarters is to visit them unceremoniously or to arouse or disturb them.

beaver bonnet ... *my sister leading the way in a very large beaver bonnet* ... {Great Expectations 13}
A woman's hat made of beaver fur, or an imitation beaver fur.

beaver glove *He carried one stained beaver glove, which he dangled before him by the forefinger as he walked or sat* ... {Martin Chuzzlewit 28}
A kind of glove, but not made from beaver.

beaver-hat *It was a close and stifling little shop full of all sorts of clothing, made and unmade, including one window full of beaver-hats and bonnets.* {David Copperfield 9}
A hat made of beaver fur, or an imitation beaver fur.

be bound *I dare be bound for that, Nell. Oh! I believe you there!* {Old Curiosity Shop 3}
Under obligation of duty or gratitude. Here disbelief is being expressed.

bed-chamber ... *his own private apartment of three rooms: his bed-chamber and two others.* {Tale of Two Cities 2-9}
Bedroom.

bed-furniture ... *and on that property married a young person in bed-furniture* ... {Great Expectations 47}
The linens and such used on a bed.

bed-gown *He had his slippers on, and a loose bed-gown, and his throat was bare for his greater ease.* {Tale of Two Cities 2-5}
A nightgown. Nightgowns were worn by both sexes.

bedight ... *and bedight with Christmas holly stuck into the top.* {A Christmas Carol 3}
Equipped, furnished, bedecked.

Bedlamite *"Why didn't you say who you were?" returned Dick, "instead of flying out of the house like a Bedlamite?"* {Old Curiosity Shop 3}
An inmate of an insane asylum. The name 'Bedlam' came from the Hospital of St. Mary of Bethlehem, which in the fifteenth century became a hospital for the insane. 'Bethlehem' was contracted to 'Bedlam'.

bed-winch *"If those eyes of yours were bed-winches," returned Miss Pross, "and I was an English four-poster, they shouldn't loose a splinter of me ... "* {Tale of Two Cities 3-14}
A kind of wrench for tightening the screws of a bed.

beef-house ... *going to a famous alamode beef-house near Drury Lane, and ordering a 'small plate' of that delicacy ...* {David Copperfield 11}
A restaurant specializing in beef dishes.

beefsteak pudding *In the whole catalogue of cookery, there is nothing I should like so much as a beefsteak pudding!* {Martin Chuzzlewit 39}
(see **pudding**)

beer-shop, beer-house *We have opened all the public-houses in the place and left our adversary nothing but the beer-shops ...* {Pickwick Papers 13}
A shop licensed for the sale of beer but not for spirits.

beforehand *Have you ever known [the English government] to be beforehand in the adoption of any useful thing?* {Little Dorrit 1-10}
Early, in advance.

Beggar my Neighbour *"What do you play, boy?" asked Estella of myself, with the greatest disdain. "Nothing but Beggar my Neighbour, miss."* {Great Expectations 8}
A simple card game for children.

Begum . . . *according to a wild legend in our family, he was once seen riding on an elephant, in company with a baboon; but I think it must have been a Baboo--or a Begum.* {David Copperfield 1}
A queen, princess, or lady of high rank in Hindustan.

behind-hand . . . *bending its figured brows upon him with a savage joy when he was behind-hand with his lessons . . .* {Little Dorrit 1-3}
Late, ill-prepared.

belated *Neither was I ever belated among wolves, on the borders of France and Spain . . .* {The Uncommercial Traveller, Nurse's Stories}
Benighted, overtaken by night before reaching shelter.

belcher handkerchief . . . *and the order of the garter on my leg, restrained from chafing my ankle by a twisted belcher handkerchief? . . .* {Old Curiosity Shop 34}
A kerchief with a blue ground and white spots, having one large blue spot in the center. Named after Jim Belcher, a famous boxer.

Beldamite *What was that you said, Beldamite?* {Dombey & Son 27}
Misspelling of Bedlamite, an inmate of an insane asylum.

belike *It shall be on table in five minutes, and this good gentleman belike will stop and see you take it.* {Edwin Drood 16}
Probably, in all likelihood.

bell-handle . . . *the appointed time was exceeded by a full quarter of an hour . . . before I could muster up sufficient desperation to pull the private bell-handle let into the left-hand door post of Mr. Waterbrook's house.* {David Copperfield 25}
A handle connected to the bell wire, a wire that rings a bell inside the house.

bell-lamp *The bell-lamp in the passage looked as clear as a soap-bubble; you could see yourself in all the tables, and French-polish yourself on any one of the chairs.* {Sketches, The Boarding-house}
A bell-shaped lamp.

bell-man *A Grand Morning Performance by the Riders, commencing at that very hour, was in course of announcement by the bell-man as they set their feet upon the stones of the street.* {Hard Times 3-7}
A town crier, one who rings a bell to attract attention and then makes public announcements.

bell-rope *"But you shall have some breakfast!" said I, with my hand on the bell-rope . . .* {David Copperfield 24}
The rope by which a bell is rung, including those ropes used to ring a bell in the servant's quarters.

bell-wether *So many bells are ringing . . . that every sheep in the ecclesiatical fold might be a bell-wether.* {The Uncommercial Traveller, City of London Churches}
A wether is a sheep. The bellwether had a bell around its neck and acted as a leader of the flock.

bell-wire *. . . this species of humor is now confined to St. James parish, where door knockers are preferred as being more portable, and bell-wires are esteemed as convenient tooth-picks.* {Nicholas Nickleby 4}
The wire connected to a handle that hung by the front door, and which, when pulled, rang a bell inside the house.

belongings *" . . . Ha'n't you no such relations, Mr. George?" Mr. George, still composedly smoking, replies, "If I had, I shouldn't trouble them. I have been trouble enough to my belongings in my day."* {Bleak House 21}
Persons related in any way, relatives.

Bench *Your case has made a noise; it is a creditable case to be professionally concerned in; I should feel on a better standing with my connexion, if you went up to the Bench.* {Little Dorrit 2-28}
Bench usually refers to a judge or a court, but here it refers to the Queens Bench Prison, which was used as a debtor's prison after 1842. Mr. Rugg, the attorney, considers the Marshalsea prison, in which Arthur finds himself, a lower-class prison.

bencher *The benchers determined to have his door broken open, as he hadn't paid any rent for two years.* {Pickwick Papers 21}
Someone who officially sits on a bench, such as a judge or a magistrate.

bender ... *this time I vin, next time you vin: never mind the loss of two bob and a bender!* {Sketches, Greenwich Fair}
Slang for a sixpence coin.

bend-sinister *Athwart the picture of my Lady, over the great chimney-piece, it throws a broad bend-sinister of light that strikes down crookedly into the hearth and seems to rend it.* {Bleak House 12}
From heraldry. Two parallel lines going from the left side of the shield to the lower right base.

benighted *The brother-in-law was riding once through a forest on a magnificent horse ... when he found himself benighted, and came to an Inn.* {The Holly Tree 1}
Overtaken by darkness before reaching shelter.

benignantly ... *Bob replaced the cork with great care, and, looking benignantly down on Mr. Pickwick, took a large bite out of the sandwich and smiled.* {Pickwick Papers 50}
With kindly manner, graciously. From the word 'benign'.

Berlin gloves ... *the bridegroom and his chosen friend, in blue coats, yellow waistcoats, white trousers, and Berlin gloves to match.* {Sketches, Hackney-coach Stands}
Gloves made from Berlin wool, a fine dyed wool.

Berlins ... *a fat man in black tights and cloudy Berlins.* {Sketches, Scotland-yard}
Berlin gloves (see **Berlin gloves**).

beseems ... *that floors are rubbed bright, carpets spread, curtains shaken out, beds puffed and patted, still-room and kitchen cleared for action--all things prepared as beseems the Dedlock dignity.* {Bleak House 40}
Suits in appearance, befits.

beshrew *Beshrew the Warden likewise for obstructing that corner, and making the wind so angry as it rushes round.* {The Uncommercial Traveller, The Calais Night Mail}
Curse.

bespeak *He has his favourite box, he bespeaks all the papers, he is down upon bald patriarchs, who keep them more than ten minutes afterwards.* {Bleak House 20}
To order or, in the sense used here, to reserve.

bespoke *... a complete outfit was bespoke that afternoon...* {David Copperfield 14}
Ordered, in the sense of ordering an article of clothing to be made to order.

best fresh *It was quite a little feast; two ounces of seven-and-sixpenny green, and a quarter of a pound of the best fresh; and Mr. Wilkins had brought a pint of shrimps, neatly folded up in a clean belcher ...* {Sketches, Miss Evans and the Eagle}
This probably refers to the best grade of fresh butter.

betide *Whatever betides... never forget that, Mary...* {Martin Chuzzlewit 14}
To happen.

betimes *She need be accustomed to such loads betimes though, neighbour, for she will carry weight when you are dead.* {Old Curiosity Shop 3}
Early, in good time.

betoken *A few small houses scattered on either side of the road betoken the entrance to some town or village.* {Pickwick Papers 28}
To signify, be a token or sign of.

between whiles *... volunteering more than one song of no inconsiderable length, and regaling the social circle between-whiles with recollections of divers splendid women who had been supposed to entertain a passion for himself...* {Nicholas Nickleby 30}
At intervals.

biddable *"A most biddable creature he is to be sure," said Mrs. Nickleby, when Smike had wished them good night and left the room.* {Nicholas Nickleby 37}
Ready to do what is bidden, obedient.

bide *The gentlefolks can't hear themselves speak, Sloppy. Bide a bit, bide a bit!* {Our Mutual Friend 1-16}
Wait. From the word 'abide.'

bier *So, they put the bier on the brink of the grave; and the two mourners waited patiently in the damp clay, with a cold rain drizzling down . . .* {Oliver Twist 5}
The movable stand on which a corpse or coffin is placed or carried.

biffin, Norfolk Biffin *. . . there were Norfolk Biffins, squab and swarthy, setting off the yellow of the oranges and lemons, and, in the great compactness of their juicy persons, urgently entreating and beseeching to be carried home in paper bags and eaten after dinner.* {A Christmas Carol 3}
1. A type of cooking apple.
Quarts of almonds; dozens of oranges; pounds of raisins; stacks of biffins; soup-plates full of nuts. --Oh, Todger's could do it when it chose! {Martin Chuzzlewit 9}
2. Also the apple baked and flattened to form a cake.

bigoted *I am not bigoted to my plans, and I can overturn them myself.* {David Copperfield 19}
Unreasonably devoted.

big-wig *. . . and we'll have a big-wig, Charley: one that's got the greatest gift of gab: to carry on his defence . . .* {Oliver Twist 43}
A person of high official standing or importance. From the large wigs formerly worn by such people as judges and government officials. Here it refers to a prominent lawyer.

bilging *The ship continued to beat on the rocks; and soon bilging, fell with her broadside towards the shore.* {Reprinted Pieces, The Long Voyage}

Having the bilge smashed. The bilge is the lowermost, rounded under-water portion of the hull of a ship.

bilious ... *to buy everything that was bilious in the shop*... {David Copper-field 5}
Refers to those diseases believed to originate from disorders of the bile, producing peevishness and ill-temper. The word is used here in the sense of foods that produce such symptoms.

bill *There was a bill, pasted on the door-post, announcing a room to let on the second floor.* {Bleak House 14}
A poster or placard bearing a public announcement.

bill-broker ... *an attorney connected with the bill-broking business* ... {David Copperfield 1}
One who negotiates the purchase and sale of monetary bills, such as bills of exchange.

billet ... *two gentlemen having by turns perused Mr. Pickwick's billet*... {Pickwick Papers 42}
1. Housing for the military, hence any place used as housing.
... *all these fuel shops with stacks of billets painted outside, and real billets sawing in the gutter* ... {Reprinted Pieces, A Flight}
2. A piece of firewood, either a short piece of log or a section of a piece of log.

billiard-marker *Tip had turned his liberty to hopeful account by becoming a billiard-marker.* {Little Dorrit 1-20}
An employee of a billiard parlor who keeps score for the persons playing billiards.

Billingsgate trade *[He went]* ... *into a general dealer's, into a distillery, into the law again, into a wool house, into a dry goods house, into the Billingsgate trade, into the foreign fruit trade, and into the docks.* {Little Dorrit 1-7}
The fish trade, from the fact that the fish market in London was called Billingsgate.

bill of exchange *My friend Mr. Thomas Traddles has . . . 'put his name,' if I may use a common expression, to bills of exchange for my accommodation.* {David Copperfield 36}
A written order to pay a given sum of money to a certain person, usually for value received but sometimes as a means of credit, or to raise money as a sort of promissory note. Mr. Traddles has co-signed the notes.

bill of mortality *Divide the lively turtles in the bills of mortality, by the number of gentlefolks able to buy 'em; and whose share does he take but his own!* {The Chimes 2}
An official list of the deaths and births in a particular district.

bind . . . *why go a binding music when you've got it in yourself?* {Little Dorrit 1-31}
To apprentice, become an apprentice.

binn . . . *one of those wooden binns with the other luggage . . .* {David Copperfield 5}
A bin, or a wooden box with an open top.

birch-broom . . . *the human helper, clearing out the next stall, never stirs beyond his pitchfork and birch-broom . . .* {Bleak House 7}
A crude broom made by tying the flexible twigs of the birch tree to a stick.

birch-rod . . . *Mr. Wopsle's great-aunt collected her energies, and made an indiscriminate totter at them with a birch-rod.* {Great Expectations 10}
A bunch of birch twigs bound together and used as a whip for punishment.

birdlime . . . *as happy as a tomtit on birdlime.* {Sketches, Mr. Minns and his Cousin}
A glue used to catch birds. If a bird landed on the glue which was spread on twigs its feet would be stuck to the twig and it could be caught. Naturally a tomtit in such a predicament would not be happy at all.

Bishop ... *although neither Burke nor Bishop had then gained a horrible notoriety, his own observation might have suggested to him how easily the atrocities to which the former has since given his name, might be committed.* {Sketches, The Black Veil}
John Bishop, too, was a body snatcher or resurrection man. He killed and sold the bodies of his victims for dissection. He was convicted of murder and hanged at Newgate in 1831.

bishop ... *we will discuss your affairs this very afternoon, over a Christmas bowl of smoking bishop, Bob!* {A Christmas Carol 5}
A sweet alcoholic drink made of wine, oranges or lemons, and sugar.

bit *Back he turned again, without the courage to purchase bit or drop, though he had tasted no food for many hours* ... {Oliver Twist 48}
1. Bit means bite, hence a bite of food. Drop here means a drop of drink, hence anything to drink.
... *Mr. Buffle begins very angry with his pen in his mouth, when the Major steaming more and more says "Take your bit out sir!* ... " {Mrs. Lirriper's Legacy 1}
The red bit, the black bit, the inkstand top, the other inkstand top, the little sand-box. {Bleak House 10}
2. A pen which, when held between the teeth across the mouth, resembled a bit in a horse's mouth. The red bit probably refers to the pen for red ink.

bitter *Shall we drink a bitter afore dinner, colonel?* {Martin Chuzzlewit 16}
A drink flavored with bitters, which originally were a medicinal extract.

bitter powder (see **powder**)

black draught ... *and Mr. Smallweed requiring to be repeatedly shaken up like a large black draught.* {Bleak House 21}
A liquid medication, a purgative, containing senna and licorice. A draught is a liquid medicine meant to be taken at one dose.

blackguard ... *which conduct I have no doubt did appear, and does appear, obtrusive--in fact, almost blackguardly.* {Bleak House 29}
A low and worthless person, often a criminal.

black hole *One day, when Private Richard Doubledick came out of the Black Hole, where he had been passing the last eight-and-forty hours, and in which retreat he spent a good deal of his time . . .* {Seven Travellers 1}
A guardroom or punishment cell. It does not necessarily refer to a solitary confinement cell in a cellar.

blacking *. . . his blacking-brushes and blacking were among his books--on the top shelf, behind a dictionary.* {David Copperfield 27}
Black shoe polish.

blacklead *. . . the half-washed-out-traces of smut and blacklead which tattooed her countenance . . .* {Nicholas Nickleby 16}
Graphite, such as is used for the lead of a pencil and for blackening stoves and other metal objects.

blacklead brush *But such wonderful things came tumbling out of the closets when they were opened--bits of mouldy pie, sour bottles, Mrs. Jellyby's caps, letters, tea, forks, odd boots and shoes of children, firewood, wafers, saucepan-lids, damp sugar in odds and ends of paper bags, footstools, blacklead brushes, bread, Mrs. Jellyby's bonnets, books with butter sticking to the binding . . .* {Bleak House 30}
The brush used for applying graphite, or blacklead, to polish metal objects.

blackleg *. . . indignities . . . outweighing in comparison any that the most heartless blackleg would put upon his groom . . .* {Nicholas Nickleby 46}
A swindler in horse racing.

blacks *I wondered . . . why he stuck them on that dusty perch for the blacks and flies to settle on, instead of giving them a place at home.* {Great Expectations 20}
Particles of soot and smut, the latter being a kind of fungus or mildew.

black-wash *We went there, early one morning, to stick bills and to black-wash their bills if we were interfered with.* {Reprinted Pieces, Bill Sticking}
A thin, black paint similar, except for color, to whitewash.

black wax *Postmark, Strand, black wax, black border, woman's hand, C.N. in the corner.* {Nicholas Nickleby 3}
Black sealing-wax, used to close the folded letter and indicating, with the black border, a death.

bladder *From my friend the noble captain--the illustrious general--the bladder, Mr. Tappertit.* {Barnaby Rudge 62}
A pretentious person, a windbag.

blade *That's the man . . . what an interesting blade he is!* {Barnaby Rudge 44}
A good, free-and-easy fellow.

blade-bone . . . *three green personages of a scaly humour, with excrescential serpents growing out of their blade-bones.* {Reprinted Pieces, Out of the Season}
Scapula, shoulder blade.

blanket-stall *On every piece of waste or common ground , some small gambler drove his noisy trade . . . ; gilt gingerbread in blanket-stalls exposed its glories to the dust . . .* {Old Curiosity Shop 19}
Stalls covered over to keep out the weather, sometimes with blankets but often with other things.

bleed . . . *Ben Allen and Bob Sawyer, who had done nothing but dodge round the group, each with a tortoise-shell lancet in his hand, ready to bleed the first man stunned.* {Pickwick Papers 51}
Treating an illness by opening a vein and releasing some blood. A commonly used but usually ineffective method.

blest *"Blest if I know," said Jerry.* {Tale of Two Cities 2-2}
Blessed.

blind-hookey . . . *it was not surprising if they sometimes lost themselves--which they had rather frequently done, as respected horse-flesh, blind-hookey . . . and the Insolvent Debtors Court.* {Hard Times 1-7}
A card game.

blind-place *In almost every yard and blind-place near, there was a church.* {Dombey & Son 56}
A place or small street closed at one end. The sense is similar to 'dead end'.

blinkers *Horses, scarcely better; splashed to their very blinkers.* {Bleak House 1}
Leather screens attached to the horse's bridle at eye level to prevent it from seeing in any direction but straight ahead.

blister *... they take medicine to an extent which I should have conceived impossible; they put on blisters and leeches with a perseverance worthy of a better cause...* {Pickwick Papers 48}
A medication applied to the skin to cause a blister to form. A commonly used and ineffective method of medical treatment.

bloater, Yarmouth bloaters *... certain small moneys, to be expended in the purchase of hot rolls, butter, sugar, Yarmouth bloaters, and other articles of housekeeping...* {Old Curiosity Shop 50}
A smoked and dried herring.

block *And saying so, he dismounted, with the aid of the block before the door, in a twinkling.* {Barnaby Rudge 10}
1. A stump of wood used as a step in mounting or dismounting a horse.
Protestants in anything but the name, were no more to be considered as abettor of these disgraceful occurrences, than they themselves were chargeable with the uses of the block, the rack, the gibbet, and the stake in cruel Mary's reign. {Barnaby Rudge 51}
2. The headsman's block, on which people were beheaded.
... the long-shore boat builders, and mast, oar, and block makers. {Great Expectations 46}
3. The nautical name for a pulley.

blockade-man *... blockade-man after blockade-man had passed the spot, wending his way towards his solitary post ...* {Sketches, The Tuggs's at Ramsgate}
A member of the anti-smuggling force, a coastguardsman.

block-tin ... *I heated the coffee in an unassuming block-tin vessel, in which Mrs. Crupp delighted to prepare it (chiefly, I believe, because it was not intended for the purpose, being a shaving pot* ... *)* {David Copperfield 25}
The metal tin, purified and cast into a block from which utensils could then be made.

blood cattle, blood horse *The sound was like that of fifty breaks with six blood cattle in each.* {Pickwick Papers 49}
Animals of good breed or pedigree.

blooded *Being promptly blooded, however, by a skilful surgeon, he rallied* ... {Barnaby Rudge 82}
Bled. Bleeding was a commonly used treatment of disease, carried out by puncturing a vein and permitting some blood to drain out. It was usually ineffective and often did the patient much harm.

bloom *Mr. Barkis rubbed his cheek with his cuff, and then looked at his cuff as if he expected to find some of the bloom upon it* ... {David Copperfield 8}
1. The crimson tint of the cheek.
The snuff of a candle, the wick of a lamp, the bloom on the peach, the down on a butterfly. {Nicholas Nickleby 27}
2. The naturally occurring light powder found on grapes and other fruit.

Bloomer trousers *The very image and presentment of a Corporal of his country's army, in the line of his shoulders, the line of his waist, the broadest line of his Bloomer trousers, and their narrowest line at the calf of his leg.* {Somebody's Luggage 2}
The bloomer costume, invented by Mrs. Amelia Bloomer, consisted of a short skirt over very wide trousers gathered closely at the ankle. The name became attached to any trouser-like garment that was very loose at the hips and gathered at the knee or below.

blotting-paper *Mr. Pickwick carefully rubbed the last page on the blotting-paper* ... {Pickwick Papers 36}
An absorbent paper used to dry the ink on paper that has been written upon with a pen.

bloused *When were travellers by wheels and hoofs seen with such red-hot cheeks as those? when were they so good-humouredly and merrily bloused?* {Martin Chuzzlewit 12}
A 'blowze' was a ruddy, fat-faced wench. The word, written 'blouse', came to mean excited and disheveled, disorderly in dress or hair.

blow ... *a most glorious nosegay, fan-shaped, some two feet and a half round, and composed of all the jolliest-looking flowers that blow.* {Dombey & Son 15}
To blossom.

blown *He was so blown himself that he couldn't get on any further until after a pause, when he added feebly, "you here?"* {The Battle of Life 3}
Out of breath.

blow up *If my mother-in-law blows him up, he whistles.* {Pickwick Papers 16}
To arouse, inflame, excite.

blow upon ... *those letters I was to have brought to your ladyship were not destroyed when I supposed they were. That if there was anything to be blown upon, it is blown upon.* {Bleak House 55}
Slang for inform on, squeal on.

blue bag *"You wouldn't, I'm sure," said Mr. Snitchey, standing a small professional blue bag against one leg of the table ...* {The Battle of Life 1}
The commonly used lawyer's brief bag was made of blue material.

blue-book *So he went in [for statistics.] He coached himself up with a blue-book or two ...* {Hard Times 2-2}
Parliamentary reports, which were bound in blue covers.

blue-bottle ... *and led a life of torment which could scarcely have been surpassed, if he had been a blue-bottle in a world of cobwebs.* {Martin Chuzzlewit 9}
The meat fly, a fly with a bluish body.

Blucher boots, bluchers ... *a young gentleman as ever stood four feet six, or something less, in his bluchers.* {Oliver Twist 8}

A strong leather half-boot or high shoe, named after Field Marshal von Blücher. In contrast with most boots, which simply were pulled on, it was laced at the front. The two leather flaps with the lacing holes are still called 'bluchers'.

Blue Chamber *Repeating his three bows he withdraws, closing the door on Volumnia's little scream, which is a preliminary to her remarking that that charmingly horrible person is a perfect Blue Chamber.* {Bleak House 53}
Mr. Pecksniff opened another door on the same floor, and shut it again, all at once, as if it were a Blue Chamber. {Martin Chuzzlewit 5}
Bluebeard's forbidden room in which he hid the bodies of his murdered wives, thus, in the first example, a dark, dangerously secretive person.

blue coaching ... *Mr. James Harthouse, with a discreet use of his blue coaching, came off triumphantly* ... {Hard Times 2-2}
Aristocratic training.

blue-coat boy ... *there's a great deal of comfort in a nightcap, as I'm sure you would confess, Nicholas, my dear, if you would only have strings to yours, and wear it like a Christian, instead of sticking it upon the very top of your head like a blue-coat boy.* {Nicholas Nickleby 37}
A student in a blue-coat school, a charity school.

bluecoat school ... *educated in the bluecoat school, and blown up in a powder-mill.* {Dombey & Son 44}
The uniform for students in a charity school included a blue coat or gown.

blue ladies *Blue ladies there are, in Boston; but like philosophers of that colour and sex in most other latitudes, they rather desire to be thought superior than to be so.* {American Notes, 3}
Learned or pedantic, always said of women. It is often used in a contemptuous sense.

blue minutes *The respectability of Mr. Vholes has even been cited with crushing effect before Parliamentary committees, as in the following*

blue minutes of a distinguished attorneys evidence . . . {Bleak House 39}
Parliamentary reports were published in a book with blue covers.

bluff *. . . the days of old King Hal, stout King Hal, bluff King Hal . . .* {The Chimes 3}
Good-natured and plain-spoken.

blunderbuss *A blunderbuss and two swords hung above the chimney-piece, for the terror of evildoers; but the blunderbuss was rusty and shattered, and the swords were broken and edgeless.* {Nicholas Nickleby 37}
A short, large bore gun that fired many balls with each shot.

blunt *Down he goes to the Commons to see the lawyer and draw the blunt . . .* {Pickwick Papers 10}
Slang for ready money.

boa *. . . an imitation ermine boa tied in a loose knot round her neck . . .* {Nicholas Nickleby 23}
A fur, shaped like a snake, used as a wrapper for the throat.

Boanerges Boiler *. . . to be steamed like a potato in the unventilated breath of the powerful Boanerges Boiler and his congregation . . .* {The Uncommercial Traveller, City of London Churches}83
The word 'boanerges' comes from a Hebrew word meaning 'sons of thunder'. It came to be applied to any very loud preacher and Dickens apparently uses it here as the first name of one such preacher.

board *At one end of the board Mrs. Jefferson Brick and two other ladies were drinking tea . . .*
1. Dining table. 'Well-spread board' suggests generous amounts of food.
And remind me to have a board done about trespassers and spring-guns and all that sort of thing, to keep the common people out. {Pickwick Papers 19}
2. A sign, such as one painted on a wooden board.

boat-cloak *In a corner was a heap of coats and boat-cloaks, and a flag, all bundled up together.* {David Copperfield 2}
A large cloak worn by officers on duty at sea.

boatswain *There I found a virtuous boatswain in his Majesty's service...* {Great Expectations 47}
A ship's officer in charge of sails and rigging.

bob *I'm at low water mark myself--only one bob and a magpie...* {Oliver Twist 8}
1. Slang for a shilling. A magpie is a halfpenny coin.
... performing, as it were, a kind of triple bob major on the peal of instruments in the female belfry... {Barnaby Rudge 7}
2. One of the changes in bell ringing. A change consists of a set of bells rung in a fixed sequence. A bob minor is rung on six bells, a bob major on eight bells.

bobbish *"The pigs is well," said Mr. Squeers, "the cows is well, and the boys is bobbish."* {Nicholas Nickleby 57}
In good health and spirits.

bobtail *We don't take in no tagrag and bobtail at our house, sir ...* {Barnaby Rudge 35}
A contemptible fellow, or rabble.

bob-wig *[A handkerchief] tied in a convenient crease of his double chin, secured his three-cornered hat and bob-wig from blowing off his head ...* {Barnaby Rudge 2}
A wig with the bottom locks turned up into short curls or bobs.

bodice, boddice *... dressed in a very juvenile manner, particularly as to the tightness of her boddice ...* {Dombey & Son 1}
The upper part of a woman's dress, also a vest-like garment worn under the dress and over the stays.

bodkin *... pen-knives, scissors, bodkins, and other small office-cutlery.* {Bleak House 10}
A sharp pointed instrument for piercing holes.

body-coat *It consisted of a brown body-coat with a great many brass buttons up the front* . . . {Old Curiosity Shop 2}
A coat fitting close to the body.

body-woman *Thirty horses stood in his stables, twenty-four male domestics sat in his halls, six body-women waited on his wife.* {Tale of Two Cities 2-7}
A woman's body servant, personal maid.

Bogle . . . *Paul looked upon the young lady with consternation, as a kind of learned Guy Faux, or artificial Bogle, stuffed full of scholastic straw.* {Dombey & Son 12}
A frightening goblin or bogy. The word is also used to mean a scarecrow.

Boguey *It's this unbearably dull, suicidal room--and old Boguey downstairs, I suppose* {Bleak House 32}
A name for the Devil (see **bogle**).

boh . . . *smirking and making great eyes at her, I'll be bound, as if you couldn't say boh! to a goose!* {David Copperfield 14}
Boo, as would now be said playfully to a child.

boiler . . . *the elder Willet and his three companions continued to smoke with profound gravity, and in a deep silence, each having his eyes fixed on a huge copper boiler that was suspended over the fire.* {Barnaby Rudge 1}
A pot for boiling foods.

bolstered *Then our fellows get nightmares, and are bolstered for calling out and waking other fellows.* {The Schoolboy's Story}
Hit with pillows or bolsters.

bombazeen, bombasine . . . *but his relict still wore black bombazeen, of such a lustreless, deep, dead, sombre shade, that gas itself couldn't light her up after dark* . . . {Dombey & Son 8}
A twilled or corded cloth made of worsted or worsted combined with silk or cotton.

bond *[The brothers] Frederick the free, was so humbled . . . and faded;*
William the bond, was so courtly, condescending . . . {Little Dorrit 1-19}
A person in bondage, not free.

bone *. . . all he hopes, is, he may never hear of no foreigner boning noth-*
ing out of no travelling chariot. {Dombey & Son 31}
To steal.

bone-house *Not a station-house or bone-house, or workhouse in the*
metropolis escaped a visit from the hard glazed hat. {Dombey & Son 25}
A morgue, as used here. It also means a charnel house, in which dead
bodies were stored.

bones *. . . seated in their chairs, were the performers on the tambou-*
rine and bones. {The Uncommercial Traveller, Mr. Barlow}
A crude musical instrument made from animal bones of various lengths,
played by one of the members of a minstrel band who was usually
addressed as Mr. Bones.

bonneting *. . . two young men, who, now and then, varied their amuse-*
ments by "bonneting" the proprietor of this itinerant coffee-house.
{Sketches, The Steam Excursion}
Crushing someone's hat down over his eyes.

booking-office *The guard's eye lighted on me as he was getting down, and*
he said at the booking-office door: "Is there anybody here for a yoong-
ster booked in the name of Murdstone . . . ?" {David Copperfield 5}
A place to obtain reservations and tickets for the coach.

book-muslin *. . . the lady in the back parlour, who was very fat, and*
turned of sixty, came in a low book-muslin dress and short kid gloves . . .
{Nicholas Nickleby 14}
A fine kind of muslin so-called because it is folded in a book-like
manner when sold by the piece.

books of practice *. . . two or three common books of practice; a jar of*
ink, a pounce box . . . {Old Curiosity Shop 33}
Law books describing methods of practice before the various courts.

boot ... *the leather hat-box was obliged to be raked up from the lowest depth of the boot to satisfy him that it had been safely packed.* {Pickwick Papers 22}
A receptacle on a coach, often under the driver's or guard's seat, for luggage or parcels.

boot-jack ... *John boldly entered the room ... and received an order for a boot-jack* ... {Barnaby Rudge 12}
A device which holds the heel of a boot down while the boot is pulled off the foot.

bootless *It were bootless to add, that if languages is required to be jabbered and English is not good enough, both families and gentlemen had better go somewhere else.* {Somebody's Luggage 1}
Useless.

boots ... *the corpulent man condescended to order the boots to bring in the gentlemen's luggage* ... {Pickwick Papers 22}
The servant whose job it was to clean and polish shoes and boots.

boot-tree ... *I can remember to have gone about my region of our house, armed with the centre-piece out of an old set of boot-trees* ... {David Copperfield 4}
A shaped block put into a boot to keep its shape.

booty, play booty *You are playing Booty with my clerk, are you Copperfield?* {David Copperfield 52}
Slang for to betray. Uriah Heep is accusing Copperfield of conspiring with Mr. Micawber to betray him.

borne upon *The harder father is borne upon, the more he needs me to lean on.* {Our Mutual Friend 1-6}
Weighed on, pressed on, made to carry burdens.

borough *In the boroughs, especially, there still remain some half-dozen old inns, which have preserved their external features unchanged* ... {Pickwick Papers 10}
1. A town, smaller than a city, able to send representatives to parliament.

He offered--not indeed to pay his debts, but to let him sit for a close borough until his own son came of age . . . {Barnaby Rudge 40}
2. A close borough is a pocket borough, a voting district in which a party so controls the election that anyone they nominate is sure to win.

botheration *. . . I am determined to be peevish after my long day's botheration.* {Tale of Two Cities 2-21}
The act of bothering. Also, as a noun, a petty vexation or annoyance. The word was often used as an exclamation.

bottle-green *. . . the bottle-green was a famous suit to wear, and I bought it very cheap at a pawnbroker's, and there was--he, he, he!--a tarnished shilling in the waistcoat pocket.* {Nicholas Nickleby 51}
The dark-green color of bottle-glass, the cheapest kind of glass from which bottles were made.

bottle of smoke *To help myself in my turn, . . . and to pass the bottle of smoke.* {Little Dorrit 1-34}
To pretend to cooperate socially, as in passing the hookah mouthpiece.

bottom of the table *. . . will you take the bottom of the table, if you please.* {Dombey & Son 5}
The seat at the foot of the table.

bound *This boy must be bound out of hand.* {Great Expectations 13}
Apprenticed.

bounty *. . . I have dared to come . . . and to take your bounty, and to thank you for it . . .* {The Haunted Man 3}
A generous gift.

bourne *He is gone to that bourne from whence no traveler returns. I hope he is appreciated there.* {Nicholas Nickleby 30}
The terminus or end goal of a journey.

bowler *"Play!" suddenly cried the bowler. The ball flew from his hand straight and swift towards the centre stump of the wicket.* {Pickwick Papers 7}
In the game of cricket, the pitcher.

bowls ... *afterplaying a pretty long game of bowls* ... {Martin Chuzzle-wit 52}
A bowling game, such as skittles.

Bow street men, Bow street officer *The constables, and the Bow Street men from London--for, this happened in the days of the extinct red-waist-coated police--were about the house for a week or two* ... {Great Expectations 16}
Bow street, a street in London in which the chief municipal police court was located. A Bow street officer or Bow street runner was a police officer.

bowstring ... *and making a loop in the air of her thread and deftly catching it into a knot with her needle, seemed to bowstring him* ... {Our Mutual Friend 4-8}
To strangle with a bowstring, a method of execution used in Turkey.

bow-window ... *a house with a wooden front and three stories of bow-window (not bay-window, which is another thing)* ... {Great Expectations 46}
A kind of curved window that bows out from the wall.

box *But his father--and his uncle--were the most profligate coachmen that ever sat upon a box.* {Bleak House 18}
1. The box under the driver's seat, hence the driver's seat itself.
... *the virgin monarch had then and there boxed and cuffed an unlucky page for some neglect of duty.* {Barnaby Rudge 1}
2. A slap on the ear with the palm of the hand, especially painful because of the percussion of the eardrum.
Mrs. Nickleby had scarcely been put away behind the curtain of the box in an arm-chair, when Sir Mulberry and Lord Frederick Veri-sopht arrived ... {Nicholas Nickleby 27}
3. The box in a theater, a group of seats enclosed on three sides.

box-seat *He went round to the coach-office, at my request, and took the box-seat for me on the mail.* {David Copperfield 55}
The driver's seat on a stagecoach, which often held one or two passengers in addition to the driver.

bracelet ... *and the unmoved policeman* ... *with his shining hat, stiff stock, inflexible great-coat, stout belt and bracelet, and all things fitting* ... {Bleak House 11}
A handcuff, hanging from his belt in the universal manner of policemen.

braces ... *the clothes hanging at some of the windows; and the men in their shirt-sleeves and braces, lolling with half their bodies out of the others* ... {Barnaby Rudge 58}
Suspenders for trousers.

bradawl ... *converted his right forefinger into an ideal bradawl or gimlet, and made as though he would screw the same into her side* ... {Barnaby Rudge 70}
A small, hand-held steel drill used to make holes for brads.

Bramah *If I was locked in a fire-proof chest vith a patent Bramah, she'd find a means to get at me, Sammy.* {Pickwick Papers 52}
A type of high-security lock with a cylindrical key invented by Joseph Bramah. For many years, in spite of the offer of a large reward, no one succeeded in picking this lock.

Bramah key ... *drawing a Bramah key from his pocket, with a small plug therein to keep the dust out.* {Pickwick Papers 53}
The cylindrical key to a Bramah lock (see **Bramah**).

brandy-balls *Even children so require sustaining under the general excitement that a pieman who has established himself for the occasion at the corner of the court says his brandy-balls go off like smoke.* {Bleak House 11}
A kind of candy.

bran-new *So, the happy schoolmaster put on a bran-new pair of gloves which he had carried in a little parcel in his pocket all the way* ... {Old Curiosity Shop 46}
Brand-new, perfectly new.

brasses *The windows, heavily shaded by trees, admitted a subdued light that made the faces around me pale, and darkened the old brasses in the pavement* ... {Bleak House 18}

Plates made of brass with designs and inscriptions, usually as memorials. They are placed in the walls and floor.

brass footman ... *from pot and kettle, face of brass footman, and black-leaded stove; bright glances of approbation wink and glow upon her.* {Martin Chuzzlewit 20}
A metal shelf made of brass on which pots could be kept near the fire.

brawn *Heaped up on the floor, to form a kind of throne, were turkeys, geese, game, poultry, brawn, great joints of meat, sucking pigs* ... {A Christmas Carol 3}
Boar meat.

brazen ... *a short truncheon, surmounted by a brazen crown* ... {Pickwick Papers 24}
Made of brass.

bread-pan ... *take them bits I've put out on the cover of the bread-pan.* {Oliver Twist 5}
The metal container in which a loaf of bread was baked.

break ... *if I could get a break and four blood horses* ... {Old Curiosity Shop 37}
A large open four-wheeled carriage. Originally it had no body, consisting of a frame with wheels and a high seat for the driver. It was used for breaking horses to harness. Later versions could seat six or more people and looked like a coach without the enclosed passenger compartment.

breakfast-cloth ... *the sofa pillows, a blanket, the table-cover, a clean breakfast-cloth, and a great-coat, made him a bed and covering, for which he was more than thankful.* {David Copperfield 25}
The tablecloth used at breakfast.

breath, take your breath *What is the Matter? Sit down and take your breath.* {Bleak House 40}
Recover free breathing after exertion, catch your breath.

breathe *At what a rate he went, to breathe the schoolmaster; and then how he lounged and loitered* . . . {Our Mutual Friend 3-10}
To put out of breath, to make tired or exhausted.

breathed *Mr. Tulkinghorn arrives in his turret-room a little breathed by the journey up, though leisurely performed.* {Bleak House 41}
Out of breath.

breeches *In breeches and gaiters, broad-brimmed hat, grey coat, speckled choaker* . . . {David Copperfield 5}
Knee breeches or small clothes. Men's pants, ending just below the knee.

brewing-place . . . *a scullery, or small brewing place, at the end of the passage.* {Oliver Twist 22}
Place in a kitchen where small amounts of ale or beer could be brewed.

brick-field . . . *they are pieces of unreclaimed land, with the withered vegetation of the original brick-field.* {Nicholas Nickleby 2}
A piece of ground where bricks are made.

bridle-road *Wasn't there a bridle-road to Mr. Pecksniff's house* . . . {Martin Chuzzlewit 20}
A road adequate for use on horseback but not suited to wheeled vehicles.

bridling . . . *Mrs. Gamp* . . . *came sidling and bridling into the room* . . . {Martin Chuzzlewit 19}
With the head up and the chin pulled back, to indicate pride, resentment, or offense.

brief *Such of the gentlemen as had a brief to carry carried it in as conspicuous a manner as possible,* . . . {Pickwick Papers 34}
A summary of the points in a law case. Carrying a brief indicated that the lawyer was employed on a case.

brimstone . . . *lighted torches; tow smeared with pitch, and tar, and brimstone;* . . . {Barnaby Rudge 63}
Sulfur.

bring-to . . . *it was settled next day that in future we would bring-to at sunset and encamp on the shore.* {English Prisoners 3}
To cause a ship to come to a standstill.

brisk up, brisk about *We want to brisk her up, and brisk her about, and give her a change.* {Our Mutual Friend 1-9}
To enliven, also to smarten up.

Bristol-board *Give him* . . . *the papers* . . . *fruit in season, a few sheets of Bristol-board, and a little claret, and he asked for no more.* {Bleak House 6}
A kind of pasteboard with a smooth surface, a light cardboard. Used, among other things, for sketching.

Britannia-metal *Mr. Jonas shook his Britannia-metal teaspoon at him* . . . {Martin Chuzzlewit 18}
An alloy of tin and antimony, resembling silver.

broadcloth . . . *little Jacob was an uncle, before the calves of his legs* . . . *had ever been encased in broadcloth pantaloons* . . . {Old Curiosity Shop 73}
Any fine, plain woven cloth, used mostly in black for men's clothing.

broadsheet . . . *he had the whole printed in great black letters on a staring broadsheet, and he caused the walls to be posted with it* . . . {Hard Times 3-4}
A large piece of paper printed on one side only.

broken fare, broken wittles *I'd take it wery koind o' your master if he'd elp a traveller* . . . *wi' a bit o' your broken wittles.* {The Uncommercial Traveller, Tramps}
Food remnants, table leavings, leftovers. 'Wittles' is dialect for 'victuals'.

broken reed . . . *she took Mr. Jonas to task for leaning so very hard upon a broken reed* . . . {Martin Chuzzlewit 11}

An unreliable person or thing. This phrase is an allusion to the Biblical phrase 'bruised reed' which has a slightly different implication (see **bruised reed**).

broker's man *[To be] a broker's man in a poor neighborhood would-n't be bad perhaps.* {Martin Chuzzlewit 5}
A broker is a person licensed to appraise or sell household furniture that has been seized for non-payment of rent. His 'man' was left in the home to see that the furniture was not removed before it could be sold, usually to the great distress of the family. This unpleasant job is described in Dickens' sketch *The Broker's Man.*

broker's shop *She would be deserted and reduced to ruin, and I should catch my death of cold in some broker's shop.* {Pickwick Papers 14}
A second-hand furniture and clothing shop.

brown loaf *. . . unpacking her basket, in which there was a piece of cold pickled pork, a little tea and sugar, and a brown loaf . . .* {Bleak House 52}
A loaf of brown bread, whole-wheat bread.

brown study *. . . sitting by the hour together in a brown study, as if he were endeavouring to recall Joe's image in his younger days . . .* {Barnaby Rudge 72}
A state of mental abstraction or musing, idle or purposeless reverie.

bruised reed *. . . I am always glad to see my old pensioner--as such, as such--and that I do--ha--extend as much protection and kindness to the--hum--the bruised reed--I trust I may so call him without impro-priety--as in my circumstances I can.* {Little Dorrit 1-31}
A Biblical reference (Isa. 42:3. "Behold my servant . . . . A bruised reed shall he not break"). The reference here is to a person injured and weakened by circumstances.

bruited *. . . this accomplishment of mine was bruited about among the boys, and attracted a good deal of notice to me . . .* {David Copperfield 7}
Noised abroad, rumored, reported. The word *bruit* is the French word for 'noise'.

bucellas ... *Mr. Hicks produced respectively a bottle of sauterne, bucellas, and sherry and took wine with everybody--except Tibbs.* {Sketches, The Boarding-house}
A Portuguese wine, named after a village in that country.

buckle-covering ... *and there ensued such toe-and-heeling, and buckle-covering, and double-shuffling, and heel-sliding, and execution of all sorts of slippery manoeuvres with vibratory legs* ... {The Haunted House 3}
A particular step in dancing, done by holding one foot so that it covers the shoe buckle of the other foot.

buckler ... *assuredly the shield and buckler of Britannia are not in present wear.* {Bleak House 19}
A kind of small round shield.

buckram *They tended their flocks severely in buckram and powder* ... {Bleak House 37}
A coarse linen stiffened with paste. The word also implies a stiffness of manner.

buckskins *There is no beau whom it takes four men at once to shake into his buckskins, or who goes to see all the executions* ... {Bleak House 12}
Leather breeches, made from the skin of a buck or from specially prepared sheepskin.

buffer ... *a fair lodging for a single buffer might be found in these parts* ... {Edwin Drood 18}
A somewhat low-grade fellow.

buff-jerkin ... *all sorts of old fellows, with great red faces and broken noses, turning up every day--buff-jerkins too--matchlocks--sarcophagus--fine place* ... {Pickwick Papers 2}
A close-fitting jacket made of buff, which is the rough-surfaced leather made from buffalo skin or ox hide. It was often worn by soldiers who owned no armor.

bugbear *What have I done to be made a bugbear of, and to be shunned and dreaded as if I brought the plague?* {Old Curiosity Shop 3}
A kind of goblin supposed to eat children, hence any object of needless dread.

Buhl table ... *marrying golden liqueur glasses to Buhl tables with sticky rings* ... {Little Dorrit 2-12}
Buhl is wood inlaid with brass, silver, tortoise shell, or other materials.

buillon ... *a row of fire-buckets--vessels calculated to be of no physical utility on any occasion, but observed to exercise a fine moral influence, almost equal to buillon, on most beholders.* {Hard Times 2-1}
Probably a misspelling of bullion.

bulks ... *to make their way, as they best could, among carts, baskets, barrows, trucks, casks, bulks, and benches* ... {Barnaby Rudge 60}
A stall built onto the front of a shop.

bull *"Him wot give him his writing and give me half a bull," says Jo in a whisper.* {Bleak House 16}
Slang for a crown, a coin worth five shillings.

bull-baiting ... *he were not a-going to be bull-baited and badgered in his own place.* {Great Expectations 18}
Setting dogs to fight bulls.

bullock ... *looking at the bullocks, as they came by, with the eye of an Australian farmer!* {David Copperfield 52}
A castrated bull, an ox.

bull's-eye ... *Mr. Bucket stops for a moment at the corner and takes a lighted bull's-eye from the constable on duty there* ... {Bleak House 22}
1. A lantern with a bull's eye lens, a hemispherical or plano-convex lens.
... *a sort of small glass lantern containing a languishing mass of bull's-eyes, which had melted in the summer and congealed in the winter until all hope of ever getting them out, or of eating them* ... *was gone forever.*
{The Haunted Man 2}
2. A kind of candy in the form of balls, like jawbreakers.

bumper *With these words Mr. Pickwick filled and drained a bumper with a trembling hand, and his eyes moistened as his friends rose with one accord and pledged him from their hearts.* {Pickwick Papers 57}
A cup or glass filled to the brim.

bumptious *You call yourself humble and sinful, but you are the most Bumptious of your sex.* {Little Dorrit 2-30}
Conceited, self-assertive in an offensive way.

bunch ... *a hatband of whole-sale capacity which was fluted behind, from the crown of his hat to the brim, and terminated in a black bunch* ... {Our Mutual Friend 2-10}
A protuberance, something bulging out.

burden *And as she sat at work, she hummed the burden of an old song, which the doctor liked.* {The Battle of Life 2}
1. The refrain or chorus of a song.
... *there is a toy-ship of considerable burden* ... {Reprinted Pieces, Our English Watering-place}
2. The capacity of a ship for carrying cargo, usually given in tons.

burgess ... *in some few of the city wards, the burgesses turned out, and without making a very fierce show, looked brave enough.* {Barnaby Rudge 67}
A magistrate or government official of a town.

burke *You don't mean to say he was burked, Sam?* {Pickwick Papers 31}
William Burke smothered his victims and sold their bodies for dissection, hence 'to burke' is to strangle or smother.

burning-glass ... *on which the sun played at a distance as on a burning-glass* ... {The Uncommercial Traveller, Travelling Abroad}
A magnifying lens used to concentrate the rays of the sun and used, on a clear day, to start a fire or to burn holes in paper or thin wood.

burn tallow ... *he was often closeted after midnight with Mr. Rugg in his little front-parlor office, and, even after those untimely hours, burnt tallow in his bedroom.* {Little Dorrit 1-25}
To burn candles made of tallow, hence to work late at night.

busk *. . . one of her most startling evolutions . . . was to grasp herself . . . by a sort of wooden handle (part of her clothing, and familiarly called a busk), and wrestle, as it were with her garments . . .* {The Battle of Life 1}
A piece of wood or whalebone used to stiffen the front of a corset.

butcher's meat *. . . their county member, as amazed that they failed to sleep in company with their butcher's meat.* {Little Dorrit 1-3}
Meat sold by butchers, distinguished from poultry, game, and fish. One source defines it as 'live animals destined for slaughter'.

but one *. . . on the next evening but one . . .* {David Copperfield 42}
Leaving out one. The last but one is the next to last.

butt *. . . whether in silver, brass, or gold, or butts of wine, or casks of gunpowder . . .* {Martin Chuzzlewit 9}
A cask or barrel.

butter-boat *. . . Mr. William, after much clattering and running about, having only gained possession of a butter-boat of gravy, which he stood ready to serve.* {The Haunted Man 1}
A vessel for serving melted butter, not a kind of ship.

but two *. . . I was going to visit a aunt of mine that lives at Chelsea--next door but two to the old original Bun House . . .* {Bleak House 54}
Leaving out two. The meaning here is 'two doors away from next door'.

bye-lane *She was awakened by the stopping of the cart, which was about to turn up a bye-lane.* {Old Curiosity Shop 15}
A lane away from the main streets. 'Bye' is here a variation of 'by'.

bye street *. . . there emerged from scores of bye streets, lanes, and nameless turnings, innumerable people carrying their dinners to the bakers' shops.* {A Christmas Carol 3}
An out-of-the-way street, a side street.

by little and little *By little and little Paul had grown stronger.* {Dombey & Son 11}
By a succession of small amounts, little by little.

by littles *I shall have a debt to pay off, by littles* ... {Our Mutual Friend 2-14}
By repeated small amounts, little by little.

by-path *Oliver reached the stile at which the by-path terminated; and once more gained the high-road.* {Oliver Twist 8}
An out-of-the-way path, a side path, side road.

by-place ... *and came to a shady by-place about which were sprinkled several little villas of quiet and secluded appearance.* {Pickwick Papers 39}
An out-of-the-way place.

by-the-by ... *I begin to feel the words I have been at infinite pains to get into my head, all sliding away, and going I don't know where. I wonder where they* do *go, by-the-by?* {David Copperfield 4}
By the way.

by times ... *reaching his fat dimpled hand up to the lips of the old woman, who was kissing it by times.* {Our Mutual Friend 1-16}
Time after time.

by-yard *In a by-yard, there was a wilderness of empty casks* ... {Great Expectations 8}
A yard set to one side, not the largest or main yard.

cab *floundering about town in a cab of his own, and doing a great deal of damage to the posts at street corners . . .* {Great Expectations 34}
A cabriolet. It does not mean a hired carriage or a taxicab (see **cabriolet**).

cabbage-net . . . *balls of packthread, ropes of onions, pounds of candles, cabbage-nets, and brushes, hung in bunches from the ceiling, like extraordinary fruit.* {The Chimes 4}
A small net in which a cabbage could be boiled.

cabinet piano . . . *the shrill complaining of a cabinet piano, wasting away, a string a day* . . . {Dombey & Son 9}
A piano of the right size for use in a private chamber or small room.

cable . . . *to wander at my cable's length about the earth* . . . {Barnaby Rudge 62}
The cable is the anchor line of a ship. The length of the cable determines how widely the ship can swing at anchor.

caboose *Fog creeping into the cabooses of collier-brigs; fog lying out on the yards and hovering in the rigging of great ships* . . . {Bleak House 1}
The cook room of a merchant ship, built on the deck.

cabriolet *Mr. Toots, like the leal and trusty soul he was, stopped the cabriolet in a winkling* . . . {Dombey & Son 44}
A light, two-wheeled carriage drawn by one horse, with a large leather folding top which could be opened over the passenger's and driver's heads. It could have a leather apron to cover their legs and laps or a wooden dashboard. It had a platform at the back on which the tiger rode (see **tiger**).

cad ... *and canvass for customers after the manner of omnibus cads*...
{Pickwick Papers 43}
The conductor or ticket taker on an omnibus.

cadger-like *A want of application, a restlessness of purpose, a thirsting after porter, a love of all that is roving and cadger-like in nature,* ...
appear to have been his leading characteristics. {Sketches, The Last Cab-driver and the First Omnibus-cad}
A cadger is a beggar, a sponger. One who wheedles money or who lives on the generosity of others.

cage ... *on the night of the wedding he was incarcerated in the village cage for having committed, in a state of intoxication, sundry excesses in the streets*... {Pickwick Papers 17}
A local prison.

Cag-Maggers *Oh Jaggerth, Jaggerth, Jaggerth! All otherth is Cag-Maggerth, give me Jaggerth!* {Great Expectations 20}
'Cag-mag' is gossip or idle talk. This person is saying that all lawyers except Mr. Jaggers are idle talkers. A possible earlier meaning of cag-mag is 'worthless scraps of meat', and then 'the cheating butchers who sold such things'. The first meaning was probably more contemporary with Dickens.

calender "... *the young man in the Eastern tale--who is described as a one-eyed almanack, if I am not mistaken, Mr. Pinch?--*" "*A one-eyed calender, I think, sir," faultered Tom.* {Martin Chuzzlewit 6}
A mendicant dervish, from the *Arabian Nights*. If it were spelled K-a-l-e-n-d-a-r, as it often is, the pun would be less appropriate.

calenture *A mild fit of calenture seizes him* ... {Edwin Drood 107}
A fever with delirium, said to be suffered by sailors who then see green fields in place of the sea.

calimanco ... *and wears a close-fitting waistcoat with black calimanco sleeves*... {Somebody's Luggage 1}
Calamanco. A woolen cloth woven so that checks are seen on one side only.

call *I ain't got no call to go and tell her so. I never said six words to her myself. I ain't a goin' to tell her so.* {David Copperfield 8}
Summons, bidding, or requirement of duty.

call a health ... *why don't you call a health, Mr. Darnay; why don't you give your toast?* {Tale of Two Cities 2-4}
Propose a 'to-your-health' toast.

calling *The Doctor occupied two floors of a large but still house, where several callings purported to be pursued by day, but whereof little was audible any day* ... {Tale of Two Cities 2-6}
Vocation, occupation.

call someone out ... *if this Dowler attempts (as I have no doubt he will) to carry into execution his threat of personal violence against myself, it will be incumbent on me to call him out.* {Pickwick Papers 38}
Challenge someone to a duel.

cambric ... *his fine frilled shirt and cambric neckcloth looked unusually soft and white* ... {David Copperfield 15}
A fine white linen, originally made at Cambray in Flanders.

came in my way *He came in my way at last.* {Oliver Twist 51}
(see **come in my way**)

came on to *By degrees [the wind] lulled and died away; and then it came on to snow.* {Old Curiosity Shop 70}
To become disagreeable. Said of night, winter, bad weather etc.

came up to time ... *and yet never sunk down or gave way to despair or wrath, but, in prize-fighting phraseology, always came up to time with a cheerful countenance, and went in to win as if nothing had happened.* {Barnaby Rudge 22}
Presented himself ready and alert at the start of a round, when the referee called 'time'.

camlet ... *with a very little second-hand camlet cloak, worn theatrically over his left shoulder* ... {Nicholas Nickleby 30}

A cloth originally made of camel's hair and silk, but since applied to material made from Angora or even wool.

camphorated spirits ... *[They] rub themselves on the slightest provocation with camphorated spirits and other lotions applicable to mumps, sore-throat, rheumatism, or lumbago.* {Sketches, The Couple Who Coddle Themselves}
Camphor dissolved in alcohol or wine and used as a liniment.

camphor julep *"Nervous," said Bob Sawyer complacently. "Camphor julep and water three times a day, and composing draught at night."* {Pickwick Papers 48}
Camphor, used as a medication, in a liquid sweetened with syrup.

can *"Make anything you like of me!" cried Hugh, flourishing the can he had emptied more than once.* {Barnaby Rudge 39}
A metal drinking cup.

cane, caning *Tickler was a wax-ended piece of cane, worn smooth by collision with my tickled frame.* {Great Expectations 2}
1. Bamboo or a bamboo-like wood, but here might be any slender piece of wood used to whip someone.
... his old schoolmaster meeting him in Cheapside, might have been unable to withstand the temptation of caning him on the spot. {Our Mutual Friend 1-4}
2. To whip with a stick of cane.

cane form *It was a bare, resounding room, smelling of stables, with cane forms along the walls ...* {Bleak House 14}
A bench made from woven strips of cane.

cankerworm *A cankerworm pegging away at your vitals in secret ...* {Somebody's Luggage 3}
A caterpillar that eats leaves and flower buds.

cannonier *... the sea cast him up against a cannon, and on the instant he became a cannonier ...* {Tale of Two Cities 2-21}
An artilleryman, a gunner.

cant *"Man," said the Ghost, "if man you be in heart, not adamant, forbear that wicked cant . . . "* {A Christmas Carol 3}
1. A manner of speaking, phraseology.
Sheep was a cant word of the time for a spy, under the gaolers. {Tale of Two Cities 3-8}
2. Slang, jargon.

canvas *I shall have the pleasure of canvassing you for the county, one of these fine mornings.* {The Battle of Life 3}
Solicit a vote, here for a seat on the next to-be-elected county council.

canvas frock *He, and his old canvas frock, and his loose stockings, and all his poor tatters of clothes . . .* {Tale of Two Cities 1-6}
A loose outer garment, coat-like (a frock), made of canvas.

canvas-lamp *This narrow street . . . [is] full of low lodging-houses, as you see by the transparent canvas-lamps and blinds, announcing beds for travellers!* {Reprinted Pieces, On Duty With Inspector Field}
An advertisement painted on a thin cloth and illuminated from behind by a lamp.

cap *"Odd," said the old gentleman, taking the gun. "Never knew one of them to miss fire before. Why, I don't see anything of the cap."* {Pickwick Papers 7}
A percussion cap, a cap-shaped piece of copper lined with a fulminating compound which, when struck by the hammer of the gun, explodes and ignites the gunpowder.

caper *. . . breathless Mr. Craggs began to doubt already, whether country dancing had been made 'too easy,' like the rest of life; and Mr. Snitchey, with his nimble cuts and capers, footed it for Self and Craggs . . .* {The Battle of Life 2}
A lively or frisky dance step.

capital *Boxes appeared in the bedrooms (where they were capital at other times), and a surprising amount of packing took place . . .* {Edwin Drood 13}
Deadly, fatal, vitally injurious.

capsicum . . . *Cayenne pepper and chopped pickled Capsicum!* {Our Mutual Friend 4-9}
A plant material, very hot and burning to the taste. Capsicum does not have the current British meaning of sweet green pepper.

capstan *On the beach, among the rough luggers and capstans groups of storm-beaten boatmen. . . watched under the lee of those objects* . . . {Reprinted Pieces, Out of the Season}
A kind of winch consisting of a vertical post turned by bars inserted in its top and around which a rope can be wound.

captain's biscuits . . . *captain's biscuits (which are always a moist and jovial sort of viand)* . . . {Martin Chuzzlewit 5}
A dry, hard biscuit, never at all moist and jovial.

caption *"Very good,"* said the attorney. *"You will have the caption made to-morrow, of course?"* {Pickwick Papers 21}
Arrest or apprehension by judicial process.

car *When I had the privillidge of being your fellow-traveller in the cars, the day before yesterday, you offered some remarks upon the Tower of London* . . . {Martin Chuzzlewit 22}
In this example the word refers to railroad cars. Before railroads it referred to any kind of wheeled vehicle.

car and griffins . . . *arrived at Greenwich in a car and griffins* . . . {Our Mutual Friend 4-4}
A car can be any kind of wheeled vehicle. Griffin is a slang term for a grim-looking vigilant guardian. Here it probably refers to a pair of rough-looking footmen.

caravan, traveling caravan *On the border of this common, and close to the hedge which divided it from the cultivated fields, a caravan was drawn up to rest* . . . {Old Curiosity Shop 26}
1. A sort of small house on wheels, a horse-drawn house trailer.
He had never seen such a fat boy, in or out of a traveling caravan . . . {Pickwick Papers 54}
2. A traveling show or menagerie.

carbine *He is no more like flesh and blood than a rusty old carbine is.* {Bleak House 47}
A kind of firearm shorter than a rifle or musket.

carbuncle ... *like a monstrous carbuncle in a fairy tale.* {Barnaby Rudge 54}
A fiery red precious stone.

card ... *see the numbers o' people as has been broughten into bein' heer, fur to weave and to card, an' to piece out a livin'* ... {Hard Times 2-5}
To use a card, a kind of wire brush, to comb wool fibers.

card of terms *Perhaps you will have the goodness to take a card of terms with you?* {Nicholas Nickleby 3}
Price list.

carking *The young gentlemen were prematurely full of carking anxieties.* {Dombey & Son 11}
Worrisome, fretting.

carman ... *Tipp, who was the carman, and wore a red jacket, used to address me sometimes as "David"* ... {David Copperfield 11}
The driver of a wagon or car.

carmine *"Some artists," said Miss La Creevy, "keep a red coat, and charge seven-and-sixpence extra for hire and carmine, but I don't do that myself, for I don't consider it legitimate."* {Nicholas Nickleby 10}
The red pigment made from cochineal, the dried bodies of small insects that live in cactus plants, mainly in Mexico. It was probably much more expensive than the mineral pigments.

carpet-bag ... *clerks and that, who hire a uniform coat to be painted in and send it here in a carpet bag.* {Nicholas Nickleby 10}
A piece of luggage made of carpet material and fitted with handles.

carpet cap ... *and divers strong men in carpet caps were balancing chests of drawers and other trifles of that nature upon their heads, and performing muscular feats which heightened their complexions*

considerably. {Old Curiosity Shop 13}
A cap made of carpet material, often worn by porters.

carpet-dance . . . *to come and play quadrilles for a carpet-dance.* {Our
Mutual Friend 1-11}
An informal dance, one in which the carpet is left down. The carpet was
always removed for large formal dances.

carriage . . . *an elderly lady . . . with a proud carriage and a handsome
face, was in the doorway as we alighted* . . . {David Copperfield 20}
1. Posture.
[She] . . . *put her hand upon his proferred arm, and got into the
carriage, which was a little, low, park carriage with a hood.* {Bleak
House 18}
2. Any wheeled vehicle for carrying people. A park carriage would be
one used mainly on the grounds of an estate, i.e., in the park of the
estate.

carriage dog . . . *the united energies of two horses, two men, four wheels,
and a plum-pudding carriage dog* . . . {Our Mutual Friend 3-4}
A coach dog, usually a Dalmatian, trained to run alongside a carriage as
a social affectation.

carriage-double . . . *we had as many as six runaway carriage-doubles at
our door in one night!* {The Chimes 4}
A double knock on the door was used to announce the arrival of visitors
by carriage. Frequently, mischievous children would knock on the door
of a house, imitating the arrival of visitors, and then run away before the
door was opened. Hence a runaway carriage-double knock.

carriage-head *There was a folding-window to the carriage-head, but I
never closed it* . . . {Bleak House 42}
The roof or top of the carriage, often a folding top.

carriage-steps *In the large inn-yards . . . horses clattered on the uneven
stones, carriage steps fell rattling down* . . . {Old Curiosity Shop 19}
The steps, usually hinged to the carriage body, for getting in and out of
the carriage. They were swung down to permit people to step down
from the carriage.

carrier ... *he was but a Carrier by the way* ... {Cricket on the Hearth 1}
A person who delivers goods and parcels.

carrying *I had seen the sheaved corn carrying in the golden fields as I came down to the river* ... {The Uncommercial Traveller, Chatham Dockyard}
Bearing, as in bearing fruit.

carrying-traffic ... *cross by an open cutting at the candelabra, seize the carrying-traffic at the console* ... {Our Mutual Friend 3-17}
The carrying of goods, the traffic of transporting goods.

carry it hollow *There are always on board ship, a Sanguine One, and a Despondent One. The latter carried it hollow at this period of the voyage, and triumphed over the Sanguine One at every meal* ... {American Notes, 16}
To win the contest, win the day. The word 'hollow' adds a sense of completeness, thoroughness.

cartel ... *there was something so exquisitely absurd in such a cartel of defiance, that Nicholas was obliged to bite his lip and read the note over two or three times* ... {Nicholas Nickleby 29}
A written challenge.

carter ... *the occasional smacking of the carter's whip* ... {Old Curiosity Shop 46}
The driver of a cart, a wagon used for hauling goods.

cart-house ... *he had gotten out by a trap in the floor which communicated with an empty cart-house below.* {Bleak House 31}
A shed or outhouse for carts.

cartridge-paper ... *there was a yellow old cartridge-paper pad upon his desk, unsoiled by ink, and reported to be twenty years of age.* {David Copperfield 35}
A rough kind of paper used for making cartridges for guns, and also for rough drawing.

ca-sa *I've noted down the amount of the taxed costs and damages for which the ca-sa was issued, and we had better settle at once and lose no time.* {Pickwick Papers 40}
Abbreviation for *capias ad satisfaciendum*, a writ permitting the imprisonment of a defendant until the plaintiff's claim is satisfied.

case, in better case ... *as if he found himself in better case.* {Our Mutual Friend 2-16}
Better off. 'In good case' means 'well off '.

case-bottle ... *and bearing in one hand a most enormous sandwich, while in the other he supported a goodly sized case-bottle, to both of which he applied himself with relish* ... {Pickwick Papers 50}
A bottle, often square, designed to fit together with others in a case.

casement ... *he saw the cheerful light of the blazing fires gleam through the old casements* ... {Pickwick Papers 29}
A window-sash hinged on its vertical side, a casement window.

casino *In the evening I used to go back to the prison, and walk up and down the parade with Mr. Micawber; or play casino with Mrs. Micawber* ... {David Copperfield 11}
A card game.

cast ... *a cast in his eye* ... {Pickwick Papers 17}
1. A squint, a permanent turning to one side of one eye.
... *he never left casting up; and he got to so many million at last that I don't believe he's ever been quite right since.* {Martin Chuzzlewit 11}
2. To cast up is to add or calculate.

castor ... *the waiter laid a cloth* ... *and put a set of castors on it.* {David Copperfield 5}
1. A small container with a perforated top, used for pepper and the like.
Pop that shawl away in my castor, Dodger, so that I may know where to find it when I cut; ... {Oliver Twist 25}
2. A hat made of beaver fur, or something to resemble beaver fur.
Mrs. Miff ... *dexterously turns him back, and runs him, as on castors,*

full at the "good lady" ... {Dombey & Son 31}
3. Small wheels on pivots used on furniture.

Casual *You're not in a state to be let come upon strange parishes 'ceptin as a Casual.* {Our Mutual Friend 3-8}
A temporary or occasional pauper, one not permitted to be a permanent inmate of a workhouse.

catamaran *"At his what?" said Peg. "Oh dear! She can never hear the most important word, and hears all the others!" whined Gride. "At his expense--you catamaran!"* {Nicholas Nickleby 53}
A quarrelsome person, especially a woman.

catawampous ... *there air some catawampous chawers in the small way too, as graze upon a human pretty strong* ... {Martin Chuzzlewit 21}
Fiercely destructive.

Catch ... *when they sung a Glee or Catch* ... {A Christmas Carol 3}
A round, a song sung in parts, especially one in which the words of the various parts combine to be ludicrous.

Catch-em-alive O ... *there was one little picture-room devoted to a few of the regular sticky old Saints, with* ... *such coats of varnish that every holy personage served for a fly-trap, and became what is now called in the vulgar tongue a Catch-em-alive O.* {Little Dorrit 1-16}
Flypaper. Sheets of paper coated with a very sticky material from which a fly, once it landed on the stuff, could not escape.

catchpole ... ... *skipping over [the kennel] and standing in delightful daring of the catchpoles on the free side* ... {The Uncommercial Traveller, On an Amateur Beat}
A sheriff's deputy. Originally a chicken chaser, from the French word *poul* meaning chicken.

catechist ... *like a docile and attentive pupil before his catechist* ... {Tale of Two Cities 2-16}
One who teaches catechism, the elementary principles of the Christian religion.

caudle ... *and a grater like a blessed infant's shoe, in tin, with a little heel to put the nutmeg in: as many times I've seen and said, and used for caudle when required within the month.* {Martin Chuzzlewit 46}
A warm drink for a sick person or a woman during childbirth. There are various recipes some of which include thin gruel, wine, and spices while others call for warm beer, spices, eggs, and sugar. The month referred to by Mrs. Gamp is the month following the birth of a child, for which she was often hired to assist the new mother.

caul *I was born with a caul, which was advertised for sale, in the newspapers, at the low price of fifteen guineas.* {David Copperfield 1}
The amnion, one of the fetal membranes, when it encloses the head of a child at birth. Superstitiously believed to protect against drowning.

cauldron ... *and turn the pens of Smithfield market into stakes and cauldrons* ... {Barnaby Rudge 37}
A very large kettle, here used as an instrument of torture.

caulker ... *and went past breaker's yards, caulkers' yards,* ... *and a great litter of such places* ... {David Copperfield 3}
A worker who caulks ships, i.e., drives a waterproofing material into the spaces between the planks of hull and deck.

causeway ... *a little causeway made of stones* ... {Great Expectations 54}
A landing pier projecting into the water.

cavatina ... *[she] proceeded to sing the popular cavatina of "Bid me discourse," accompanied on the piano by Mr. Tippin* ... {Sketches, The Tuggs's at Ramsgate}
A short musically simple song.

cellerage ... *Mr. Grewgious's sleeping-room was across the common stair; and he held some not empty cellerage at the bottom of the common stair.* {Edwin Drood 11}
Cellars, the place in cellars.

cellar-board ... *fitting visionary feet and legs into a cellar-board full of boots and shoes* ... {Sketches, Meditations in Monmouth-street}
A sale-board, having on it many of the goods sold in the store, at the

level of the cellar. This was present when the business was conducted from a store in the cellar.

cellar-flap . . . *a tipsy man fell through the cellar-flap of an empty house . . . and wasn't found till the new tenant went in . . .* {Nicholas Nickleby 41}
A hinged door placed flat on the ground and leading into the cellar.

censer *Gently with your light, friend. You swing it like a censer.* {Barnaby Rudge 34}
A carrier for burning incense, swung to and fro to spread the scent.

centinel *The smoking centinel at the door interposed in this place, and without taking his pipe from his lips, growled, "Here's the gal a comin' down."* {Old Curiosity Shop 11}
Sentinel.

centre-bit *Crape, keys, centre-bit, darkies--nothing forgotten?* {Oliver Twist 22}
A drill for drilling holes in wood, having a projecting central point. Known as a burglar's tool in the nineteenth century.

cesspool *Alleys and archways, like so many cesspools, disgorged their offences of smell, and dirt . . .* {A Christmas Carol 4}
A hole dug to receive liquid waste from any source, usually toilets, which retains the solid materials and allows the water to seep away.

cestus *Instantly, Miss Skiffins stopped it with the neatness of a placid boxer, took off that girdle or cestus as before, and laid it on the table.* {Great Expectations 37}
A belt or girdle for the waist worn in ancient times, especially by brides.

chace . . . *boats and seamen stationed there for the chace of the pirates.* {English Prisoners 1}
Chase, a naval term that means the pursuit of a ship.

chaff . . . *he poses the drowsy bench with legal "chaff," inexplicable to the uninitiated and to most of the initiated too . . .* {Bleak House 19}
1. Annoying banter, without anger, but exasperating.

He has bought two specimens of poultry, which, if there be any truth in adages, were certainly not caught with chaff. . . {Bleak House 49}
2. Worthless material, the remains after the grain has been removed from wheat.

chaff-biscuits *Salt meat and new rum; pease-pudding and chaff-biscuits.* {Nicholas Nickleby 22}
To chaff, in bread making, is to form dough into a ball so as to make a round loaf. In that sense a chaff-biscuit would be like a roll. Chaff also means the husk of the grain, and chaff-bread is a coarse, poor quality bread.

chaffering *. . . in a shrill cracked voice that somehow makes itself heard, above all the chaffering and vending hum.* {Reprinted Pieces, Our French Watering-place}
Bargaining or chattering.

chain-cable *These were succeeded by anchor and chain-cable forges, where sledge hammers were dinging upon iron all day long.* {Dombey & Son 9}
A ship's anchor line, made from chain.

chair *. . . see if Dolly has finished dressing, and to tell her that the chair that was ordered for her will be here in a minute . . .* {Barnaby Rudge 13}
An enclosed chair carried on poles by two men. Often called a sedan, or a sedan chair.

chairmen *The very chairmen seemed favored rivals as they bore her down the street.* {Barnaby Rudge 13}
Those whose occupation it was to carry a sedan chair. Two men were required for each chair.

chaise *Meanwhile, the other man sat very composedly in his vehicle, which was a kind of chaise with a depository for a large bag of tools . . .* {Barnaby Rudge 2}
Any light horse-drawn vehicle, usually without a driver's seat and often without the shafts that were attached to the horse's harness.

chaise and four *Chaise and four directly! Out with 'em!* {Pickwick Papers 9}
A chaise drawn by four horses. Being very light, a chaise drawn by four horses would be very fast.

chaise-cart ... *Uncle Pumblechook ..., who was a well-to-do corn-chandler in the nearest town, and drove his own chaise-cart.* {Great Expectations 4}
A light cart for carrying goods, but also suitable for riding in.

challenge *The watch found at the Weir was challenged by the jeweller as one he had wound and set for Edwin Drood ...* {Edwin Drood 16}
The word is here used in an old sense of 'to claim'.

chamberlain *In those times a bed was always to be got there at any hour of the night, and the chamberlain ... showed me straight into the bedroom ...* {Great Expectations 45}
The attendant at an inn in charge of the bedchambers, or bedrooms.

chamber-robe ... *Monsieur the Marquis walked to and fro in his loose chamber-robe, to prepare himself gently for sleep ...* {Tale of Two Cities 2-9}
A kind of bathrobe or dressing gown, worn informally indoors.

chambers *It was because I was thoroughly glad to see you ... that I gave you this address instead of my address at chambers.* {David Copperfield 27}
The rooms occupied by a lawyer. Also sometimes used to mean a set of rooms meant to be lived in by one person.

chamomile tea *They likewise indulge in chamomile tea and such-like compounds ...* {Sketches, The Couple Who Coddle Themselves}
A medicinal tea made from camomile flowers.

champing ... *licking, and even champing the moister wine-rotted fragments [of the wine cask.]* {Tale of Two Cities 1-5}
Biting hard on something.

chancel *Within the grill-gate of the chancel . . . white robes could be dimly seen . . .* {Edwin Drood 9}
The eastern part of a church, separated by a grill or screen, and reserved for those officiating at the services.

chancery *Thirty or forty years ago, before losses and chancery suits came upon it, it was a thriving place . . .* {Oliver Twist 50}
1. The court of the Lord Chancellor of England, which heard cases that might not properly fit into the courts of common law.
The Chicken himself attributed this punishment [to his face] to his having had the misfortune to get into chancery early in the proceedings . . . {Dombey & Son 44}
2. In boxing, his head gripped under his opponent's left arm, his face being pummeled by his opponent's right fist.

chandler *We were so fortunate as to find one . . . over a chandler's shop . . .* {David Copperfield 32}
A retail dealer in provisions. Originally, one who dealt in candles, a candler or chandler, but later applied more generally.

chaney *. . . three or four sheets of writing paper . . . a orange, and a Chaney mug with his name upon it.* {The Holly-Tree 2}
China, porcelain.

'Change *. . . Scrooge's name was good upon 'Change, for anything he chose to put his hand to.* {A Christmas Carol 1}
The Exchange, the place where business was transacted.

changes, ring the changes *. . . but would sometimes ring the changes backwards and forwards on all possible moods . . .* {Barnaby Rudge 7}
Changes are the variations in the sequence in which the bells in a set are rung. The specific variations are given names such as bob minor, bob major, nine tailors, etc.

chapel-of-ease *[The parochial workhouse beadle] is, in right and virtue of his office, possessed of all the excellences and best qualities of humanity; and that to none of those excellences, can mere companies' beadles, or court-of-law beadles, or even chapel-of-ease beadles . . . lay*

the remotest claim. {Oliver Twist 27}
A chapel built for the convenience of parishioners who live far from the church.

chaplet *Chaplets of flowers, plumes of feathers, jewels, laces, silks and satins . . .* {Dombey & Son 40}
A wreath or garland worn on the head.

chapter-house *Fragments of old wall, saint's chapel, chapter-house, convent, and monastery . . .* {Edwin Drood 3}
The building outside the church in which meetings of the members of a religious order were held.

character *She had a written character . . . and according to this document could do everything.* {David Copperfield 44}
A formal testimony given by an employer as to the qualities and habits of someone who has been in his or her employ.

charcoal *. . . they have both arrived at the conclusion that they are a terribly persecuted pair of unfortunates and have no recourse but clandestine matrimony or charcoal.* {Pickwick Papers 54}
To suffocate by the fumes of burning charcoal, hence to commit suicide.

charing *Goes out charing and washing by day . . .* {Pickwick Papers 33}
The word 'chare' corresponds to the word 'chore' in the United States. Charing is doing household chores or household cleaning, day work.

chariot *At nine, accordingly, we went out in a little chariot, and drove to London.* {David Copperfield 54}
A light four-wheeled vehicle with only back seats, but having a coach box for the driver.

chariot and pair *"Do you want to rob me, or to murder me? Which is it?" "Did you ever know a man come out to do either, in a chariot and pair, you ridiculous old vampire?"* {Oliver Twist 32}
Chariot drawn by two horses.

charity boy ... *much as a charity boy with a very good memory might get his catechism said*... {Edwin Drood 11}
A boy brought up in a private charitable institution or charity school.

charwoman *Judy*... *begins to collect in a basin various tributary streams of tea, from the bottoms of cups and saucers and from the bottom of the teapot for the little charwoman's evening meal.* {Bleak House 21}
A cleaning woman (see **charing**).

chase *Outside, the stately oaks, rooted for ages in the green ground which has never known ploughshare, but was still a chase when kings rode to battle with sword and shield*... {Bleak House 16}
Unenclosed ground reserved for hunting.

chatterbox *A set of idle chatterboxes, how should they know!* {Old Curiosity Shop 20}
Contemptuous name for a person who talks compulsively.

chaunt ... *they were not a little surprised to hear a human voice, chaunting with a highly elaborated expression of melancholy, and in tones of suffocation which a human voice might have produced from under five or six feather-beds*... {Nicholas Nickleby 49}
A variation of 'chant', to sing, especially with a prolonged or drawling intonation.

cheap jack *I am a Cheap Jack, and my own father's name was Willum Marigold.* {Doctor Marigold 1}
A traveling hawker, or street seller, who sets a price and then gradually cheapens it in a sort of reverse auction.

checks *But when they were once past the pay-place and tearing away for very life with their checks in their hands; and above all, when they were fairly in the theatre, and seated*... {Old Curiosity Shop 39}
Theater tickets, in the same sense as the check given when a coat is checked in a cloakroom.

check string ... *Mr. Squeers suddenly tugged at the check string with all his might, and cried, "Stop!" "What are you pulling a man's arm off*

for?" said the coachman, looking angrily down. {Nicholas Nickleby 38}
A string used to signal the coachman to stop. From context here, it was
apparently tied to the driver's arm.

cheek *"What does he come here cheeking us for, then?" cried Master
Kiddermaster, showing a very irascible temperament.* {Hard
Times 1-6}
Insolence, effrontery.

cheesemonger *... reference was made to Mrs. Green, lodger, at the
cheesemonger's round the corner...* {Old Curiosity Shop 21}
A seller of cheeses.

chemical *Here Camilla put her hand to her throat and began to be
quite chemical as to the formation of new combinations there.* {Great
Expectations 11}
An allusion to the formation of new substances by chemistry, here referring to the formation of previously unknown sounds.

chemist *... the baker, who in his turn folded his arms and stared at the
grocer, who stood at his door and yawned at the chemist.* {Great
Expectations 8}
A druggist or pharmacist.

chemists' lamps *... and not sicken and turn green as chemists' lamps...*
{Barnaby Rudge 9}
Blue and green bottles were illuminated in the chemists' (pharmacists')
shop windows.

chemists' shops *... pigs... with long strings at their legs, running
into clean chemists' shops and being dislodged with brooms by 'pren-
tices...* {Old Curiosity Shop 46}
Drug stores or pharmacies.

Cheshire *To these succeed, by command of Mr. Smallweed, "three
Cheshires," and to those "three small rums."* {Bleak House 20}
A kind of cheese.

cheval glass ... *an immense variety of superb dresses and materials for dresses: some arranged on stands, others laid carelessly on sofas, and others again, scattered over the carpet, hanging on cheval glasses, or mingling in some other way, with the rich furniture* ... {Nicholas Nickleby 10}
A tall mirror, swung in a frame, allowing the whole body to be viewed.

chickabiddies *Why, my dear, who'd murder sich chickabiddies as you?* {Barnaby Rudge 59}
A term of endearment, usually used with children.

chicken *"This is Christopher Nubbles, isn't it, that come in last night for felony?" said the man. His comrade replied that this was the chicken in question.* {Old Curiosity Shop 61}}
Usually a young person, but also slang for man.

chid *She gently chid me for being rude* ... {David Copperfield 2}
Chided, scolded.

chiffonier *Mr. Micawber had a few books on a little chiffonier, which he called the library* ... {David Copperfield 11}
A small cupboard with the top forming a sideboard.

chilblains ... *to think of the days when papa used to bring me here the least of girls a perfect mass of chilblains to be stuck upon a chair with my feet on the rails* ... {Little Dorrit 2-23}
Swelling and discoloration of the skin of the feet and hands, caused by exposure to cold.

chimney-board *He was just leaving the kitchen, and I was preparing to descend, when down came the infernal chimney-board with a tremendous crash.* {Sketches, A Passage in the Life of Mr. Watkins Tottle}
A large wooden board used to close the opening of a fireplace during the summer.

chimney-cowl ... *the wind was coming in gusts* ... *twirling the rusty chimney-cowls and weathercocks* ... {Little Dorrit 1-29}
A hood placed on top of the chimney, designed to turn with the wind so as to prevent the wind from blowing down the chimney.

chimney-glass *. . . and the chimney-glass, reflecting Mr. Dombey and his portrait at one blow, seemed fraught with melancholy meditations.* {Dombey & Son 5}
A mirror on the chimney-piece, above the mantel of a fireplace.

chimney-piece *He leaned against the chimney-piece, brooding . . .* {David Copperfield 16}
The ornamental structure over and around the fireplace, or the shelf above it. Includes the mantel shelf or mantelpiece.

chimney-pot *I suppose you have hardly seen anything but chimney-pots and bricks and mortar all your life, Sam . . .* {Pickwick Papers 16}
An earthenware or metal extension for the top of a chimney.

chin *. . . an air with variations on the guitar, by Miss Tippin, accompanied on the chin by Master Tippin.* {Sketches, The Tuggs's at Ramsgate}
Chin music is talk, chatter. Master Tippin was chattering away while his sister was singing.

chink *[The burning ashes from the stove] chink when they shoot out here . . .* {The Haunted Man 2}
The sound made by metal, as in coins knocking against one another.

chip *. . . while the general growth of people seem to have come into existence, buds, I seem to have come into existence a chip.* {Edwin Drood 9}
1. Something worthless.
. . . in a white chip bonnet and a dress of celestial blue! {David Copperfield 33}
2. Chip means 'wood fibers' or thin strips of wood. A chip bonnet is a hat woven from that material.

chip or tan *. . . two dry little elderly ladies, dressed in black, and each looking wonderfully like a preparation in chip or tan of the late Mr. Spenlow.* {David Copperfield 41}
Chip is thin strips of wood, such as those used in making chip baskets or chip bonnets. Tan is pieces of the bark of trees either before or after being used in the tanning of leather. The implication is that the two ladies, related to Mr. Spenlow, resembled a rough sculpture of him.

chit ... *she invariably affected to regard all male bipeds under thirty as mere chits and infants* ... {Barnaby Rudge 9}
An expression of contempt, usually used to refer to a young person.

choak ... *my tears dropped upon my bread-and-butter, and trickled into my tea, and choaked me.* {David Copperfield 4}
Choke.

choaker *In breeches and gaiters, broad-brimmed hat, grey coat, speckled choaker* ... {David Copperfield 5}
A large neckerchief worn high around the throat.

chocolate *His chocolate and toast stood upon a little table at his elbow* ...
{Barnaby Rudge 75}
Hot chocolate drink, cocoa.

choleric *Now Mr. Bumble was a fat man, and a choleric;* ... {Oliver Twist 2}
Irascible, hot-tempered.

chop-house *I dined at what Herbert and I used to call a geographical chop-house* ... {Great Expectations 47}
An eating house where chops and other meat cuts are served.

chopper ... *Mr. Lorry went into his room with a chopper, saw, chisel, and hammer* ... {Tale of Two Cities 2-19}
Axe or other tool for chopping.

choused ... *if I ain't* ... *been choused this last week into as bad luck as ever a poor devil* ... *met with!* {Tale of Two Cities 2-1}
Swindled, tricked, cheated, or defrauded.

Christmas Waits *The Christmas Waits were playing somewhere in the distance, and, through his thoughtfulness, he seemed to listen to the music.* {The Haunted Man 1}
Strolling woodwind players and singers who performed Christmas carols and accepted tips for doing so. The word 'waits' originally referred only to the woodwind instruments such as the flute and hautboy or oboe.

chuck-farthing ... *they presently fell to pitch and toss, chuck-farthing, odd or even, dog-fighting, and other Protestant recreations.* {Barnaby Rudge 37}
A game in which coins are pitched at a mark. The person whose coin comes closest to the mark may then throw all the coins at a hole and keep those that go into the hole.

chuckle-head *He was of a chuckle-headed high-shouldered make ...* {Little Dorrit 1-21}
A blockhead, a stupid person.

chummy ... *vereas, he 'ad been a chummy--he begged the cheerman's parding for usin' such a wulgar hexpression--more nor thirty year--he might say he'd been born in a chimbley ...* {Sketches, The First of May}
A chimney sweeper's helper, usually a small boy.

chump-end ... *three defaced bibles (shaped as if they had been unskilfully cut off the chump-end of something) more illegibly printed at the best than any curiosities of literature I have since met with ...* {Great Expectations 10}
The thick, blunt end of anything.

church-rates *I think the Church-Rates guesses who I am, and I know the Waterworks does because I drew a tooth of his when I first came down here.* {Pickwick Papers 38}
Taxes, usually local, earmarked for use by the church. In this quotation Bob Sawyer is referring to the collector of the tax rather than to the tax itself.

church-warden *It arose out of a scuffle between two church-wardens, one of whom was alleged to have pushed the other against a pump ...* {David Copperfield 29}
A lay honorary officer of a parish who assists in the duties of the minister and represents the parishioners.

circle at Astley's *Our fondness for that red cab was unbounded. How we should have liked to have seen it in the circle at Astley's!* {Sketches, The Last Cab-driver and the First Omnibus-cad}

Astley's was an amphitheater where equestrian shows, races, acrobats, clowns, etc. performed. It was very popular and actually was the first circus.

circus ... *the curtain that hid such gorgeous mysteries; the clean white sawdust down in the circus; the company coming in and taking their places; the fiddlers looking carelessly up at them while they tuned their instruments* ... {Old Curiosity Shop 39}
The circular area in which the performance would take place.

claptrap, clap-trap ... *it was mere professional claptrap.* {Tale of Two Cities 2-20}
There was a moral infection of clap-trap in him. {Hard Times 1-7}
Language designed to get applause, cheap and showy sentiment.

clarionet ... *playing a clarionet as dirty as himself* ... {Little Dorrit 1-7}
Clarinet.

clasp-knife ... *taking out his clasp-knife and falling upon a great piece of bread and meat* ... {Old Curiosity Shop 10}
A knife with a blade that folds into the handle, and usually locks open.

clasped book *They pretend that Sophy has a lock of [my hair] in her desk, and is obliged to shut it in a clasped book, to keep it down.* {David Copperfield 41}
A book with a strap and clasp designed to keep it closed.

clay-pit *We have orphans, I know* ... *over at the clay-pits; but they are employed by relations or friends* ... {Our Mutual Friend 1-9}
The place or hole from which clay is dug.

clean out *He has cleaned me out. But I can go and earn some more, when I like* ... {Oliver Twist 39}
Slang for to strip of money.

clear-starch *There is no King George the Fourth now* ... *to set the dandy fashion; there are no clear-starched jack-towel neckcloths, no short-waisted coats, no false calves, no stays.* {Bleak House 12}
Clear, or colorless, starch. In modern usage the word 'clear' is dropped.

clear-starcher *In this happy retreat are colonized a few clear-starchers, a sprinkling of journeymen bookbinders . . . and a seasoning of jobbing-tailors.* {Pickwick Papers 32}
One who clear starches linen, i.e, stiffens the cloth with clear, or colorless, starch.

cleave *. . . with his tongue cleaving to his mouth . . .* {Pickwick Papers 21}
To stick fast or adhere.

cleaver (see **marrowbones**)

clift *. . . the footprints of an extinct creature, hoary ages upon ages old, that geologists have identified on the face of a clift . . .* {The Uncommercial Traveller, On an Amateur Beat}
Cliff.

clock, eight-day *. . . and an eight-day clock which hadn't gone for eighteen years at least and of which the minute-hand had been twisted off for a tooth-pick.* {Old Curiosity Shop 5}
A clock that would run for eight days on one winding. A convenience since it needed winding only once a week. Earlier clocks and watches required winding at least daily.

clod-hopping *. . . a common, paltry, low-minded, clod-hopping, pipe-smoking alehouse . . .* {Martin Chuzzlewit 7}
'Clodhoppers' meant clumsy, heavy shoes used for walking on plowed fields or rough terrain, from 'clod', a clump of earth, and 'grasshopper'. It soon came to mean a stupid country man, a hick, the kind of person who wore clodhoppers.

clogs *She comes back every evening at dusk, adding clogs and an umbrella to the bonnet on wet nights . . .* {Dombey & Son 51}
Wooden-soled overshoes worn to lift the shoes above the wet street.

close *A few oil-lamps were scattered at long distances, but they only served to mark the dirty entrance to some narrow close or to show where a common stair communicated . . .* {Pickwick Papers 49}
1. An enclosure about or beside a building. A court, yard, or quadrangle.

Keeping his place of retirement very close, that he may not be visited too often by affectionate grandsons and their devoted friends . . . {Old Curiosity Shop 13}
2. Concealed, secret.
. . . *a mouldy sort of establishment in a close neighborhood* . . . {David Copperfield 19}
3. Enclosed, confined, hence crowded.

closet . . . *they walked into that gentleman's private closet, and remained there in close conversation for some quarter of an hour* . . . {Old Curiosity Shop 38}
Any small room.

clothes-horse . . . *dividing his attention between the frying-pan and a clothes-horse, over which a great number of silk handkerchiefs were hanging.* {Oliver Twist 8}
A wooden frame with horizontal bars on which clothes are hung to dry or air.

coach . . . *they agreed to occupy the seat at the back of the coach, where they could all sit together.* {Pickwick Papers 2}
A large four-wheeled vehicle with seats inside and outside for conveying passengers.

coach and six . . . *the three passengers shut up in the narrow compass of one lumbering old mail-coach* . . . *were mysteries to one another, as complete as if each had been in his own coach and six* . . . {Tale of Two Cities 1-3}
A coach drawn by six horses.

coach-bill . . . *left his carawan some years ago and took to carrying coach-bills about London* . . . {Old Curiosity Shop 19}
Advertisements for coach companies.

coach-box . . . *for a long time his Wednesday hardly ever came round, without my entertaining a misgiving that he would not be on the coach-box as usual.* {David Copperfield 17}
The seat for the driver of a coach, so-called because it is also a box

into which goods could be stowed. A passenger or two often rode on the box with the driver.

coaches *What do you call it, when Lords break off door-knockers, and beat policemen, and play at coaches with other peoples money, and all that sort of thing?* {Nicholas Nickleby 15}
This may refer to the driving of coaches as a sport, as was done by members of four-in-hand clubs, and to the propensity of some gentlemen of the time to live on borrowed money. A coach-match is a chariot race, and play is gambling, so this reference may, instead, be to betting on coach races.

coach-horser *The attorney was in high glee, for the embarrassed coach-horser was ordered to be discharged forthwith.* {Pickwick Papers 42}
A person whose business it was to supply horses for use by the coaches. The system of coach transportation was extensive, and large numbers of horses had to be supplied.

coachman *... it reached, instead, the coachman on the box, who thanked him kindly, and stuck it in his button hole.* {Martin Chuzzlewit 11}
Coach driver or guard.

coach-office *I was at the coach-office to take leave of her and see her go ...* {David Copperfield 26}
An office in which passengers and parcels were booked for the coach and where the coach was boarded.

coach-top *They were soon on the coach-top and rolling along the road.* {Barnaby Rudge 25}
The outside seats on the top of the coach.

coach trimming *... a yellow waistcoat, with a coach trimming border.* {Pickwick Papers 37}
Lace of a kind used to trim the interior of a coach.

coaling *... took in his victuals much as if he were coaling; with a good deal of noise, a good deal of dropping about, and a puff and snort occasion-*

ally . . . {Little Dorrit 1-13}
The taking on of coal by a steamship or locomotive.

coal-scuttle . . . *he had . . . so far forgotten himself as to carry a coal-scuttle up to the second floor.* {Pickwick Papers 37}
A kind of bucket or pail for holding coal, which could then be poured into the fireplace.

coalheaver . . . *calling to a full-grown coalheaver, in a waggon, who for a moment blocked the way, "Now, young 'un, who trusted* YOU *with a cart?"* {Martin Chuzzlewit 27}
One who hauls and shovels coal. He would have been strong and muscular and not a person to challenge casually.

coal-hole . . . *and doesn't she do all sorts of things, and grope into all sorts of places, coal-holes and pantries and I don't know where, that can't be very agreeable* . . . {David Copperfield 8}
A dark and dingy place in the cellar, often built into the cellar wall, in which coal for the fireplace was stored. It can also refer to a hole in the ground at the side or front of the house through which coal was delivered to the coal cellar.

coal-whipper . . . *here were colliers by the score and score, with the coal-whippers plunging off stages on deck, as counterweights to measures of coal swinging up* . . . {Great Expectations 54}
A person who hauls buckets of coal from the hold of a ship by means of a pulley and rope.

cob *He was well-mounted upon a sturdy chestnut cob, and had the graceful seat of an experienced horseman* . . . {Barnaby Rudge 10}
A stout, short-legged horse, usually one that has not been castrated.

cobbler *Mr. Pickwick at length yielded a reluctant consent to his taking lodgings by the week of a bald-headed cobbler who rented a small slip-room in one of the upper galleries.* {Pickwick Papers 44}
1. A mender or maker of shoes.
This wonderful invention, sir . . . is called a cobbler. Sherry cobbler when you name it long; cobbler, when you name it short. {Martin

Chuzzlewit 17}
2. A drink made with wine, sugar, and fruit juices, served over crushed ice.

cobbler's-wax *Either this boy sticks to it like cobbler's-wax or there is something out of the common here that beats anything that ever came my way at Kenge and Carboy's.* {Bleak House 19}
A resinous material used by shoemakers to rub on thread, which was then used to sew leather.

cockade *The red cap and tri-colour cockade were universal, both among men and women.* {Tale of Two Cities 3-1}
A ribbon, knot of ribbons, or rosette worn in the hat.

cockchafer *... a chaos of subjects, in which mackarel, and Mr. F's Aunt in a swing, had become entangled with cockchafers and the wine trade.* {Little Dorrit 2-23}
A kind of beetle, also called May beetle, or June bug.

cock-crow *... up and ringing her bell at cock-crow.* {David Copperfield 4}
The crowing of a rooster, usually considered to be at dawn.

cocked-hat *... under an old cocked-hat like a three-cornered spittoon, and over a great muffler for the chin and throat ...* {Tale of Two Cities 1-3}
A hat with a sharply turned up brim, especially a three-cornered hat.

cock-loft *... went all over the dismal house ... from cellar to cock-loft.* {Our Mutual Friend 1-15}
A room under the ridgepole of a house, the highest room in the attic.

cock's feather corps *... as a hatter, he is in a cock's feather corps ...* {The Uncommercial Traveller, Arcadian London}
A corps of Rifle Volunteers whose headgear featured a cockade.

cock-shy *"What are you doing to the man?" ... "Making a cock-shy of him" ...* {Edwin Drood 5}
An object at which things are thrown, as a form of amusement. The

word 'shy' means 'throw'. The original cock-shy took place on Shrove Tuesday, when a stick was thrown at a rooster. The thrower who knocked the bird off its feet and caught it before it got up, kept it. The phrase later came to mean any carnival type of game in which something was thrown at a target.

coeval ... *a corpulent man, with a fortnight's napkin under his arm and coeval stockings on his legs* ... {Pickwick Papers 22}
Of the same age. His stockings also were two weeks old.

coffee-biggin ... *ladies would fly out at their doors crying, "Mr. Baptist--dust-pan!" "Mr. Baptist--flour-dredger!" "Mr. Baptist--coffee-biggin!"* {Little Dorrit 1-25}
A coffee pot with a strainer inside it to keep the grounds out of the infusion. Biggin was the name of its inventor.

Coffin-plate *His legs, too, were encased in coffin plates as though in armour; and over his left shoulder he wore a short dusky cloak which seemed made of a remnant of some pall.* {Nicholas Nickleby 6}
A metal plate set into the lid of a coffin with the name of the deceased and possibly dates of birth and death.

cognovit *You gave them a* cognovit *for the amount of your costs after the trial, I'm told?* {Pickwick Papers 46}
An acknowledgment by a defendant that the plaintiff's case is just, thus permitting judgment against the defendant.

collected *Demented Traveller ... plunges at the door, rattles it.... Collected Guard appears. "Are you for Tunbridge, sir?"* {Reprinted Pieces, A Flight}
Calm and composed, by contrast with the demented traveler.

collier *Of barges, sailing colliers, and coasting traders, there were perhaps as many as now* ... {Great Expectations 54}
A ship used for carrying coal.

collier-brig *Fog creeping into the cabooses of collier-brigs; fog lying out on the yards and hovering in the rigging of great ships* ... {Bleak House 1}

A collier is a ship used for transporting coal. A brig is a kind of two-masted sailing ship; hence, a collier-brig is a coal-carrying ship rigged as a brig.

collops ... *plates of pig's face, cold ham, salt beef; or perhaps a mess of smoking hot collops.* {American Notes, 2}
Thin slices of meat, especially bacon.

colloquy ... *he never passed in at my door--never sat in colloquy with me until midnight.* {Little Dorrit 2-20}
Conversation.

columbine ... *let us at once confess to a fondness for pantomimes--to a gentle sympathy with clowns and pantaloons--to an unqualified admiration of harlequins and columbines--to a chaste delight in every action of their brief existence* ... {The Pantomime of Life}
A female character in the Harlequinade, or pantomime, who was the mistress of Harlequin.

comb-and-curlpaper ... *and the daring Miss Ferdinand had even surprised the company with a sprightly solo on the comb-and-curlpaper* ... {Edwin Drood 13}
Thin paper wrapped around the teeth of a comb and hummed into produces a sound similar to that of a kazoo.

come in for it *"What do you mean?" said Joe, adding in an undertone as he approached him again, "You'll come in for it presently, I know you will!"* {Barnaby Rudge 1}
Due to receive punishment or incur trouble.

come in my way *He'd start up from a marble coffin, to come in my way!* {Oliver Twist 33}
To be where I am, to be in my path.

come on *What could the wretched Joe do now* ... *but stand up to his journeyman, and ask him what he meant by interfering betwixt himself and Mrs. Joe; and further, whether he was man enough to come on?* {Great Expectations 15}
A challenge of defiance, a challenge to a fight.

come out ... *Walter was a little bashful at first, and might be expected to come out shortly.* {Dombey & Son 10}
To show oneself publicly, make a public declaration of opinion.

come over ... *you must put your boots on overnight; and have a telescope at each eye ... if you want to come over him.* {Oliver Twist 25}
To get the better of.

comet vintage ... *he has the moist and vinous look, and eke the boots, of one acquainted with 'Twenty port and comet vintages.* {The Uncommercial Traveller, City of London Churches}
Wine made in a year when a comet was seen, supposed to be of finer flavor.

come up *"Then come up," said the carrier to the lazy horse ...* {David Copperfield 5}
A call to a horse to start moving, such as get up, or git up, or giddy-up.

come up to time (see **came up to time**)

come Yorkshire ... *it's not exactly what we understand by 'coming Yorkshire over us' in London.* {Nicholas Nickleby 42}
To cheat or dupe someone.

comforter *The weather-beaten pea-coat, and a no less weather-beaten cap and comforter ...* {Dombey & Son 56}
A long woolen scarf.

command of feature ... *he had acquired a strong command of feature, and ... [his] face changed no more than a wall.* {Our Mutual Friend 3-5}
Control over the features, the parts of the face and its expression.

commercial-room *It was in the evening, however, that the "commercial room" was filled with a social circle, whose characters and manners it was the delight of Mr. Tupman to observe ...* {Pickwick Papers 14}
A room in an inn for the accommodation of commercial travelers (traveling salesmen) and their customers.

commercials ... *a waiter came in and said, "The commercials underneath sent up their compliments, and it wasn't the Tumbler's Arms,"* ...
{Great Expectations 13}
The commercial travelers, or traveling salesmen, in the commercial room below.

Commission de lunatico, commission of lunacy ... *if they'd just get up a pretty little Commission de lunatico at the Gray's Inn Coffee House and give me the job* ... {Old Curiosity Shop 37}
... *they'd have got out a commission of lunacy, or some dreadful thing.*
{Nicholas Nickleby 25}
An official authority to investigate and rule upon the sanity of some person.

common *On the border of this common, and close to the hedge which divided it from the cultivated fields, a caravan was drawn up to rest* ...
{Old Curiosity Shop 26}
A field not privately owned, supposedly for the use of the entire community.

commoney ... *his 'ally tors' and his 'commoneys' are alike neglected* ...
{Pickwick Papers 34}
Children's name for the ordinary, or common, type of marble used in the game of marbles.

common room ... *the ruddy gleam of the fire, streaming through the old red curtains of the common room* ... {Barnaby Rudge 2}
The public room of an inn.

commons ... *the gruel was served out; and a long grace was said over the short commons.* {Oliver Twist 2}
The share of provisions to which each member of a company is entitled. Short commons is a very small share.

company ... *the way is long, and there is much company out of doors tonight.* {Our Mutual Friend 2-15}
Numbers of people. 'Much company' means 'many people'.

compass *If what you say be true, he takes much needless trouble, sir, to compass his design.* {Barnaby Rudge 29}
1. To attain, or accomplish.
Dear sisters, let us live and die, if you list, in this green garden's compass; only shun the gloom and sadness of a cloister, and we shall be happy. {Nicholas Nickleby 6}
2. A circumscribed area or space.

compassionate *As I stood compassionating her, and thinking how in the progress of time I too had come to be part of the wrecked fortunes of that house . . .* {Great Expectations 49}
To treat with compassion.

compeer *. . . neither was Mr. Stryver, already fast shouldering his way to a large and lucrative practice, behind his compeers in this particular . . .* {Tale of Two Cities 2-5}
Equals in rank.

compittance *. . . we live on a compittance, under the will of a diseased governor.* {Our Mutual Friend 1-5}
Dialect for a competence, an income sufficient to live comfortably.

compliments *. . . she was jolly . . . and desired her compliments . . .* {David Copperfield 3}
Formal respects, greetings.

compo *I wonder whether I'm meant to be a footman or a groom or a gamekeeper or a seedsman. I look like a sort of compo of everyone on 'em.* {Pickwick Papers 12}
A slang shortening of the word 'composition', meaning a mixture.

composing draught *That done, they gave him cordial and some toast, and presently a pretty strong composing-draught, under the influence of which he soon fell into a lethargy . . .* {Barnaby Rudge 66}
A sedative or tranquilizing medication

composition *The account is now favorably balanced: my creditor has accepted a composition.* {Bleak House 19}
1. The settling of a debt or claim by some mutual arrangement.

... the figure of Venus on the first landing looked as if she were ashamed of the composition-candle in her right hand ... {Sketches, The Bloomsbury Christening}
2. A mixture. Here, a candle made from a mixture of materials instead of from tallow or a single kind of wax.

concourse *... and the concourse, which had been rapidly augmenting for some hours, and still received additions every minute, waited with an impatience which increased with every chime of St. Sepulchre's clock ...* {Barnaby Rudge 77}
An assemblage of people, a crowd.

Condemned Hold *... you were put into a species of Condemned Hold at the back, where you meditated on a misspent life ...* {Tale of Two Cities 2-1}
The cell in which a prisoner condemned to death is kept.

condign *... at one time or other contemplated the infliction of condign punishment, which they had only been restrained from administering by considerations of mercy ...* {Nicholas Nickleby 29}
Appropriate.

condition *Doctor, your clients are people of condition.* {Tale of Two Cities 3-10}
Of high rank, position, or quality.

condole *Tim Linkinwater's sister lamented; the housekeeper condoled; and both kept thrusting their heads out of the second-floor window to see if the boy was "coming" ...* {Nicholas Nickleby 37}
Grieve with, or express sympathy with other persons in their affliction.

confident *Rose also explained her reasons for not making a confident of her friend Mr. Losborne ...* {Oliver Twist 41}
Confidant, one in whom someone confides.

confined, confinement *No genteel lady was ever yet confined--indeed, no genteel confinement can possibly take place--without the accompanying symbol of a muffled knocker.* {Nicholas Nickleby 36}
To give birth, giving birth.

conkey ... *that was done by Conkey Chickweed,* ... {Oliver Twist 31}
Slang for inquisitive, nosy.

connexion *He had married a meek little dancing-mistress, with a toler-able connexion* ... *and had worked her to death* ... {Bleak House 14}
The visions rising before his mercenary mind, of the many ways in which this connexion was to be turned to account ... {Our Mutual Friend 1-5}
A contact with a person, here in the sense of having business or social value. The word also often refers to family relationships.

conning *Yet there he sat patiently conning the page again and again* ...
{Nicholas Nickleby 12}
Learning by repetition, poring over.

Consol *It was originally, I think, eight thousand pounds, Consols?*
{David Copperfield 44}
Abbreviation for 'Consolidated Annuities', bonds issued by the British government, a popular conservative investment for people with moderate amounts of capital.

Constantia ... *a glass of Constantia and a home-made biscuit.* {Edwin Drood 10}
A red wine from the Constantia farm near Cape Town, South Africa.

consumption ... *what do* you *know of the gradual sinking beneath consumption or the quick wasting of fever* ... {Pickwick Papers 21}
A wasting disease, usually tuberculosis.

consumptive *"He's been consumptive for a long time past," said Mr. Roker, "and he's taken wery bad in the breath to-night* ... " {Pickwick Papers 44}
Suffering from a wasting disease, usually tuberculosis.

controul *Circumstances beyond my controul* ... {David Copperfield 49}
A different spelling of 'control'.

contumely *But if the various banking-houses refuse to avail themselves of Mr. Micawber's abilities, or receive the offer with contumely, what*

is the use of dwelling upon that *idea?* {David Copperfield 28}
Contemptuous, insolent, insulting language or treatment.

conventicle *All slangs and twangs are objectionable everywhere, but the slang and twang of the conventicle . . . should be studiously avoided . . .* {The Uncommercial Traveller, Two Views of a Cheap Theatre}
A private religious meeting, originally of an illegal or clandestine kind.

conversable *Mrs. Bardell let lodgings to many conversable single gentlemen, with great profit, but never brought any more actions for breach of promise of marriage.* {Pickwick Papers 57}
Easy and pleasant in conversation, fond of talking.

conversazione *. . . at the evening conversazione at school, charged two-and-sixpence in the half-year's bill . . .* {The Uncommercial Traveller, Refreshments for Travellers}
An evening meeting, usually of a learned society, at which the work of the society is presented and discussed.

converse *Encouraging each other with such converse as this; but keeping very close together . . .* {Oliver Twist 28}
Conversation.

conveyancer *In dirty upper casements, here and there, hazy little patches of candlelight reveal where some wise draughtsman and conveyancer yet toils for the entanglement of real estate in meshes of sheep-skin, in the average ration of about a dozen of sheep to an acre of land.* {Bleak House 32}
A lawyer who prepares documents for the conveyance of property. Legal documents were written on parchment, made from sheepskin.

convolvulus *. . . even the wild convolvulus and rose and sweetbriar, are the worse for his going by, and need time to recover from the taint of him in the air.* {The Uncommercial Traveller, Tramps}
Morning glory and similar plants.

cookery *. . . everybody felt disposed to do justice to the meal, notwithstanding that the meat had been purchased and dressed, and the pie made*

and baked, at the prison-cookery hard by. {Pickwick Papers 44}
A kitchen or cook shop.

copper ... *the two young Cratchits hustled Tiny Tim, and bore him off into the wash-house, that he might hear the pudding singing in the copper.* {A Christmas Carol 3}
A large boiler or very large cooking pot made of copper or iron, and sometimes supported on a base of bricks. It was often too large for the kitchen and so was used in one of the outbuildings

copper-plate ... *a connubial copper-plate Mr. and Mrs. Veneering, requesting the honour of Mr. and Mrs. Boffin's company at dinner...* {Our Mutual Friend 1-17}
Material such as invitations and calling cards printed from engravings made on plates of copper.

copper-stick *It was Christmas Eve, and I had to stir the pudding for the next day with a copper-stick, from seven to eight by the Dutch clock.* {Great Expectations 2}
This probably refers to a large wooden stick used for stirring the food being cooked in a copper (see **copper**).

coppice-wood ... *a quiet coppice-wood, in which many leaves of burning red and golden yellow still remained upon the trees.* {Tale of Two Cities 1-3}
A wood or grove of small trees, grown for the purpose of periodic cutting.

copy-book ... *dog's-eared lesson-books, cracked slates, tear-blotted copy-books, canings, rulerings, hair-cuttings, rainy Sundays ...* {David Copperfield 7}
Usually a book containing materials to be copied by pupils, but the fact that they were tear-stained suggests that they were the books in which the students made their copies of assigned material.

copyhold *Think of the laws appertaining to real property... to leasehold, freehold, and copyhold estate ...* {The Battle of Life 1}
An ancient legal way of having the use of land granted by the lord of a manor.

corbel ... *the dim angel's heads upon the corbels of the roof, seeming to watch their progress.* {Edwin Drood 12}
Originally a construction jutting out from a wall and supporting the weight above. It has been used here to mean a carved corbel.

cordially ... *beginning to hate him, he began to hate him cordially.* {Nicholas Nickleby 50}
Heartily, with all one's heart. Used here with sarcasm.

cords ... *a servant, most wonderful got up in milk-white cords and tops* ... {Going into Society}
Corduroy breeches.

corked ... *I perceived that I was in the presence of Mr. Barlow--corked!* {The Uncommercial Traveller, Mr. Barlow}
Face blackened with a burnt cork for a performance in a minstrel show.

cork-jacket *Whether sea-going people were short of money about that time, or were short of faith and preferred cork-jackets, I don't know* ...
A sailor's life jacket, made of cork for flotation.

corn *I am at present, my dear Copperfield, engaged in the sale of corn upon commission.* {David Copperfield 27}
British corn is American wheat, though the word may mean any kind of grain.

corn-chandler ... *Uncle Pumblechook* ... *who was a well-to-do corn-chandler in the nearest town* ... {Great Expectations 4}
A retail dealer in grains. The word 'chandler' originally meant a maker of candles. It later came to mean a retail dealer in general supples, and then, in phrases like 'corn-chandler', a retail dealer in the specified merchandise.

corner pin *Why, lord set you up like a corner pin, we've a reg'lar playground o' children here.* {Little Dorrit 1-6}
In bowling or skittles, the pins at the corners of the pattern of pins.

Cornet of Dragoons *Now this gentleman had a younger brother of still better appearance than himself, who had tried life as a Cornet of Dragoons, and found it a bore* . . . {Hard Times 2-2}
A officer of junior rank in a cavalry unit.

cornfactor, corn-factor *There were, within sight, an auctioneer's and a fire-agency office, a cornfactor's, a linen-draper's* . . . {Pickwick Papers 7}
One who deals in grains, selling on commission.

corn-sheaves *The last soft light of the setting sun had fallen on the earth, casting a rich glow on the yellow corn-sheaves* . . . {Pickwick Papers 6}
Bundles of wheat.

cornelian . . . *the coral necklace which rested on her neck, supporting, outside her frock, a lonely cornelian heart* . . . {Nicholas Nickleby 39}
A variety of chalcedony, a reddish quartz stone.

corpse candles *I had heard of corpse candles, and at last I persuaded myself that this must be a corpse bell tolling of itself at midnight for the dead.* {Barnaby Rudge 1}
A superstition. Flickering lights supposed to be seen in a churchyard or by a grave, predicting a death or the route of a funeral.

corse *For my sake--for mine, Lenville--forego all idle forms, unless you would see me a blighted corse at your feet.* {Nicholas Nickleby 29}
Corpse. A theatrical, Shakespearian word.

cosmography . . . *astronomy, geography, and general cosmography* . . . {Hard Times 1-2}
The science that maps the general features of the earth and heavens. It is now considered a part of astronomy.

cosmorama *The temples and saloons and cosmoramas and fountains glittered and sparkled before our eyes* . . . {Sketches, Vauxhall-gardens by Day}
A peep show containing views of many places in the world, seen through a magnifying glass placed in a small hole in the end of the view-box.

costermonger *Covent Garden market, and the avenues leading to it, are thronged with carts of all sorts, sizes, and descriptions, from the heavy lumbering waggon, with its four stout horses, to the jingling costermonger's cart, with its consumptive donkey.* {Sketches, The Streets--Morning}
A street-seller of fruits, vegetables, or other things, who had a barrow or cart to hold his goods.

cot *... the rushes among which it was the intention of himself and Mrs. Blimber to dwell, and the bee that would hum around their cot.* {Dombey & Son 60}
A poetic word for a small house or cottage.

cottage-bonnet *... a young lady brought me home a chip cottage-bonnet, with white and green trimming, and green persian lining...* {Nicholas Nickleby 10}
A woman's hat of the kind seen in early portraits of Queen Victoria. A bonnet had the shape of an inverted flower pot, with a wide brim turned up at the front and down at the back. A cottage-bonnet was smaller and less fancily decorated. It was sometimes made of straw.

cottage-loaf *... the refection had the appearance of a small cottage-loaf and a pennyworth of milk.* {Our Mutual Friend 3-16}
A loaf of bread made from two lumps of dough, a smaller one being stuck on top of the larger.

cottage piano *My dear girl had a cottage piano there and quietly sat down to sing some of Richard's favourites...* {Bleak House 60}
A small upright piano.

cotter *... windy weather suggested by every cotter's little rick, with its thatch straw-ridged...* {The Uncommercial Traveller, The Shipwreck}
A peasant who occupies a cottage and rents a small plot of land from a farm, often in exchange for work on the farm.

cotton *... it is a world wrapped up in too much jeweler's cotton and fine wool...* {Bleak House 2}
Cotton wool, cotton balls.

cottons ... *the gentlemen who condescended to appear in plush shorts and cottons for a quarterly stipend* ... {Pickwick Papers 47}
Cotton clothing.

cotton to *"I don't object to Short," she says, "but I cotton to Codlin."* {Old Curiosity Shop 37}
To be drawn to, or attached to.

couch *He's a very nice old man* ... *He used to draw my couch.* {Dombey & Son 12}
Paul Dombey is referring to a sort of wheelchair in which he was wheeled to the beach when he was too ill to walk there.

coulisse ... *there was a rustic theatre, open to the sky; the stage a green slope; the coulisses, three entrances upon a side* ... {Reprinted Pieces, To Be Read at Dusk}
The wings of a stage.

counsellor *A field-marshal has his uniform* ... *a counsellor his silk gown; a beadle his cocked hat.* {Oliver Twist 37}
An attorney, a barrister.

counsellors' bands *The litter of rags* ... *might have been counsellors' bands and gowns torn up.* {Bleak House 5}
Strips of cloth, extensions of the collar, worn in formal dress by, among others, lawyers.

countenance *You have much too open and generous a countenance for that.* {Nicholas Nickleby 27}
The expression of one's face.

counter *Mrs. Kenwigs, my dear, will you sort the counters?* {Nicholas Nickleby 14}
Pieces of metal, ivory, or other materials used to keep track of scores in games.

countermine *I should be glad to countermine him, respecting the handsome gal, your friend.* {Our Mutual Friend 4-8}
Originally, an exploding mine placed so as to destroy a mine planted by

the enemy; but figuratively, a plot or ploy designed to foil someone else's plot.

counterpane *Mr. Cruncher reposed under a patchwork counterpane, like a Harlequin at home.* {Tale of Two Cities 2-1}
An ornamental bed cover.

counting-house *The confined room, strong of parchment-grease, is warehouse, counting-house, and copying-office.* {Bleak House 10}
A room for bookkeeping and business correspondence, an office.

coupé ... *it was our destiny always to clatter through it, in the coupé of the diligence from Paris* ... {Reprinted Pieces, Our French Wateringplace}
A closed carriage seating two with the driver outside.

couper *Tally-ho Thompson was a famous horse-stealer, couper, and magsman.* {Reprinted Pieces, The Detective Police}
A dealer in horses and cattle, a dishonest one in this context.

course *They had been lectured at from their tenderest years; coursed like little hares.* {Hard Times 1-3}
To pursue rabbits with greyhounds.

courser *Sometimes, there was the clash of armour, and the gleaming of the moon on caps of steel; and, at others, jaded coursers were spurred up to the gate, and a female form glided hurriedly forth, as if eager to demand tidings of the weary messenger.* {Nicholas Nickleby 6}
A swift horse.

court ... *the Dodger and Charley Bates had filed off down the first convenient court they came to.* {Oliver Twist 10}
A yard, or courtyard, enclosed by buildings.

cove, covey *Two coves in vite aprons--touches their hats wen you walk in.* {Pickwick Papers 10}
Slang for man. In the United States the word would be 'guy'.

Coventry *You are the Hand they have sent to Coventry, I mean?* {Hard Times 2-4}
To be sent to Coventry is to be ostracized, excluded from any contact with people.

cover ... *we found that lady in the midst of a voluminous correspondence, opening, reading, and sorting letters, with a great accumulation of torn covers on the floor.* {Bleak House 23}
The wrapping of a letter or package, also the envelope.

coverlet *"... I dare say," returned Sir Mulberry, tossing his arm restlessly upon the coverlet.* {Nicholas Nickleby 38}
The uppermost covering of a bed, the counterpane.

covert *A thick wood skirted the meadow-land in another direction; but they could not have gained that covert for the same reason.* {Oliver Twist 35}
Shelter, a hiding place.

coverture ... *Madame Mantalini appeared to make reference, more than once, to certain debts incurred by Mr. Mantalini previous to her coverture ...* {Nicholas Nickleby 21}
A legal term for the condition of a woman during her marriage, when she is supposed to be under the protection and authority of her husband.

cowcumber ... *I don't think anybody but a man as was stone-blind would mistake Fixem for [a gentleman]; and as for me, I was as seedy as a cheap cowcumber.* {Sketches, The Broker's Man}
A form of 'cucumber' used in the seventeenth and eighteenth centuries.

cow-heel ... *but I fear his father dealt in pork, and that his business did once involve cow-heel and sausages ...* {Barnaby Rudge 15}
Jellied cow feet or ox feet.

cow on the chimney-pots *Who could continue to exist where there are no cows but the cows on the chimney-pots ...* {Pickwick Papers 7}
A device on top of a chimney that turns with the wind and keeps the

wind from blowing down the chimney. It was probably originally called a chimney-cowl, rather than a chimney-cow.

cowslip wine *Peggoty's promised letter... arrived... and with it a cake in a perfect nest of oranges, and two bottles of cowslip wine.* {David Copperfield 7}
Wine made from the flowers of the cowslip, a wild plant.

coxcombical *For he is, by heaven, the most self-satisfied, and the shallowest, and the most coxcombical and utterly brainless ass!* {Bleak House 18}
Foolishly conceited. From 'coxcomb', a cap worn by a professional fool, resembling the comb of a rooster.

crack *The crib's barred up at night like a jail; but there's one part we can crack, safe and softly.* {Oliver Twist 19}
1. Slang for a burglary.
... a snug little shop at the crack end of the Yard ... {Little Dorrit 2-13}
2. Preeminent, first-class, the best.

crackers *... and she started when I let them off, as if they had been crackers.* {David Copperfield 48}
Firecrackers.

cracksman *You'll be a fine young cracksman ...* {Oliver Twist 25}
Slang for burglar, housebreaker.

crack up *Our backs is easy ris. We must be cracked-up, or they rises, and we snarls. We shows our teeth, I tell you, fierce. You'd better crack us up, you had!* {Martin Chuzzlewit 33}
To praise or eulogize.

cramp-bones *Such mean little boys, when they were not dancing, with string, and marbles, and cramp-bones in their pockets ...* {Bleak House 38}
The kneecap of a sheep, superstitiously believed to protect against cramps.

cranky   . . . *his friend appeared to be rather 'cranky' in point of temper* . . . {Old Curiosity Shop 7}
Irritable, of uncertain temper.

crape   . . . *taking off his hat, to see that the black crape band was all right; and finding that it was, putting it on again* . . . {Martin Chuzzlewit 20}
Crepe, a thin silk or imitation silk fabric.   When black, it is used as a symbol of mourning.

cravat   *His cravat was in hue and pattern, like one of those mantles which hair-dressers are accustomed to wrap about their clients* . . . {Martin Chuzzlewit 4}
A kerchief tied around the neck with a bow in front.

craze   *"A poor fellow with a craze, sir,"* said Mr. Dick, *"a simpleton, a weak minded person."* {David Copperfield 45}
A mental flaw or defect.

crazy   . . . *the floor of the crazy stairs and landing cracked beneath the tread of the other travellers who were passing to their beds* . . . {Old Curiosity Shop 19}
Cracked, damaged, likely to fall apart.

crest   . . . *grinning again with a pen in his mouth, like some nobleman's or gentleman's crest.* {Old Curiosity Shop 33}
An animal form above the coat of arms, often shown holding something in its mouth.

crib   *The crib's barred up at night like a jail; but there's one part we can crack, safe and softly.* {Oliver Twist 19}
1. Slang for house.
Child, being fond of toys, cribbed the necklace, hid it, played with it, cut the string, and swallowed a bead. {Pickwick Papers 32}
2. Steal, snitch.
. . . *a mean little airless lodging, a mere closet for one, a mere crib for two* . . . {Hard Times 3-9}
3. A narrow room.

Cribb, Thomas *"No worse than yerself," retorted Bailey, guarding his head, on a principle invented by Mr. Thomas Cribb. "Ah! Come Now! Do that agin, will yer!"* {Martin Chuzzlewit 9}
Tom Cribb was a famous champion boxer who defeated Jem Belcher, the fighter for whom the Belcher kerchief is named.

cried the game *... others playing at ball with some adventurous throwers outside, others looking on at the racket-players or watching the boys as they cried the game.* {Pickwick Papers 45}
Shouted encouragement and so forth in response to the course of the game.

crier *The crier was sent round, in the morning, to proclaim the entertainments ...* {Nicholas Nickleby 24}
A person appointed to make public announcements, usually shouted, or cried, in the streets.

criminate *... but I still do not see anything in it to criminate the poor child.* {Oliver Twist 31}
Incriminate, or prove one guilty of a crime.

crock *... and the boy grimed with crock and dirt from the hair of his head to the sole of his foot ...* {Great Expectations 7}
Smut, soot, dirt.

Crockford's *The third [member of Parliament], who was at Crockford's all night, has just gone home to put a clean shirt on, and take a bottle or two of soda water, and will certainly be with us in time to address the meeting.* {Nicholas Nickleby 2}
Crockford's was a gambling house noted for high stakes.

crook *... with a hook in one hand and a crook in the other ...* {Martin Chuzzlewit 20}
A staff with a curved, hooked end used for catching sheep by the legs.

crop *... with her hair--it had more than a tinge of red, and she wore it in a crop--curled in five distinct rows, up to the very top of her head ...* {Nicholas Nickleby 9}
Closely cut, short hair.

cross-bill ... *between the registrar's red table and the silk gowns, with bills, cross-bills, answers, rejoinders, injunctions, affidavits, issues, references to masters, masters' reports, mountains of costly non-sense piled before them.* {Bleak House 1}
A motion filed in Chancery court by a defendant against the plaintiff.

crossing-sweeper ... *making himself as cheap as crossing-sweepers.* {Old Curiosity Shop 19}
Streets in the nineteenth century were filled with horse manure. A boy or man could earn some money by sweeping the street at the corner when someone wanted to cross.

croup ... *noises... natural to a person of middle age who had been afflicted with a combination of inflammatory sore throat, croup, and hooping-cough from his earliest infancy.* {Pickwick Papers 39}
A disease of the throat, in children, having a characteristic sharp cough.

crown bowl ... *he had finished his first pipe and disposed of half a dozen glasses out of a crown bowl of punch* ... {Nicholas Nickleby 52}
A crown, or five shilling's worth.

crownpiece ... *such a trifling loan as a crownpiece* ... {Martin Chuzzlewit 4}
A one-crown coin, worth five shillings.

crow to pluck with someone *Remember me kindly if you please to old Mr. Willet, and tell him that whenever he comes here I have a crow to pluck with him.* {Barnaby Rudge 13}
To have a matter of dispute to clear up, to pick a bone with someone.

cruet *There was a gorgeous banquet ready spread for the third act, consisting of two pasteboard vases, one plate of biscuits, a black bottle, and a vinegar cruet* ... {Nicholas Nickleby 24}
A small bottle for vinegar or oil.

cruet stand ... *a private box, fitted up with red curtains, white table-cloth, and cruet stand complete* ... {Old Curiosity Shop 39}
The frame or stand which holds the cruets for use on the table.

crumb ... *in proof of her desperate thoughts, she made a lunge as she spoke, which would have scarcely disturbed the crumb of a half-quartern loaf.* {Nicholas Nickleby 31}
The center of a loaf of bread or a roll, not the crust. The meaning is reversed in modern British English.

crunched ... *a fiery-faced matron attired in a crunched bonnet* ... {Martin Chuzzlewit 45}
Crushed or squashed.

cry ... *and people were crying flowers up and down the street* ... {Martin Chuzzlewit 48}
Hawking or selling goods on the street by shouting out what is for sale.

cucumber-frame ... *I strolled into the garden, and strolled all over it. It was quite a wilderness, and there were old melon-frames and cucumber-frames in it* ... {Great Expectations 11}
A low box with a glazed covering for seedlings.

cue ... *and my uncle was in thoroughly good cue.* {Pickwick Papers 49}
Mood or frame of mind.

cuff ... *the virgin monarch had then and there boxed and cuffed an unlucky page for some neglect of duty.* {Barnaby Rudge 1}
A blow with the fist or open hand.

cupping-glass ... *snails were constantly discovered holding on to the street doors* ... *with the tenacity of cupping-glasses.* {Dombey & Son 8}
A small glass, shaped like a drinking glass. When heated, the open mouth of the glass was placed on the skin to apply suction (a medical treatment that was commonly used but ineffective).

curacoa *Worn out by worry and excitement* ... *and reluctantly revived with curacoa* ... {Our Mutual Friend 1-10}
A common misspelling of curaçao, an orange liqueur named after the Caribbean island of Curaçao.

curb-chain *A busy little man he always is, in the polishing at harness-house doors, of stirrup-irons, bits, curb-chains, harness bosses,*

anything in the way of a stable-yard that will take a polish . . . {Bleak House 66}
1. A chain acting as a curb or preventer. Part of the harness of a horse. *He had a gold watch and a gold curb-chain with large gold seals* . . . {Pickwick Papers 35}
2. The watch-chain which attached the watch to the clothing.

curl-papers *Standing before the dressing-glass was a middle-aged lady in yellow curl-papers, busily engaged in brushing what the ladies call their 'back hair'.* {Pickwick Papers 22}
Pieces of paper around which the hair was twisted and allowed to set to produce curls.

curricle *Gride and Nickleby! Good pair for a curricle. Oh roguery! roguery! roguery!* {Nicholas Nickleby 47}
A very fast, light, two-wheeled carriage pulled by two horses abreast. It seated two and was popular with young men-about-town until it was replaced by the cabriolet, a safer vehicle. Because the harness included a bar that went across the horses' backs both horses had to be of exactly the same height.

curtain lecture *I am going to give you your first curtain lecture.* {Our Mutual Friend 4-5}
A reproof given to a husband by a wife, usually in bed.

curtain-pegs *The ladies smiled, curtseyed, and glided into chairs, and dived for dropped pocket-handkerchiefs: the gentlemen leant against two of the curtain-pegs* . . . {Sketches, The Boarding-house}
Pegs inserted into the window frame and then used to hold the curtains to the side.

curveting . . . *on horse-back, galloping first to one place and then to another, and backing his horse among the people, and prancing and curveting, and shouting in a most alarming manner* . . . {Pickwick Papers 4}
A leap of a horse in which the forelegs are raised and advanced together, then the hind legs jumped from the ground before the forelegs touch down.

custom *"Ah!" said the old lady, "painters always make ladies out prettier than they are, or they wouldn't get any custom, child."* {Oliver Twist 12}
The practice of customarily going to a certain shop or place of business, hence business patronage or customers.

cut *Chapter 44 Mr. Ralph Nickleby cuts an old acquaintance.* {Nicholas Nickleby 44}
1. To snub a person, pretend not to see them in a social setting.
Fezziwig 'cut'--but so deftly, that he appeared to wink with his legs, and came upon his feet again without a stagger. {A Christmas Carol 2}
2.A dance step done by leaping from the ground and moving the feet alternately back and forth very rapidly.
Pop that shawl away in my castor, Dodger, so that I may know where to find it when I cut . . . {Oliver Twist 25}
3. To run away, or simply to leave.
. . . he purchased a knife with seven blades in it, and not a cut (as he afterwards found out) among them. {Martin Chuzzlewit 5}
4. A cut in anything, made by a blade. The implication here is that all seven blades were dull and the knife was worthless.

cutlass *. . . the guard of the Dover mail . . . keeping an eye and a hand on the arm-chest before him, where a loaded blunderbuss lay at the top of six or eight loaded horse-pistols, deposited on a substratum of cutlass.* {Tale of Two Cities 1-2}
A short sword with a flat curved blade, commonly used by sailors.

cut my stick *"And now that the nag has got his wind again," said Mr. Chuckster, rising in a graceful manner, "I'm afraid I must cut my stick."* {Old Curiosity Shop 40}
Leave, depart.

cut off *"A good night for cutting off in," said Orlick. "We'd be puzzled how to bring down a jail-bird on the wing tonight."* {Great Expectations 15}
To run away.

cut one's mutton ... *a verbal invitation* ... *to come and cut his mutton in Brig Place on some day of his own naming* ... {Dombey & Son 17} Slang for eat dinner.

cutting leaves *Mr. Pickwick, perceiving that there was some embarrassment on the old gentleman's part, affected to be engaged in cutting the leaves of a book that lay beside him* ... {Pickwick Papers 56} Book pages were printed on sheets of paper, several pages to a sheet, which were then folded to bring the pages into correct sequence. Since the folds were not cut by the printer, the purchaser had to cut the pages apart before reading the book.

cyphering-book ... *he brought no greater amount of previous knowledge to the subject than certain dim recollections of two or three very long sums entered into a cyphering-book at school* ... {Nicholas Nickleby 37} An arithmetic book, one in which children did their work.

D *He has sold himself to the D.* {David Copperfield 49}
The Devil.

dab *I have had Frenchwomen come, before now, and show themselves dabs at pistol-shooting.* {Bleak House 24}
1. A skillful or expert person.
... dined in a sumptuous manner off boiled dabs ... {David Copperfield 3}
2. Any kind of small flat fish.
... dabbing two dabs at him with her needle, as if she put out both his eyes. {Our Mutual Friend 4-8}
3. A sharp and abrupt little blow or thrust.

Daffy *... it's what I'm obliged to keep a little of in the house, to put into the blessed infants Daffy, when they ain't well ...* {Oliver Twist 2}
Daffy's *Elixir Salutis,* a soothing syrup given to infants. Gin was often added to the mixture.

dale *... there was the same noble country, the same broad expanse of hill and dale ...* {Pickwick Papers 36}
A valley.

damask *... there was a picture of him in the house with a damask nose.* {David Copperfield 41}
The color of the Damask rose, a dark red.

Dame-Schools *He had business everywhere, going down all the turnings, looking into all of the wells ... dashing into the midst of all the Dame-Schools, fluttering all the pigeons ...* {Cricket on the Hearth 2}
A private elementary school, usually run by an old woman or widow.

dame's house ... *a pear tree, formerly growing in a garden near the back of his dame's house at Eton* ... {Little Dorrit 2-12}
A boarding house at a school, kept by a dame, or matron.

damme *"And damme, sir," cried Gabriel, "with your pardon for the word* ... " {Barnaby Rudge 26}
Damn.

damp *The imprisoned air, the imprisoned light, the imprisoned damps, the imprisoned men, were all deteriorated by confinement.* {Little Dorrit 1-1}
A noxious gas or vapor.

damson pie ... *a pelisse the colour of the interior of a damson pie* ...
{Sketches, Mr. Minns and his Cousin}
A pie made from the dark purple Damson plum.

damson syrup *Spoons are waved in the air, legs appear above the table-cloth in uncontrollable ecstasy, and eighty short fingers dabble in damson syrup.* {Sketches, The Couple Who Dote Upon Their Children}
Syrup made from sugar and Damson plums.

dark-lantern ... *drawing a dark-lantern from his pocket, and throwing the glare full on Oliver's face* ... {Oliver Twist 22}
A lantern with a candle and one opening for the light to emerge, covered by a slide that can be moved aside when light is needed.

darky *Crape, keys, centre-bit, darkies--nothing forgotten?* {Oliver Twist 22}
Slang for dark lantern.

dart *Mr. Bucket had certainly picked him up at a dart.* {Bleak House 62}
1. With a sudden rapid motion.
... *he watches the spasmodic shoots and darts that break out of her face and limbs* ... {Edwin Drood 1}
2. A sudden motion, or a sudden glance.

dash *"I--so I have understood," said Arthur, dashing at the assertion.*
{Little Dorrit 1-8}
To depress or discourage, here becoming discouraged.

Davy lamp ... *he indeed would have been a very Davy lamp of refuge.*
{Dombey & Son 11}
The miner's safety lamp invented by Sir Humphry Davy. It could burn
safely even in the presence of the explosive gases often found in mines.

daw ... *for Christmas daws to peck at* ... {A Christmas Carol 3}
Jackdaw, a small kind of crow.

day-book *The undertaker... was making some entries in his day-book by
the light of a most appropriately dismal candle* ... {Oliver Twist 4}
A book or journal in which the transactions of the day were entered.

daygo ... *his physician said something else, and a leg of mutton somehow
ended in daygo.* {Our Mutual Friend 1-2}
Day-going is the going of the day, or end of day. Daygo, therefore, is
the day's end.

day week ... *your papa, whom we all perfectly adore and dote upon, is to
be married to my dearest Edith this day week.* {Dombey & Son 30}
One week from the day mentioned.

dead beat ... *the kettle, being dead beat, boiled over, and was taken off the
fire.* {Cricket on the Hearth 1}
Totally exhausted.

dead image *"You drew her portrait perfectly," said Mr. Harthouse.
"Presented her dead image."* {Hard Times 2-9}
Exact image.

dead-light ... *I would reopen my outer dead-light and my inner sliding-
window... and would look out at the long-rolling, lead coloured, white-
topped waves* ... {The Uncommercial Traveller, Aboard Ship}
A metal cover over a vent or window.

dead set *Here everybody laughed again; and the stout gentleman by the fire whispered in our ear that Griggins was making a dead set at us.* {The Funny Young Gentleman}
A persistent, determined attack.

dead-wall *he came to the dead-wall of the King's Bench prison.* {David Copperfield 12}
A uniform and continuous wall, unrelieved by breaks or interruptions.

deal *Having himself deposited the important stone in a small deal box...* {Pickwick Papers 11}
Pine boards about seven inches wide. Boxes, tables, and other items were often made from deal.

Debtor's Door *... the last man who paid the same great debt at the same small Debtor's Door.* {The Uncommmercial Traveller, The City of the Absent}
When the place of execution was moved from Tyburn to London a gallows that could hang a dozen or so people at one time was built outside Newgate prison, abutting on a door to the prison. The door was called the Debtor's Door and it led directly to the gallows.

deception *... I was a light porter to a stay and mantua maker, in which capacity I was employed to carry about, in oilskin baskets, nothing but deceptions--which soured my spirits and disturbed my confidence in human nature...* {The Battle of Life 2}
Probably refers to false bosoms and/or false hips. In the United States, pads used to enlarge women's breasts were sometimes referred to as 'gay deceivers'.

decompose *"Ah, what has decomposed you, ma'am?" inquired Mrs. Rogers.* {Pickwick Papers 46}
Literally to disintegrate, used here in the sense of 'to emotionally upset'.

deep file *... he was a long-headed man, a dry one, a salt fish, a deep file, a rasper...* {Martin Chuzzlewit 38}
A file is a person, or man. To be deep is to be profoundly cunning.

deep trimmings *I told him that, without deep trimmings, the family was disgraced.* {Great Expectations 11}
Expensive, elaborate mourning effects.

delf ... *a few rough chairs and a table, a corner cupboard with their little stock of crockery and delf...* {Old Curiosity Shop 15}
The original spelling of Delft, the Dutch town from which that kind of earthenware came.

delicate, delicacy *My aunt evidently liked the offer, though she was delicate of accepting it.* {David Copperfield 15}
... you can have no delicacy in speaking plainly. {Martin Chuzzlewit 12}
Modest, modesty.

demogalize *That out-dacious Oliver has demogalized them all!* {Oliver Twist 17}
To 'mogue' is to mislead, to gammon. Mr Bumble has made up this word as an emphatic way of saying that Oliver has gained the sympathy of the other inmates of the workhouse by lying to them.

Denmark satin ... *Denmark satin shoes, and open-worked stockings ...* {Sketches, Miss Evans and the Eagle}
A shiny worsted fabric woven with a satin twill and used in shoemaking.

dentistical *To know that he is always keeping a secret from her, that he has under all circumstances to conceal and hold fast a tender double tooth, which her sharpness is ever ready to twist out of his head, gives Mrs. Snagsby, in her dentistical presence, much the air of a dog who has a reservation from his master and will look anywhere rather than meet his eye.* {Bleak House 25}
Pertaining to a dentist or teeth. Here it refers to the analogy between Mr. Snagsby's secret and an aching molar tooth.

derange *Do not let me derange you; pray be tranquil.* {Little Dorrit 2-30}
Disturb.

descant ... *and leaning back in his arm-chair, he descants at considerable length upon its beauty, and the cost of maintaining it.* {Sketches,

London Recreations}
To comment on, discuss, or criticize.

descry *Indeed, he could descry no security from the pitfalls that were yawning for Polly* . . . {Mugby Junction 2}
Catch sight of, discover, see.

desert *After glancing at herself as a comparatively worthless vessel, but still one of some desert* . . . {Barnaby Rudge 22}
Worthiness of recompense, meritoriousness.

design *I don't complain that you design to keep me here.* {Our Mutual Friend 4-6}
Plan or scheme.

despond, desponding *But its of no use to despond.* {Martin Chuzzlewit 36}
Lose heart, become despondent.

detainer *Nobody else went to the expense of lodging a detainer*... {Nicholas Nickleby 47}
A writ whereby a person arrested by the suit of one creditor can be detained at the suit of another.

detaining creditor *I am his detaining creditor for seventeen hundred pounds.* {Nicholas Nickleby 47}
A creditor who has obtained a detainer (see **detainer**).

determine . . . *when that person discloses, my part in this business will cease and determine.* {Great Expectations 36}
Come to an end, terminate.

deuce-and-all . . . *she was taught to be the deuce-and-all of education.* {Hard Times 1-6}
Deuce is a euphemism for Devil, hence the Devil and all, or absolutely everything.

deuce is in it *"Don't apologise, for the world," replied Sir John sweetly; "old friends like you and I, may be allowed some freedom, or the deuce*

is in it." {Barnaby Rudge 43}
An expression of impatience implying some sort of mischief or involvement of the Devil.

developed ... *extra bills of three feet long by nine inches wide, were dispersed in all directions, ... thrust under knockers, and developed in all the shops.* {Nicholas Nickleby 24}
1. Unfolded or unrolled.
[The girls were] wearing miraculously small shoes, and the thinnest possible silk stockings: the which their rocking-chairs developed to a distracting extent. {Martin Chuzzlewit 17}
2. Revealed.

Devil ... *there are few comestibles better, in their way, than a Devil.* {David Copperfield 28}
The drumstick of a turkey or goose, grilled and highly spiced.

devil's tattoo ... *sitting down again and beating the devil's tattoo with his boot on the patternless rug.* {Bleak House 39}
The act of idly drumming the fingers on a table. A tattoo is a military drumbeat, played in the evening.

dial *Punctual as the counting-house dial, which he maintained to be the best time-keeper in London* ... {Nicholas Nickleby 37}
A clock of any kind, derived by contraction from the word 'sundial'.

dial-plate ... *he basked in the strip of summer-light and warmth that shone upon his table and the ground as if they were a crooked dial-plate, and himself the only figure upon it.* {Dombey & Son 22}
The face plate of a clock, the plate upon which the numbers appear.

diamond-pane lattices *Its windows were old diamond-pane lattices* ... {Barnaby Rudge 1}
Windows made of lozenge- or diamond-shaped pieces of glass.

dickey ... *three people were squeezed into it besides the driver, who sat in his own particular little dickey at the side* ... {Pickwick Papers 46}
A small separate seat on a carriage for either the driver or a servant.

The cabriolet, into which the three people were squeezed, was built to hold only two passengers.

dietary *Do I understand that he asked for more, after he had eaten the supper allotted by the dietary?* {Oliver Twist 2}
The allowance of food for an inmate.

digester *Ben, my fine fellow, put your hand into the cupboard and bring out the patent digester.* {Pickwick Papers 38}
A tightly closed metal vessel in which materials can be exposed to water at high temperatures and pressures, similar to a pressure cooker.

diligence *As soon afterwards as might be, in those Diligence days, Mr. Meagles rang the cracked bell at the cracked gate, and it jarred open . . .* {Little Dorrit 2-33}
A public stagecoach.

diminishing glass *In her eyes Tracy Tupman was a youth; she viewed his years through a diminishing glass.* {Pickwick Papers 7}
A negative lens. When looked through, it shows a smaller-than-life image.

dimity *. . . a smart little house on wheels, with white dimity curtains festooning the windows . . .* {Old Curiosity Shop 26}
A stout, white cotton cloth.

dinner-cloth *Below stairs the dinner-cloth had not been taken away, but had been left ready for breakfast.* {Bleak House 5}
Tablecloth used at dinner.

dinner-cover *. . . surrounded by such a plentiful collection of bright potlids, well-scoured saucepans, burnished dinner-covers, gleaming kettles, and other tokens of her industrious habits . . .* {The Battle of Life 2}
The metal cover placed over a dinner plate to keep the food warm.

dinner-mats *But such wonderful things came tumbling out of the closets when they were opened-- . . . letters, tea, forks, odd boots and shoes of*

children . . . nutshells, heads and tails of shrimp, dinner-mats, gloves,
coffee-grounds, umbrellas . . . {Bleak House 30}
Place mats.

dint *. . . the disagreeable dints I have formerly described in his nostrils*
coming and going with his breath . . . {David Copperfield 25}
1. A dent or depression.
. . . Mrs. Wititterly, who, by dint of lying on the same sofa for three
years and a half, had got up a little pantomime of graceful
attitudes, . . . now threw herself into the most striking of the series . . .
{Nicholas Nickleby 28}
2. By means of, also implying persistence and force.

dip *Half a dozen gas-lamps out of the street wouldn't have lighted the*
entry too well, so you may suppose that it was pretty dark with
Scrooge's dip. {A Christmas Carol 1}
A dip-candle (see **dip-candle**).

dip-candle *. . . being but faintly illuminated through the agency of one*
low-spirited dip-candle and no snuffers. {Great Expectations 10}
A candle made by repeatedly dipping a length of wick into melted
tallow or wax.

direction *. . . he put a piece of paper with a direction written on it in the*
lady's hand, saying it was in case she should forget. {Dombey & Son 52}
Instructions on how to get to a particular place, an address.

disburden *. . . now that we have disburdened our conscience, we shall*
proceed . . . {Pickwick Papers 4}
Unburden.

discompose *The profound astonishment with which her son regarded*
her during this long address . . . in no way discomposed Mrs. Nickleby,
but rather exalted her opinion of her own cleverness . . . {Nicholas
Nickleby 55}
Disturb the composure of someone.

discounting profession *There the young gentleman improved his*
mind . . . and . . . gradually elevated himself into the discounting profession.

{Bleak House 21}
The work of a discounter, one who buys debts or obligations at a discount to later recover the full amount.

disgrace-jacket *He put his hand before his own eyes, and the breast of his disgrace-jacket swelled as if it would fly asunder.* {The Seven Poor Travellers 1}
A special uniform tunic without belt or facings. It was worn by soldiers when under arrest or being punished.

dissenter ... *it was with him my great-grandfather went to school; for I know the master of his school was a dissenter* ... {Nicholas Nickleby 49}
A Catholic or other person who separates himself from the established Church of England.

distraint ... *he looked far more like a man in possession of his house under a distraint, than a commercial Colossus bestriding his own hearthrug* ... {Little Dorrit 2-12}
A legal term referring to the seizure of goods in order to force a person to fulfill an obligation.

distress *It was a distress for half a year's rent--two pound ten, I think.* {Sketches, The Broker's Man}
A legal seizure of someone's property to force the payment of a debt.

Divan ... *Mr. Quilp determined to use it, both as a sleeping place by night and as a kind of Divan by day* ... {Old Curiosity Shop 11}
A smoking room. Originally a Turkish council, then the cushions the Turks sat upon, then that style cushion sat upon while smoking, finally a smoking room.

divers ... *had a share in the ventures of divers mates of East Indiamen, smoked his smuggled cigars under the very nose of the custom House* ... {Old Curiosity Shop 4}
Diverse, various.

doat *Me who doat upon her with the demdest ardour!* {Nicholas Nickleby 34}
Dote.

dock ... *a dirty frowsy room, at the upper end of which was a raised platform railed off from the rest, with a dock for the prisoners* ... {Oliver Twist 43}
An area, usually enclosed by a railing, where the prisoners sat or stood during their trial.

Doctors' Commons *"The Wellingtons has gone to Doctors' Commons." "No," said the little man. "Yes, for a license."* {Pickwick Papers 10}
Originally the common dining room of the College of Doctors of Civil Law. Here it refers to the buildings and the several civil courts which they contained. These included admiralty, probate, marriage, and divorce courts.

dodge *He loves a dodge for its own sake; being ... the dodgerest of dodgers.* {Our Mutual Friend 3-13}
A trick for the purpose of cheating or eluding.

do for ... *when they broke his second [rib], and did for him.* {David Copperfield 5}
To damage fatally, ruin, destroy.

dog-cart ... *people will flatten their noses against the front windows of a chemist's shop when a drunken man who has been run over by a dog-cart in the street is undergoing a surgical inspection in the back-parlour.* {Pickwick Papers 25}
A commonly used carriage drawn by a single horse with the rear wheels larger than the front. It usually had no top. There were two seats, back to back, each holding two persons. The seats were built over a box-like structure that originally held the owner's dogs (hence the name), but was later used like an automobile trunk is now used. The word does not refer to a cart drawn by a dog. Those carts were prohibited by law after 1855.

dog-days *He carried his own low temperature always about with him; he iced his office in the dog-days; and didn't thaw it one degree at*

Christmas. {A Christmas Carol 1}
The days associated with the rising of Sirius, the dog star. Considered the hottest and most unwholesome time of the year.

dog-hutch ... *a drunken face tied up in a black bundles, and flaring out of a heap of rags on the floor of a dog-hutch which is her private apartment* ... {Bleak House 22}
A box-like dog house.

dog-shores *Then, to go over the side again and down among the ooze and wet to the bottom of the dock, in the depths of the subterranean forest of dog-shores and stays that hold [the ship] up* ... {The Uncommercial Traveller, Chatham Dockyard}
Short timbers supporting a ship under construction, and the last to be removed before launching.

dog sleep *This was Gabriel Varden's state, as, nodding in his dog sleep, and leaving his horse to pursue a road with which he was well acquainted, he got over the ground unconsciously, and drew nearer and nearer home.* {Barnaby Rudge 3}
Light, fitful sleep.

dog's nose ... *those delectable drinks Purl, Flip, and Dog's Nose.* {Our Mutual Friend 1-6}
A drink made of beer and gin, or of ale and rum. It included sugar and nutmeg.

domino ... *slips him on a mask and domino, and mixes with the masquers.* {Barnaby Rudge 4}
A kind of cloak worn with a mask.

donkey-tandem *Poor Paul's little bedstead is carried off in a donkey-tandem.* {Dombey & Son 59}
A cart drawn by two donkeys hitched one behind the other, in tandem, instead of in the usual way, side-by-side.

door-plate ... *no domestic object which was capable of collecting dirt, from a dear child's knee to the door-plate, was without as much dirt*

as could well accumulate upon it. {Bleak House 30}
A metal plate at the door of the house, with the name of the resident.

dormitory ... *sitting at his desk in his parlour or standing before the dressing-glass in his dormitory* ... {Pickwick Papers 12}
Bedroom.

dormouse *she would come a little way out of her wrappers, like a feminine dormouse* ... {Hard Times 1-9}
A small hibernating rodent, in size between squirrels and mice.

Dorset, tub of weekly ... *the latter gentleman was seated on a tub of weekly Dorset, behind the little red desk with a wooden rail* ... {Sketches, The Tuggs's at Ramsgate}
Mr. Tuggs was a grocer, and the tub probably contained the butter from the farming county of Dorset which was delivered to his store once a week.

dose ... *old woman, you shall have a dose, old woman, such a dose!* {Little Dorrit 1-16}
A quantity of medicine. It is used figuratively here to refer to a dose of unpleasant medicine or a punishment.

doth *We won't go home till morning, till daylight doth appear.* {Pickwick Papers 7}
Does.

double-diamond *A magnum of the double-diamond, David, to drink the health of Mr. Linkinwater.* {Nicholas Nickleby 37}
Dixon's Double Diamond port wine was a favored and high quality wine.

double eye-glass *Sir Leicester, quite unconscious, reads on through his double eye-glass, occasionally stopping to remove his glass and express approval* ... {Bleak House 29}
A pair of eyeglasses. An eyeglass was a single eyeglass, a monocle.

double knock *[Miss Tox's house] was in the dullest of No-Thorough-fares, rendered anxious and haggard by distant double knocks.*

{Dombey & Son 7}
A double knock announces the arrival of the Major ... {Dombey
& Son 31}
Two knocks in quick succession announcing the arrival of a visitor or of
a carriage.

double monkey ... *the inimitable manner in which Bill Thompson can
"come the double monkey," or go through the mysterious involutions of
a sailor's hornpipe.* {Sketches, The Streets--Night}
To 'come the double monkey' is to take more than one's share, something Mr. Thompson probably did in his comic sketches.

double sight *A parishioner here suggested that this might be termed
"taking a double sight," but the observation was drowned in loud cries
of "Order!"* {Sketches, The Election for Beadle}
This is a joke on the gesture of taking a sight (see **taking a sight**).

double tooth ... *looking at him as if he would like to try the effect of ex-
tracting a double-tooth or two* ... {Our Mutual Friend 2-5}
Molar tooth.

doubtful Old Master *When the agreement was ready in duplicate (the
landlord having worked at it like some cherubic scribe, in what is con-
ventionally called a doubtful, which means not at all doubtful, Old
Master) it was signed by the contracting parties* ... {Our Mutual
Friend 1-4}
Dickens is comparing the appearance of the landlord to that of a
cherub in an Italian Renaissance painting, supposedly painted by a
master of a school of painting. Such cherubs were shown doing things
appropriate to the subject of the painting in which they appeared, including writing. A doubtful Old Master would be a picture whose
painter was not known with certainty.

dovecot ... *there were no pigeons in the dovecot, no horses in the stable* ...
{Great Expectations 8}
A house for pigeons.

dowerless ... *can even I believe that you would choose a dowerless girl* ...
{A Christmas Carol 2}

Without a dowry (the money and goods a woman brought to a marriage and which became her husband's property).

down, downy *The hair of Withers was radiant with pomatum, in these days of down, and he wore gloves and smelt of the waters of Cologne.* {Dombey & Son 37}
Oh, you're a downy fellow, Steerforth, so you are ... {David Copperfield 22}
Wide-awake, knowing.

downs *I don't know how many sail* ... *were then lying in the downs. Some of these vessels were of grand size* ... {Bleak House 45}
The Downs is a channel to the sea lying off the east coast of Kent.

drab *Rendered complete by drab pantaloons and a buff waistcoat, I thought Mr. Barkis a phenomenon of respectability.* {David Copperfield 10}
1. A kind of woolen cloth, also the color of that clothing (a light brown, or yellowish brown).
I began well; and, but for babbling drabs, I would have finished as I began. {Oliver Twist 51}
2. A drab is also a harlot, slattern, slut.

drabs ... *a new green shooting-coat, plaid neckerchief, and closely fitted drabs.* {Pickwick Papers 1}
Trousers made of the cloth called drab.

drag *When the heavy drag had been adjusted to the wheel, and the carriage slid down hill, with a cinderous smell, in a cloud of dust* ... {Tale of Two Cities 2-8}
1. An iron plate, attached by a chain to the front of a carriage, placed under the rear wheel when going down hill to prevent its rotating, thus slowing the descent of the carriage.
... *a couple of waterside men, bearing between them certain machines called drags* ... {Old Curiosity Shop 49}
2. Grapnels, ropes with hooks for dragging a river.
... *did homage to Bella as if she were a compound of a fine girl, thor-*

ough-bred horse, well-built drag, and remarkable pipe. {Our Mutual
Friend 3-5}
3. A privately owned four-horse carriage built like a stagecoach.

draggle-tailed *And a pretty figure you'll cut then, with a draggle-tailed
wife and a crowd of squalling children* . . . {The Chimes 1}
With skirts dragging in the mud.

dragoon trot . . . *clattering at a heavy dragoon trot over the uneven town
pavement* . . . {Tale of Two Cities 3-1}
Dragoons are cavalry, usually armed with firearms.

drain *"A drain for the boy," said Toby, half-filling a wine-glass. "Down
with it, innocence."* {Oliver Twist 22}
Slang for gin or other alcoholic drinks.

dram *The umpires, having partaken of a dram, shook hands and
departed* . . . {Pickwick Papers 55}
A small glass of liquor.

draught . . . *and after being drugged with black draughts and blue pills, to
an extent which Demple (whose father was a doctor) said was enough to
undermine a horse's constitution, received a caning and six chapters
of Greek Testament for refusing to confess.* {David Copperfield 7}
1. A liquid medicine meant to be taken in one dose. Black draught is a
purgative containing senna, magnesium sulfate, and licorice.
. . . *the child looked wistfully in each, doubtful at which to ask for permission to rest awhile, and buy a draught of milk.* {Old Curiosity Shop 15}
2. A swallow, or drink.
*The people were none the richer for the wreck, for it was the season
of the herring-shoal--and who could cast nets for fish and find dead
men and women in the draught?* {The Uncommercial Traveller, The
Shipwreck}
3. The quantity of fish taken with one casting of a net.

draught-board . . . *a notched and disfigured bench, immoveable from the
wall, with a draught-board rudely hacked upon it with a knife* . . . {Little
Dorrit 1-1}
Checkerboard.

draughts . . . *sat playing draughts with a younger girl* . . . {Our Mutual Friend 1-4}
1. The game of checkers.
. . . *a set of draughts, made of old buttons and soup bones* . . . {Little Dorrit 1-1}
2. The checkers, used in the game of checkers or draughts.

draughtsman . . . *artistical effects achieved in bygone times by some imprisoned draughtsman in his leisure hours.* {Pickwick Papers 41}
A draftsman, one who makes drawings or plans.

draw a tooth . . . *I drew a tooth of his when I first came down here.* {Pickwick Papers 38}
Pull a tooth, as a dentist does.

drawer *Then bring me another pint of this wine, drawer* . . . {Tale of Two Cities 2-4}
One who draws wine or liquors from the keg into the serving glass, hence a tapster (as in 'beer on tap') or simply a waiter.

drawers *His boots were, on a small scale, the boots of a ploughman, while his legs, so crossed and recrossed with scratches that they looked like maps, were bare below a very short pair of plaid drawers finished off with two frills of perfectly different patterns.* {Bleak House 14}
A name for various garments covering the body from the waist down, not underwear. Here it means a pair of shorts.

drawing bills . . . *his son, who, I have heard, ran very wild, and was in the habit of drawing bills upon him without the least authority!* {The Chimes 3}
Running up charges for goods and services.

drawing-master *In the same house were also established, as I gathered from the plates on the door, a drawing-master, a coal-merchant . . . and a lithographic artist.* {Bleak House 14}
A teacher of drawing.

drawing-room *He led the way to a drawing-room, which he speedily lighted up . . .* {Dombey & Son 45}
A withdrawing room. A room reserved for the reception of company and to which the ladies withdrew after dinner.

drawn the ball *. . . a discovery which made a considerable impression on everybody but the doctor, who had drawn the ball about ten minutes before.* {Oliver Twist 31}
Extracted the bullet.

draw upon *I have been tempted in these two short interviews, to draw upon that fellow, fifty times.* {Barnaby Rudge 27}
To draw a sword, initiate a sword fight.

draw water *The rest of the class go and draw water up, till somebody tells you to leave off . . .* {Nicholas Nickleby 8}
To get water from a well. A laborious task involving the hauling up of full buckets of water from the depths of the well.

dray *. . . and away went the huge vehicle, with the noise of half a dozen brewer's drays at least.* {Nicholas Nickleby 38}
A low cart without sides, commonly used by brewers for hauling kegs and barrels of beer.

drayman *There were two good-tempered burly draymen letting down big butts of beer into a cellar . . .* {Martin Chuzzlewit 53}
The man who drives a dray, usually a brewer's dray (see **dray**).

dreadnought *It lay in the usual place--the Carrier's dreadnought pocket . . .* {Cricket on the Hearth 2}
1. A thick woolen coat worn in bad weather.
. . . whose only articles of dress (linen not included) were a pair of dreadnought trousers; a blue jacket, formerly admired upon the Thames at Richmond; no stockings; and one slipper. {American Notes, 2}
2. Trousers made from the same thick-piled wool as a dreadnought coat.

dress *. . . a stone kitchen, fitted with coppers for dressing the prison food . . .* {Oliver Twist 52}

1. To prepare or make ready.
... the trodden vegetable refuse which is so like their own dress that perhaps they take the Market for a great wardrobe ... {Our Mutual Friend 4-9}
2. Clothing.
True, it was yet a matter of doubt whether Casio would be enabled to get into the dress which had been sent for him from the masquerade warehouse. {Sketches, Mrs. Joseph Porter}
3. Costume, as in a fancy dress ball.

dress at *Mr. Sapsea "dresses at" the dean; has been bowed to for the Dean, in mistake ...* {Edwin Drood 4}
To dress in a manner calculated to gain the affection of a person.

Dresser *... his services might at any moment be required as Dresser.* {Little Dorrit 2-12}
1. One who attires another person or assists him in dressing.
... the magistrates and clerk were bowed in by the house-surgeon and a couple of young men who smelt very strong of tobacco-smoke--they were introduced as "dressers" ... {Sketches, The Hospital Patient}
2. A surgeon's assistant. One who dresses wounds and applies bandages.

dresses *Men who had been into the cellars, and had staved the casks, rushed to and fro stark mad, setting fire to all they saw--often to the dresses of their own friends--and kindling the building in so many parts that some had no time for escape ...* {Barnaby Rudge 55}
Clothing.

dressing-glass *... Mr. Chester rising slowly, pulling off the loose robe he wore, and sitting down before the dressing-glass.* {Barnaby Rudge 23}
A mirror, usually full-length, used while getting dressed.

drest *I would have her branded on the face, drest in rags, and cast out in the streets to starve.* {David Copperfield 10}
An earlier spelling of 'dressed'.

drift *... the wheels sent the road drift flying about our heads like spray from a water-mill.* {Bleak House 6}
The dust and sand of the road.

driving-boxes *On the sideboard [were] some very cloudy fish-sauce cruets, a couple of driving-boxes, two or three whips and as many travelling-shawls . . .* {Pickwick Papers 14}
The box on which the driver of a coach sat. In eighteenth-century coaches it was portable, and had a cushion placed on its top. Later the driver's seat was built into the coach, but was still often referred to as the box.

drop *It wouldn't have loosened the knot: or kept the drop up, a minute longer.* {Oliver Twist 9}
1. The trap door of the gallows, on which the condemned stands.
Back he turned again, without the courage to purchase bit or drop, though he had tasted no food for many hours . . . {Oliver Twist 48}
2. Something to drink.

dropsical *But Bitherstone . . . is extremely inky; and his lexicon has got so dropsical from constant reference that it won't shut . . .* {Dombey & Son 41}
Suffering from dropsy, a disease state in which fluid accumulates in the body, which then becomes swollen. It is used here figuratively.

dross *These . . . ever regarded gold as dross . . .* {Our Mutual Friend 1-17}
Originally, the scum thrown off when a metal was melted; then, any worthless or impure material.

drover *. . . with several chaste and extremely correct imitations of a drover's whistle, delivered in a tone of peculiar richness and volume.* {Pickwick Papers 33}
One who drives groups of cattle or sheep, called droves. Also a dealer in cattle, and sometimes any kind of dealer.

drum *. . . incidents like these, arising out of drums and masquerades and parties at quadrille . . .* {Barnaby Rudge 16}
1. An evening party of fashionable people at a private house.
They were ready for a dance in half a second . . . and the Drum was on the very brink of leathering away with all his power . . . {The Chimes 4}
2. The drummer.

druggett ... *the druggett-covered carpet* ... {David Copperfield 13}
A coarse woolen material.

dry rot ... *mingled by day with the scent of dry rot and by night with various exhalations which arise from damp cloaks* ... {Pickwick Papers 31}
A decayed condition of wood in which it crumbles to a dry powder, caused by various fungi.

dry-saltery ... *everything, the stove excepted, was wet, and shining with soft soap and sand, the smell of which dry-saltery impregnated the air.* {Dombey & Son 23}
The place of business of a drysalter, who dealt in pickles, tinned meats, oils, and other foods. The name probably came from the practice of preserving meats by packing them in salt.

Duck *If any true friend and well-wisher could make you a bankrupt, you would be a Duck; but as a man of property you are a Demon!* {Our Mutual Friend 3-15}
A term of endearment.

ducks and drakes *He soon made ducks and drakes of what [money] I gave him* ... {David Copperfield 47}
Throw away idly or carelessly. From the pastime of 'ducks and drakes', which is throwing flat stones so they skip on the surface of water.

dudgeon ... *instead of being impressed by the speaker's strong common sense, they took it in extraordinary dudgeon.* {Hard Times 1-6}
A feeling of anger or offense.

duffer ... *the prey of ring-droppers, pea and thimble riggers, duffers, touters, or any of those bloodless sharpers, who are, perhaps, a little better known to the Police.* {Martin Chuzzlewit 37}
A duffer is a counterfeit coin or article. Here it refers to the passers of such counterfeits.

Duke Humphry ... *Diggory Chuzzlewit was in the habit of perpetually dining with Duke Humphry.* {Martin Chuzzlewit 1}

Dining with Duke Humphry was a euphemism for 'going without dinner'.

dull *"From Sir Mullberry," replied Pyke. "You must be very dull here." "Rather dull, I confess," said Mrs. Nickleby.* {Nicholas Nickleby 27}
Depressed, listless. The implication in this example is one of boredom.

dumb-ague *But for him, I might never have heard of the "dumb-ague," respecting which malady I am now learned.* {The Uncommercial Traveller, Chatham Dockyard}
A mild form of malaria in which there are no chills.

dumb church organ *Sitting with her hands laid separately upon the desk . . . she looked as if she were performing on a dumb church organ.* {Little Dorrit 1-5}
An organ keyboard not operating the organ pipes, used for silent practice.

dumb-foundered *Why, Daisy, old boy, dumb-foundered!* {David Copperfield 28}
Dumbfounded.

dumb nod *[Miss Pleasant] answered with a short dumb nod.* {Our Mutual Friend 2-12}
Dumb means silent, without speech. Hence a silent nod.

dumb-waiter *He . . . cleared the table; piled everything on the dumb-waiter; gave us our wine-glasses; and, of his own accord, wheeled the dumb-waiter into the pantry.* {David Copperfield 28}
Usually a pole bearing one or more revolving shelves which held table necessities and was placed near the dining table. In this quotation the dumb-waiter is wheeled out, so it must be a small table on wheels, similar to a teacart.

dunder-headed *. . . how can dunder-headed Mr. Sapsea be otherwise than a credit to Cloisterham, and society?* {Edwin Drood 4}
Very stupid, thick-headed.

dun-haunted ... *there are yet nooks and comers where dun-haunted students may look down from their dusty garrets, on a vagrant ray of sunlight* ... {Barnaby Rudge 15}
Constantly set upon, dunned, by creditors.

duodecimo ... *the open scrap book, displayed in the midst of some theatrical duodecimos that were strewn upon the table* ... {Nicholas Nickleby 24}
A book in which the size of each page is one-twelfth of a full sheet of paper.

durst *She durst not refuse me then.* {Oliver Twist 44}
Dare.

dust *The man ... whose name is Harmon, was the only son of a tremendous old rascal who made his money by Dust.* {Our Mutual Friend 1-2}
Trash, refuse.

dust-binn ... *a little, pale, wall-eyed, woebegone inn like a large dust-binn of two compartments and a sifter.* {Bleak House 39}
Trash bin.

dust-cellar ... *they dragged Oliver, struggling and shouting, but nothing daunted, into the dust-cellar, and there locked him up* ... {Oliver Twist 6}
A room in the cellar for trash.

dust-heap *Sam was sitting with his eyes fixed upon the dust-heap outside the next gate* ... {Pickwick Papers 39}
Trash or garbage pile.

dustman ... *I had not seen Peepy on the occasion of our last call (when he was not to be found anywhere, and when the cook rather thought he must have strolled away with the dustman's cart)* ... {Bleak House 14}
In the United States, the equivalent is a garbage man.

dust-yard *"Did you see anything?" "Nothing but the dust-yard."* {Our Mutual Friend 2-7}
Trash yard or junkyard.

Dutch cheese *He gives Dutch cheese too, eating Cheshire, sir, himself.* {Barnaby Rudge 8}
Poor quality cheese, contrasted with better quality Cheshire cheese.

Dutch clock *... here's the Dutch clock a-working himself up to being equal to strike eight ...* {Great Expectations 7}
A kind of clock, originally imported from Holland.

Dutch drops *... Tom Pinch, in his guilty agitation, shook a bottle of Dutch Drops until they were nothing but English Froth ...* {Martin Chuzzlewit 24}
A balsam, originally from Holland. A liquid used as a medication.

Dutch oven *"The town's as flat, my dear feller,"replied Mr. Chuckster, "as the surface of a Dutch Oven."* {Old Curiosity Shop 56}
A portable oven in which hot coals were placed and cooking done on the flat top.

Dutch Pin *So he sat for half an hour, quite motionless, and looking all the while like nothing so much as a great Dutch Pin or Skittle.* {Barnaby Rudge 78}
A kind of bowling pin used in the game of ninepins.

dyer's pole *... and pointed to a dyer's pole hard by, where a dangling suit of clothes bore some resemblance to a man upon a gibbet.* {Old Curiosity Shop 60}
The sign of a dyer's shop, a pole with clothing hung on it.

dyspepsia *All work and no play, Mr. Headstone, will not make dulness, in your case, I dare say; but it will make dyspepsia, if you don't take care.* {Our Mutual Friend 4-11}
A vague term meaning various disorders of the digestive organs, supposedly causing weakness, depression, and loss of appetite.

earnest *Mr. Weller touched his hat as an earnest of his obedience . . .*
{Pickwick Papers 39}
Security or pledge.

earthen jar *. . . a solitary specimen . . . in the inmost recesses of an earthen jar.* {Pickwick Papers 1}
A jar made of earthenware, or ceramic.

ear-trumpet *. . . vying with each other in paying zealous . . . attentions to the old lady . . . one holding her ear-trumpet, another an orange, and a third a smelling-bottle . . .* {Pickwick Papers 6}
A wide-mouthed tube, the small end of which is placed in the ear to improve one's hearing.

earwig *. . . earwigged by the parson . . .* {Oliver Twist 42}
Slang for to worm information out of someone.

Eastern pipe *. . . Clennam produced his Eastern pipe, and handed Mr. Pancks another Eastern pipe . . .* {Little Dorrit 2-13}
Mr. Clennam had spent many years in China, so the pipe was probably a Chinese pipe made of brass, pewter, or gun-metal. It had a water-jacket for cooling the smoke.

easy shave *. . . arter late hours nothing freshened up a man so much as a easy shave.* {Martin Chuzzlewit 29}
A shave given by a professional barber, including hot towels and other things to make the shave more comfortable.

easy shaver *The bird-fancier was an easy shaver also, and a fashionable hair-dresser also . . .* {Martin Chuzzlewit 19}
Someone who provides shaves, as does a barber.

easy shaving-shop ... *that complicated whiff which ... saluted every nose that was put into Sweedlepipe's easy shaving-shop.* {Martin Chuzzlewit 26}
A place in which shaving was done, as in a barbershop.

ebullition *Having given vent to this cruel ebullition of deadly malice and cold-blooded triumph* ... {Pickwick Papers 51}
A sudden outburst.

écarté *Do you play* écarté, *sir?* {Pickwick Papers 13}
A card game for two persons using all the cards except those from two to six. During the game the players may discard cards from their hands and replace them with fresh cards from the deck.

ecod *Oh! ecod, you had better ask father that.* {Martin Chuzzlewit 8}
A mild oath, like egad or oh God.

edge-tool ... *cut his fingers with his own edge-tools.* {Martin Chuzzlewit 28}
Any tool, such as a knife or chisel, with a sharp edge.

effect, give every effect *Preparations ... were incessantly made at Minerva House to give every effect to the forthcoming ball.* {Sketches, Sentiment}
Pleasing appearance, pleasing impression.

egg-hot ... *she ... made a little jug of egg-hot ... to console us* ... {David Copperfield 11}
A hot drink made of beer, beaten eggs, sugar, and nutmeg.

eight-day clock *An old eight-day clock, of solemn and sedate demeanor, ticked gravely in one corner* ... {Pickwick Papers 5}
A clock that is wound only once in eight days, or once a week. Early watches and small clocks required winding at least daily.

eke *A favourite at the Old Bailey, and eke at the Sessions* ... {Tale of Two Cities 2-5}
In addition.

elbow (of a chair)   *But Paul got his hand free as soon as he could, and rubbing it gently to and fro on the elbow of his chair, as if his wit were in the palm, and he were sharpening it . . .*   {Dombey & Son 8}
The arm of a chair, short, and designed to support only the elbow.

elbow-chair   *They were both elbow-chairs, of ancient mahogany . . .*
{Martin Chuzzlewit 49}
A chair with arms made to support just the elbows.

electric fluency   . . . *You expect a cove to be a flash of lightening. I wish I was the electric fluency . . . I'd have a shock at somebody that would settle their business.*   {Dombey & Son 52}
Electricity was at first believed to be a fluid, and Rob probably meant to say 'electric fluid'. There is also a pun here, since 'fluence' means 'to influence', and 'to put the fluence' means to overcome by mental force.

electrifying machine   . . . *a clock, a violin, an astronomical telescope, an electrifying machine . . .*   {Our Mutual Friend 1-17}
A device for passing electricity into a person, in this case probably a static electricity generator.

electrotyped   *She had called [Great-uncle Chopper's gift] shabby, electrotyped, second-hand, and below his income.*{Reprinted Pieces, Holiday Romance 1}
A method of printing in which a mold, made from the original lead type, is plated with metal and reinforced to make a harder and more durable plate for printing. In spite of the disparaging reference in this quotation the method actually provided superior print quality, especially when large numbers of copies were printed.

elder-wine   *Long after the ladies had retired did the hot elder-wine, well qualified with brandy and spice, go round and round and round again . . .*   {Pickwick Papers 28}
Wine made from the berries of the elder, elderberry wine.

elephant and castle   . . . *some books were brought in . . . on which he always sat from that time--carrying them in and out himself on after occasions, like a little elephant and castle.*   {Dombey & Son 12}
The castle is the tower carried on the back of a battle elephant.

eligible   . . . *Miss Panky moaning long afterwards, in the least eligible chamber, and Mrs. Pipchin now and then going in to shake her.* {Dombey & Son 8}
Fit or suitable.

ell . . . *a troublesome class of persons who, having an inch conceded them, will take an ell.* {Barnaby Rudge 30}
A measure of length. The English ell is 45 inches. The Flemish ell is 27 inches.

elope *Hastily cloaked and muffled, and stealing away. She elopes!* {Hard Times 2-11}
To run away or escape. Here it does not mean for the purpose of marrying.

elysium *[The workhouse was] a tavern where there was nothing to pay; . . . a brick-and-mortar elysium, where it was all play and no work* . . . {Oliver Twist 9}
The abode of the blessed after death, a place or state of ideal happiness.

endue *Miss Tox endued herself with the pair of ancient gloves, like dead leaves, in which she was accustomed to perform these avocations* . . . {Dombey & Son 29}
To put on.

engage for *Mr. Lorry readily engaged for that, and the conference was ended.* {Tale of Two Cities 2-19}
To be answerable for, to promise.

engross . . . *he barked at my old friend* . . . *with such* . . . *pertinacity, that he* . . . *engrossed the conversation.* {David Copperfield 44}
To gain or keep exclusive possession of something.

ensign-staff *When [the ship] struck, a number of men climbed up the ensign-staff, under an apprehension of her immediately going to pieces.* {Reprinted Pieces, The Long Voyage}
The flagstaff at the stern of a ship from which the national flag is flown.

entail *"Well, then, my dear, I'm afraid he'll never come to the title,"
said my uncle . . . "You have cut off the entail, my love."* {Pickwick Papers
49}
1. The succession of a landed estate, thus to cut off the entail is to prevent the continued inheritance.
. . . besides entailing . . . the risk of funeral expenses . . . {David Copperfield
5}
2. To impose upon, to bring on by necessary consequence.

entertainment *When dinner was done, and the cloth was cleared away
(the entertainment had been brought from a neighboring eating
house) . . .* {Dombey & Son 4}
1. A meal, especially a formal or elegant meal. It does not mean an act
or show.
*Ten years ago, I took my credentials to an English gentleman . . . . He
engaged me by the six months, and my entertainment was generous.*
{Reprinted Pieces, To Be Read at Dusk}
2. Provision, pay.

entreat *I entreat you, good gentlemen, do not come near us, do not
speak, do not move!* {Tale of Two Cities 1-6}
To beseech, to solicit pressingly.

environing *The trees environing the old chateau, keeping its solitary
state apart, moved in a rising wind . . .* {Tale of Two Cities 2-23}
Encircling.

epergne *A corpulent straddling epergne, blotched all over as if it had
broken out in an eruption rather than been ornamented . . .* {Our
Mutual Friend 1-11}
A centerpiece for the table, usually branched and holding small dishes
or flower vases.

equipage *More than enough of bad roads, bad equipages, and bad
horses . . .* {Tale of Two Cities 3-1}
Carriage, horses, driver, and footmen all taken together. It may sometimes refer to the carriage alone.

erewhile . . . *Mr. Mortimer Lightwood, erewhile called in the news-papers eminent solicitor.* {Our Mutual Friend 1-8}
Some time ago, a while ago.

escrutoire . . . *a chest of drawers with an escrutoire top* . . . {David Copperfield 17}
Should be 'escritoire', a writing desk.

espial . . . *had not withdrawn his eye from this place of espial for five minutes* . . . {Oliver Twist 42}
The act of keeping watch or spying.

Esquimaux . . . *Spear of Esquimaux make* . . . {Edwin Drood 4}
Eskimo.

ether *Oh blessed star of Innocence, wherever you may be, how did you glitter in your home of ether, when the two Miss Pecksniffs put forth, each her lily hand* . . . {Martin Chuzzlewit 5}
The imaginary substance supposed to suffuse the universe, and through which light waves moved.

eulogium *Then, he launched into a general eulogium on the Commons.* {David Copperfield 26}
A laudatory discourse, a formal expression of praise.

evening-tide . . . *by coming in the evening-tide among the desks and writing implements she shed a feminine . . . grace upon the office.* {Hard Times 2-1}
Eventide, the time of evening.

ewer . . . *a washing-table, with a jug and ewer, that might have been mistaken for a milk-pot and slop-basin.* {Martin Chuzzlewit 17}
A pitcher with a wide spout, often used to bring water for washing of hands.

exciseable articles *Exciseable articles were remarkably cheap at all the public-houses* . . . {Pickwick Papers 13}
Articles and goods subject to excise taxes. Here it refers to alcoholic beverages.

exciseman *With this little boy, the only pledge of her departed exciseman . . .* {Pickwick Papers 34}
An officer employed to collect excise taxes and prevent infringement of the excise laws.

execution *. . . Mr. Micawber will be constantly arrested, or taken in execution.* {David Copperfield 44}
Having the goods or person of a debtor seized by the sheriff, in execution of a judgment of a court.

exordium *This exordium, and Miss Pross's two hands in quite agonised entreaty clasping his, decided Mr. Cruncher.* {Tale of Two Cities 3-14}
The beginning of anything, especially the introductory part of a speech.

experientia *. . . experientia does it--as papa used to say.* {David Copperfield 11}
Latin word for experience.

exploded *We are great in obsolete seals, and in faded pin-cushions, and in rickety camp-stools, and in exploded cutlery . . .* {Reprinted Pieces, Our English Watering-place}
Discarded, disused, or out of fashion.

express *. . . we must hold 'em at a distance; we must send expresses out to stop 'em short upon the road, and bring 'em on a mile or two a day, until we're properly prepared to meet 'em* {The Battle of Life 2}
A message sent by a special messenger.

extinguisher *. . . a great extinguisher for a cap . . .* {A Christmas Carol 2}
1. A cone-shaped metal device used to extinguish the flame of a candle by placing it over the candle. Large ones were affixed to the railings of a house for link boys to extinguish their links (see **link**).
. . . and Mr. Weller, removing the extinguisher from Pott, set him free with a caution. {Pickwick Papers 51}
2. The wrestling grip binding an opponent's arms to his sides, by analogy with the tight fit of a candle extinguisher.

extinguisher-topped   . . . *a round room, in one of the chateau's four extinguisher-topped towers.* {Tale of Two Cities 2-9}
Towers with an inverted cone-shaped roof, resembling a huge candle extinguisher.

extras *They are neither of Miss Twinkleton's inclusive regulars, nor of her extras.* {Edwin Drood 3}
In a private school, those courses or classes for which an extra payment was required.

facer *I have administered a succession of facers to them* . . . {David Copperfield 17}
A blow on the face.

facings . . . *a red coat with deep blue facings* . . . {Pickwick Papers 27}
The material of collar, cuffs, and lapels, often different from that of the rest of the garment and of a different color.

factious *Admit it for your factious purposes, and make it worse.* {A Christmas Carol 3}
Proceeding from or pertaining to faction, the tendency to form parties and act for party purposes.

faculty *The faculty don't consider it a healthy custom, I believe, Mr. Richard, to carry one's handkerchief in ones hat--I have heard it keeps the head too warm* . . . {Old Curiosity Shop 59}
Referring to the medical faculty, or medical learning in general.

fag . . . *he had passed his whole life in the dancing-school and had done nothing but teach and fag, fag and teach, morning, noon, and night!* {Bleak House 14}
1. To do something tiring or wearisome.
What set this fag to be jealous of his master's actions . . . {Nicholas Nickleby 59}
2. The junior student, in an English public school, who is obliged to perform menial duties for a more senior student.

fag end . . . *the tremulous tones of old Gride's voice, as it feebly chirruped forth the fag end of some forgotten song* . . . {Nicholas Nickleby 51}
The last part or remnant of anything, after the best part is used.

faggot ... *a large faggot and a plentiful supply of coals being heaped upon the fire, the appearance of things was not long in mending* ... {Nicholas Nickleby 6}
A bundle of twigs or small branches used as fuel for a fire.

fain *But as we grow older, we grow wiser--better, I would fain hope* ... {Barnaby Rudge 29}
1. Disposed to or inclined to.
... *perplexed his mind to that degree that he was fain, several times, to take off his hat to scratch his head.* {Tale of Two Cities 1-3}
2. Necessitated or obliged to.

fair-copy ... *she could ingross, fair-copy, fill up printed forms with perfect accuracy* ... {Old Curiosity Shop 33}
To make a final copy of a document after all corrections are made.

Fairy-rings *Why, even to sit watching for the Fairy-rings in the fields* ... *was a pleasant occupation* ... {Cricket on the Hearth 2}
A circular band of grass of a color different from the surrounding grass, supposed to be caused by fairies dancing there.

fall *"Did you ever try a fall with a man when you were young, master?" said Hugh. "Can you make any play at single-stick?"* {Barnaby Rudge 35}
A bout of wrestling. So-named from the bout ending with a fall, which occurs when the loser falls to the ground.

fall of the leaf *My uncle's great journey was in the fall of the leaf, at which time he collected debts, and took orders in the north;* ... {Pickwick Papers 49}
Autumn. By contraction of this phrase the word 'fall' came to mean the season.

fall out, fell out ... *and thus it fell out that she became the unconscious means of bringing them together.* {Our Mutual Friend 3-9}
To happen, to come to pass.

false calves *There is no King George the Fourth now* ... *to set the dandy fashion; there are no clear-starched jack-towel neckcloths, no short-*

waisted coats, no false calves, no stays. {Bleak House 12}
Padding for the calves, to give the legs a better appearance.

false collar *[Mr. Chuckster] ... was pounced upon by the fair enslaver, and had a false collar plucked up by the roots, and his hair very much dishevelled, before the exertions of the company could make her sensible of her mistake ...* {Old Curiosity Shop 61}
A collar not sewn to the shirt but removable.

family *He warn't one of the family at that time ...* {Oliver Twist 31}
Slang for fraternity of criminals.

fancy *It's nothing but fancy.* {David Copperfield 1}
Fantasy or imagination.

fancy work *"A little fancy work?" suggested Fagin.* {Oliver Twist 42}
Slang for prostitution.

fanfaronade *...And hark! fanfaronade of trumpets...* {Somebody's Luggage 2}
Fanfare.

fan-light *The eye he had was unquestionably useful, but decidedly not ornamental: being of a greenish grey, and in shape resembling the fan-light of a street door.* {Nicholas Nickleby 4}
A semicircular window with panes shaped like a hand-held fan.

fantail *The wheeling and circling flights of runts, fantails, tumblers, and pouters ...* {Barnaby Rudge 1}
A fancy kind of pigeon, as are runts, tumblers, and pouters.

fantail hat *... he would reappear, with a tied-up broken head, in fantail hat and velveteen smalls, like an accursed goblin ...* {Our Mutual Friend 4-14}
A hat with a fan-shaped leather flap on the back, worn by dustmen to protect the neck while carrying trash.

Fantoccini *... Punch comes, the Fantoccini come, the Tumblers come, the Ethiopians come; Glee-singers come at night and hum and vibrate (not*

always melodiously) under our windows. {Reprinted Pieces, Our English Watering-place}
A kind of puppet show in which the puppets are moved mechanically by strings or rods.

farden ... *I laid it out honest to the last brass farden.* {Edwin Drood 23}
Dialect for farthing (see **farthing**).

farinagholkajingo ... *Miss Billsmethi, sir, who I hope will have the pleasure of dancing many a quadrille, minuet, gavotte, country-dance, fandango, double-hornpipe, and farinagholkajingo with you, sir.* {Sketches, The Dancing Academy}
A made-up word meant to exaggerate the complicated and foreign-sounding names of dances.

farrago ... *all the farrago of noted places with which the brain of a traveller is crammed* ... {Reprinted Pieces, Lying Awake}
A medley of fact and fancy.

farrier *In knowledge of horseflesh he was almost equal to a farrier, in stable learning he surpassed his own head groom* ... {Barnaby Rudge 47}
One who shoes horses. Also one who treats the diseases of horses.

farthing ... *he had quite settled the only terms that could be accepted, and had resolved not to abate one single farthing.* {Nicholas Nickleby 30}
A coin the value of a quarter of a penny, not in use but named to indicate a trivial amount.

farthingale ... *Here is the green farthingale* ... {Great Expectations 33}
A hooped petticoat. The farthingale is actually the framework of hoops.

farthing-candle ... *the feeblest farthing-candle ray of light* ... {Little Dorrit 2-12}
A candle costing only a farthing, a small cheap one.

fast *In all the rooms, the mouldering shutters were fast closed: and the bars which held them were screwed tight into the wood;* ... {Oliver Twist 18}
Firmly fixed in place.

father-in-law *The fact is, I am not their father, Mr. Squeers. I'm only their father-in-law.* {Nicholas Nickleby 4}
Step-father. This is an incorrect use of the '-in-law' construction which occurs in several places in Dickens' writings. The mistake was common in the early nineteenth century.

fathom *Bright eyes they were. Eyes that would bear a world of looking in before their depth was fathomed.* {The Chimes 1}
To measure a depth or sound a depth.

favours *A group of humble mourners entered the gate: wearing white favours; for the corpse was young.* {Oliver Twist 33}
A ribbon, cockade, or the like worn at a ceremony.

feather *I'm in wonderful feather, sir.* {Little Dorrit 2-32}
To be in good feather is to be in good spirits, in good health.

feather-bed ... *between the feather-bed and the mattress* ... {Pickwick Papers 8}
Bedding consisting of a large sack filled with feathers, often used instead of, or in addition to, a mattress.

feathering *The neatness of the young man's attire, the dexterity of his feathering* ... {Pickwick Papers 33}
The plumage of a bird, hence by analogy the decoration of his clothing.

fee (someone) ... *[he] was glad to fee a link-boy to escort him home.* {Barnaby Rudge 16}
Pay someone for a service.

feint ... *I [was] surprised by the feint everybody made, then, of not having been asleep at all* ... {David Copperfield 5}
Pretense.

fell ... *he was stopped by Joe's suddenly working round him with every demonstration of a fell pugilistic purpose.* {Great Expectations 18}
Exceedingly great, huge.

fell out ... *and relates what fell out upon their way thither.* {Martin Chuzzlewit 8}
Happened, came to pass.

fen *When mists arose from dyke, and fen, and river.* {The Haunted Man 1}
Marshland, land covered, at least from time to time, with shallow water.

fence ... *you covetous, avaricious, in-sa-ti-a-ble old fence* ... {Oliver Twist 13}
Slang for a receiver of stolen goods.

fender ... *Mr. Bucket made me sit down in a corner by the fire and take off my wet shoes, which he turned up to dry upon the fender, talking all the time.* {Bleak House 59}
1. A metal frame in front of the fireplace, meant to keep coals from rolling out into the room.
... *out at last upon the clearer river, where the ships' boys might take their fenders in* ... {Great Expectations 54}
2. Pads, usually made of rope, hung over the sides of ships to prevent damage and abrasion.

ferret ... *Mr. Snagsby has dealt in all sorts of blank forms of legal process; in skins and rolls of parchment* ... *in red tape and green ferret* ... {Bleak House 10}
A stout tape, like red tape, used to tie up bundles of legal documents. It has the same figurative sense of obstructive bureaucracy as does red tape.

fetch ... *the very fetch and ghost of Mrs. Gamp, bonnet and all, might be seen hanging up, any hour of the day, in at least a dozen of the second-hand clothes shops about Holborn.* {Martin Chuzzlewit 19}
The apparition or supernatural double of a person.

fetter . . . *how she had made chains of dandelion-stalks for youthful vowers of eternal constancy . . . and how soon those fetters had withered and broken.* {Dombey & Son 29}
A chain or shackle used to bind the ankles or wrists.

fibbed . . . *he was severely fibbed by the Larkey one, and heavily grassed.* {Dombey & Son 44}
Struck by blows delivered in rapid succession.

fig *Whenever I see a beadle in full fig, coming down a street on a Sunday at the head of a charity school, I am obliged to turn and run away, or I should hit him.* {Little Dorrit 1-2}
In full uniform or dress.

figure *Away went Mr.Pickwick--hands across--. . . pousette everywhere-- loud stamp on the ground--ready for the next couple . . . all the figure over once more . . .* {Pickwick Papers 28}
A set of movements in a dance.

file *The Dodger . . . desired the jailer to communicate 'the names of them two files as was on the bench'.* {Oliver Twist 43}
An artful or shrewd person, also a man, a guy.

fillet *A doll she had dressed lay near upon the ground. I took it up, and saw that she had made a green fillet such as she wore herself, and fastened it about its mimic eyes.* {American Notes, 3}
A headband or a ribbon worn to hold the hair back.

fillip *And whenever Mrs. Pipchin caught herself falling forward into the fire, and woke up, she filliped Master Bitherstone on the nose for nodding also.* {Dombey & Son 8}
A blow delivered by bending the thumb against the last joint of the first finger and suddenly releasing it.

fillyillially *It's very fillyillially done, you know; but you are flattering your father.* {Mugby Junction 3}
A misconstruing of the word 'filially'.

fin *"Smauker, my lad, your fin," said the gentlemen with the cocked hat.* {Pickwick Papers 37}
Slang for hand.

find   *... and asked me how I found myself...* {David Copperfield 3}
Used in the sense of the greeting 'How are you?'.

find out *... Nell had no difficulty in finding out Miss Monflather's boarding and Day Establishment ...* {Old Curiosity Shop 31}
To come upon by searching or inquiry, to find.

fine, in fine *In fine, Paul looked on until the clock had quite recovered its familiar aspect.* {Dombey & Son 14}
Latin for in the end, at last.

finger-glass *He finding ... a piece of orange flower somewhere in the lobbies now approached undetected with the same in a finger-glass ...* {Our Mutual Friend 4-4}
A glass holding water for rinsing the fingers after a meal.

finger-post *They had stopped to rest beneath a finger-post where four roads met ...* {Old Curiosity Shop 17}
A post set up at a parting of the roads, with one or more arms, often terminating in pointing fingers, to indicate the directions of the towns to which the roads lead.

fire *She fired when she asked the last question, and she slapped my face with such force as she had, when I answered it.* {Great Expectations 11}
To show sudden anger.

fire-agency *There were, within sight, an auctioneer's and a fire-agency office, a cornfactor's, a linen-draper's ...* {Pickwick Papers 7}
A fire insurance agency.

fire-balloon *... and other rustic sports; lotteries for toys, roundabouts, dancing on the grass to the music of an admirable band, fire-balloons and fireworks.* {Reprinted Pieces, Our French Watering-place}
A balloon sent up with fireworks that are ignited in the air.

fire-box *He carried in his pocket, too, a fire-box of mysterious and unknown construction . . .* {Old Curiosity Shop 47}
A box containing materials for lighting a match, before self-striking matches.

fire-bucket *The wit of the counting-house became in a moment as mute as the row of leathern fire-buckets hanging up behind him.* {Dombey & Son 13}
A leather bucket kept filled with water, to be used in case of fire.

fire-damp *I ha' fell into a pit that ha' been wi' th' fire-damp crueller than battle.* {Hard Times 3-6}
The miner's name for methane, an explosive gas often found in mines. The word 'damp' means gas or vapor.

firedogs *. . . none of your free-and-easy companions, who would scrape their boots upon the firedogs in the common room . . .* {Barnaby Rudge 10}
Andirons. The iron bars within either side of the fireplace, on which logs are placed

fire-guard *Lumber-room as usual. Old fire-guard, old shoes, two fish-baskets, washing-stand on three legs, and a poker.* {A Christmas Carol 1}
A wire frame or semicircular railing in front of a fireplace to keep children out of the fire.

fire-irons *The little dog retreated under the sofa on my approaching him, and was with great difficulty dislodged by the fire-irons.* {David Copperfield 38}
Implements for tending a fire, usually poker, tongs, and shovel.

firemen-watermen *There were two firemen-watermen in the boat, lying by until somebody was exhausted . . .* {Sketches, The Loving Couple}
A river-boatman who also acted as a steamship fireman, shoveling fuel into the ship's boiler.

fire office ... *the head accountant, who was to get him into the fire office.*
{Dombey & Son 58}
1. A fire insurance office.
He would have been invaluable to a fire-office; never was a man with
such a natural taste for pumping engines, running up ladders, and
throwing furniture out of two-pair-of-stairs' windows ... {The Public
Life of Mr. Tulrumble}
2. From the context it seems to mean a fire-station, though that definition for fire office is not in any of the standard sources.

fire-ship ... *they got to the corner of Brig Place without any molesta-*
tion from that terrible fire-ship [Mrs. MacStinger] ... {Dombey &
Son 23}
Not a fire-fighting ship, but a ship filled with combustibles and set afire
to drift among other ships and destroy them. A much feared weapon in
the days of wooden ships.

fire-shovel *"Jolly sort of lodgings," said Mark, rubbing his nose with the*
knob at the end of the fire-shovel, and looking round the poor cham-
ber ... {Martin Chuzzlewit 13}
The small shovel kept by the fireplace, one of the fire irons.

firing *And even if you exchanged blankets for the child--or books and*
firing--it would be impossible to prevent their being turned into liquor.
{Our Mutual Friend 1-9}
Materials for a fire, here referring to wood or coal.

fish ... *tell me something about the Chinese ladies whether their eyes are*
really so long and narrow always putting me in mind of mother-of-
pearl fish at cards ... {Little Dorrit 1-13}
The counters used in card games, like chips are used in poker. They
were often made of materials like bone, ivory, and, as here, mother-of-
pearl shaped like fish.

fish-basket *Lumber room as usual. Old fire-guard, old shoes, two*
fish-baskets, washing-stand on three legs, and a poker. {A Christmas
Carol 1}
Basket in which fish are transported.

fish-kittle *As to a fish-kittle, Mrs. Crupp said, well! would I only come and look at the range.* {David Copperfield 24}
Dialect for fish kettle.

fisticuffs, fisty-cuffs *... one of those ... fellows, who, if they are ever beaten at fisticuffs, or other kind of warfare, never know it, and go on coolly till they win.* {Barnaby Rudge 35}
[A sewing society] which holds meetings, passes resolutions, never comes to fisty-cuffs or bowie-knives as sane assemblies have been known to do elsewhere... {American Notes, 3}
Fist fighting.

Fives' Court *... the adventurous pair of the Fives' Court will after-wards send round a hat, and trust to the bounty of the lookers-on for the means of regaling themselves...* {Nicholas Nickleby 1}
'Fives' is slang for fist, and 'a fives' means a fist fight. Hence the 'fives court' is the boxing ring.

fixtures *I have therefore taken a 'ouse in that locality, which in the opinion of my friends, is a hollow bargain (taxes ridiculous, and use of fixtures included in the rent), and intend setting up professionally for myself there forthwith.* {Bleak House 64}
Accessories to the house, which may include outbuildings, stables, or equipment.

flagellation *... adjusting the wax-end which was twisted round the bottom of his cane, for purposes of parochial flagellation.* {Oliver Twist 7}
Flogging, whipping.

flageolet *... the shrill flageolet and deafening drum...* {Old Curiosity Shop 19}
A small wind instrument having six finger holes and a mouthpiece.

flagon *... a table decorated with a white cloth, bright pewter flagons, and other tempting preparations for a well-cooked meal...* {Barnaby Rudge 2}
A large metal bottle, usually with a top that screws on.

flambeau ... *preceded by running-footmen bearing flambeaux...* {Barnaby Rudge 16}
A torch, especially one made of several thick wicks dipped in wax.

flap-brimmed hat ... *putting on a low-crowned flap-brimmed hat, goes softly out.* {Edwin Drood 12}
A hat with a brim that hangs down like earflaps.

flapped waistcoat ... *and had the shoe buckles and flapped waistcoat the least reconcilable to human reason ...* {Dombey & Son 4}
An old-fashioned (in Dickens' time) waistcoat with flaps for decoration.

flash *Not by flash Toby Crackit?* {Oliver Twist 19}
Slang for well-dressed, fancily dressed.

flash notes ... *a third [man] dressed as a farmer well to do in the world with his top-coat over his arm and his flash notes in a large leathern pocket-book ...* {Nicholas Nickleby 50}
Counterfeit banknotes.

flat ... *being told that Mr. Jinkins and party paid [for theater tickets] observ[ed] that "they must be nice flats, certainly;"* ... {Martin Chuzzlewit 11}
1. Slang for a stupid person.
... *a common stair communicated, by steep and intricate windings, with the various flats above.* {Pickwick Papers 49}
2. Apartment.
... *of all the trying sisters a girl could have, she did think the most trying sister was a flat sister.* {Little Dorrit 2-14}
3. Dull or depressed.
... *the large dining-room ... presented a strange jumble of flats, flies, wings, lamps, bridges, clouds, thunder and lightening ... and various other messes in theatrical slang included under the comprehensive name of "properties."* {Sketches, Mrs. Joseph Porter}
4. Painted scenery, so-called because it consists of flat sheets of canvas stretched over a wooden frame.

flat-candle *I read the service over with a flat-candle on the previous night . . .* {David Copperfield 36}
A short, thick candle often used in a bedroom.

flat-iron *. . . I thought they'd a wery strong flavour o' warm flat-irons.* {Pickwick Papers 37}
An iron with a flat face for smoothing cloth, an ordinary iron.

flaunting *She . . . looked bold, and haggard, and flaunting, and poor . . .* {David Copperfield 22}
Obtruding boastfully, impudently, or defiantly on the public view.

flaxen *Sir Matthew Pupker especially, who had a little round head with a flaxen wig on top of it, fell into such a paroxysm of bows, that the wig threatened to be jerked off every instant.* {Nicholas Nickleby 2}
Of the color of flax, a white or yellow fiber.

Flemish ell *. . . having snipped off a Flemish ell . . .* {Barnaby Rudge 30}
A unit of length, 27 inches.

flies *. . . the large dining-room . . . presented a strange jumble of flats, flies, wings, lamps, bridges, clouds, thunder and lightening . . . and various other messes in theatrical slang included under the comprehensive name of "properties."* {Sketches, Mrs. Joseph Porter}
Painted scenery suspended across the top of the stage.

flint *And your own flesh and blood might come to want too, might they, for anything you cared? Oh you precious old flint!* {Martin Chuzzlewit 18}
1. A miser, a skinflint.
He took out a blackened pipe, filled it, lighted it with flint and steel, pulled at it until it was in a bright glow . . . {Tale of Two Cities 2-23}
2. A hard, grey rock that produces sparks when struck against a piece of steel. Flint and steel were carried to start a fire, in the days before matches.

flip *We had a hot supper on the occasion, graced by the inevitable roast fowl, and we had some flip to finish with.* {Great Expectations 19}

A drink made of beer mixed with spirits and sugar, then heated with a hot iron.

flitch ... *to claim the flitch of bacon.* {Our Mutual Friend 2-16}
A side of an animal, a side of bacon. Here it refers to a prize given to a married couple who have not quarreled for a year and a day.

flock mattress ... *and for some time he lay gasping on a little flock mattress* ... {Oliver Twist 1}
A mattress stuffed with flock, which consists of coarse tufts of cotton or wool, or pieces of cloth torn apart by machinery.

floor-clothed *He found himself in a little floor-clothed room* ... {Nicholas Nickleby 16}
A floor covered with a substitute for carpeting, such as linoleum or oilcloth.

floored ... *ever since that time when I was floored in Eden* ... {Martin Chuzzlewit 43}
Overthrown, overpowered, done for.

flouncing ... *she is as pert and flouncing a minx as ever you met with in all your days!*{Reprinted Pieces, Holiday Romance 4}
Moving with self-awareness and in a way to attract attention.

flour-dredger ... *ladies would fly out at their doors crying, "Mr. Baptist--dust-pan!" "Mr. Baptist--flour-dredger!" "Mr. Baptist--coffee-biggin!"* {Little Dorrit 1-25}
A tin for sprinkling flour.

floury ... *"and he said in a very plain manner----" "Floury, if you please," interrupted Malderton again* ... {Sketches, Horatio Sparkins}
(see **flowery**)

flowed *"The shop-door was unbolted and unlocked, and Mr. Gills gone." "Gone!" roared the Captain. "Flowed, sir," returned Rob.* {Dombey & Son 25}
To flow is the opposite of to stand or stay, hence, the colloquial meaning is to leave or take off.

flowers of type *Flaming placards are rife on all the dead walls in the borough, public-houses hang out banners, hackney-cabs burst into full-grown flowers of type . . .* {Reprinted Pieces, Our Vestry}
So many posters and bills have been attached to the cabs that they look like flowers made of printed materials.

flowery *But don't be hard upon me! Don't be flowery, Jacob! Pray!* {A Christmas Carol 1}
Full of fine words and showy expressions. The terrified Scrooge would like Marley's ghost to be brief.

flue *The clothes of this gentleman were much bespeckled with flue . . .* {Nicholas Nickleby 21}
Fluffy particles of cotton, down, etc. Lint.

fluffy *Fluffy and snuffy strangers stare into the kitchen-range as curiously as into the attic clothes-press.* {Dombey & Son 59}
Covered with fluff, lint, or feathery material.

flummox *. . . if your governor don't prove a alleybi, he'll be what the Italians call reg'larly flummoxed . . .* {Pickwick Papers 33}
To bring to confusion, to bewilder, confound.

flunkey *. . . speculating on the number of families . . . who lived in such hutches of their own free flunkey choice.* {Little Dorrit 1-10}
A flunky is an obsequious person, a toady. Hence a choice made by a flunky in submission to someone of higher rank.

fly *One night he wos took very ill; sends for a doctor; doctor comes in a green fly . . .* {Pickwick Papers 44}
1. Any covered carriage pulled by one horse, such as a cab or hansom, for hire.
"It was quite right of you to say nothing about the lady the other night . . . You can't be too quiet, Jo." "I am fly, master." {Bleak House 25}
2. Knowing, wide-awake, sharp.

fly-away *. . . dressed in such a free and fly-away fashion, that the long ends of his loose red neckcloth were streaming out behind him . . .* {Martin

Chuzzlewit 5}
When said of clothing it means streaming, loose.

fly-cage *A paper fly-cage dangled from the ceiling . . .* {Oliver Twist 37}
A flytrap so arranged that flies can crawl into it but not out.

fly-driver *. . . the fly-driver who stopped to drive the happy pair to the spot where they proposed to take steamboat to Ryde . . .* {Nicholas Nickleby 25}
The driver of a fly, a one-horse carriage.

flying the garter *Who do you suppose will ever employ a professional man when they see his boy playing at marbles in the gutter or flying the garter in the horse-road?* {Pickwick Papers 38}
A child's game, resembling leapfrog, in which players jump from a line of stones (the garter) across the back of another player.

fly van *[She] is only waiting for a fly van, going to-night to Brighton on private service, which is to call for her, by private contract, and convey her home.* {Dombey & Son 59}
A light wagon drawn by one horse, usually hired.

fob, fob-pocket *. . . Mr. Nickleby replaced his watch in his fob, and, fitting on his gloves to a nicety, turned upon his way . . .* {Nicholas Nickleby 3}
. . . and a gold watch in his fob-pocket . . . {Pickwick Papers 28}
A small pocket in the vest or in the waistband of trousers, in which a watch was usually carried.

foetid *. . . both of whom observed the foetid effluvia and regarded them as being emitted from the premises in the occupation of Krook, the unfortunate deceased.* {Bleak House 33}
Fetid. Having an offensive smell.

fogle *. . . if you don't take fogles and tickers-- . . .* {Oliver Twist 18}
Slang for pocket handkerchief.

foil *. . . one gentleman . . . whispered to a neighbor in green-foil smalls that Tuckle was in spirits to-night.* {Pickwick Papers 37}

Setting something off or adorning it by virtue of a contrasting color. The neighbor was wearing knee breeches that were decorated in green.

folio ... *and with the air of some old necromancer appeared to be profoundly studying a great folio volume that lay open on a desk* ... {Barnaby Rudge 25}
A book made up of sheets of paper folded only once, hence the largest sized volume. It can be as large as 20" x 12½".

follerers ... *he was nothing but a follerers. When he first came to lodge here, I didn't know what he was, and I confess that when I found out I gave him notice.* {Bleak House 15}
(see **follower**)

follower *Five servants kept. No man. No followers.* {Nicholas Nickleby 16}
A man who calls at a house to court a maidservant.

fomentation ... *holding her pocket handkerchief to her chest, like a fomentation, with both hands.* {Bleak House 38}
A cloth soaked in a hot medication and applied to the skin as a medical treatment.

font *There were the seats where the poor old people sat* ...; *the rugged font where children had their names, the homely alter where they knelt* ... {Old Curiosity Shop 17}
Baptismal fountain.

foolscap *Mr. Swiveller took a large sheet of foolscap, and with a countenance of profound gravity, began to make a very small note in one corner.* {Old Curiosity Shop 35}
A kind of writing or printing paper about twelve by fifteen inches in size.

foot-board ... *Mr. Wardles carriage, which in common humanity, had a dicky behind for the fat boy, who, if there had been a foot board instead, would have rolled off and killed himself in his very first nap.* {Pickwick Papers 54}

A small platform at the back of a carriage on which the footman stands.

foot-boy ... *in the window hung a long and tempting array of written placards, announcing vacant places of every grade, from a secretary's to a foot-boy's.* {Nicholas Nickleby 16}
A boy in livery to assist or replace the footman.

foot-passengers *Young Piper and young Perkins, as members of that restless juvenile circle which is the terror of the foot-passengers in Chancery Lane...* {Bleak House 33}
Pedestrians, people walking in the street.

footpad *At that time, too, all the roads in the neighborhood of the metropolis were infested by footpads or highwaymen...* {Barnaby Rudge 2}
A robber on the highways who robs on foot rather than on horseback.

foraging-cap ... *the gentleman in the foraging-cap, who plays the harp...* {Sketches, The River}
A kind of cap worn by infantry soldiers. Foraging is searching for or raiding for provisions.

forbear, forborne ... *I have forborne, and forborne, as long as it was in the nature of man to do it.* {Tale of Two Cities 2-10}
To abstain from, or refrain from, something.

forcemeat *Count up your injuries, in its side-dishes of ailing sweet-breads in white poultices, of apothecaries' powders in rice for curry, of pale stewed bits of calf ineffectually relying for an adventitious interest on forcemeat balls.* {The Uncommercial Traveller, Refreshments for Travellers}
Finely chopped meat or fish, usually with eggs or cereal added.

forcer ... *Miss Blimber meant it--though she was a forcer.* {Dombey & Son 14}
One who forces others to do things.

fore-boot *"Is the red bag in?" "All right, sir." "And the striped bag?"*
"Fore-boot, sir." "And the brown-paper parcel?" "Under the seat,
sir." {Pickwick Papers 22}
The stowage box, or boot, at the front of a coach.

foreign post night ... *and returns to the office, from which, if it is not*
foreign post night, he again sallies forth in about half an hour.
{Sketches, Thoughts about People}
Mail to a particular foreign country would be sent from a post office
only on selected days of the week; therefore, a businessman would need
to post all his letters to that country by the evening of the selected day
or his mail would not go out for another week.

forensic ... *and having worn for five-and-twenty years the forensic wig*
which hung on a block beside him. {Pickwick Papers 31}
Relating to the law, hence a lawyer's wig.

forfeits ... *and here we all wait, until the clock strikes twelve, to usher*
Christmas in, and beguile the time with forfeits and old stories. {Pick-
wick Papers 28}
Games in which a player gives up something of his own (the forfeit) and
must do something ludicrous to redeem it.

fork, fork out *"The watchword to the old min is--fork." "Is what?"*
demanded Quilp. "Is fork, sir, fork," replied Mr. Swiveller, slapping
his pocket {Old Curiosity Shop 3}
Slang for pay up, hand over money.

form ... *a long, bare, melancholy room, made barer still by lines of*
plain deal forms and desks. {A Christmas Carol 2}
A long bench without a back.

forsooth *You tell me! Tell me, forsooth!* {Our Mutual Friend 1-10}
In truth, truly.

fortnight *Commission to the extent of two and ninepence in a fortnight*
cannot, however limited our ideas, be considered remunerative.
{David Copperfield 28}
A period of fourteen nights, hence two weeks.

foster-mother *"Miss Haredale, I am told, is a very charming creature." "I am her foster-mother, and should know . . . "* {Barnaby Rudge 27}
A woman who helps bring up another's child, as a nurse.

foster-sister *[She]had ever since been the humble friend of Miss Haredale, whose foster-sister she was . . .* {Barnaby Rudge 20}
A girl nursed at the same breast with another child.

foul *It was the Inn where friends used to put up, and where we used to go to see parents, and to have salmon and fouls, and be tipped.* {The Holly-Tree 1}
Fowl. Chicken and the like.

found *Russel Place, Russel Square; offers eighteen guineas; tea and sugar found.* {Nicholas Nickleby 16}
Supplied, usually by an employer, as part of or in lieu of wages.

Foundation-boy *As time went on, I became a Foundation-boy on a good foundation, and I cost Brother Hawkyard nothing.*{Reprinted Pieces, George Silverman's Explanation 6}
A student with a scholarship and stipend supplied by a charitable foundation.

founded *Caddy, while she was observant of her husband and was evidently founded upon him, had acquired a grace and self-possession of her own . . .* {Bleak House 38}
Based, grounded.

founder *. . . perhaps the wealthiest brass and copper founder's family known to mankind.* {Martin Chuzzlewit 9}
To found metal is to cast metal. A founder is one who casts metal, and a foundry is the place in which it is done.

fourgon *. . . leave the carriages and fourgon at Martigny . . .* {Little Dorrit 2-1}
A horse-drawn baggage wagon or luggage van. The word was originally French and referred to a coach of French design and construction. The front of the wagon had seats, covered by a folding top, for the

servants who traveled with the fourgon, usually in advance of the family. The rear of the vehicle was a large rectangular body that held the boxes of clothing and other family needs.

four-in-hand . . . *what an easy thing it is to drive a four-in-hand when you have had as much practice as he has.* {Pickwick Papers 28}
A vehicle with four horses driven by one person. So-called because the reins for all four horses were held in one hand.

Four-in-hand Club . . . *it should be laid out with highway roads, turnpikes, bridges, miniature villages, and every object that could conduce to the comfort and glory of Four-in-hand Clubs* . . . {Sketches, Full Report of the Second Meeting of the Mudfog Association}
Gentlemen who drove large carriages and coaches as a hobby formed clubs at whose meetings they demonstrated their skills. Such four-in-hand clubs still exist in the United Kingdom.

fowling-piece . . . *with dog and hatchet, goat-skin cap and fowling-pieces . . .* {Martin Chuzzlewit 5}
A light gun for shooting wild fowl.

fox's martyr . . . *the more that I was torn to pieces sir the more I'd say it though I may not be a fox's martyr.* {Dombey & Son 44}
John Foxe (1516-1587) wrote a book, popularly called *The Book of Martyrs*, which was an account of the people who suffered persecution for being Protestants.

franks . . . *shabby figures in quest of franks, flit restlessly to and fro . . .* {Nicholas Nickleby 16}
The signature of a member of parliament written on an envelope in place of a postage stamp. It permitted the letter to be mailed free.

freehold *Think of the laws appertaining to real property . . . to leasehold, freehold, and copyhold estate . . .* {The Battle of Life 1}
A lease that is held for life.

free of *"Let's have the seafaring man in," says the voice. "Let's vote him free of the Club, for this night only."* {Message from the Sea 4}

Allowed the use or enjoyment of a place. Here, allowed to be part of the club.

free-school *It's a poor boy from the free-school, sir . . .* {Oliver Twist 7}
A private charity school.

French bedstead *It was not a turn-up bedstead, nor yet a French bed-stead, nor yet a four-post bedstead . . .* {Martin Chuzzlewit 49}
A bedstead with a high headboard and high footboard. It was meant to be placed against a wall, with a frame attached to the wall for the curtains that surrounded the bed.

French lamps *. . . pastrycooks' men with green boxes on their heads, and rout-furniture-warehouse carts, with cane seats and French lamps, hurrying to the numerous houses where an annual festival is held in honour of the occasion.* {Sketches, The New Year}
Oil lamps with tubular wicks, invented in France by Aimé Argand in the eighteenth century. They were brighter than the ordinary oil lamp with a flat wick.

fresh and fresh *. . . it was your business to take . . . a personal interest and sympathy in a hundred gentlemen fresh and fresh . . .* {Somebody's Luggage 1}
Not deteriorated by time, remaining fresh.

frill *. . . round his neck was tattered child's frill, only half concealed by a coarse, man's neckerchief.* {Nicholas Nickleby 7}
A wavy or fluted edging, usually on a shirt.

fringe *How handsome her eyes looked when she was stooping over him! Such long lashes, such delicate fringe!* {Nicholas Nickleby 47}
Bangs, the front hair brushed forward and cut short.

frippery *. . . eyed the gaudy frippery about him with very little concern . . .*
{Nicholas Nickleby 10}
Tawdry finery of clothing.

frizzled ... *to mention such supplementary items as marmalade, eggs, water-cresses, salted fish, and frizzled ham* ... {Edwin Drood 20}
Fried or grilled with a sputtering noise.

frogged *His coat, in colour blue, and of a military cut, was buttoned and frogged, up to his chin.* {Martin Chuzzlewit 4}
Having frogs on it, ornamental fastenings with a spindle-shaped button on one side and a fancy loop on the other.

from home ... *Mr. Pickwick and Sam Weller were from home all day long* ... {Pickwick Papers 57}
Away from home.

front *"You dogs!" said the Marquis, but smoothly and with an unchanged front, except as to the spots on his nose* ... {Tale of Two Cities 2-7}
1. Expression of the face.
If you take notice ... what a very few shirts there are, and what a many fronts, you'll penetrate the mystery of his packing. {Martin Chuzzlewit 17}
2. A dicky, the separate front part of a shirt without sleeves. It was less expensive to buy and to launder than a shirt.
The shabby little old man ... is standing in the porch, and has put his hat on the front--for he is quite at home there, being sexton. {Dombey & Son 57}
3. The forehead. He has casually pushed his hat forward.

front glass *"Halloa!" cried the doctor, letting down the front glass in a great hurry and shouting to the postilion* ... {Oliver Twist 36}
The window in front of the passenger compartment of a carriage through which the passengers could communicate with the coachman or, in this case, with the man who drove the coach by riding one of the wheel horses.

frousy, frouzy, frowsy ... *screened ... from the cold air without, by a frousy curtaining of miscellaneous tatters* ... {A Christmas Carol 4}
... *the place is rendered close, by the steams of moist acts of Parliament and frowsy petitions* ... {Nicholas Nickleby 16}
Having an untidy or soiled appearance, dirty, neglected, unkempt.

froward ... *and the arrogant and the froward and the vain, fretted, and chafed, and made their usual uproar.* {Little Dorrit 2-34}
Perverse, ungovernable, naughty.

fruiterer *The poulterers' shops were still half open, and the fruiterers' were radiant in their glory.* {A Christmas Carol 3}
A dealer in fruit, a fruit seller.

fugleman *"One cheer more," screamed the little fugleman in the balcony, and outshouted the mob again, as if lungs were cast-iron with steel works.* {Pickwick Papers 13}
Originally, an especially expert soldier placed in front of a company as an example to the others in their exercises; hence, one who acts as leader for responses of the crowd or who gives signals for their responses.

full-blown *A slatternly full-blown girl who seemed to be bursting out at the rents in her gown and the cracks in her shoes* ... {Bleak House 43}
In full bloom.

full habit ... *part of his income was derived from the pilotage of timid women (mostly of full habit and past the middle term of life)* ... {Tale of Two Cities 2-14}
There are two possible meanings. 'Full', in the sense of rounded, plump, or protuberant, with 'habit' in the sense of bodily condition; hence, a plump or large woman. The second possibility takes 'habit' in the sense of clothing or dress, and 'full' in the sense of excess material in the form of folds or tucks of cloth; hence, a dress made with much extra material. The context seems to make the first meaning more likely.

full-stop ... *a round brazen door-handle ... like a brazen full-stop.* {Hard Times 1-11}
The period which marks the end of a sentence.

furbelow ... *some fine lady, monstrously hooped and furbelowed, and preceded by running-footmen bearing flambeaux* ... {Barnaby Rudge 16}
A decorative flounce used on cloth or clothing.

furnace of proof ... *passing through the furnace of proof and coming out dross.* {Our Mutual Friend 3-5}
The furnace in which samples of metals were melted to test them for purity.

furniture, horse's furniture ... *making Hugh sensible that he must dismount, sunk the horse's furniture in a pool of stagnant water, and turned the animal loose.* {Barnaby Rudge 68}
The furnishings of the horse, including the saddle, bridle, etc.

furze ... *and nothing grew but moss and furze, and coarse, rank grass.* {A Christmas Carol 3}
Gorse, a spiny evergreen shrub that grows as a weed on wasteland.

fustian ... *a hairy cap and fustian overalls* ... {Pickwick Papers 33}
A kind of coarse cloth, usually of a dark color.

fusty *Two miserable little white mice, left behind by their owner, are running up and down in a fusty castle made of pasteboard and wire* ... {David Copperfield 5}
Something that has lost its freshness, smelling of mold or damp. Also old-fashioned or fogyish.

gable-ends *Now and then a village with its modest spire, thatched roofs, and gable-ends, would peep out from among the trees* ... {Old Curiosity Shop 43}
The triangular-topped end wall of a building with a peaked roof.

gaby *"That gaby." "Who?" said Little Dorrit. "My dear child ... how slow you are! Young Sparkler."* {Little Dorrit 2-6}
A simpleton.

gain on *She don't gain on her papa in the least. How can one expect she should, when she is so very unlike a Dombey.* {Dombey & Son 5}
To win favor.

gaiters *Snawley was a sleek, flat-nosed man, clad in sombre garments, and long black gaiters* ... {Nicholas Nickleby 4}
A legging, a covering for the legs from ankle to knee.

gallipot ... *set traps [for flies] of vinegar and sugar in gallipots* ... {Little Dorrit 1-6}
A small glazed pot used for ointments or other medicines.

gallows *"... Now, young gallows." This was an invitation for Oliver to enter through a door* ... {Oliver Twist 11}
Someone deserving hanging, but also used to mean mischievous children.

galvanic *Don't be galvanic, sir!* {David Copperfield 35}
Electrical, hence shocking. Also used in the sense of twitching, as though from electrical shocks.

galvanic start *And so drops asleep, and has galvanic starts all over him.*
{Our Mutual Friend 1-10}
A twitch or jerking movement resembling those produced by the application of a galvanic, or electric, current.

gamboge-coloured *The cab stopped, and out jumped a man in a coarse Petersham greatcoat, whitey-brown neckerchief, faded black suit, gamboge-coloured top-boots, and one of those large crowned hats, formerly seldom met with, but now very generally patronised by gentlemen and costermongers.* {Sketches, A Passage in the Life of Mr. Watkins Tottle}
Gamboge is a bright yellow pigment obtained from the resin of certain Cambodian trees.

game-cock *A game-cock in the stable-yard, deprived of every spark of his accustomed animation, balanced himself dismally on one leg in a corner...* {Pickwick Papers 51}
A cock, or rooster, bred and trained for the sport of cock-fighting.

gaming *Gaming, the vice which ran so high among all classes (the fashion being of course set by the upper)...* {Barnaby Rudge 16}
Gambling.

gaming-room *Every club and gaming-room has rung with it. There has been a good song made about it, as I am told...* {Nicholas Nickleby 38}
Gambling room.

gammon *That's the way they gammon each other, sir.* {Martin Chuzzlewit 23}
Lies, or nonsense, often meant to deceive.

gangway *Mother, will you be so good as to put a chair for the other lady and get out of the gangway.* {Bleak House 38}
Any kind of passageway in a house or building.

gaoler *Two gaolers, who had been standing there, went out, and the prisoner was brought in, and put to the bar.* {Tale of Two Cities 2-2}
Jailer, jail guard.

gape *He finds that nothing agrees with him so well as to make little gyrations on one leg of his stool, and stab at his desk, and gape.* {Bleak House 20}
Yawn or open the mouth wide.

garden-engine ... *if the Major had played on him with the garden engine ... there would have been words betwixt the Major and me.* {Mrs. Lirriper's Legacy 1}
A portable pump for watering the garden.

Garraway's *Let me read the first [letter]: "Garraway's, twelve o'clock. Dear Mrs. B---- Chops and Tomata sauce. Yours, Pickwick." Gentlemen, what does this mean?* {Pickwick Papers 34}
Garraway's was a popular London coffee house. Gentlemen often spent considerable time there reading newspapers, socializing, gossiping, and drinking a variety of things including coffee.

garret ... *looking up he could just discern the face of Gride himself, cautiously peering over the house parapet from the window of the garret.* {Nicholas Nickleby 59}
A room on the top floor of a house just under the roof, an attic.

garter ... *for the sake of a ribbon, star, or garter...* {Martin Chuzzlewit 10}
A garter was a band of cloth tied around the leg to hold up a stocking. A fancy garter is worn as part of the insignia of the highest order of English knighthood, *The Most Noble Order of the Garter.*

gas ... *a storehouse of awful implements of the great torture of the law--a place not to be entered after the gas is turned off.* {Bleak House 10}
Gas light.

gas jet ... *lighting his candle at the gas jet in the bar before stalking moodily up stairs to his own room ...* {Martin Chuzzlewit 13}
A narrow tube through which illuminating gas is released and is ignited to produce a flame. One was kept burning at a bar to light cigars and candles.

gas microscope *"Yes, I have a pair of eyes," replied Sam, "and that's just it. If they wos a pair o' patent double million magnifyin' gas micro-scopes of hextra power, p'raps I might be able to see through a flight o' stairs and a deal door; but bein' only eyes, you see, my wision's limited."* {Pickwick Papers 34}
A kind of projection microscope which cast a magnified image on a screen. The light was produced by a gas jet using oxygen and hydrogen gas.

gauze blind *It was a shop-front, fitted up with a gauze blind and an inner door . . .* {Nicholas Nickleby 16}
A curtain made of gauze, a thin almost transparent cloth.

general post *Sam not forgetting to drop his letter into a general post-office as they walked along.* {Pickwick Papers 33}
The mail sent from the General Post Office in London to all the post offices in the kingdom, as contrasted with the twopenny post which was local.

general shop *At the general shop, at the butcher's and at the public-house . . .* {Our Mutual Friend 4-6}
General store.

Geneva ware *. . . in Mr. Pinch's eyes, however, [the watches] were small-er than Geneva ware . . .* {Martin Chuzzlewit 5}
Swiss watches, made in Geneva.

genius *"What are you then?" asked the baron. "A genius," replied the figure. ". . . I am the Genius of Despair and Suicide . . . "* {Nicholas Nickleby 6}
1. A spirit, or sometimes a muse.
. . . her evil genius [was] writhing on the roof . . . {David Copperfield 26}
2. Everyone was supposed to be attended through life by two spirits, or geniuses, one evil the other good.

genteel *. . . I have always looked forward to his marrying well, for a genteel provision for myself in the autumn of life . . .* {Barnaby Rudge 12}
Things suited to the station in life of a gentleman or gentlewoman.

gentian . . . *amazing infusions of gentian, peppermint, gilliflower, sage, parsley, thyme, rue, rosemary, and dandelion* . . . . {Edwin Drood 10}
A medicinal plant from which a bitter tonic was made.

German-merchants . . . *from a hasty glance at the directions of some packages which were lying about, Nicholas supposed that the Brothers Cheeryble were German-merchants.* {Nicholas Nickleby 35}
Importers of goods from Germany.

get up linen *Her mother got up linen; and was called to Heaven when She was born.* {The Chimes 1}
To prepare linen clothing, such as shirts, for wearing. This included such things as ironing and forming frills.

get someone on *Mr. Headstone has always got me on . . . and of course if he was my brother-in-law he wouldn't get me on less, but would get me on more.* {Our Mutual Friend 2-15}
To help someone get ahead, get forward, prosper.

gewgaw *"Trim off these gewgaws," said his father, plucking the scraps of ribbon and feathers from his hat* . . . {Barnaby Rudge 69}
1. A trivial ornament, a petty thing of little value.
"There is little need," said the monk . . . "to fritter away the time in gew-gaws which shall raise up the pale ghosts of hopes of early years."
{Nicholas Nickleby 6}
2. Vanities.

gibbet . . . *a gibbet, with some chains hanging to it which had once held a pirate.* {Great Expectations 1}
1. An upright pole with a projecting arm from which were hung, in chains, the bodies of criminals after execution.
Protestants in anything but the name, were no more to be considered as abettors of these disgraceful occurrences, than they themselves were chargeable with the uses of the block, the rack, the gibbet, and the stake in cruel Mary's reign. {Barnaby Rudge 51}
2. Gallows, for hanging.

gig *I drove down in a gig that afternoon to look after that boy.* {Bleak House 57}
A light two-wheeled carriage drawn by one horse. It seated two, the owner-driver and a passenger. It was the commonest middle-class carriage.

gig umbrella *Mrs. Gamp had a large bundle with her, a pair of pattens, and a species of gig umbrella* . . . {Martin Chuzzlewit 19}
An umbrella meant to be fitted to, or carried in , a gig.

gill *I'd bet a gill of old Jamaica* . . . *that I know what you're smiling at.* {Dombey & Son 17}
One quarter of a pint.

gilliflower . . . *amazing infusions of gentian, peppermint, gilliflower, sage, parsley, thyme, rue, rosemary, and dandelion* . . . {Edwin Drood 10}
Gillyflower is a clove or one of several other plants with a clove-like scent.

gimlet . . . *I have thought of nothing but hammers, nails, screw-drivers, and gimlets, morning, noon, and night.* {Nicholas Nickleby 38}
A sharp pointed drill with a T-handle, used for boring holes in wood by hand.

ginger-beer . . . *a close-shaved gentlemen in white trousers and a white hat* . . . *who calls in at the shell-fish shop as he comes along and drinks iced ginger-beer.* {Bleak House 19}
A carbonated, nonalcoholic, drink flavored with ginger, that resembles beer in color and in the way that it foams. It is close to what is called ginger ale in the United States.

gipsy dinner . . . *they remain there until nine at night, solaced by gipsy dinners, not abundant in quantity, from the cook's shop* . . . {Bleak House 39}
An open-air dinner, a picnic dinner.

gipsy party . . . *we allotted the various household duties, as if we had been on a gipsy party, or a yachting party, or a hunting party, or were*

shipwrecked. {The Haunted House 1}
A group of people going picnicking.

girandole *It was a scene of gaiety, glitter, and show; of richly dressed people, handsome mirrors, chalked floors, girandoles, and waxed candles* . . . {Pickwick Papers 35}
A branched candleholder.

give in . . . *there have been times when there were too many for me, and I have given in* . . . {David Copperfield 17}
We burst out crying. The colonel gave in second, and came to first; but he gave in strong. {Reprinted Pieces, Holiday Romance 1}
Give up, surrender. In the second example it means to surrender to sobbing.

gives on *The doorway of the staircase gives on the little court-yard close to the left here* . . . {Tale of Two Cities 1-5}
Opens on, opens into.

glass . . . *and walking slowly to and fro--stopping now and then to glance at himself in the mirror, or survey a picture through his glass, with the air of a connoisseur* . . . {Barnaby Rudge 15}
1. A single eyeglass, or monocle.
With these words, the father, who had been arranging his cravat in the glass, while he uttered them in a disconnected careless manner, withdrew, humming a tune as he went. {Barnaby Rudge 15}
2. Looking-glass or mirror.
"I was afraid the ground would have been wet," said the doctor, "for my glass fell yesterday." {Martin Chuzzlewit 19}
3. A barometer, being made from a glass tube, was referred to as a glass. What fell was the level of the liquid in the tube, indicating a fall in air pressure and the probable onset of rainy weather.

glass-coach *Married! Church, parson, clerk, beadle, glass-coach, bells, breakfast, bride-cake* . . . {Cricket on the Hearth 2}
Originally a coach with glass windows, but later a private coach which was available for hire and was considered a cut above a hackney coach.

glass office . . . *Jonas took the candle from the table, and walking into the glass office, produced a bunch of keys from his pocket.* {Martin Chuzzlewit 18}
The office separated from the rest of the apartment by glass partitions.

glazed hat . . . *and made appointments on 'Change with men in glazed hats and round jackets pretty well every day.* {Old Curiosity Shop 4}
Some fabrics were given a high shine by rubbing them with a metal-faced wooden block. The process was called 'glazing'. Hats with a glazed finish were apparently common middle-class attire.

glazed stocks *Officers were running backwards and forwards . . . and even the very privates themselves looked from behind their glazed stocks with an air of mysterious solemnity . . .* {Pickwick Papers 4}
Neckcloths having a smooth shiny surface, giving a glassy appearance. This was the style for soldiers' uniforms (see **glazed hat**).

glee *Street bands are on their mettle in Golden Square; and itinerant glee-singers quaver involuntarily as they raise their voices within its boundaries.* {Nicholas Nickleby 2}
A song for three or more voices with two or more contrasted movements and (in strict use) without accompaniment.

glim *"Let's have a glim,"* said Sikes, *"or we shall go breaking our necks . . . "* {Oliver Twist 16}
Slang for a light or candle.

gloaming *The gate commands a cross bye-path, little used in the gloaming . . .* {Edwin Drood 14}
Twilight.

Globes *Indeed, whenever Miss Pupford . . . tells how Minerva sprang, perfectly equipped, from the brain of Jupiter, she is half supposed to hint, "So I myself came into the world, completely up in Pinnock, Mangnall, Tables, and the use of the Globes."* {Tom Tiddler's Ground 2}
Young ladies who went to small, private schools during the nineteenth century were taught how to use both the terrestrial globe (the globe of the earth) and the celestial globe (with the constellations, the zodiac, the

plane of the ecliptic, and other heavenly things indicated on it). Pinnock is William H. Pinnock, a nineteenth-century writer on laws and usages of church and clergy who wrote many 'catechisms'. Richmal Mangnall was headmistress of a ladies' school and wrote a book, *Questions*, which was the terror of many generations of school-girls. The tables referred to are the ordinary tables of arithmetic, multiplication, money, and weights and measures as taught in school.

Glory ... *Mrs. Lupin almost wondered not to see a stained-glass Glory, such as the Saint wore in the church, shining about his head.* {Martin Chuzzlewit 3}
A circle of light, the halo around the head of holy figures in religious paintings.

glow-worm *They were not meteors; they were too low. They were not glow-worms; they were too high.* {Pickwick Papers 39}
An insect, the female of which is wingless and produces a light like that of a firefly.

Glue Monge *"... he's a-shaking all over, like--" Blight's simile is perhaps inspired by the surrounding dishes of sweets--"like Glue Monge."* {Our Mutual Friend 3-17}
This is a pun on 'blancmange', a white, sweet desert of a jelly-like consistency. Dickens must have thought that it tasted like glue.

go *"Here's a go!" cried Mr. Squeers ... "Here's a delicious go!"* {Nicholas Nickleby 38}
1. An unexpected turn of affairs.
Commodius ... kills [a hundred lions] off in a hundred goes! {Our Mutual Friend 1-5}
2. An attempt, a try.

gobbled *Never was taught a stitch, young man ... Just gobbled and gobbled, till I found out how to do it.* {Our Mutual Friend 4-16}
A gobble stitch is one made too long through haste, carelessness or lack of skill.

go-cart *... she sits glowering at me like Fate in a go-cart ...* {Little Dorrit 1-24}

A light framework on castors for supporting a baby while it learns to walk, or a variety of light vehicles.

go down ... *it ain't worth hearing, and it won't go down with me.*{Our Mutual Friend 3-15}
Be acceptable.

go in *"Tottle, will you 'go in'?" inquired Mr. Gabriel Parsons* ... {Sketches, A Passage in the Life of Mr. Watkins Tottle}
Enter the game, become a player.

going forward ... *and Mr. Simmery, having by this time killed all the flies and taken all the bets, strolled away to the stock Exchange to see what was going forward.* {Pickwick Papers 55}
Going on, happening.

gold-beater *Here was the strong arm of the law, coming down with twenty-gold-beater force, upon two offenders from the metropolis itself*... {Pickwick Papers 24}
A goldbeater was one whose daily job was hammering plates of gold until they became thin leaves of foil. Twenty goldbeaters would produce a mighty series of blows.

Golden Balls ... *certain entertainments, so splendid and costly in their nature that he emphatically calls them "Golden Balls."* {Martin Chuzzlewit 1}
A pun on the three golden balls that are the sign of a pawn shop.

gonoph ... *I am obliged to take him into custody. He's as obstinate a young gonoph as I know. He won't move on.* {Bleak House 19}
Slang for pickpocket, from the Hebrew word for thief.

goods train ... *I could see the goods train running smoothly along the embankment in the valley.* {The Haunted House 1}
Freight train.

go off *Miss Malderton was as well known as the lion on the top of Northumberland House, and had an equal chance of "going off."* {Sketches, Horatio Sparkins}

To go off is to get married and also to start into sudden action. There is a play on both meanings here.

go off like smoke *Even children so require sustaining under the general excitement that a pieman who has established himself for the occasion at the corner of the court says his brandy-balls go off like smoke.* {Bleak House 11}
To disappear like smoke, hence to sell rapidly.

goosing ... *when you have a animosity towards a Indian ... which can hardly hold you from Goosing him audible when he's going through his war dance ...* {Going Into Society}
Hissing like a goose to express disapproval.

go up *Mayors have been knighted for "going up" with addresses ...* {Edwin Drood 12}
To be ruined financially, socially, or politically.

governess ... *made an inquiry, in a very low tone of voice, relative to some situation as governess, or companion to a lady.* {Nicholas Nickleby 16}
A female teacher employed in a private household.

grab *"Hold your noise,"* remonstrated the Dodger, looking cautiously round. *"Do you want to be grabbed, stupid."* {Oliver Twist 12}
Slang for take into custody, arrest.

grampus ... *went about the building coughing like a grampus.* {Dombey & Son 5}
A person who puffs and blows like a grampus fish.

grand chain ... *Breakfasting at nine ... Going to the City at ten ... Coming home at half-past five ... Dining at seven, and the grand chain.* {Our Mutual Friend 1-11}
The grand chain was a figure in a dance, in which the couples paraded around the ballroom. Dickens here is giving the daily activities of a businessman as names to figures of the dance, ending with a legitimate name for a dance figure.

grassed . . . *he was severely fibbed by the Larkey one, and heavily grassed.* {Dombey & Son 44}
Knocked to the ground. Boxing was against the law, and bouts were often held on open ground.

gravelled . . . *he never had been so gravelled . . .* {Our Mutual Friend 4-12}
1. Confounded, nonplused, puzzled.
. . . it is our misfortune to do that kind of thing now and then. We don't want to do it; but if men will be gravelled, why--we can't help it. {Little Dorrit 2-28}
2. Aground, stranded, on the way to destruction, as a ship aground on gravel.

grazier . . . *a low-crowned broad-brimmed white hat, such as a wealthy grazier might wear . . .* {Nicholas Nickleby 35}
One who grazes or feeds cattle for the market.

greatcoat *Greatcoats, riding-whips, bridles, top-boots, spurs, and such gear, were strewn about on all sides . . .* {Barnaby Rudge 47}
A large, heavy overcoat.

green *Further, he often sees damaging letters produced in evidence and has occasion to reflect that it was a green thing to write them.* {Bleak House 53}
1. Inexperienced.
It was quite a little feast; two ounces of seven-and-sixpenny green, and a quarter of a pound of the best fresh; and Mr. Wilkins had brought a pint of shrimps, neatly folded up in a clean belcher . . . {Sketches, Miss Evans and the Eagle}
2. Probably vegetable greens (see **greens**).

greengrocer . . . *the stout greengrocer Collegian in the corduroy knee-breeches . . .* {Little Dorrit 1-19}
A seller of vegetables and fruit.

green-hearted *He is such a cheery fellow. No worldliness about him. Fresh and green-hearted!* {Bleak House 37}
Youthful, simple.

Greenland *"Where did he come from?" "Greenland . . . "* {Oliver Twist 8}
A greenhorn is an inexperienced person who does not know his way
around, and a greenhorn would surely come from Greenland.

greens *Mr. Bagnet hospitably declares that he will hear of no business
until after dinner and that his friend shall not partake of his counsel
with out first partaking of boiled pork and greens.* {Bleak House 27}
Green vegetables boiled for the table. In London, usually small cab-
bages and cabbage sprouts.

Grenadier wooden measure *. . . on her head a most wonderful bonnet like
a Grenadier wooden measure . . .* {Tale of Two Cities 1-4}
This may have been a nickname for a kind of measuring cup, since it
does not appear to be an official name for one. It might possibly refer
to a wooden measuring cup in the form of a grenadier's hat, also called
a bearskin. It was a very tall fur-covered cylindrical hat with a rounded
top.

gridiron *. . . candle-boxes, and gridirons, and that sort of necessaries . . .*
{David Copperfield 27}
A cooking utensil made of parallel bars of iron in a frame, upon which
meat or fish could be grilled.

griffin *. . . arrived at Greenwich in a car and griffins . . .* {Our Mutual
Friend 4-4}
Griffin is a slang term for a grim-looking vigilant guardian. It probably
refers here to a pair of rough-looking footmen.

grig *I shall be merry as a grig among these gentry.* {Old Curiosity
Shop 50}
Proverbial small-sized creature, a cricket on the hearth.

grill-gate *Within the grill-gate of the chancel . . . white robes could be dimly
seen . . .* {Edwin Drood 9}
A gate made from crisscrossing metal strips in the form of a grill.

gripe *Avarice, hard dealing, griping cares? They have brought him to
a rich end, truly!* {A Christmas Carol 4}
1. Distressful, oppressing, squeezing.

The piece of money I had put into the claw of the child I had overturned was clawed out of it, and was again clawed out of that wolfish gripe . . . {The Uncommercial Traveller, On an Amateur Beat}
2. Grip.

grog . . . *took his first cigar and mixed his first glass of grog.* {Old Curiosity Shop 5}
A mixture of rum and water.

groined . . . *a chamber of no describable shape, with a groined roof . . .* {Edwin Drood 18}
Groins are ribs formed by the intersection of two vaults, such as those often seen in the interior of large churches.

grot *With one of his keys, he opened a cool grot at the end of the yard, and they all went in.* {Our Mutual Friend 1-3}
A grotto, cave, or cavern, either natural or artificial.

groundsel *There was fresh groundsel, too, for Miss Maylie's birds . . .* {Oliver Twist 32}
A common European weed used to feed cage birds.

grout . . . *the ceilings were so fantastically clouded by smoke and dust, that old women might have told fortunes in them, better than in grouts of tea . . .* {Little Dorrit 1-5}
Sediment, here referring to the dregs of tea leaves left in the cup.

grub . . . *you want grub, and you shall have it . . .* {Oliver Twist 8}
1. Slang for food.
The red-nosed man warn't by no means the sort of person you'd like to grub by contract. {Pickwick Papers 22}
2. To feed, provide grub for.

grubber *As if, instead of being his proprietors grubber, he were the triumphant proprietor of the Marshalsea, the Marshal, and all the turnkeys . . .* {Little Dorrit 1-32}
One who lives laboriously, ploddingly. Here it may also mean money grubber, someone sordidly intent on acquiring money.

gruel *If you had kept the boy on gruel, ma'am, this would never have happened.* {Oliver Twist 7}
A light, liquid food, usually made by boiling a small amount of oatmeal in a large amount of water.

guard-chain *The merry old gentleman ... a snuff-box in one pocket ..., a note-case in the other, and a watch in his waistcoat-pocket: with a guard-chain round his neck ... trotted up and down the room ...* {Oliver Twist 9}
A chain used to secure something, such as a watch or brooch, to an article of clothing.

Guernsey *... pleasant to see the watch off duty mustered and come in: best hats, best Guernseys, washed hands and faces, smoothed heads.* {The Uncommercial Traveller, Aboard Ship}
A heavy knitted shirt worn by sailors.

guinea *Russel Place, Russel Square; offers eighteen guineas; tea and sugar found.* {Nicholas Nickleby 16}
An English gold coin worth twenty-one shillings, one shilling more than a pound.

gull *... the blundering cheat--gull that he was, for all his cunning ...* {Martin Chuzzlewit 28}
One who is gulled, a dupe, a sucker.

gulled *... he was really ashamed of his share in the transaction, and deeply mortified by the misgiving that he had been gulled.* {Nicholas Nickleby 50}
Duped, tricked, taken in.

Gum-Tickler *"Will you mix [your rum] Mr. Wegg?" "I think not, sir. On so auspicious an occasion, I prefer to take it in the form of a Gum-Tickler".* {Our Mutual Friend 4-3}
The first drop or drink taken.

gutter *... tied up to posts by the gutter side were long lines of beasts and oxen, three or four deep.* {Oliver Twist 21}

A hollow channel at the side of a street to carry away surface water, the kennel.

guy ... *a person without the use of his lower extremities, carried up-stairs similarly to a guy?* {Bleak House 55}
An effigy of Guy Fawkes, usually crudely made, to be burned on Guy Fawkes' Day.

Guy Faux ... *Newman Noggs standing bolt upright in a little niche in the wall like some scarecrow or Guy Faux laid up in winter quarters* ...
{Nicholas Nickleby 28}
Refers to the 'guy' of Guy Fawkes' Day (see **guy**).

habited *Mr. Bob Sawyer, who was habited in a coarse blue coat . . .*
{Pickwick Papers 29}
Dressed. From 'habit' in the sense of clothing.

hack *My horse, young man! He is but a hack hired from a roadside posting house, but he must carry me to London to-night.*
{Barnaby Rudge 2}
Short for hackney, a hired horse, or sometimes just an ordinary horse.

hack-cabriolet, hackney-cabriolet *. . . bribing the drivers of hackney cabriolets to come suddenly round the corner and dash among them . . .*
{Old Curiosity Shop 37}
A cabriolet for hire (see **cabriolet**).

hack cob *Here's the pony run right off his legs, and me obliged to come home with a hack cob, that'll cost fifteen shillings besides other expenses . . .* {Nicholas Nickleby 13}
A hired cob, a kind of horse.

hackney-chair *Long stands of hackney-chairs and groups of chairmen . . . obstructed the way . . .* {Barnaby Rudge 16}
Sedan chair for hire.

hackney-coach *We then took a hackney-coach and drove away to the neighborhood of Leicester Square.* {Bleak House 24}
A coach for hire.

hair-chain *. . . she can draw, paint, work all manner of pretty things for ornamenting stools and chairs: slippers, Peg, watch-guards, hair-chains, and a thousand little dainty trifles.* {Nicholas Nickleby 51}
A chain of braided hair, used as an ornament.

hair-guard ... *with his decent silver watch in his pocket and its decent hair-guard round his neck* ... {Our Mutual Friend 2-1}
A string braided from hair and used to retain a watch or jewelry.

hair papers ... *dressed in a dimity night-jacket; with her hair in papers; she had also a dirty nightcap on* ... {Nicholas Nickleby 7}
Curling papers.

hair-powder *[She] presented her uncongenial cheek, the little wrinkles in it filled with hair-powder, to Dora to be kissed.* {David Copperfield 27}
A scented powder sprinkled on the hair or wigs, most common in the eighteenth century, but worn by menservants until the beginning of the twentieth century.

hair trunk ... *opened a battered and mangy old hair trunk, found it empty* ... {Hard Times 1-6}
A trunk covered with leather on which the hair is still present.

half *Peggotty's promised letter* ... *arrived before 'the half' was many weeks old.* {David Copperfield 7}
Until about the middle of the nineteenth century, British schools were on a semester system with the school year divided into two halves.

half-boots ... *a stoutly-built fellow of about five-and-thirty, in a black velveteen coat, very soiled drab breeches, lace-up half-boots, and grey cotton stockings* ... {Oliver Twist 13}
A boot reaching halfway to the knee.

half-door ... *putting his arm over the half-door of the bar, coolly unbolting it, and leisurely walking in.* {Pickwick Papers 27}
A door of half the usual height, in this case the height of the bar.

half-price to the play *He takes me half-price to the play, to an extent which I sometimes fear is beyond his means* ... {Martin Chuzzlewit 32}
Admission only to the second half of the performance, which was at a reduced price.

half-quartern loaf *... and related ... an agreeable anecdote about the removal of a tumour on some gentleman's head, which he illustrated with an oyster-knife and a half-quartern loaf...* {Pickwick Papers 30}
A quartern-loaf is a loaf of bread made from a quartern (a quarter pound) of flour, hence a loaf of bread half the size of a quartern-loaf.

half-sheet *What do you say to Mrs. Bucket having, within this half-hour, secured the corresponding ink and paper, fellow half-sheets and what not?* {Bleak House 54}
Small sheets of paper produced when larger sheets are cut, and used for letter writing.

half-year (see **half**)

hall *Good things have been said about it by blue-nosed, bulbous-shoed old benchers in select port-wine committee after dinner in hall.* {Bleak House 1}
Here refers to the official meeting place of an institution.

hall-fire *Mercury does not consider himself called upon to leave his Olympus by the hall-fire to let the young man out.* {Bleak House 29}
Hall fireplace, the fireplace in the entrance vestibule of a house.

halt *... a halt in his gait...* {Pickwick Papers 17}
A limp.

halves *... there's two pair of halves in the commercial...* {Pickwick Papers 10}
Half boots. The 'commercial' refers to the commercial room of the inn.

hammercloth *... carriages guided by short-legged coachmen in flaxen wigs, deep sunk into downy hammercloths...* {Bleak House 56}
The cloth upholstery covering the driver's seat on a coach.

hamper *A few hampers, half-a-dozen broken bottles, and such like rubbish...* {Nicholas Nickleby 2}
A wicker box with a cover.

hand-basin ... *all the fathers could dance upon rolling casks, stand upon bottles, catch knives and balls, twirl hand-basins, ride upon anything* ... {Hard Times 1-6}
A basin in which water was placed for washing the hands.

hand-bills ... *she brought forth specimens ... in the shape of hand-bills, some of which were couched in the form of parodies on popular melodies* ... {Old Curiosity Shop 27}
A one-page printed advertisement, meant to be handed out.

hand-carriage *"There have been wheels here," said Mr. Slinkton. "And now I look again, the wheels of a hand-carriage!"*{Reprinted Pieces, Hunted Down 4}
Since the person being wheeled about is the crippled Major Banks, this probably refers to a Bath chair or wheelchair.

hand-chaise ... *the little hand-chaises are dragged wearily along, the children are tired, and amuse themselves and the company generally by crying* ... {Sketches, London Recreations}
A small carriage meant to be pushed or drawn by hand. A baby carriage.

hand gallop ... *going round St. James's Square at a hand gallop, and coming slowly into Pall Mall by another entry, as if, in the interval, his pace had been a perfect crawl.* {Martin Chuzzlewit 27}
An easy gallop, not at excess speed.

hand in *They say you're the best maker of lobster salads in London. ... Is it a good one, this morning--is your hand in? How does the breakfast look?* {Barnaby Rudge 77}
To be in practice, with skill maintained.

hand is out ... *he forgets the long-familiar cry of 'knuckle down', and at tip-cheese or odd and even, his hand is out.* {Pickwick Papers 34}
Out of practice.

handmaiden *"Get along with you, you wretch," said the handmaiden, obviously not ill-pleased with the compliment, however.* {Pickwick

Papers 14}
A female personal attendant or servant.

handpost *"Maybe, maybe," returned the blind man, with a sigh, and yet with something of a smile upon his face, "that's likely. Handposts and milestones are dumb, indeed, to me."* {Barnaby Rudge 45}
A guidepost at the parting of roads, also called a fingerpost, that shows the towns to which the roads lead.

hand-screen *It happens that the fire is hot where my Lady sits and that the hand-screen is more beautiful than useful, being priceless but small.* {Bleak House 2}
A fan-like device held in the hand to screen the face from the heat of a fire.

hands-four-round *What would your sabbath enthusiasts say to . . . a general hands-four-round of ten-pound householders, at the foot of the Obelisk in St. George's-Fields?* {Sketches, The First of May}
A round dance, one in which the dancers go around in a circle.

handsome *It would be handsome in me to begin to bind Mrs. Boffin at this time of day.* {Our Mutual Friend 1-8}
Generous, magnanimous. Since it is said when Boffin is about to make a will that does not bind her at all, it is said here with sarcasm.

hang-dog *Your manners have been of that silent and sullen and hang-dog kind . . .* {Tale of Two Cities 2-11}
Low, degraded, having a base or sneaking appearance, fit only to be hanged like a dog.

hangings *There was the old grisly four-post bedstead, without hangings, and with a jail-like upper rim of iron and spikes . . .* {Our Mutual Friend 1-15}
Curtains which usually hang from the upper frame of a bed and enclose it.

hard-bake *The commodities chiefly exposed for sale in the public streets are marine stores, hard-bake, apples, flat fish, and oysters.* {Pick-

wick Papers 2}
A sweet made of boiled sugar or treacle with blanched almonds.

hard by ... *first having brought some water from a running stream hard by, and washed his wound, and laved his hands and face* ... {Barnaby Rudge 69}
Close by, near.

hard-favoured *Betsy Snap was a withered, hard-favoured, yellow old woman* ... {The Poor Relation's Story}
Having a hard or unpleasing appearance, ugly.

hardly *Is it not enough that you have made a beggar of me, and that I have sacrificed my whole store, so hardly earned, to preserve this home?* {Barnaby Rudge 46}
The word 'hard' in its adverbial form. It does not mean 'barely' but 'in a hard way'.

hard-nibbed pen *[Sam] requested to be served with a sheet of the best gilt-edged letter-paper and a hard-nibbed pen which could be warranted not to splutter.* {Pickwick Papers 33}
A quill pen with a hard tip, which could be made of metal, ruby, horn, or tortoise shell. It could also be a simple quill pen with a very small slit, making the nib less flexible.

hare and hounds ... *when you come to see him at hare and hounds, taking the fence and ditch by the finger-post, and sliding down the face of the little quarry, you'll never forget it.* {Old Curiosity Shop 52}
A game in which a person, the hare, runs off leaving a trail of torn paper for the other players, the hounds, to follow. Also called 'paper chase'.

hare-skin ... *one o' the precise and tidy sort, as puts their feet in little india-rubber fire-buckets wen its wet weather, and never has no other bosom friends but hare-skins* ... {Pickwick Papers 44}
Rabbit skin.

harmonic meeting ... *going to the theatre--supping at harmonic meetings--eating oysters by the barrel--drinking stout by the gallon--* ...

{Sketches, The Dancing Academy}
A music and comedy performance, usually given in a tavern or inn. There was a sort of master of ceremonies and both amateur and professional performers. The audience sat at tables and ate and drank during the performance. This was in the days before music halls.

harmonium ... *I found myself... singing the praises of a summer's day to the harmonium, and my small but highly respected friend the fifer blazing away vocally* ... {The Uncommercial Traveller, The Short-timers} An organ-like musical instrument with a keyboard and bellows but using vibrating reeds instead of pipes.

harness boss *A busy little man he always is, in the polishing at harness-house doors, of stirrup-irons, bits, curb-chains, harness bosses, anything in the way of a stable-yard that will take a polish* ... {Bleak House 66}
Metal studs applied to a leather harness for ornamentation, usually made of brass and requiring frequent polishing.

harrow *It was a wonderful equipage, with six great coronets outside, and ragged things behind for I don't know how many footmen to hold on by, and a harrow below them to prevent amateur footmen from yielding to the temptation.* {Great Expectations 20}
1. A large frame with many teeth projecting downward, meant to be dragged over the ground to pulverize the soil. Here it is hung on the coach to prevent anyone from jumping onto the back, where the footmen rode.
I have got some of you under the harrow. {David Copperfield 52}
2. To be 'under the harrow' is to be trapped in an uncomfortable, tortured situation.

hartshorn *The landlady... soon came running in with a little hot brandy and water, followed by her servant girl, carrying vinegar, hartshorn, smelling salts, and such other restoratives* ... {Old Curiosity Shop 46}
A kind of smelling salt.

harum-scarum . . . *I'm a harum-scarum sort of good-for-nought that more kicks than halfpence come natural to* . . . {Bleak House 34}
Reckless, heedless.

hatchment *There was a christening party at the largest coffin-maker's, and a funeral hatchment had stopped some great improvements in the bravest mansion.* {Nicholas Nickleby 32}
A tablet bearing the coat of arms of a deceased person. It was attached to the front of the house as a public indication that a death had occurred.

hat-peg . . . *an old ricketty desk and two stools, a hat-peg, and ancient almanack, an inkstand with no ink* . . . {Old Curiosity Shop 5}
A wooden peg attached to the wall on which to hang a hat.

hawker . . . *a bit of a waggoner, a bit of a haymaker, a bit of a hawker, a bit of most things that don't pay and lead to trouble* . . . {Great Expectations 42}
One who goes from place to place selling goods, often in the street.

hayband . . . *keeping his rags together with a hayband, and warming his dinner by sitting upon it* . . . {Our Mutual Friend 3-6}
A rope made from twisted hay, used to tie up a bale of hay.

hay-rick *[The leaves] crept under the eaves of houses, and clung tightly to the sides of hay-ricks, like bats* . . . {Martin Chuzzlewit 2}
A stack of hay, a haystack.

hazard, French hazard . . . *large amounts were constantly changing hands on such hazards.* {Martin Chuzzlewit 11}
1. Bets, or betting games.
There were . . . *half-a-mile of club-houses to play* in *and there were* rouge-et-noir, *French hazard, and other games to play* at. {Nicholas Nickleby 50}
2. French hazard is a gambling game of dice in which the play is made complicated by arbitrary rules.

head ... *you are most positively prohibited from making any inquiry on this head* ... {Great Expectations 18}
"Certainly, sir," returned Brass, taking out his pocket-book and pencil. "I'll take down the heads if you please, sir." {Old Curiosity Shop 51}
1. The chief point or topic, or division of a subject.
... *they generally fuddled themselves before they began to do anything, lest it should make head and get the better of them.* {Martin Chuzzlewit 19}
2. To make head is to advance or press forward.
Charley Hexam was a master now, in another school, under another head. {Our Mutual Friend 4-7}
3. Headmaster or principal of a school.

head drawer ... *the head drawer of the Royal George Hotel opened the coach-door as his custom was.* {Tale of Two Cities 1-4}
Headwaiter (see **drawer**).

headpiece *I am afraid I am but a shallow, surface kind of fellow, Jack, and that my headpiece is none of the best.* {Edwin Drood 2}
Brain.

head-voice *He has a remarkable head-voice, and will commence as a chorister.* {David Copperfield 36}
Voice in a high register, as soprano or falsetto.

heart, have all the heart *He had had all the heart to leave his son a beggar* ... {Pickwick Papers 21}
To find it in one's heart, to be hardhearted enough.

heath ... *the house where he lay was out of London, and away on the borders of a fresh heath* ... {Dombey & Son 60}
Bare, open, uncultivated ground.

heavy coach *When Mr. Pecksniff and the two young ladies got into the heavy coach at the end of the lane, they found it empty* ... {Martin Chuzzlewit 8}
A large stagecoach.

heavy-swell *Look at his togs!--superfine cloth, and the heavy-swell cut!* ... *Nothing but a gentleman* ... {Oliver Twist 16}

A man of showy or impressive appearance, one dressed in the height of fashion.

hedger *He wore thick shoes, and thick leather gaiters, and thick gloves like a hedger's.* {Our Mutual Friend 1-5}
A person who trims hedges, a kind of gardener.

heel-tap, heeltap *"As there was a proper objection to drinking her in heel-taps," said the voice, "we'll give her the first glass in the new magnum. Little Kate Nickleby!"* {Nicholas Nickleby 32}
Liquor left behind in a glass after drinking from it.

henbane *The prospect of finding anybody out in anything, would have kept Miss Miggs awake under the influence of henbane.* {Barnaby Rudge 9}
A medicinal plant used to induce sleep.

hermitical *The same hermitical state of mind led to her renunciation of made dishes and wines at dinner . . .* {Hard Times 2-8}
Pertaining to a hermit.

Hessian boots *But one of the seven mild men unexpectedly leaped into distinction, by saying* he *had known him, and adding--"always wore Hessian boots!"* {Dombey & Son 36}
A high boot, with the front of the boot coming up higher than the back. It usually had tassels at the top of the front.

higgler *. . . higgler's baskets of small shaving-glasses, laces, braces, trouser-straps, and hardware . . .* {Martin Chuzzlewit 36}
A wandering dealer in small goods who often exchanged them for poultry and dairy products.

high *. . . you'll find some of the gentlemen rather high at first, you know, but they'll soon come round.* {Pickwick Papers 37}
Haughty, pretentious, arrogant.

High 'Change, time of High 'Change *. . . at about the time of High 'Change, Pressure began to wane, and appalling whispers to circulate . . .* {Little

Dorrit 2-25}
The time of greatest activity on the stock exchange.

high-dried ... *looked as if he would have [been] ground immediately into high-dried snuff.* {Edwin Drood 9}
Very dry, exceedingly dry.

high feather *Mr. Trundle was in high feather and spirits, but a little nervous withal.* {Pickwick Papers 28}
Good health, good spirits.

Highlander ... *the business was of too modest a character to support a life-size Highlander, but it maintained a little one on a bracket on the doorpost* ... {Little Dorrit 1-18}
The figure of a Scottish Highlander used as a sign of a tobacco shop.

high-low ... *gentlemen in muddy high-lows, soiled white hats, and rusty apparel* ... {Pickwick Papers 20}
A boot laced up the front and reaching above the ankle.

high-road ... *a rusty old chariot with post-horses* ... *had turned out of the high road and driven unexpectedly to the Blue Dragon [Inn]* ...
{Martin Chuzzlewit 3}
A main road, a highway.

high ropes *Yes, I went there the night before last, but she was quite on the high ropes about something, and was so grand and mysterious, that I couldn't make anything of her* ... {Nicholas Nickleby 31}
Elated and/or disdainful.

highwayman *Do you suppose highwaymen don't dress handsomer than that?* {Barnaby Rudge 1}
A robber on the highways who is mounted on a horse.

Hilary Term *What the two drank together, between Hilary Term and Michaelmas, might have floated a king's ship.* {Tale of Two Cities 2-5}
A session of the High Court of Justice in England.

hind *I became, at ten years old, a little laboring hind* . . . {David Copperfield 11}
A servant, in later use a farm servant.

hind-boot . . . *dragged Mr. Pickwick's portmanteau from the hind-boot, into which it had been hastily thrown when they joined the coach at Eatanswill* . . . {Pickwick Papers 16}
The boot, or stowage box, at the back end of the coach.

hipped *I am not about to be hipped again* . . . {David Copperfield 22}
Affected with hypochondria, morbid, depressed, in low spirits.

hippo-comedietta . . . *the highly novel and laughable hippo-comedietta of The Tailor's Journey to Brentford.* {Hard Times 1-3}
A short comic performance done at a circus. 'Hippo' implies that horses appeared.

hitch *"Very easily said!" remarked Camilla, amiably repressing a sob, while a hitch came into her upper lip, and her tears overflowed.* {Great Expectations 11}
A quick, jerky movement.

hoarding . . . *a church with hoarding and scaffolding about it* . . . {Little Dorrit 2-6}
A temporary fence made of boards, put in place during repairs or construction.

hoar frost *I smell the fog that hung about the place; I see the hoar frost, ghostly, through it* . . . {David Copperfield 9}
Frozen dew, a whitish frost.

hoary . . . *the very bell-rope in the porch was frayed into a fringe, and hoary with old age.* {Old Curiosity Shop 17}
Gray or grayish white, the color of hoarfrost.

hob . . . *the tea kettle had been singing gaily on the hob full twenty minutes, chirping as kettle never chirped before* . . . {Barnaby Rudge 80}
An iron shelf at the side of a grate in a fireplace, or at the side of a stove, where things can be set to warm.

hobbledehoy ... *there was a terrific roaring on the grass in front of the house, occasioned by all the men, boys, and hobbledehoys attached to the farm* ... {Pickwick Papers 28}
A clumsy or awkward youth.

hock ... *and down their four-and-twenty throats went four-and-twenty imperial pints of such rare old hock that they smacked their eight-and-forty lips, and winked again.* {Nicholas Nickleby 6}
A German white wine, originally the one produced at Hochheim. Queen Victoria liked it and made it popular.

hocussed *Said the Dog was the perfect picture of the old aunt from whom he had expectations. Found him particularly like her when hocussed.* {Little Dorrit 1-10}
Stupefied by liquor to which laudanum (a form of opium) was added.

hod *"What's he been a doing of?" asked a labourer with a hod of bricks* ... {Nicholas Nickleby 38}
A V-shaped receptacle, with one end of the V closed, mounted on a pole and used to carry bricks, mortar, plaster, and the like.

hogshead *If I lend him a helping hand, the only difference is, that he may, upon the whole, possibly drink a few gallons, or puncheons, or hogsheads, less in this life then he otherwise would.* {Barnaby Rudge 40}
A large cask, containing around fifty gallons of wine.

hoity-toity *"Why, he don't mean to say he's going!" exclaimed Mrs. Grudden ... "Hoity-toity! Nonsense."* {Nicholas Nickleby 29}
An expression of surprise and contempt at something flighty or showing undue assumption.

holden ... *there were articles to carry ... in reference to the adjustment and disposition of which, councils had to be holden by the Carrier and the senders* ... {Cricket on the Hearth 2}
An early form of the past participle of hold.

hole in the water *I don't know why I don't go and make a hole in the water, I'm sure I don't.* {Bleak House 46}
Commit suicide by drowning.

holland *Chesney Wold is shut up, carpets are rolled into great scrolls in corners of comfortless rooms, bright damask does penance in brown holland, carving and gilding puts on mortification, and the Dedlock ancestors retire from the light of day.* {Bleak House 29}
Holland-cloth, a linen originally made in Holland.

Hollands *... by mixing together in a pewter vessel certain quantities of British Hollands and the fragrant essence of the clove ...* {Pickwick Papers 16}
Hollands Geneva, or gin. A gin originally made, as might be expected, in Holland.

holster-case *... but, I only had a stick, having imprudently left my pistols in their holster-case with the landlord's son.* {Barnaby Rudge 6}
The leather case, or holster, for a pistol or pistols.

homely *Their teapots and such things were set out on tables ready for their afternoon meal, when I saw their room: and it had a homely look.* {The Uncommercial Traveller, On an Amateur Beat}
Not ugly but home-like, homey. Also simple, plain.

hood *[She] put her hand upon his proffered arm, and got into the carriage, which was a little, low, park carriage with a hood.* {Bleak House 18}
A folding top, usually waterproof, that covers the passengers.

hoodwinked *... Mrs. General's apartment--hoodwinked by a narrow side street with a low gloomy bridge in it ...* {Little Dorrit 2-4}
1.Covered from sight, concealed.
   ... deserted by all in whom I have ever trusted, hoodwinked and beset by all who should help and sustain me ... {Martin Chuzzlewit 10}
2. Deceived, from the original meaning of covering the eyes with a hood.

hookah *... teeming with ... tigers, elephants, howdahs, hookahs, umbrellas, palm trees, palanquins, and gorgeous princes of a brown complexion ...* {Dombey & Son 4}
The water-cooled pipe of India.

hooped ... *some fine lady, monstrously hooped and furbelowed, and preceded by running-footmen bearing flambeaux* ... {Barnaby Rudge 16}
Wearing a hooped skirt, a skirt expanded into a wide bell-like shape by hoops in the underskirt.

hooping-cough ... *he thought of measles, scarlet fever, thrush, hooping-cough, and a good many other sources of consolation besides.* {Pickwick Papers 29}
Whooping cough, pertussis.

hoop-stick *He had drawn out the plan of attack on a piece of paper, which was rolled up round a hoop-stick.* {Reprinted Pieces, Holiday Romance 1}
A common toy in the nineteenth century. A child would run alongside a hoop while striking it on top with a short wooden stick to keep it rolling.

hop-garden ... *I have worked in many a market-garden afore now, and in many a hop-garden too.* {Our Mutual Friend 2-14}
A field in which hops are grown.

hoptalmy *Why, the sight of you, Mr. Fagin, would cure the hoptalmy!* {Oliver Twist 26}
Ophthalmia, an inflammation of the eye. From 'hopthalmia', medical student's slang.

Horner, Mr. ... *Mr. Horner (not the young gentleman who ate mince-pies with his thumb, but the man of Colosseum notoriety)* ... {Sketches, Greenwich Fair}
The Colosseum was a huge rotunda designed for a panorama in 1824. The first show there was of Thomas Hornor's (Dickens has misspelled the name) bird's-eye views of London, which he painted from a precarious perch in a crow's nest on top of St. Paul's cathedral.

hornpipe ... *a dancing step, extremely difficult in its nature* ... *which is commonly called The Frog's Hornpipe.* {Martin Chuzzlewit 11}
A sailor's dance, originally performed to the sound of a wind instrument partly made of horn.

horn spectacles *At the bedside sat a short old man in a cobbler's apron, who, by the aid of a pair of horn spectacles, was reading from the Bible aloud.* {Pickwick Papers 44}
Eyeglasses with frames made from material obtained from animal horn.

horse ... *various extremely diminutive articles of clothing were airing on a horse before the fire* ... {Nicholas Nickleby 36}
A clotheshorse, a wooden frame with horizontal bars on which clothes are hung to dry or air.

horse chanter *"Oh, him!" replied Neddy. "He's nothing exactly. He was a horse chanter; he's a leg now."* {Pickwick Papers 42}
One who sells horses fraudulently.

horsecloth ... *a fly-driver, coming by with his carriage, dropped a horsecloth.* {David Copperfield 13}
A rug or cloth used to cover a horse.

horsehair ... *room, furnished in a funereal manner with black horsehair, and ... heavy dark tables.* {Tale of Two Cities 1-4}
Furniture upholstered in material made from horsehair, hairs from the manes and tails of horses. This material was also used to cover trunks.

horse-pistol ... *the arm-chest ... where a loaded blunderbuss lay at the top of six or eight loaded horse-pistols, deposited on a substratum of cutlass.* {Tale of Two Cities 1-2}
A large pistol carried at the pommel of the saddle when on horseback.

horse-road ... *his boy playing at marbles in the gutter or flying the garter in the horse-road* ... {Pickwick Papers 38}
A road cut for the use of horses rather than carriages.

horses to *Then when the horses were to, in he came like a Harlequin* ... {Old Curiosity Shop 47}
To 'put the horses to' is to hitch them to the vehicle.

horse-trough ... *immersing Mr. Stiggin's head in a horse-trough full of water* ... {Pickwick Papers 52}

A large trough, often at the side of the road or street kept filled with water for horses.

horsing long stages *The insolvent gentleman . . . had contracted a speculative but imprudent passion for horsing long stages, which had led to his present embarrassments . . .* {Pickwick Papers 42}
Supplying horses for use on those stagecoaches which traveled over long distances, called 'long stages'.

hosier *. . . I went to the hatter's, and the bootmaker's, and the hosier's, and felt rather like Mother Hubbard's dog whose outfit required the services of so many trades.* {Great Expectations 19}
A maker and seller of hosiery, socks and stockings, and knitted underwear.

host *. . . Mr. Ralph Nickleby had reckoned without his host; for however fresh from the country a young lady (by nature) may be . . .* {Nicholas Nickleby 19}
Ralph Nickleby is giving this party, thus he is the 'host' in the modern sense of the word. Host here means 'guest', apparently an earlier meaning.

hostler *. . . at last he come to be hostler at the Maypole for his board and lodging and a annual trifle . . .* {Barnaby Rudge 11}
One who attends to horses at an inn, also a stableman or groom.

hot and hot *Mutton chops, which were brought in hot and hot, between two plates.* {Dombey & Son 8}
Food served as soon as it is cooked, especially dishes served in succession as fast as they are ready.

hot boiled beans *. . . like the children in the game of hot boiled beans and very good butter . . .* {Edwin Drood 18}
A game like hide-and-seek, using the words 'Hot boiled beans and very good butter / If you please to come to supper'.

hot-pieman *"Put 'em under the pump," suggested a hot-pieman.* {Pickwick Papers 2}
A seller of hot meat pies, or pastys.

hot pot . . . *when there was "hot pot" in the bill of fare* . . . {The Uncommercial Traveller, Aboard Ship}
Meat and vegetable stew.

hot-pressed . . . *a letter . . . in which Nicholas said, all through four sides of closely-written, gilt-edged, hot-pressed, Bath post letter paper, that he responded to the call of his fellow-townsmen* . . . {The Public Life of Mr. Tulrumble}
Paper made smooth and glossy by being pressed between glazed boards and hot metal plates.

House is up . . . *[he] is much addicted to stopping 'after the House is up'* . . . {Sketches, A Parliamentary Sketch}
The House is up when it is adjourned at the end of a daily session, when the members get up to leave the chambers.

house-lad *[He was] informed that he was to go, that night, as general house-lad to a coffin-maker's* . . . {Oliver Twist 4}
A male household servant, not necessarily a boy.

house of (public) entertainment *It looked as if it had once been a large house of entertainment; but the roof had fallen in, in many places, and the stairs were steep, ragged, and broken.* {Pickwick Papers 49}
A tavern or inn. The word 'entertainment' here refers to meals, not to performances.

house-top *Monsieur Gabelle* . . . *went out on his house-top alone . . . [and] . . . glanced down from behind his chimneys . . .* {Tale of Two Cities 2-23}
The roof of a house.

howbeit . . . *Orlick was perhaps confirmed in some suspicion that I should displace him; howbeit, he liked me still less.* {Great Expectations 15}
Nevertheless.

howdah . . . *teeming with . . . tigers, elephants, howdahs, hookahs, umbrellas, palm trees, palanquins, and gorgeous princes of a brown complexion . . .*

{Dombey & Son 4}
The seat and canopy carried by an elephant.

Hue-and-Cry ... *and then, with a horrible grin, re-seated himself at the table: where he was soon deeply absorbed in the interesting pages of the Hue-and-Cry.* {Oliver Twist 15}
The *Hue-and-Cry* and *Police-Gazette* was a popular newspaper. It later made the *Police-Gazette* the more prominent part of its name.

hugger-mugger ... *my little sister that lives with you in a secret, stealthy, hugger-muggering kind of way and with no manner of enjoyment* ...
{Old Curiosity Shop 2}
Secretly, clandestinely.

hulk ... *the scourings of the jails and hulks, living within the shadow of the gallows itself* ... {Oliver Twist 40}
A dismantled ship, unfit for service at sea, kept floating and used as a prison.

Hummums ... *country gentlemen who are sleeping at the Hummums for the first time.* {Sketches, The Streets--Morning}
A Turkish bath, or bathhouse, from the Arabic word 'hammam', meaning a hot bath.

humour *"How could I be so cruel! cruel!" cried the dwarf. "Because I was in the humour. I'm in the humour now."* {Old Curiosity Shop 50}
Mood, or temper.

hunch ... *the shopman took his mug of tea and hunch of bread-and-butter on a sack of peas in the front premises.* {Great Expectations 8}
A thick or clumsy piece, a hunk.

hundredweight ... *and the whole blown to atoms with ten thousand hundredweight of gunpowder* ... {Bleak House 9}
A weight of about a hundred pounds, the exact amount varying according to local usage.

hunks ... *you become the sole inheritor of the wealth of this rich old hunks* ... {Old Curiosity Shop 7}
An old miser.

hunting-watch *He took out of his pocket the most respectable hunting-watch I ever saw* ... {David Copperfield 21}
A watch with a hinged metal cover to protect the glass. Originally used to prevent damage while hunting.

hurdle ... *he'll be drawn on a hurdle to be half hanged, and then he'll be taken down and sliced* ... {Tale of Two Cities 2-2}
A kind of frame or sledge on which the condemned was dragged to the place of execution. Its less brutal use was for hauling large stones and other very heavy things.

husbandman *Never was there a lighter-hearted husbandman, a creature more popular with young and old, a blither or more happy soul than Barnaby* ... {Barnaby Rudge 82}
A farmer.

hustings ... *Mr. Winkle had undertaken to escort that lady to a house-top in the immediate vicinity of the hustings* ... {Pickwick Papers 13}
A temporary platform on which candidates for parliament stood while addressing the electorate. By extension, the whole business of running for office.

hyseters ... *the attentions that I've shown to that man! The hyseters he has eat, and the pints of ale he has drank in this house--!* {Nicholas Nickleby 36}
Dialect for oysters.

idea *Which makes it the more probable that she may be tired of his idea . . . and not indisposed to exchange it for the newer one of another lover, who presents himself . . . under romantic circumstances . . .* {The Battle of Life 2}
Nature or character.

ideal *. . . but the acute pain in his shoulders when he attempted to rise assured him that the kicking of the goblins was certainly not ideal.* {Pickwick Papers 29}
Of the nature of an idea or mental image, imaginary.

ideality *In respect of ideality, reverence, wonder, and other such phrenological attributes, it is now worse off than it used to be.* {Bleak House 21}
Opposite of reality, existence in idea only.

ill-omened *. . . to find her linked mysteriously with an ill-omened man, alarmed at his appearance, yet favoring his escape, was a discovery that pained as much as startled him.* {Barnaby Rudge 6}
Inauspicious, ill-starred.

ill-used *I was not actively ill-used. I was not beaten . . .* {David Copperfield 10}
Abused.

imbrued *. . . and Mr. Wopsle was imbrued in blood to the eyebrows.* {Great Expectations 18}
Soaked, saturated, stained.

impending *. . . with a crazy wooden verandah impending over the water . . .* {Our Mutual Friend 1-6}
Hanging over, overhanging.

Imperial *I had two ample Imperials on the roof, other fitted storage for luggage in front, and other up behind...* {The Uncommercial Traveller, Travelling Abroad}
A special luggage case for the top of a coach.

imperial pint *... it was the coachman with the hoarse voice, who took an imperial pint of vinegar with his oysters without betraying the least emotion.* {Pickwick Papers 55}
A liquid measure slightly larger than a U.S. pint.

impersonation *... the face of a pretty, laughing, girl; dimpled and fresh, and healthful--the very impersonation of a good-humour and blooming beauty.* {Barnaby Rudge 4}
A person representing an idea or principle, a personification. It does not have the implication of a pretense.

import *The only popular legend... is a dark Old Bailey whisper... importing how the black creature who holds the sun-dial there, was a negro who slew his master...* {The Uncommercial Traveller, Chambers}
Signify, mean.

impress into service *... the impressment [of the saucepan] into the service of boiling my egg...* {David Copperfield 5}
Impressment refers to enforced service in the army or navy, to be drafted.

impression *... I think I would introduce that something into a Posting-Bill, and place a large impression in the hands of an active sticker.* {Reprinted Pieces, Bill-sticking}
Printing, the number of copies of a piece printed in a single run of the press.

improve *Their interview being interrupted... Toots had no opportunity of improving the occasion...* {Dombey & Son 12}
To make good use of, to turn to advantage.

imputation *... he is not worthy of such a daughter, which is no imputation on him...* {Tale of Two Cities 2-6}

Attributing a fault or a crime to someone. The sense here is that he is not at fault, but that his daughter is so much more worthy.

in a string ... *an ancient spinster, with her lapdog in a string*... {Barnaby Rudge 15}
Tied to a string, on a leash.

incommodious *It was very small, very dark, very ugly, very incommodious.* {Tale of Two Cities 2-1}
Causing inconvenience, or annoyance. Of a place, uncomfortable, or small, narrow.

indented ... *having procured a very small card with the Signor's address indented thereon, walked straight at once to the Signor's house* ... {Sketches, The Dancing Academy}
Printed with the lettering depressed below the surface of the paper, embossed.

indentures *Mr. Bumble was at once instructed that Oliver Twist and his indentures were to be conveyed before the magistrate, for signature and approval, that very afternoon.* {Oliver Twist 3}
A contract binding an apprentice to his master.

independence *I wish to leave the poor girls some little independence, as well as a good name.* {Bleak House 37}
A competency, enough money to make it unnecessary to earn a living.

index *The treadle and index at the tollhouse (a most ingenious contrivance for rendering fraud impossible), were invented by Mr. Lethbridge* ... {Reprinted Pieces, Down With the Tide}
From context this must be some mechanical way of counting the people using the bridge and ensuring that the toll was paid and recorded. It probably consisted of a metal plate (the treadle) that when stepped on advanced a pointer (the index) on a dial.

Indiaman ... *this would be one of the great Indiaman's boats*... {Bleak House 45}
A large commercial sailing ship engaged in trade with India. Usually refers to one owned by the East India company.

Indian ink *The view from my Lady Dedlock's own windows is alternately a lead-coloured view and a view in Indian ink.* {Bleak House 2}
Black drawing ink containing a pigment made from lampblack and gum. It is called 'India ink' in the United States. Lampblack is finely powdered carbon, obtained by allowing a smoky oil-lamp flame to deposit carbon on a cool, metal surface.

india-rubber cloak *There was one young gentleman in an india-rubber cloak, who smoked cigars all day . . .* {Pickwick Papers 35}
A cloak made of rubber, for use in the rain.

India van *. . . the India vans lumbering along their stone tramway . . .* {The Uncommercial Traveller, Wapping Workhouse}
Vans were large, closed, horse-drawn wagons. The India vans were those used to carry from the docks the enormous quantity of goods brought to England from India by the ships of the English East India Company. They traveled on tracks made of dressed stones.

indifferent *. . . striking out at Mrs. Boffin with a pair of indifferent shoes . . .* {Our Mutual Friend 1-16}
Not very good.

indite *. . . and often indited square-folded letters to his mother, inclosing a shilling or eighteen pence . . .* {Old Curiosity Shop 38}
To put into written words, to write.

inexplicables *He usually wore a brown frock-coat without a wrinkle, light inexplicables without a spot, a neat neckerchief with a remarkably neat tie, and boots without a fault . . .* {Sketches, Mr. Minns and his Cousin}
A euphemism for trousers or pants.

inexpressibles *. . . the same suit of coffee-colour minus the inexpressibles, which were then of a pale nankeen.* {Dombey & Son 4}
Another euphemism for trousers or pants. It does not mean underwear.

infantine *With that he fell into a quiet slumber:--subsided into such a gentle, pleasant sleep, that it was quite infantine.* {Barnaby Rudge 24} Infantile, like an infant.

in fine *In fine, he traced them to the Notary's house; learnt the destination of the carriage . . . [and] darted round to the coach office without more ado . . .* {Old Curiosity Shop 48} Latin for finally, at the end.

infirmary *The jail might have been the infirmary, the infirmary might have been the jail . . .* {Hard Times 1-5} A part of a building set aside for caring for the sick.

in full blow *. . . when they're gone to be in full blow elsewhere.* {Barnaby Rudge 27} Fully blossomed, full-blown.

ingross *. . . she could ingross, fair-copy, fill up printed forms with perfect accuracy . . .* {Old Curiosity Shop 33} Write out in a special handwriting used in courts of law.

in hand *I have not heard anything more about it. It's in hand though . . .* {Hard Times 2-10} Being dealt with, in process.

inkstand *. . . when he had arrived at the end of this little manuscript, carefully refolded and replaced it in the inkstand drawer . . .* {Pickwick Papers 37} A stand holding one or more bottles of ink, with trays or a drawer for pens and, sometimes, paper.

in little *There you have Harold Skimpole in little.* {Bleak House 37} In miniature, in a nutshell.

inn of court *. . . could not be a barrister without being entered at an inn of court as a student.* {David Copperfield 36} The four sets of buildings, including Lincoln's Inn and Gray's Inn, owned by the legal societies which have the exclusive right to teach for, examine for, and admit to the practice of law.

inn-yard ... *he would stand about the inn-yards, and look mournfully at every one who passed* ... {Oliver Twist 8}
The courtyard of an inn.

inodorous ... *the point* ... *at which one could take the river (if so inodorously minded) bore the   appellation   Break-Neck-Stairs.* {No Thoroughfare 1}
Without odor. The phrase 'inodorously minded' means 'of a mind to disregard odors'.

in place ... *how cook would dress, being a bridesmaid, conjointly with her sister "in place" at Fulham* ... {Sketches, The Young Couple}
Having a servant's place, being employed as a servant.

insides ... *to put it in vun o' the coach-pockets, vich 'ud be a temptation to the insides.* {Pickwick Papers 56}
The fortunate passengers of a coach who rode inside the body of the coach and not on the open seats outside.

in someone's way *As it was very easy for Kit to persuade himself that the old house was in his way, his way being anywhere* ... {Old Curiosity Shop 14}
1. On his way.
... *I have purposely put myself in her way more than once or twice* ...
{Barnaby Rudge 26}
2. In someone's path, near to someone.

instinct *The Phantom, with an evil smile, drew closer to the chair* ... *and looking down into his face with searching eyes, that seemed instinct with fire, went on* ... {The Haunted Man 1}
Imbued or charged with.

intercourse *Madam, bear with me, and remember my intercourse with Mr. Dombey, and my knowledge of him, and my reverence for him, almost from childhood* ... {Dombey & Son 37}
Ordinary social contact and communication between people. Does not have the current sexual connotation.

interesting situation *She has always been in an interesting situation through the same long period, and has never been confined yet.* {Reprinted Pieces, The Begging-letter Writer}
A euphemism for pregnant. Pregnancy was rarely referred to directly in nineteenth-century literature.

in the road *We'll go down this way, as you may like to see the yard, and it's all in the road.* {Our Mutual Friend 1-15}
On the way, on our way.

ironmaster *He is called, I believe--an--ironmaster.* {Bleak House 28}
A manufacturer of iron, or master of an iron foundry.

ironmonger *It was a remarkable instance of want of forethought on the part of the ironmonger who had made Mrs. Crupp's kitchen fire-place, that it was capable of cooking nothing but chops and mashed potatoes.* {David Copperfield 24}
A dealer in ironware, a seller and maker of goods made of iron and of fireplaces.

ironmongery *The table-cloths and pillow-cases . . . are what discourage me most, Copperfield. So does the ironmongery--candle-boxes, and gridirons, and that sort of necessaries . . .* {David Copperfield 27}
The goods dealt in by an ironmonger, also the place where the business of an ironmonger is carried on (see **ironmonger**).

iron-mould *. . . speckled all over with iron-mould . . .* {Great Expectations 10}
Stains caused by rust or ink.

ironwood *. . . [she] gives it back to him, asking what wood it is? Ironwood.* {Edwin Drood 14}
A name given to any very hard wood, usually referring to different trees in different localities.

irruption *But there was no loud irruption into the courtyard, as he had expected, and he heard the gate clash again, and all was quiet.* {Tale of Two Cities 3-2}
The action of bursting in or breaking in, a violent entry or invasion.

isinglass ... *our friend who long lived on rice pudding and isinglass* ... {Our Mutual Friend 1-2}
A kind of clear gelatin obtained from sturgeon.

Italian image boy, lad ... *I had been very much frightened by an Italian image boy that very morning.* {Nicholas Nickleby 27}
Images were cheap statuettes of famous people, often sold in the streets by Italian immigrants.

Italian iron ... *a toy horse without a head; the said horse being composed of a small wooden cylinder, not unlike an Italian iron, supported on four crooked pegs* ... {Nicholas Nickleby 16}
A cylindrical iron used for fluting or crimping of frills.

italian-ironing ... *between the italian-ironing of frills, the flouncing of trousers, the trimming of frocks* ... {Nicholas Nickleby 52}
Using an Italian iron (see entry immediately above).

jack *No other company was in the house than the landlord, his wife, and a grizzled male creature, the "jack" of the little causeway* . . . {Great Expectations 54}
1. Any man or boy, especially a low-level servant or a person who does odd jobs.
. . . no murmur of it was audible above the clatter of plates and dishes, the hissing of the frying-pan, the bubbling of the saucepans, the low monotonous waltzing of the jack . . . {The Battle of Life 3}
2. The roasting jack, a device that turned meat over the fire.

jackanapes . . . *not sitting upon, or dropping himself into a seat, as any common jackanapes would: but letting himself gradually and slowly down into a chair* . . . {Oliver Twist 17}
An impertinent upstart, one who behaves like an ape or monkey.

jack-boots . . . *two centaurs with glazed hats, jack-boots, and flowing manes and tails,* . . . {Bleak House 12}
A large boot that comes above the knee.

Jack-in-the-green . . . *falling about* . . . *first on one side, and then on the other, like a "Jack-in-the-green," on May-day* . . . {Sketches, The Bloomsbury Christening}
A man or boy enclosed in a wood or wicker pyramidal framework covered with leaves. He was a traditional figure in the May-Day celebrations of the chimney sweeps.

Jack-in-the-water *"Would you prefer a wessel, sir?" inquired another, to the infinite delight of the "Jack-in-the-water."* {Sketches, The Steam Excursion}
An attendant at the waterman's stairs, leading down into the river, who didn't mind getting his feet and legs wet to help a customer get into a boat. He, of course, expected to be tipped.

Jack Ketch ... *murder him yourself if you would have him escape Jack Ketch* ... {Oliver Twist 26}
The hangman (see **Ketch**).

jack-knife ... *his jack-knife and his pack of cards* ... {Great Expectations 41}
A large clasp knife, or folding knife.

Jack of the swamps ... *the driver's lantern dancing on like its namesake Jack of the swamps and marshes* ... {Old Curiosity Shop 46}
Jack o' Lantern or Will o' the Wisp. Methane gas, produced in swamps, will spontaneously ignite and produce flickering intermittent lights.

jack-towel *Here's a sink, with water laid on, sir, and a clean jack-towel behind the door.* {Pickwick Papers 25}
A long towel sewed into a loop and hung on a roller for many people to use.

jade *"What a handy jade it is!" said the locksmith to Mrs. Varden, who stood by with folded hands--rather proud of her husband too--while Miggs held his cap and sword at arms length* ... {Barnaby Rudge 41}
... *you jade of a magpie, jackdaw, and poll-parrot, what do you mean* ... {Bleak House 21}
A contemptuous name for a woman, used playfully or teasingly in the first example, and nastily, in the second.

jail-delivery ... *made a jail-delivery of her pocket-handkerchief and held it before her eyes.* {David Copperfield 4}
Deliverance from jail or imprisonment. Hence, she took her handkerchief from its place of confinement.

jail fever *He sank under a contagious disorder, very prevalent at that time, and vulgarly termed the jail fever.* {Barnaby Rudge 82}
Typhus fever. Spread by body lice, it was endemic in jails and other places in which people were crowded together for long periods. It caused many deaths and frequently beat the executioner to his job.

jalousie-blind *A small lofty room, with its window wide open, and the wooden jalousie-blinds closed* ... {Tale of Two Cities 2-9}

A blind made of slats which slope up (from the outside) keeping out rain but admitting some light and air.

japan ... *he applied himself to a process which Mr. Dawkins designated as 'japanning his trotter-cases'* ... {Oliver Twist 18}
To polish, by analogy with the shiny appearance of japanned articles (see **japanned**).

japanned ... *he retired in company with a japanned candlestick to one side of the house, while Mr. Pickwick and another japanned candlestick were conducted ... to another.* {Pickwick Papers 22}
Painted with a hard, black varnish which was originally obtained from Japan.

javelin-man *Would a javelin-man do?--Or there's Philips the constable--he's disengaged* ... {Barnaby Rudge 61}
A man carrying a spear or pike in the retinue of a sheriff.

jean ... *he took out a common frock of coarse dark jean* ... {Martin Chuzzlewit 46}
A twilled, cotton cloth, named after the city Genoa.

jemmy .. *the singular coincidence of 'jemmies' being a cant name [for sheep's heads] and also ... an ingenious implement much used in his profession.* {Oliver Twist 20}
1. Burglar's tool, a jimmy.
... if I'd been your friend in the green jemmy--damn me--punch his head ... {Pickwick Papers 2}
2. A greatcoat.
The man in the shop, perhaps, is in the baked "jemmy" line, or the firewood and hearth-stone line, or any other line which requires a floating capital of eighteen-pence or thereabouts: ... {Sketches, Seven-dials}
3. A sheep's head cooked as food.

jerkin ... *they did on many occasions lead their leather-jerkined soldiers to the death* ... {Martin Chuzzlewit 1}
A kind of close-fitting jacket.

jessamine *The heavy rain beat down the tender branches of vine and jessamine, and trampled them in its fury* . . . {Martin Chuzzlewit 43}
Jasmine.

jeweller's cotton . . . *sitting before the fire, with her bonnet tied over her left arm, stopping her ears with jeweller's cotton.* {David Copperfield 1}
Ordinary cotton, as in cotton balls.

job, to job *[The carriage] belonged to a job-master in a small way, who drove it himself, and who jobbed it by the day, or hour* . . . {Little Dorrit 1-33}
Hired out for a specific job, or for a limited time. The jobmaster was usually the owner of the vehicles and the one who hired them out (see **jobmaster**).

jobbery *Jobbery was suspected by the malicious* . . . {Little Dorrit 2-12}
Turning a public office or trust for private gain, the actions of a corrupt public official or, in the United States, the run-of-the-mill politician.

jobbing tailor . . . *several small housekeepers who are employed in the docks, a handful of mantua-makers, and a seasoning of jobbing tailors.* {Pickwick Papers 32}
A tailor who does piecework or takes on small jobs.

jobmaster . . . *had introduced him to a marker who taught billiards, a Life-Guard who taught fencing, a jobmaster who taught riding* . . . {Dombey & Son 22}
The operator of a livery stable who also rents out horses and carriages by the job, or for any time period. By the time the railroads began to appear, some jobmasters had huge businesses and owned several thousand horses and hundreds of carriages.

jog-trot . . . *a surprise is worth having in such a little jog-trot place.* {No Thoroughfare, Act 1}
Slow, monotonous, uniform, humdrum.

joint-stock piano *Firstly, there is a joint-stock piano in a great many of the boarding-houses.* {American Notes, 4}

A piano made by a joint stock company, one with a small, limited number of stockholders. The implication is of a company organized to manufacture something recently patented and perhaps of low quality.

jointure *the family are not wealthy--they're poor, indeed--and she lives upon a small jointure* ... {Dombey & Son 21}
Lands or estate held jointly by husband and wife but made over to the wife on the husband's death.

jolter-headed *As to corporations, parishes, vestry-boards, and similar gatherings of jolter-headed clods* ... {Bleak House 13}
Heavy-headed or thick-headed, a blockhead.

jorum ... *a steaming jorum: of which, the first gulp brought the water into Mr. Bumble's eyes.* {Oliver Twist 37}
A large drinking bowl.

journeyman *Now Joe kept a journeyman at weekly wages* ... {Great Expectations 15}
A person who had completed his apprenticeship and is qualified to receive wages for his work.

journey-work ... *as poor a piece of journey-work as ever this world saw.* {The Haunted House 1}
Inferior or hack work. So-called because a journeyman did not do as good work as a master.

junketting ... *fresh from journeying and junketting in foreign lands* ... {Little Dorrit 1-5}
Dickens here means 'going on a pleasure trip' (an expression used in the United States). The original meaning is 'banqueting' or 'feasting'.

jury droop *[The lawyer] strengthened as usual with his double-eyeglass and his little jury droop* ... {Little Dorrit 2-12}
A lawyer in court would normally bow to the jury, but this became a perfunctory and minimal gesture. The lawyer here is an obsequious person and would have bowed to almost everyone.

keep in the way *Jerry, if you wish to take something to eat, you can. But, keep in the way.* {Tale of Two Cities 2-3}
Stay close by.

ken *Is he to be kidnapped to the other ken . . .* {Oliver Twist 13}
1. Slang for a house, a house of thieves.
The . . . lamplighter . . . laughed out loudly as the Spirit passed: though little kenned the lamplighter that he had any company that Christmas. {A Christmas Carol 3}
2. To know or be aware of.

kennel *The kennel . . . ran down the middle of the street . . .* {Tale of Two Cities 1-5}
1. The gutter of a street, the ditch that carries off the surface water.
But never did that dog live, in kennel, stable-yard, or house, whose life was half as hard as Mr. Pecksniff's with his gentle child. {Martin Chuzzlewit 30}
2. A dog house.

kept it up *You know the blue Dragon, Mr. Westlock: you kept it up there, once or twice, yourself.* {Martin Chuzzlewit 39}
To prolong a carouse.

kept the house *Mr. Creakle kept the house from indisposition . . .* {David Copperfield 7}
Stayed in the house, remained at home.

kerb-stone *Mr. Tuckle no sooner got into the open air than he was seized with a sudden desire to lie on the kerb-stone . . .* {Pickwick Papers 37}
Curbstone, one of the stones forming the curb of a street.

kerseymere trousers *So there was I, on my wedding night, in the light kerseymere trouser, fancy waistcoat, and blue coat, that I had been married in in the morning, in a back kitchen chimney . . .* {Sketches, A Passage in the Life of Mr. Watkins Tottle}
Kersymere is a twilled cloth with a special texture produced by raising one-third of the warp threads (the longitudinal threads) for each thread of the woof (the transverse threads).

Ketch, Mr. Ketch, Jack Ketch *. . . we half expected to see a brass plate, with the inscription "Mr. Ketch;" for we never imagined that the distinguished functionary could by possibility live anywhere else!* {Sketches, Criminal Court}
Jack Ketch was a seventeenth-century hangman who became notorious, apparently for his cruelty. His name was soon given to the hangman in the Punchinello puppet plays and then became the common name for a hangman.

kettle-holder *On the front of his sale-board hung a little placard, like a kettle holder, bearing the inscription in his own small text . . .* {Our Mutual Friend 1-5}
A rectangular piece of cloth for holding a hot kettle in the hand, a pot holder. It usually hung from a loop at one corner.

key-bugle *The lively notes of the guard's key-bugle vibrate in the clear cold air and wake up the old gentleman inside . . .* {Pickwick Papers 28}
A bugle fitted with five or six keys, small levers which moved a pad thereby uncovering a hole in the side of the instrument. The keys increased the number of notes that could be played.

key-note *. . . playing the accompaniment without notes . . . he followed her lips most attentively . . . softly hinting at the key-note from time to time.* {Edwin Drood 7}
The first note of the scale in a key of music, the one from which the key is named.

kickshaw *. . . he sang . . . that evening, no kickshaw ditties . . .* {Edwin Drood 12}
Dainty and elegant, but trifling, of little value.

Kidderminster carpet *And such a parlour as it was! Beautiful Kidderminster carpet--six bran-new cane-bottomed stained chairs--three wine-glasses and a tumbler on each sideboard--farmer's girl and farmer's boy on the mantel-piece* . . . {Sketches, The Mistaken Milliner}
A kind of carpet with a pattern made by the intersections of two differently colored yarns. It was originally made in the town of Kidderminster.

kiddy or stage-coach way . . . *it was his ambition to do something in the celebrated "kiddy" or stage-coach way, and he had even gone so far as to invest capital in the purchase of a rough blue coat with wooden buttons* . . . {Sketches, Making a Night of it}
A kiddy was a professional thief who dressed in a flashy way. The word was later applied to any flashy dresser.

killibeate *"Ah," said Mr. John Smauker, "you disliked the killibeate taste, perhaps?"* {Pickwick Papers 37}
Should be spelled c-h-a-l-y-b-e-a-t-e, meaning 'impregnated with iron'. The taste is that of iron in the water.

kinchin, kinchin lay *"The kinchin lay." "What's that?" demanded Mr. Claypole.* {Oliver Twist 42}
Kinchin is a child. The kinchin lay is robbing children who have been sent on errands (see **lay**). These are slang words.

kindling *How beautiful the landscape kindling in the light* . . . {The Battle of Life 3}
Making bright or glowing.

kissing [one's own] hand . . . *and kissing his left hand in token of friendship* . . .
{Martin Chuzzlewit 7}
A polite gesture used on parting.

kit . . . *I ought to know something of the piano, and I ought to know something of the kit too, and consequently I have to practise those two instruments* . {Bleak House 38}
A small, narrow fiddle formerly much used by teachers of dancing.

knee-breeches ... *his flapped waistcoat and drab plush knee-breeches.*
{Oliver Twist 4}
Breeches, or trousers, that come down only to the knee, or to just below
the knee.

knee-cords ... *in a green coat, knee-cords, and tops.* {Pickwick Papers 14}
Knee-breeches made of corduroy.

knee-shorts *Pursuing his more quiet occupation of barber, he
generally subsided into an apron not over-clean, a flannel jacket,
and corduroy knee-shorts.* {Martin Chuzzlewit 26}
Another word for knee-breeches.

knee-smalls ... *his knee-smalls unbraced* ... {David Copperfield 16}
Knee-breeches.

knocker *She recovered damages to the amount of 1,000 £., which the
unfortunate knocker was compelled to pay.* {Sketches, The Board-
ing-house}
This is not slang but refers to Dickens' earlier description of Mr. Calton
as resembling "a chubby street-door knocker, half-lion, half-monkey."

knock up *You don't know the value of money, you live hard, you'll knock
up one of these days, and be ill and poor* ... {Tale of Two Cities 2-11}
1. To break down, become unserviceable, to be exhausted
*Haven't you slept enough, growler, that you're not to be knocked up
for once?* {Barnaby Rudge 34}
2. To awaken, as by knocking on the door.
*"What has been doing in the city to-day?" "Trap, bat, and ball, my
dear," said Mr. Orange; "and it knocks a man up."* {Reprinted Pieces,
Holiday Romance 4}
3. To tire out, to fatigue.

knot, porter's knot ... *by the public-house, the knots of those who rested
and regaled within, were piled from morning until night.* {Martin
Chuzzlewit 9}
A shoulder pad used by porters when carrying loads.

knout ... *the great Pott, accoutered as a Russian officer of justice with a tremendous knout in his hand* ... {Pickwick Papers 15}
A whip made of a two-foot stick of wood with a three-and-a-half foot piece of leather attached to it. It is also described as having leather strips wrapped with wire.

knouted ... *I was going to be knouted by a noble personage in a fur cap, boots, and earrings* ... {The Uncommercial Traveller, Travelling Abroad}
Whipped with a knout (see **knout**).

knowing *[The house] looked so knowing, with the front garden, and the green railing, and the brass knocker, and all that--I really thought it was a cut above me.* {Sketches, Mr. Minns and his Cousin}
Stylish, smart.

knuckle-down ... *his 'ally-tors' and his 'commoneys' are alike neglected; he forgets the long-familiar cry of 'knuckle down'* ... {Pickwick Papers 34}
The act of placing one's knuckles on the floor in preparation for shooting a marble, or taw, in the child's game of marbles.

kye-bosk *"Hooroar," ejaculates a pot-boy in parenthesis, "put the kye-bosk on her, Mary!"* {Sketches, Seven-dials}
Dialect for 'kibosh', to dispose of, finish off.

Lady-day ... *he'll be twenty-one next Lady-day* ... {Reprinted Pieces, The Lamp-lighter}
Annunciation day, 25 March.

lagged ... *they'll ask no questions arter him, fear they should be obliged to prosecute, and so get him lagged.* {Oliver Twist 16}
Transported, or exiled.

lamp-iron *"Listen to him", cried the same scowling red-cap. "As if it was not a favour to be protected from the lamp-iron."* {Tale of Two Cities 3-1}
A projecting rod of iron used to hang a lamp over the street, also used during the French Revolution as a makeshift gallows.

lamplighter ... *the lamplighter on his rounds went flashing past, leaving behind a little track of smoke mingled with glowing morsels of his hot red link.* {Barnaby Rudge 18}
The person who lit the street lamps after dark. Lamplighters were noted for the speed with which they ran up their ladders and moved from lamp to lamp carrying a small torch.

Lamps *"Are you a porter?" "On Porter's wages, sir. But I am Lamps."* {Mugby Junction 1}
The lamp-man, one whose job it was to tend the lamps. Railroad lamps of the time were oil lamps and needed filling, wick-trimming and changing, and much attending to.

lancet ... *how can you pretend to be wool-gathering, Dick, when you are as sharp as a surgeon's lancet?* {David Copperfield 13}
A surgeon's knife, most commonly used to 'bleed' patients.

Lancashire manner ... *an impromptu wrestle with my friend Bound-erby in the Lancashire manner* ... {Hard Times 3-2}
In Lancashire wrestling, the contestants were in stocking feet and were permitted to grasp any part of their opponent's body, in contrast with other forms of wrestling in which only the upper body could be held. It was considered a somewhat barbarous form of wrestling because bat-tling on the ground was permitted. In the more gentlemanly bouts, the wrestling was ended if one contestant fell.

lanthorns ... *after having cut several wax-candles in pieces, and stuck them up in various parts of the round-house, and lighted up all the glass lanthorns he could find, took his seat* ... {Reprinted Pieces, The Long Voyage}
Lanterns.

lappets ... *if the late Mr. Grimaldi had appeared in the lappets of Mrs. Siddons, a more complete effect could not have been produced.* {Martin Chuzzlewit 22}
Streamers attached to a lady's hat as decoration.

larboard *I hope she steered herself, skiffed herself, paddled herself, larboarded herself and starboarded herself, or whatever the tech-nical term may be* ... {Our Mutual Friend 4-17}
The port side of a boat, the left side looking forward from the stern. The other side is starboard. Because 'larboard' was easily confused with 'starboard' the word was eventually replaced by the word 'port'.

larder ... *and in one corner an illustrious larder, with glass doors, developing cold fowls and noble joints, and tarts* ... {Martin Chuz-zlewit 12}
A room or closet in which foods are stored, possibly named for lard because it may have originally referred to the storage of bacon.

Lascar *Lying, also dressed and also across the bed* ... *are a Chinaman, a Lascar, and a haggard woman.* {Edwin Drood 1}
An East-Indian sailor.

last but one *The fashion of the last Louis but one ... --the fourteenth Louis ...* {Tale of Two Cities 2-9}
Next to last.

last importance *And let me entreat you to consider that the clearing up of this mystery and the discovery of the real perpetrator of this deed may be of the last importance to others besides yourself.* {Bleak House 52}
Utmost importance, as important as anything can get.

lath *Mrs. Skewton heaved a gentle sigh, supposed to cast a shadow on the surface of that dagger of lath, whereof her susceptible bosom was the sheath ...* {Dombey & Son 27}
Lath is a piece of thin, flat, narrow wood. A dagger of lath is therefore a wooden, or imitation, dagger.

latterly *Latterly, he appears to have devoted the greatest pains to making these results ... plain and clear ...* {Dombey & Son 53}
Lately, recently.

lattice-blind *But in the day-time, when the lattice-blinds (now closely shut) were opened, and the light let in ...* {Dombey & Son 54}
A window blind made of laths crossed to form diamond patterns.

lattice window *It was a little lattice window, about five feet and a half above the ground ...* {Oliver Twist 22}
A window made of small diamond-shaped panes held together by lead or wood strips arranged in the form of a lattice.

laudanum *"What do you mean by 'hocussing' brandy and water?"* inquired Mr. Pickwick. *"Puttin' laud'num in it,"* replied Sam. {Pickwick Papers 13}
A solution of opium in alcohol or wine, used here as a knockout drop. The use and sale of opium was not regulated in nineteenth-century Britain, and it was freely available. It was used as a pain-killer, as a tranquilizer, and to induce sleep. Addiction to laudanum was not unusual.

lave ... *first having brought some water from a running stream hard by, and washed his wound, and laved his hands and face* ... {Barnaby Rudge 69}
Wash or bathe.

lavender *[they were required] to assume this courtly dress, and kept it constantly in lavender for their convenience.* {Barnaby Rudge 8}
Lavender flowers were placed in the folds of freshly washed clothing to perfume it.

law-hand *Some of the inscriptions I have enumerated were written in law-hand, like the papers I had seen in Kenge and Carboy's office* ... {Bleak House 5}
A special style of writing used for legal documents.

law-stationer *Her mother's brother, gentlemen, failed for eight hundred pounds, as a law-stationer.* {Pickwick Papers 55}
A tradesman who sells stationery and other articles needed by lawyers. In Great Britain, one who also takes in manuscripts and legal documents to be copied.

lawn sleeves   *a bishop--a real bishop--with his arms in lawn sleeves and his head in a wig.* {Pickwick Papers 17}
Lawn is a kind of fine linen which was commonly used for the sleeves of a bishop's dress.

lay *Since our people have moved this boy on, and he's not to be found on his old lay, if Mr. Snagsby* ... *[will] point him out, we can have him here in less than a couple of hours' time.* {Bleak House 22}
Slang for occupation, job, or some activity one does more-or-less regularly.

lay by ... *and folding her mantle ready for laying by* ... {Tale of Two Cities 2-6}
To put away in storage, or for future disposal.

lay-down collar ... *all night long I dreamt of nothing but a black gentleman, at full length, in Plaster-of-paris, with a lay-down collar tied with two tassels* ... {Nicholas Nickleby 27}

Probably the opposite of a stand-up collar, hence a collar which lies flat on the shirt.

lay-figure ... *he only wanted me for a dramatic lay-figure, to be contradicted and embraced and wept over and bullied* ... {Great Expectations 15}
A crude, jointed wooden human figure used by artists as a model.

lay precentor ... *being so much respected as Lay Precentor, or Lay Clerk, or whatever you call it* ... {Edwin Drood 2}
A precentor is the one who leads the singing of a church choir or congregation. A lay precentor is one who is not a member of the clergy.

lay the cloth, lay a meal or **lay the table** ... *she laid the cloth, assisted by Belinda Cratchit, second of her daughters.* {A Christmas Carol 3}
To set a table for a meal, or simply to set a table. The cloth referred to is the tablecloth.

lay-to ... *at daybreak next day, we found ourselves forced to lay-to. ... towards noon the next day, it lulled a little, and we made sail again.* {Message from the Sea 4}
To bring a boat into a stationary position with its bow to the wind.

lazar-house ... *the same poisoned fountains that flow into our hospitals and lazar-houses, inundate the jails, and make the convict-ships swim deep* ... {Dombey & Son 47}
A house for diseased people, usually those afflicted with Hansen's disease (leprosy).

leads ... *he opens the French window and steps out upon the leads.* {Bleak House 41}
The sheets or strips of metallic lead used to cover a roof.

lazzarone *In the Neapolitan country, where everybody was a spy, a soldier, a priest, or a lazzarone* ... {The Uncommercial Traveller, The Italian Prisoner}
A beggar or bum.

leal *Mr. Toots, like the leal and trusty soul he was, stopped the cabriolet in a winkling . . .* {Dombey & Son 44}
Loyal, faithful.

leaping-pole *. . . using his tall staff as a leaping-pole, come flying over ditch or hedge or five-barred gate . . .* {Barnaby Rudge 25}
A pole used for jumping, as in pole-vaulting.

learn of *He's a dear good fellow, miss; but he can't write yet--he's going to learn of me--and I wouldn't shame him for the world!* {Bleak House 36}
Local speech for 'learn from'.

leasehold *Think of the laws appertaining to real property . . . to leasehold, freehold, and copyhold estate . . .* {The Battle of Life 1}
Real estate held by a lease.

leather-jerkin *. . . they did on many occasions lead their leather-jerkined soldiers to the death . . .* {Martin Chuzzlewit 1}
A jerkin, a close-fitting short jacket, made of leather.

leather-legginned *. . . a tall, raw-boned gamekeeper and a half-booted, leather-legginned boy . . .* {Pickwick Papers 19}
Leggings are coverings for the legs, usually from ankle to knee and are often made from leather.

leathern *. . . grinning assent from under a leathern portmanteau . . .* {Martin Chuzzlewit 17}
Made of leather.

leathers *. . . wore a short smock-frock over his leathers . . .* {Oliver Twist 42}
1. Leather breeches or leather leggings.
Out of the vay, young leathers. {Pickwick Papers 19}
2. A person wearing leather breeches or leather leggings.

leaving shop *. . . she was an unlicensed pawnbroker, keeping what was popularly called a Leaving Shop . . .* {Our Mutual Friend 2-12}
Slang for an unlicensed pawnshop.

ledger *From this ledger he drew forth a couple of whip-lashes, three or four small buckles* . . . {Pickwick Papers 43}
The word is used here in the sense of 'pocket-book', as the context indicates. It does not mean a record book.

lee, lees . . . *scrawled upon a wall with his finger dipped in muddy wine-lees* . . . {Tale of Two Cities 1-5}
Lee is the sediment cast down by wine.

leech . . . *they take medicine to an extent which I should have conceived impossible; they put on blisters and leeches with a perseverance worthy of a better cause* . . . {Pickwick Papers 48}
A bloodsucking aquatic worm applied to the skin to draw blood, as a method (generally ineffective) of medical treatment.

leg *"I beg pardon," said Mr. Datchery, making a leg with his hat under his arm* . . . {Edwin Drood 17}
1. A bow, made by drawing one leg back and bending the other.
He was a horse chanter; he's a leg now. {Pickwick Papers 42}
2. Slang for a blackleg, a swindler at horse races.

leg-bail . . . *he has us now if he could only give us leg-bail again* . . . {Oliver Twist 19}
Slang for escape. To make bail with your legs.

leggings, leggins . . . *a tall, raw-boned gamekeeper and a half-booted, leather-leggined boy, each bearing a bag of capacious dimensions, and accompanied by a brace of pointers.* {Pickwick Papers 19}
Coverings for the legs, usually from ankle to knee, and often made of leather.

lenity *Into the midst of this fray, Mr. and Mrs. Tetterby both precipitated themselves with great ardour* . . . *and having* . . . *laid about them without any lenity, and done much execution, resumed their former relative positions.* {The Haunted Man 3}
Mildness, gentleness.

let ... *til this coach-house and stable gets a better let, we live here cheap.* {The Chimes 2}
1. Rental.
... *places to see the execution were let at high prices* ... {Barnaby Rudge 77}
2. Rented or hired.

lettings ... *he now got more money out of his own wretched lettings, unquestioned, than anybody with a less knobby and less shining crown could possibly have done.* {Little Dorrit 1-13}
Places rented out.

let into ... *a looking-glass let into the wall* ... {Tale of Two Cities 3-2}
Fitted into, built into.

let out *It'll be a deuced unpleasant thing if she takes it into her head to let out when those fellows are here, won't it?* {Pickwick Papers 32}
To give vent to anger or other emotions.

letter-cart, flushed letter cart ... *nearly run down by a flushed letter-cart* ... {Our Mutual Friend 2-16}
The red-painted mail cart of the British postal system.

levee days ... *and on levee days, was sometimes known to have as many as twenty half-pay officers waiting their turn for polishing.* {Barnaby Rudge 82}
A levee is a morning assembly held by a king or prince.

lexicon *But Bitherstone* ... *is extremely inky; and his lexicon has got so dropsical from constant reference that it won't shut* ... {Dombey & Son 41}
A dictionary, usually of Greek or Hebrew.

lieve *"Thankee, sir," said Mark. "I'd as lieve stand."* {Martin Chuzzlewit 13}
Should be 'lief'. 'I'd as lief' means 'I would rather'.

Life Guards *But, it being whispered that a detachment of Life Guards had been sent for, they took to their heels with great expedition, and left*

the street quite clear. {Barnaby Rudge 43}
Two regiments of the royal household cavalry are named Life Guards.

life-preserver ... *two or three heavy bludgeons which stood in a corner, and a 'life-preserver' that hung over the chimney-piece.* {Oliver Twist 19}
A stick or bludgeon weighted with lead, meant as a self-defense weapon but often used by criminals.

lifer *They know what a clever lad he is; he'll be a lifer.* {Oliver Twist 43}
Slang for someone sentenced to be transported (usually to Australia) for life.

lift ... *mechanical lifts for the housemaids, with all their brushes and brooms ...* {Hard Times 1-3}
An elevator.

ligature ... *tied to the wrists of those who carried them, with strips of linen and fragments of dress; ligatures various in kind ...* {Tale of Two Cities 3-2}
Anything used in tying something.

light, to light someone ... *the portly man stepped back to the garden-gate, and helped his companion to put up the gig: while Brittles lighted them, in a state of great admiration.* {Oliver Twist 31}
Hold a candle to give light for someone.

lightermen ... *roaring curses over the bulwarks at respondent lightermen ...* {Great Expectations 54}
A lighter is a boat or barge used for unloading, or lightening, a large vessel that cannot come close enough to a pier or wharf. The lightermen are the sailors who operate a lighter.

light guinea *I wouldn't for a light guinea that he should never go a wooing agin ...* {Barnaby Rudge 3}
A guinea coin that was of reduced value, because it was worn down or had been trimmed.

light porter ... *against the door of which strong chamber the light-porter laid his head every night* ... {Hard Times 2-1}
A porter hired for light work rather than heavy carrying.

lights, in lights of, bumpy, bony *And as to being regarded in lights, there's bumpey lights as well as bony* {Our Mutual Friend 2-7}
Mr. Venus, who deals in human bones, was rejected by a young lady who told him that she did not want to be regarded in a particular light if she married him, specifically 'in that bony light'. When Mr. Wegg bumps his head he makes a joke of this by complaining that there are bumpy lights as well as bony.

lightsome ... *I was a lightsome young creature.* {Oliver Twist 41}
Lighthearted, cheerful.

ligneous ... *Mr. Boffin again shook hands with that ligneous sharper [Mr. Wegg]* ... {Our Mutual Friend 1-5}
Wooden.

like *There was one young man sketching his face in a little note-book. He wondered whether it was like, and looked on when the artist broke his pencil point,* ... {Oliver Twist 52}
1. Of a portrait, bearing a faithful resemblance to the original.
He may come to that before he dies. It's like enough. {Barnaby Rudge 37}
2. Likely enough, likely to happen.

liking, on liking ... *he is a very young man on liking, and we don't like him.* {Our Mutual Friend 4-4}
Being tried out for a job. If the boss likes him, he gets the job.

limber *I goes a-nutting in your woods, and breaks--who don't?--a limber branch or two.* {The Chimes 3}
Easily bent.

lime *"You're a damned rogue," says the old gentleman, making a hideous grimace at the door as he shuts it. "But I'll lime you, you dog, I'll lime you!"* {Bleak House 21}

An allusion to catching birds by smearing tree branches with lime, which traps them. What is meant here is 'I'll trap you'.

limekiln ... *the appointed place was the little sluice-house by the limekiln on the marshes* ... {Great Expectations 52}
The oven in which limestone is heated to make lime.

line ... *in the line he was called Chops;* ... *partly because his real name, if he ever had any real name (which was very dubious), was Stakes.* {Going Into Society}
1. A branch of business or activity, a line of work. Here it refers to the part of the entertainment business now called the side show.
... *Toby Crackit has been hanging about the place for a fortnight; and he can't get one of the servants into a line.* {Oliver Twist 19}
2. Slang for persuading someone to become an accomplice.

linen *His linen* ... *was white as the tops of the waves that broke upon the neighboring beach* ... {Tale of Two Cities 1-4}
Shirts, whether made of linen or other cloth.

linen-draper *There were, within sight, an auctioneer's and a fire-agency office, a cornfactor's, a linen-draper's* ... {Pickwick Papers 7}
A retailer of linen and other fabrics.

linen roller ... *there were files of moth-eaten letters hanging up against the walls; and linen rollers, and fragments of old patterns, and odds and ends of spoiled goods* ... {Martin Chuzzlewit 11}
The wooden rods on which cloth was rolled up.

lines *A grand review was to take place upon the Lines. The manoeuvres of half a dozen regiments were to be inspected* ... {Pickwick Papers 4}
1. The military formation when a unit is deployed in ranks.
... *my lines is strained* ... {Tale of Two Cities 2-1}
2. The word 'line' means 'one's appointed lot in life'. In this phrase it may relate to 'hard lines', meaning 'bad luck'.

link ... *the fog and darkness thickened so, that people ran about with flaring links, proffering their services to go before horses in car-*

riages, and conduct them on their way. {A Christmas Carol 1}
A torch, commonly used to light one's way in the streets.

link-boy, linkman ... *he who had been ... most valiant at the supper-table ... was glad to fee a link-boy to escort him home.* {Barnaby Rudge 16}
At last, the guests were all gone, and the linkmen too; and the street, crowded so long with carriages, was clear ... {Dombey & Son 36}
A boy or man employed to carry a link (see **link**).

list ... *and water spread itself wheresoever it listed ...* {A Christmas Carol 3}
1. Pleasure or wish. Hence the water went where it pleased.
... *I'm sure I should go and list for a soldier ...* {Old Curiosity Shop 2}
2. Enlist.
... *the drunken old chap, in a pair of list slippers and a nightcap ...* {Our Mutual Friend 1-3}
3. The somewhat coarse material used as the selvage or edge of fabric. Such things as slippers, shoes, and cushions for billiard tables were made from list.

lint *Down by the Docks, the apothecary sets up in business on the wretchedest scale--chiefly on lint and plaster for the strapping of wounds--and with no bright bottles, and with no little drawers.* {The Uncommercial Traveller, Bound for the Great Salt Lake}
A soft, fleecy material made from scraped linen and used for bandages.

Little Go *[Our Vestry] is even regarded by some of its members as a chapel of ease to the House of Commons: a Little Go to be passed first.* {Reprinted Pieces, Our Vestry}
College slang for the first of the examinations for the Bachelor of Arts degree.

liver wing *Mr. Pumblechook helped me to the liver wing, and to the best slice of tongue ...* {Great Expectations 19}
The right wing of the fowl was usually trussed for cooking with the liver tucked under it.

livery *Just as he was turning into Holborn, he ran against a young gentleman in a livery.* {Martin Chuzzlewit 26}
The uniform of a servant, especially a footman.

living *He was warmly attached to church and state, and never appointed to the living in his gift any but a three-bottle man and a first rate foxhunter.* {Barnaby Rudge 47}
An income, from lands or other sources, associated with a church appointment.

loaded to the muzzle *[It was understood] that if his mother ever met his father, she would shoot him with a silver pistol, which she carried, always loaded to the muzzle, for that purpose.* {Reprinted Pieces, Our School}
When firearms were loaded from the muzzle it was possible to fill the entire barrel of the gun with powder and shot, increasing the firepower of the weapon enormously--if the barrel did not explode.

loadings *There's a quarter pound of powder in the case, and I have got two newspapers in my pocket for the loadings.* {Pickwick Papers 2}
The powder, wadding, and ball put into a muzzle-loading firearm. The newspaper was used as wadding over the powder.

loadstone *As truly as the loadstone draws iron towards it, so he, lying at the bottom of his grave, could draw me near him when he would.* {Barnaby Rudge 62}
Lodestone, a naturally magnetic, iron-containing mineral.

loaf *On the table before him stood a pot of ale, a cold round of beef, and a very respectable-looking loaf . . .* {Pickwick Papers 23}
A loaf of bread.

loaf and fish trade ashore *[To] prosper in the private loaf and fish trade ashore . . .* {Little Dorrit 1-34}
The profits of jobbery, which is using a public office for private profit.

loblolly boy *. . . the conventional unintelligibility of his orders in the ears of uncommercial land-lubbers and loblolly boys, though they were always intelligible to the crew, was hardly less pleasant.* {The Uncom-

mercial Traveller, The Short-timers}
A ship's surgeon's assistant.

lobster   ... *but had a dismal light about it, like a bad lobster in a dark cellar.* {A Christmas Carol 1}
The context implies that a putrefying lobster becomes luminescent. It should be possible to determine this experimentally if a suitably ventilated laboratory could be found. However, lobsters in England in Dickens' time were not the same as Maine lobsters of the United States now; consequently, the experiment might not work.

lock, lock-house *And to think of a sweet little cherub being born inside the lock!* {Little Dorrit 1-6}
1. Prison, the jail.
"I am the Lock," said the man. "The Lock?" "I am the Deputy Lock, on job, and this is the Lock-house..." {Our Mutual Friend 3-8}
2. The lock of a canal is the arrangement of solid gates which can be opened and shut to permit the water level to rise or fall. Here the operator of the lock is referred to as the Lock. The lock-house is the small dwelling for the lock operator.

locofoco *Here's full particulars of the patriotic locofoco movement yesterday, in which the whigs was so chawed up...* {Martin Chuzzlewit 16}
An ordinary match, of a type which can be struck anywhere. Also, a cigar with a match head embedded in its tip to make it self-igniting. The word also became used as the name for a splinter group of the Democratic party, and that is the meaning in this example. The political name was acquired when the faction struck locofocos after the lights went out during a political meeting.

locomotive   ... *and to dance in the open air to the music of a locomotive band...* {Nicholas Nickleby 52}
The single gentleman, it is true, could do nothing [of the work] himself, but he overlooked everybody else and was more locomotive than anybody. {Old Curiosity Shop 69}
Moving from one place to another. It does not have to have the sense of self-propelled by machinery.

lodge, keeper's lodge ... *we ran out of the wood ... and made for a keeper's lodge which was close at hand.* {Bleak House 2}
A house occupied by a caretaker, usually at the entrance gate to an estate.

lodge-gate *[I] retraced the way by which I had come, and never paused until I had gained the lodge-gate, and the park lay sullen and black behind me.* {Bleak House 36}
A gate near which there is a lodge, the hut or enclosed place where the gatekeeper stayed.

lodging-bill *The chief features in the still life of the street are green shutters, lodging-bills, brass door-plates, and bell-handles* ... {Pickwick Papers 32}
Bills, or posters, of lodging for rent.

loft-room *There is a bed in the wholesome loft-room by the stable; we had better keep him there till morning, when he can be wrapped up and removed.* {Bleak House 31}
The room over a stable.

London Pantechnicon *I had merely shut myself for half a minute, in a German travelling chariot that stood for sale in the Carriage Department of the London Pantechnicon.* {The Uncommercial Traveller, Travelling Abroad}
A two-acre complex of warehouses, stables, wine vaults, and carriage houses where many things could be bought.

long and long ... *hundreds of years hence, when the digging for gold in Australia shall have long and long ceased out of the land.* {The Uncommercial Traveller, The Shipwreck}
Throughout a long period, for a very long time.

long-clothes ... *his first long-clothes were made from a blue bag.* {Bleak House 20}
The gown of an infant.

long-headed *You are a long-headed fellow, Fledgeby.* {Our Mutual Friend 2-5}
Shrewd, farseeing.

long stages (see **horsing long stages**)

look out *Having looked out from among the old furniture the handsomest and most commodious chair he could possibly find, which he reserved for his own use* ... {Old Curiosity Shop 11}
To find, or choose, by looking. To pick out.

looking-glass ... *a draped table with a gilded looking-glass ... that I made out at first sight to be a fine lady's dressing-table.* {Great Expectations 8}
A mirror.

loophole ... *showing in the clear atmosphere their every scrap of tracery and fretwork, and every niche and loophole.* {Barnaby Rudge 77}
A narrow vertical opening in a wall.

loose-box ... *the pony in the loose-box in the corner.* {Bleak House 7}
A stall large enough for an animal to move about freely.

loo table *"Augustus, my love," said Miss Pecksniff, "ask the price of the eight rosewood chairs, and the loo table."* {Martin Chuzzlewit 46}
A kind of round table originally used for the game of loo, a card game involving the formation of tricks as in whist or bridge. The loo is a money penalty for breaking a rule or failing to take a trick.

lose *Poor fellow, he loses time, and time is money as the good proverb says* ... {Barnaby Rudge 23}
You had nearly imposed upon me, but you have lost your labour. {Martin Chuzzlewit 24}
Waste. In these examples, waste time and wasted labor.

losing hazard *My life's a burden to me. If it wasn't for weangeance, I'd play at pitch and toss with it on the losing hazard.* {Barnaby Rudge 27}
A card game in which the loser wins the stakes.

loth ... *she would entreat Mr. Swiveler to relax as though she were not by, which Mr. Swiveler, nothing loth, would readily consent to do.* {Old Curiosity Shop 36}
Reluctant; hence, 'nothing loth' means 'not at all reluctant'.

love-nots ... *the dark brown dining-room, which no confectioner can brighten up, let him garnish the [carvings on the walls] with as many flowers and love-nots as he will.* {Dombey & Son 31}
Should be love-knot, a ribbon tied in a particular kind of bow and supposed to be a token of love.

lover *She never had a lover, and the governor proposed old Bounderby, and she took him.* {Hard Times 2-3}
A suitor, one who is courting or in love with someone. Does not have the current connotation of sexual partner (as in the United States).

low ... *oxen were tied up for sale in the long narrow streets, butting and lowing, and receiving blows on their blunt heads* ... {Dombey & Son 55}
The moo sound made by cattle.

low-lived ... *I was much more ignorant than I had considered myself last night; and generally that I was in a low-lived bad way.* {Great Expectations 8}
Living a low life, one of low degree or value.

lowering *The sky had been dark and lowering for some time, and the commencement of a violent storm of rain drove Ralph for shelter to a tree.* {Nicholas Nickleby 44}
Sinking, crouching. The sense is gloomy, threatening. In some contexts it means depressing, also literally becoming lower.

lucifer-match, lucifers *I would get my living by selling lucifers.* {Bleak House 32}
A wooden match that can be struck on any rough surface.

lucky, make one's lucky ... *wot's the use o' runnin arter a man as has made his lucky and got to t'other end of the borough by this time.* {Pickwick Papers 10}
Slang for escape, make one's escape.

lucubration ... *[Mr.] Wolf, not to be left behind-hand, recited the leading points of one or two vastly humorous articles he was then preparing. These lucubrations ... were highly approved ...* {Martin Chuzzlewit 28}
A learned discourse, in writing.

lugger *On the beach, among the rough luggers and capstans groups of storm-beaten boatmen ... watched under the lee of those objects ...* {Reprinted Pieces, Out of the Season}
A sailboat carrying a lugsail, one supported by a long spar that usually extends fore and aft of the mast diagonally across the sail.

luke *Let me have nine penn'orth o' brandy and water, luke, and the inkstand, will you miss?* {Pickwick Papers 33}
Lukewarm.

lull ... *her voice had dropped, so that she spoke low, and with a dead lull upon her ...* {Great Expectations 8}
A lulled or stupefied condition.

lumber ... *the pain that I shall feel when those old jugs and bottles are swept away as lumber!* {Nicholas Nickleby 40}
Odds and ends, unused furniture, junk, useless things in general. Does not mean planks of wood (as it does in the United States).

lumbering *The furniture, at once spare and lumbering, hid in the rooms rather than furnished them ...* {Little Dorrit 1-5}
Tending toward being lumber, or like old and unused articles (see **lumber**).

lumber-room ... *a kind of antipodean lumber-room full of old chairs and tables upside down.* {Bleak House 66}
Storage room for unused furniture and the like (see **lumber**).

lummy *To think of Jack Dawkins--lummy Jack--the Dodger--The Artful Dodger--going abroad for a common twopenny-halfpenny sneeze-box!* {Oliver Twist 43}
Slang for great, first-rate.

lush ... *piece of double Glo'ster; and to wind up all, some of the rightest sort you ever lushed.* {Oliver Twist 39}
To drink.

lustre *Every chandelier or lustre, muffled in holland, looked like a monstrous tear* ... {Dombey & Son 3}
1. A lustre is the glass ball, or cut-glass pendant, used to refract light in a chandelier. The word may also mean the chandelier itself.
... *my fancy* ... *has shed a lustre on your name.* {The Haunted Man 2}
2. Brilliance, splendor, glory.

luxurious ... *but he came of a rich family, and was idle and luxurious.* {Reprinted Pieces, George Silverman's Explanation 7}
Pleasure loving, fond of luxury.

lying-in hospital ... *everything was fact between the lying-in hospital and the cemetery* ... {Hard Times 1-5}
Maternity hospital.

lymphatic ... *she was of an unusually lymphatic temperament* ... {The Haunted House 1}
Having the characteristics supposed, in ancient medical theories, to be due to too much lymph. Flabby muscled, pale, and mentally sluggish.

Macassar Oil ... *she turned to a walking advertisement of Rowland's Macassar Oil, who stood next to her* ... {Sketches, The Tuggs's at Ramsgate}
A hair oil made by Rowland and Son, very popular in the early nineteenth century. It was claimed to be made from ingredients obtained from Macassar, a district in the island of Celebes. Because the oil on gentlemen's heads stained the upholstery of high-backed chairs, doilies were pinned to the chairs at head height. They were called antimacassars.

mace *There is the registrar below the judge, in wig and gown; and there are two or three maces, or petty-bags, or privy purses, or whatever they may be, in legal court suits.* {Bleak House 1}
An official of the court who carries a mace, a heavy staff or club, as a symbol of office.

madcap *....when from alley close at hand some shouts of revelry arose, and there came straggling forth a dozen madcaps, whooping and calling to each other* ... {Barnaby Rudge 18}
Someone behaving in a wild, impulsive, or reckless manner.

made-dish *The flying waiter then flew across Holborn for the soup, and flew back again, and then took another flight for the made-dish, and flew back again* .... {Edwin Drood 11}
A dish composed of several ingredients.

mad hospital *What now? Are you a subject for the mad hospital?* {Tale of Two Cities 1-5}
Hospital for the insane.

mag . . . .*if he don't keep such a business as the present as close as possible it can't be worth a mag to him . . .* {Bleak House 54}
Slang for a halfpenny coin, a shortening of 'magpie'.

magazine . . . *what magazine he mightn't blow up, without meaning of it.* {Dombey & Son 39}
A place for the storage of gunpowder and ammunition.

magic-lantern *Jo stands amazed in the disk of light, like a ragged figure in a magic-lantern, trembling to think that he has offended against the law in not having moved on far enough.* {Bleak House 22}
An early kind of slide projector with circular lenses. In order to transmit the maximum amount of light, the entire area of the lens was used. The light was not projected as a rectangle but as a disk.

magnetic slumber . . . *with as much thought or consciousness of what he was doing as if he had been in a magnetic slumber.* {Nicholas Nickleby 7}
A hypnotic sleep. From the term 'animal magnetism', the first name for hypnosis.

magpie . . . *only one bob and a magpie . . .* {Oliver Twist 8}
Slang for a halfpenny coin.

magsman *Tally-ho Thompson was a famous horse-stealer, couper, and magsman.* {Reprinted Pieces, The Detective Police}
Slang for swindler.

mail . . . *the waking from a sound nap as the mail came dashing past like a highway comet . . .* {Old Curiosity Shop 46}
1. Short for mail coach, a coach which carried the mail and passengers. They ran on precise schedules and were usually the fastest coaches.
. . . *a railway terminus, with the morning mails coming in . . .* {The Uncommercial Traveller, Night Walks}
2. Short for the railroad train that carried both mail and passengers, the mail train.

There were suits of mail standing like ghosts in armour here and there . . . {Old Curiosity Shop 1}
3. A kind of body armor, usually made of many linked rings of metal.

mail-guard . . . *the sound of the mail-guard's horn came cheerily upon their ears* . . . {Martin Chuzzlewit 2}
The guard on a mail coach.

maintenon cutlet . . . *Mr. Alexander Trott sat down to a fried sole, maintenon cutlet, Madeira, and sundries* . . . {Sketches, The Great Winglebury Duel}
A cutlet named, for no good reason, after the Marquise de Maintenon, secret wife of Louis XIV.

make good a story . . . *Mr. Pinch has a proud spirit* . . . *and when he left us* . . . *he scorned to make his story good, even to me.* {Martin Chuzzlewit 43}
To support a story with evidence, to prove the truth of a story.

make love *"Has he been making love to either of you?" "Yes," said Kate.* {Nicholas Nickleby 41}
To court or woo. Does not have the current sexual connotation.

make one *"Remember, Tim," said brother Charles, "that we dine at half-past five to-day instead of two o'clock; . . . Mr. Nickleby, my dear sir, you will make one."* {Nicholas Nickleby 37}
Be one of the party.

make up to *Though he called me Mr. Pip, and began rather to make up to me, he still could not get rid of a certain air of bullying suspicion* . . . {Great Expectations 18}
To make advances toward, perhaps in the sense of to attempt to settle a dispute.

make-weight . . . *somebody, who appeared to be a make-weight, and was not introduced at all.* {Nicholas Nickleby 19}
A person of little value thrown in to fill a space, in this case at a dinner party.

making belief *Sometimes he stopped at the fire-place, and sometimes at the door; making belief that he was staring with all his might into shop-windows.* {Oliver Twist 9}
An incorrect substitute for 'making believe'.

mangle *... a small home with a large mangle in it, at the handle of which machine stood a very long boy ...* {Our Mutual Friend 1-16}
A machine for pressing cloth. The earlier versions consisted of a heavily weighted box, arduously pulled back and forth over several rollers. The cloth was placed between the rollers and a polished board. Later improved models were made of two rollers, worked by a crank, between which the cloth was rolled.

mangling, take in *He's got a wife, Ma'am, as takes in mangling, and is as 'dustrious and hard-working a young 'ooman as can be ...* {Sketches, The Pawnbroker's Shop}
The phrase is the same as 'take in ironing' (see **mangle**).

Mangnall (see **globes**)

mangold-wurzel *... and become a part proprietor in turnips or mangold-wurzel.* {Tom Tiddler's Ground 1}
Mangel-wurzel, a variety of large beet raised for cattle feed.

man of oil *Bah, you man of oil, have I no eyes to see how you have angled with him from the first?* {Martin Chuzzlewit 18}
An oily, flattering, slippery kind of person.

man's estate *... a good looking youth, newly arrived at man's estate, ... stepped forward from the doorway ...* {Martin Chuzzlewit 2}
Adulthood.

mantelshelf *The mantelshelf was ornamented with a wooden inkstand, containing one stump of a pen ...* {Pickwick Papers 14}
A shelf projecting forward from the mantelpiece of a fireplace.

mantle *The daylight mantled in his gleaming hat and boots, as in a polished glass.* {Martin Chuzzlewit 27}
Reflect.

mantua-maker ... *the mantua-makers upstairs, who were busy on the family mourning.* {Dombey & Son 2}
A mantua is a loose gown, open in front to show an underskirt, worn by women in the seventeenth and eighteenth centuries. The word mantua-maker came to mean 'dressmaker'.

marine stores *She had stopped at a shop over which was written* KROOK, RAG AND BOTTLE WAREHOUSE. *Also, in long thin letters,* KROOK, DEALER IN MARINE STORES. {Bleak House 5}
A general name for the cordage, sails, and other things with which ships need to be supplied.

mark ... *the French class becomes so demoralized that the mark goes round as briskly as the bottle at a convivial party* ... {Edwin Drood 3}
In some schools a child was given a badge, called the mark, to wear when he did something wrong. He got rid of it by passing it on to another child whom he detected in some wrongdoing.

marker ... *had introduced him to a marker who taught billiards* ... {Dombey & Son 22}
The person who keeps the score in the game of billiards.

market-cross ... *a dull little town with a church-spire, and a marketplace, and a market-cross, and one intensely sunny street and a pond with an old horse cooling his legs in it* ... {Bleak House 18}
Originally, a cross erected at a market as a public monument, but in the nineteenth century it came to mean a polygonal building with open arches at the sides. It was used as a shelter when there was rain during a market.

market-garden ... *where the railways still bestride the market-gardens that will soon die under them.* {Our Mutual Friend 2-1}
A commercial vegetable garden, a truck garden. The word 'truck' does not mean a vehicle but is another word for 'produce'.

market-gardener ... *but when it came to know me well, and love me, it was sure to marry a market-gardener.* {Old Curiosity Shop 56}
One who raises fruits and vegetables for sale at markets. A truck gardener (see **market-garden**).

market-town *On the day following, Oliver and Mr. Maylie repaired to the market-town, in the hope of seeing or hearing something of the men there* ... {Oliver Twist 35}
A town, usually the largest in the district, which has been granted the privilege of having the market for its region.

Marplot ... *you are such a beloved little Marplot for putting one out* ... {Little Dorrit 2-15}
One who foils a plan by officious intervention. From the name of a character in an eighteenth-century play who did just that.

marquee *The wickets were pitched, and so were a couple of marquees for the rest and refreshment of the contending parties.* {Pickwick Papers 7}
A large tent.

marrow ... *winking in the sun there were such heaps of drooping pods, and marrows, and cucumbers, that every foot of ground appeared a vegetable treasury* ... {Bleak House 18}
1. A kind of gourd used as a table vegetable.
"Now, Small," says Mr. Guppy, "what would you recommend about pastry." "Marrow puddings," says Mr. Smallweed instantly. {Bleak House 20}
2. Marrow pudding could be made from vegetable marrows or from beef marrow, the fatty material in beef bones.

marrowbones *The men who play the bells have got scent of the marriage, and the marrowbones and cleavers too, and a brass band too.* {Dombey & Son 31}
A crude kind of musical instrument made, at first by butchers, from hollow animal bones. The tones were produced by striking the bones with knives (cleavers). The players became street musicians who traditionally were paid to play at weddings, but they were often paid more for not playing.

mash *There is likewise the Honourable Bob Staples, who can make warm mashes with the skill of a veterinary surgeon and is a better shot than most gamekeepers.* {Bleak House 28}
A mixture of boiled grains given to animals as a hot food.

mast-house *The old pensioners, who for the moderate charge of a penny, exhibit the mast-house, the Thames and shipping, the place where men used to hang in chains, and other interesting sights, through a tele-scope . . .* {Sketches, Greenwich Fair}
A long building in which ship's masts were made, repaired, and stored. One end of the building was at the water's edge and was tall enough to contain a crane for raising the mast and placing it on a ship.

match *Their legs are so hard . . . that they must have devoted the greater part of their . . . lives . . . to pedestrian exercises and the walking of matches.* {Bleak House 49}
A contest of any kind in which two individuals are pitted against one another.

matchlock *. . . buff-jerkins too--matchlocks--sarcophagus--fine place--old legends too--strange stories . . .* {Pickwick Papers 2}
A musket in which the powder is ignited by a slowly burning fuse, brought into contact when the trigger is pulled. The fuse is called a 'slow-match' and the mechanism that operates it the 'lock'.

matter *. . . have you anything more to say to me? I think there can be nothing else. You have been short, but full of matter!* {Little Dorrit 1-5}
Things of substance, things of importance.

maw *. . . if he knew how empty of learning my young maw was at his time of life.* {Hard Times 1-7}
Stomach.

mazy *. . . in remembrance of her with whom I shall never again thread the windings of the mazy . . .* {Old Curiosity Shop 56}
Resembling the nature of a maze, full of windings and turnings. Here the word means simply 'maze'.

mean . . . *if you could have been aware how small and flabby and mean you was, dear me, you'd have formed the most contemptible opinions of yourself.* {Great Expectations 7}
Common, inferior in rank or quality.

meat-safe . . . *the coal-cellar, the candle-box, the salt-box, the meat-safe, were all padlocked.* {Old Curiosity Shop 36}
A cupboard used for storing meat and made of perforated metal or wire screening.

meat-screen . . . *when we go to see a kitchen-fender and a meat-screen . . .* {David Copperfield 43}
A metal screen placed so as to reflect the heat of the fire back on roasting meat.

meed *My thanks, and my congratulations, are equally the meed of Mr. Dorrit and of Miss Dorrit.* {Little Dorrit 2-15}
Reward.

meet *An ancient city, Cloisterham, and no meet dwelling-place for any one with hankerings after the noisy world.* {Edwin Drood 3}
Fitting, suitable.

melon-frame . . . *I strolled into the garden, and strolled all over it. It was quite a wilderness, and there were old melon-frames and cucumber-frames in it . . .* {Great Expectations 11}
A glass-covered, low box in which seeds are planted for an early start. It is named after the seeds planted in it.

member *"Our member has come down express," returned the landlord . . .* {Martin Chuzzlewit 35}
Short for member of Parliament.

memorialize *Mr. Jaggers was querulous and angry with me for having "let it slip through my fingers," and said we must memorialize by-and-by, and try at all events for some of it.* {Great Expectations 55}
To write a statement of facts, in the form of a petition or remonstrance, to a person in authority or to a government.

mercer ... *Sheen and Gloss's the mercers* ... {Bleak House 58}
A dealer in fabrics, especially expensive ones.

merino ... *carpet, merino, muslin, bombazeen, or woolen-stuff.* {Oliver Twist 48}
A fine woolen material, resembling cashmere, made originally from the wool of merino sheep.

metempsychosis *It was as if the original Barbox had ... thither caused to be conveyed Young Jackson ... and had effected a metempsychosis and exchange of persons with him.* {Mugby Junction 2}
Transmigration of a soul, at death, into a different body. A kind of reincarnation.

mews ... *Mr. Turveydrops great room, which was built out into a mews at the back and was lighted by a skylight.* {Bleak House 14}
A mews is a yard with stables for carriages and carriage horses. The Mews may refer to the royal stables at Charing Cross.

Michaelmas *What the two drank together, between Hilary Term and Michaelmas, might have floated a king's ship.* {Tale of Two Cities 2-5}
A festival celebrated on 29 September in honor of the Archangel Michael. It is one of the four quarter-days of the English business year.

Michaelmas term *London. Michaelmas term lately over, and the Lord Chancellor sitting in Lincoln's Inn Hall.* {Bleak House 1}
The term of the High Court of Justice that began soon after Michaelmas.

might be ... *Mrs. Wititterly sighed and looked on, as if she felt the honour, but had determined to bear it as meekly as might be.* {Nicholas Nickleby 28}
Could be.

mignonette *There's the same mignonette box in the middle of the window, and the same four flower-pots, two on each side, that I brought with me when I first came.* {Nicholas Nickleby 35}
A kind of plant, having fragrant flowers.

milestone *"Roving stones gather no moss, Joe," said Gabriel. "Nor milestones much," replied Joe.* {Barnaby Rudge 3}
A pillar set in the roads at intervals of one mile, with the number of miles from the last, or to the next, town marked on it.

milk-punch *It smells, I think, like milk-punch.* {Pickwick Papers 50}
A mixture of milk, brandy, oranges or lemons, and sugar.

milksop *"Look at the snivelling milksop!" said my uncle.* {The Poor Relation's Story}
Literally, a piece of bread soaked in milk. It came to mean a spiritless man, without courage or manliness.

milk-walk *I went to pieces when I was in a milk-walk, thirty year ago; arterwards, when I was a fruiterer, and kept a spring-wan . . .* {Sketches, A Passage in the Life of Mr. Watkins Tottle}
The regular route of a milkman selling milk.

mill *[The prize fighter was] in the country, training (at Toots's cost) for his great mill with the Larkey boy.* {Dombey & Son 41}
1. A prize fight or boxing match.
What mill!--why, the *mill--the mill as takes up so little room that it'll work inside a Stone Jug . . .* {Oliver Twist 8}
2. Slang for treadmill. Walking the treadmill was a form of punishment. The Stone Jug was a nickname for Newgate prison.

Millbank *Bow Street, Newgate, and Millbank, are a poor return for general benevolence . . .* {Sketches, The Last Cab-driver and the First Omnibus-cad}
Millbank Penitentiary. The dismal location in which it was built is described in *David Copperfield.*

mill-weir *It was but for an instant that I seemed to struggle with a thousand mill-weirs and a thousand flashes of light; that instant passed, I was taken on board the galley.* {Great Expectations 54}
A mill-dam, a dam constructed in the stream just above the waterwheel of a mill.

mim *"Master's come home, mim," cried Miggs, running before him into the parlour.* {Barnaby Rudge 7}
Regional speech for Ma'am.

mine ... *temporary fortifications had been erected, the citadel was to be attacked and taken, and a mine was to be sprung.* {Pickwick Papers 4}
An explosive charge of gunpowder buried in a tunnel. To spring a mine means to explode it.

mite *Mr. Pardiggle ... was always talking about his mite, or Mrs. Pardiggle's mite, or their five boy's mites.* {Bleak House 30}
The small sum which is all a person can afford to give to charity.

mixed biscuit ... *refreshed with just a sip of something comfortable and a mixed biscuit or so ...* {Nicholas Nickleby 38}
Biscuits (cookies to an American) could be purchased all of a single style or with several styles in one box. The latter were called mixed biscuits and were somewhat less expensive than those purchased unmixed.

mob-cap ... *his eyes fixed on a very fat old lady in a mob-cap--evidently the proprietress of the establishment ...* {Nicholas Nickleby 16}
A woman's cap which covered the hair and had side pieces that covered the ears and fastened under the chin. It was made of a soft cloth and could be worn alone, if it was a fancy one, or under a bonnet.

moddley-coddley *Don't moddley-coddley, there's a good fellow.* {Edwin Drood 2}
A variation of mollycoddle, from 'coddle' meaning 'to nurse or pamper'.

mode *It is a young lady's walking-shoe. It is in the present mode.* {Tale of Two Cities 2-24}
The current fashion.

moderator lamp ... *a small table with two moderator lamps hanging over it, and an ornamental looking-glass let into the wall.* {The Uncommercial Traveller, In the French-Flemish Country}
A lamp that burned rapeseed oil and had a regulator which mechanical-

ly controlled the flow of oil to the lamp in order to give an even light as the quantity of oil in the reservoir fell.

moiler, moiling ... *I am a toiler and a moiler* ... {Bleak House 25} One who performs labor or drudgery.

moisten your clay *Moisten your clay, wet the other eye, drink, man!* {Old Curiosity Shop 62} Have a drink.

momus ... *the Mississippi Momuses, nine in number, were announced to appear in the town-hall, for the general delectation, this last Christmas week.* {The Uncommercial Traveller, Mr. Barlow} As is apparent from the context of the story, the Mississippi Momuses is the name Dickens gives to a troupe giving a minstrel show. Momus is the Greek god of ridicule, hence his choice of the name.

money-broker ... *cannot be too strongly recommended to the notice of capitalists, both large and small, and more especially of money-brokers and bill-discounters.* {Nicholas Nickleby 1} A dealer in money, a moneylender or arranger of loans.

monthly ... *never did I think till I know'd you, as any woman could sicknurse and monthly likewise, on the little that you takes to drink.* {Martin Chuzzlewit 25} A nurse hired for the month following the birth of a child.

moon-calf *Why didn't I say firmly, "You have no right to such secrets, and I demand of you to tell me what this means," instead of standing gaping at her, like an old moon-calf as I am!* {Barnaby Rudge 6} A congenital idiot.

moonshine ... *Mr. Casby had taken all the profits, all the ethereal vapor, and all the moonshine, as his share* ... {Little Dorrit 2-32} Foolish ideas and plans.

Moorish band ... *the place for dancing ready chalked for the company's feet--and a Moorish band playing at one end of the gardens* ... {Sketches, Miss Evans and the Eagle}

This may refer to bands that play a mixture of exotic music ranging from minstrel songs to westernized Oriental music.

morning-gown *He had exchanged his riding-coat for a handsome morning-gown, his boots for slippers* . . . {Barnaby Rudge 15}
A loose gown worn indoors before dressing for the evening.

morrice *"Now then! Morrice!* {Oliver Twist 8}
Slang for to hurry."

mortified bonnet *Again, the cocked hat and the mortified bonnet stand in the background at the marriage hour* . . . {Dombey & Son 31}
Meaning not clear. Could be 'abstemious' or 'not of the pleasures of the world', hence not attractive.

Mosaic Arab . . . *the friend of gentlemen, Mosaic Arabs and others, usually to be seen at races* . . . {Household Words, Gone Astray}
Mosaic does not refer to pictures made from pieces of stone, but to things relating to Moses. The word 'Arab' refers to Semites, hence the phrase simply means the Semitic people who followed the laws of Moses, or Jews.

moss-rose *When those learned gentlemen begin to raise moss-roses from the powder they sow in their wigs, I shall begin to be astonished too!* {Bleak House 60}
A small garden flower that grows low to the ground.

Mother-in-Law *"Wy, Sammy," said the father, "I han't seen you for two year and better." "Nor more you have, old codger," replied the son. "How's Mother-in-Law?"* {Pickwick Papers 20}
Used here incorrectly to mean stepmother. This incorrect usage was apparently common in the first part of the nineteenth century but has since disappeared.

motion . . . *he had only one brief and a motion . . . in twenty years* . . . {Oliver Twist 41}
1. An application to a court to obtain a ruling or court order.
Inspector Field's hand is the well-known hand that has collared half the

people here, and motioned their brothers, sisters, fathers, mothers, male and female friends, inexorably to New South Wales. {Reprinted Pieces, On Duty With Inspector Field}
2. In this example the word still has its legal meaning but, since the Inspector was not a lawyer, the motions were probably instigated, but not actually made, by Inspector Field.

mould-candle ... *put two mould-candles in the back parlour, and charge 'em to this gen'lm'n's account* ... {Sketches, A Passage in the Life of Mr. Watkins Tottle}
A candle made by pouring wax into a metal mold, as opposed to a dip-candle made by repeatedly dipping a wick into molten wax.

mountebank *Men who had lounged all night in smock-frocks and leather leggings, came out in silken vests and hats and plumes, as jugglers or mountebanks* ... {Old Curiosity Shop 19}
From 'mount-on-a-bench', an itinerant quack who sold pills and nostrums. A charlatan. Also, one who resorts to degrading means to obtain notoriety.

mourning brooch ... *Captain Cuttle again assumed his ankle-jacks and mourning brooch, and issued forth on his second expedition.* {Dombey & Son 17}
A brooch, usually made of black material such as jet and worn as a memorial to someone who has died.

mourning-ring ... *and twining her hands in his long black hair, tore therefrom about enough to make five or six dozen of the very largest-sized mourning-rings.* {Pickwick Papers 25}
A ring worn as a memorial to someone who has died. It could be made of any material, including braided hair.

mouth-organ ... *he breathed a hornpipe tune into that sweet musical instrument which is popularly termed a mouth-organ, without at all changing the mournful expression of the upper part of his face* ... {Old Curiosity Shop 37}
Harmonica.

move ... *he might have got into trouble if we hadn't made our lucky; that was the move, wasn't it Charley?* {Oliver Twist 18}
Slang for a trick or scheme.

moving panorama *Knowing Mr. Barlow to have invested largely in the moving panorama trade* ... {The Uncommercial Traveller, Mr. Barlow}
Large scenes painted on canvas wound on rollers which were slowly turned to provide motion to the painting.

mow *Florence she seldom sees, and when she does, is angry and mows at.* {Dombey & Son 41}
A grimace, especially one which is derisive.

mud-cart *Pitching somebody into a mud-cart* ... {Our Mutual Friend 4-16}
A two-wheeled vehicle for hauling mud, earth, or refuse.

mudlark *A compound of Newgate, Bedlam, a Debtors' Prison in the worst time, a chimney-sweep, a mudlark, and the Noble Savage!* {Tom Tiddler's Ground 1}
A gutter child, ragamuffin, also called, in Dickens' time, a street Arab. A young child who runs about the streets unsupervised.

muff *[Dando adds], in an undertone, to somebody by him, "Blowed if hever I see sich a set of muffs!"* ... {Sketches, The River}
An awkward, clumsy, impractical person.

muffin-bell ... *and then a muffin-bell rings, and the curtain drops.* {Sketches, Greenwich Fair}
A bell such as that rung by the muffin boy as he walked the streets selling muffins.

muffin boy, muffin youth ... *it considers the Muffin Boys, as presently constituted, wholly undeserving the confidence of the public* ... {Nicholas Nickleby 2}
... *the pot-boy, the muffin youth, and the baked-potato man.* {Pickwick Papers 32}
A boy who sells muffins.

muffin-cap . . . *seeing the new boy promoted to the black stick and hat-band, while he, the old one, remained stationary in the muffin-cap and leathers.* {Oliver Twist 6}
A flat, woolen cap, resembling in shape an English muffin, worn by charity school boys.

muffler *"Bedlam broke loose!" said Tackleton under his breath. "We shall arrive at the strait-waistcoat and mufflers soon."* {Cricket on the Hearth 2}
1. A cloth wrapped around the face to prevent someone from speaking. A kind of gag.
"Dinner-time, eh!" repeated Toby, using his right-hand muffler like an infantine boxing-glove, and punishing his chest for being cold. {The Chimes 1}
2. A glove or mitten.

mug *His mug is a fortun' to him.* {Oliver Twist 22}
Slang for face.

mull . . . *and whenever he misses him, yelps out "Mulled agin!" and tries to atone for the failure by taking more correct and vicious aim.* {Edwin Drood 5}
In sports, to fail at something. Here it means 'to miss a target'.

mumchance *Have they no liberty, no will, no right to speak? Are they obliged to sit mumchance, and to be ordered about till they are the laughing-stock of young and old?* {Barnaby Rudge 3}
Silent, dumb.

mummery . . . *there was a motley assemblage of feasting, laughing, talking, begging, gambling, and mummery.* {Nicholas Nickleby 50}
Dumb-show acting, miming.

mushroom-ketchup . . . *salt, vinegar, blacking, red-herrings, station-ery, lard, mushroom-ketchup, staylaces, loaves of bread* . . . {The Chimes 4}
Ketchup is a sauce made from the juice of a variety of foods, not just tomatoes. Walnut ketchup and mushroom ketchup were once popular.

music-desk *[The piano player] had got behind the bars of the piano music-desk, and there presented the appearance of a captive languishing in a rosewood jail.* {Our Mutual Friend 1-11}
A stand that holds sheet music.

musket *The heavy ringing of the musket-stocks upon the ground, and the sharp and rapid rattling of the ramrods in their barrels* . . . {Barnaby Rudge 57}
An early, infantry firearm with a smoothbore barrel. Originally it was fired by a matchlock. The stock of the weapon is the wooden piece that was placed against the shoulder.

must *The gloom, and must, and dust of the whole tenement* . . . {Little Dorrit 2-10}
Mold, mildew.

muster *I went up to the house you told me of, and got put upon the muster* . . . {Barnaby Rudge 40}
The muster roll, or list of soldiers. To put oneself on the muster is to enlist.

mute . . . *I once had the honor of being on intimate terms with a mute, who in private life and off duty was as comical and jocose a little fellow as ever chirped out a devil-may-care song* . . . {Pickwick Papers 29}
A hired mourner at a funeral.

nab *It makes you nervous, Bill--reminds you of being nabbed, does it?* {Oliver Twist 44}
Slang for to arrest or capture.

nail one's colors to the mast *"It is not to be supposed," [said Mr. Dombey]. (Mrs. Chick had nailed her colors to the mast, and repeated "I know it isn't," but he took no notice of it.)* {Dombey & Son 5}
To adopt an unyielding attitude. From the fact that a flag nailed to the mast could not be lowered in surrender.

nankeen *She has an extensive acquaintance at Bath among appalling old gentlemen with thin legs and nankeen trousers, and is of high standing in that dreary city.* {Bleak House 28}
A yellow cotton cloth.

natives *... his eyes rested on a newly-opened oyster-shop, on a magnificent scale, with natives laid, one deep, in circular marble basins in the window, together with little round barrels of oysters ...* {Sketches, The Misplaced Attachment of Mr. John Dounce}
An oyster reared in British waters, and mostly those reared in artificial beds. It usually meant a superior grade of oyster.

natural *... the lad's a natural, und can be got to do anything if you take him the right way.* {Barnaby Rudge 49}
1. Someone naturally deficient in intellect, a half-wit.
Let us understand each other; I see we may safely do so. What are these boys;--natural children? {Nicholas Nickleby 4}
2. Illegitimate.

Nature's Nobs *... the high principle that Nature's Nobs felt with Nature's Nobs, and true greatness of soul sympathized with true greatness of*

soul . . . {Martin Chuzzlewit 7}
A nob is a person of wealth or distinction. The implication here is that of persons born to those characteristics, but with some sarcasm.

navvy *Sometimes the "navvy" on tramp . . . will take a similar part in a job of excavation, and will look at it without engaging in it, until his money is all gone.* {The Uncommercial Traveller, Tramps}
A laborer who did work like ditch digging was called a navigator, and the word was shortened to navvy.

near cut . . . *the Metropolitan Representatives found it a near cut, and many other foot passengers followed their example.* {Sketches, Scotland-yard}
Short cut.

nearly . . . *it is only that you may hear something that has occurred: something very dreadful, Mr. Nickleby, which concerns you nearly.* {Nicholas Nickleby 60}
Closely. It does not mean 'almost'.

near sight . . . *with an awkward and hesitating manner; with a shambling walk, and with what is called a near sight* . . . {Edwin Drood 9}
Nearsightedness, myopia.

neat wine *Upon the bright green shutters [of the inn], there were golden legends about beer and ale, and neat wines, and good beds; and an affecting picture of a brown jug frothing over at the top.* {The Battle of Life 3}
Wine undiluted with water.

neck and crop . . . *we're going in neck and crop for fashion.* {Our Mutual Friend 1-15}
Completely, totally.

neckankecher . . . *your bereaved form was attired in a white neckankecher, and you was took on from motives of benevolence at The George and Gridiron, theatrical and supper.* {Somebody's Luggage 1}

Dialect for 'neck-handkerchief', a neckerchief or kerchief worn around the neck.

neck or nothing ... *he'll fill his wehicle with passengers, and start off in the middle of the road, neck or nothing, to the Devil!* {Martin Chuzzlewit 52}
A phrase that expresses willingness to take any risk.

negus *However, I could take some toast and some hot negus* ... {Bleak House 57}
A drink invented by Colonel Francis Negus, a mixture of wine, hot water, sugar, and flavoring.

nem. con. *Suffice it to say, that the single ladies unanimously voted him an angel, and that the married ones,* nem. con., *agreed that he was decidedly the finest baby they had ever beheld--except their own.* {Sketches, The Bloomsbury Christening}
An abbreviation of the Latin legal phrase *nemine contradicente* 'with no one contradicting'.

nervous *With such a well directed nervous blow, that down he went, as heavily and true as if a charge of a Life-Guardsman had tumbled him out of a saddle.* {Martin Chuzzlewit 52}
Vigorous, powerful.

netting *Mrs. Sparsit netting at the fire-side* ... {Hard Times 1-11}
Making a net from string. Small net bags and reticules were frequently homemade.

Newmarket *He imparted to her the mystery of going the odd man or plain Newmarket for fruit, ginger-beer, baked potatoes, or even a modest quencher* ... {Old Curiosity Shop 36}
A coin-tossing game, a heads-or-tails game.

Newmarket coat ... *round his neck he wore a flaming red worsted comforter, whereof the straggling ends peeped out beneath his threadbare Newmarket coat, which was very tight and buttoned all the way up.* {Nicholas Nickleby 29}
A close-fitting coat for men, originally worn for riding.

newsmonger ... *some officers of the jail who are waiting there, congratulate him in their rough way on his release. The newsmonger is of the number, but his manner is not quite hearty* ... {Old Curiosity Shop 68}
Someone who collects and sells news, but also, as used here, it may mean just a gossiper.

next day but one *There were the two sons of a man who lay under sentence of death, and who was to be executed along with three others, on the next day but one.* {Barnaby Rudge 63}
The day after the next day, the day after tomorrow.

nib *Shall it be a hard or a soft nib?* {Nicholas Nickleby 9}
The point of a pen.

nice question *I quite understand it to be a nice question.* {Tale of Two Cities 2-19}
Difficult to decide or settle, demanding close consideration or thought.

nigh *Which road are you takin'? We go the nighest.* {Old Curiosity Shop 17}
Near, most direct.

nightcap ... *she took out of her bundle a yellow nightcap, of prodigious size, in shape resembling a cabbage* ... {Martin Chuzzlewit 25}
1. A close-fitting head covering worn at night, usually while sleeping.
You'll never have the laugh at me, though, unless it's behind a nightcap. {Oliver Twist 15}
2. Slang for the cap placed on the head of someone about to be hanged.

night-cellar *The palace, the night-cellar, the jail, the mad-house* ... {Oliver Twist 46}
A cellar serving as a tavern for persons of the lowest class.

night-coach *But the night-coach had a punctual character, and it was time to join it at the office* ... {Martin Chuzzlewit 11}
A coach that traveled during the night.

night-house *The coach-stands in the larger thoroughfares are deserted; the night-houses are closed; and the chosen promenades of profli-*

gate misery are empty. {Sketches, The Streets--Morning}
A tavern which stays open all night.

night-porter ... *the gates are shut; and the night porter, a solemn warder with a mighty power of sleep, keeps guard in his lodge.* {Bleak House 32}
A porter who was supposed to stay awake at night, a sort of night watchman or night doorman.

ninepin ... *planted in her chair again, ready to be bowled down like a ninepin.* {Bleak House 21}
A bowling pin. Various bowling games used different numbers of pins, nine or ten being common.

Nixon *"Vell, now," said Sam, "you've been a-prophecyin' away wery fine, like a red-faced Nixon as the sixpenny books give picturs on."* {Pickwick Papers 43}
A writer named Nixon who made prophecies. He was called the Cheshire Prophet, and his books were popular in Dickens' time.

nob *"One for his nob!" said Gobler.* {Sketches, Mr. Minns and his Cousin}
In the card game cribbage, a jack of the same suit as the turned-up card. It counts one point.

Nobbs *Some tip-top "Nobbs" come down occasionally--even Dukes and Duchesses.* {Reprinted Pieces, Our English Watering-place}
People of high position in life. It is usually spelled with only one 'b'.

nobby ... *we are in fact what would be popularly called a nobby place.* {Reprinted Pieces, Our English Watering placc}
Fashionable or first class.

noggin ... *a slight lunch of a bushel of oysters, a dozen or so of bottled ale, and a noggin or two of whisky to close it up with.* {Pickwick Papers 49}
A quantity of whiskey, usually a quarter of a pint.

nonage *There was the interminable Sunday of his nonage; when his mother . . . would sit all day behind a bible . . .* {Little Dorrit 1-3}
The period in life of being underage, a minor.

nonce, for the nonce *then converting the parlour, for the nonce, into a private tiring room, she dressed her, with great care . . .* {Dombey & Son 6}
For the time being, temporarily.

noodle *I'd be a match for all noodles and all rogues . . .* {Great Expectations 15}
A simpleton.

noontide *It was high noontide, when two dusty men passed through his streets . . .* {Tale of Two Cities 2-15}
Noon, midday.

Norfolk Biffin (see **Biffin**)

nose-bag *I had scarcely had time to enjoy the coach and to think how like a straw yard it was, and yet how like a rag-shop, and to wonder why the horses nose-bags were kept inside . . .* {Great Expectations 20}
A canvas or leather bag containing feed, hung over the face of a horse so that it could eat while still hitched to a vehicle.

nose-gay *She had such an exquisite nosegay in her hand.* {Bleak House 17}
A bunch of flowers, especially sweet-smelling flowers.

Notary *"I am very glad of any cause, sir." said the Notary, "which procures me the honour of this visit."* {Old Curiosity Shop 38}
A notary public.

notch . . . *they notch in here--it's the best place in the whole field . . .* {Pickwick Papers 7}
1. To notch is to keep score. A notch is a run at cricket.
All-Muggleton had notched some fifty four while the score of the Dingley Dellers was as blank as their faces. {Pickwick Papers 7}
2. To score, succeed in getting a run at cricket.

notes of admiration *They require the additional aid of whole rows of notes of admiration* ... {Reprinted Pieces, Our Vestry}
Notes of exclamation, exclamation points.

note of hand ... *his dirty note of hand for a wretched sum payable on the occurrence of a certain event* ... {Our Mutual Friend 2-5}
A promissory note, an agreement to pay something.

nothing to say to someone ... *I had already had the honor of telling your son that I wished to have nothing whatever to say to him.* {Little Dorrit 1-20}
A euphemism for not intending to accept a proposal of marriage.

No-Thoroughfare *[Miss Tox's house] was in the dullest of No-Thoroughfares, rendered anxious and haggard by distant double knocks.* {Dombey & Son 7}
A street on which through traffic is not permitted, usually a dead-end street.

notice-board *Of course, they will be punished with the utmost rigour of the law, as notice-boards observe* ... {Hard Times 2-8}
A kind of bulletin board on which legal notices, police notices, and the like could be posted.

notorious *It was perfectly notorious to the assemblage that the largest body, which comprehended about two thirds of the whole, was designed for the attack on Newgate.* {Barnaby Rudge 63}
Obvious, conspicuous.

nurse ... *Mrs. Gabriel Parsons drank four glasses of port on the plea of being a nurse just then* ... {Sketches, A Passage in the Life of Mr. Watkins Tottle}
1. The implication is that Mrs. Parsons has an infant child and is breast-feeding. She uses this as an excuse to drink more wine than might be considered otherwise proper.
Then Caddy hung upon her father and nursed his cheek against hers as if he were some poor dull child in pain. {Bleak House 3}
2. To hold caressingly as a nurse does a child.

nursing *"They were all fine babies," said Mr. Lumbey. And Mr. Lumbey went on nursing the baby with a thoughtful look.* {Nicholas Nickleby 36}
Taking care of. Here it does not have the sense of breast feeding.

oaken ... *a couple of oaken presses that would have held the baggage of a small army* ... {Pickwick Papers 14}
Made of oak wood.

oakum ... *the boy opened the door and thrust in his head, which was like a bundle of badly-picked oakum.* {Old Curiosity Shop 5}
Pieces of rope, picked apart and used for stuffing into boat seams.

oakum head *I might have been assassinated three hours ago by that one-eyed monster with the oakum head.* {Sketches, The Great Winglebury Duel}
In the illustration by Cruikshank, the man being referred to, the boots, is shown with disheveled hair resembling oakum, but the phrase may imply a head filled with oakum.

obtain *"There is such a feeling sometimes, no doubt," I replied; "but I don't think it obtains to any great extent."* {Reprinted Pieces, Hunted Down}
To be prevalent.

objurgation *While the good lady was bestowing this objurgation on Mr. Ben Allen, Bob Sawyer and Mr. Pickwick had retired in close conversation to the inner room* ... {Pickwick Papers 48}
A sharp or severe rebuke.

occasion *Some of us at Tellson's are getting old, and we really can't be troubled out of the ordinary course without due occasion.* {Tale of Two Cities 2-21}
A set of circumstances requiring action.

ochre ... *pay your ochre at the door* ... {Hard Times 1-6}
Money. Ochre is a yellow-colored pigment, sometimes the color of gold.

octavo ... *carried under their arms goodly octavos, with a red label behind* ... {Pickwick Papers 34}
A book in octavo, i.e., one in which the leaves are one-eighth the full-sized sheet on which it was printed.

odd man *He imparted to her the mystery of going the odd man or plain Newmarket for fruit, ginger-beer, baked potatoes, or even a modest quencher* ... {Old Curiosity Shop 36}
A coin-tossing game for three players. The odd man either wins or loses, that having been decided in advance.

odd-or-even ... *the idlest boys, who, growing bolder with impunity, waxed louder and more daring; playing odd-or-even under the masters eye, eating apples openly and without rebuke* ... {Old Curiosity Shop 25}
A children's game. One player holds either one or two objects in one hand, the other guesses the number of objects.

odds ... *It only brought him Wexation [said Mr. Chivery.] "How vexation, Chivery?" "No odds," returned Mr. Chivery. "Never mind ... "*
{Little Dorrit 1-19}
'No odds', or 'it makes no odds', means 'it makes no difference', 'it doesn't matter'.

offer *[The cat would]* ... *never offer at the birds when I was here unless I told her to it.* {Bleak House 14}
Make an attempt to do violence.

off-hand ... *but his 'prentice: which is a very clever lad: sent 'em some medicine in a blacking bottle, off-hand.* {Oliver Twist 5}
At once, without deliberation or preparation.

Officier de l'Octroi *No article liable to local duty have I with me, Monsieur l'Officier de l'Octroi* ... {The Uncommercial Traveller, The Calais Night Mail}

The octroi was a tax on goods brought into a city, a sort of municipal import duty.

office *The fact is, that there was considerable difficulty in inducing Oliver to take upon himself the office of respiration* ... {Oliver Twist 1}
1. The operation of a bodily or mental function, the proper action of an organ or faculty.
Then Mr. Boffin, with his stick at his ear, like a Familiar spirit explaining the office to him, sat staring at a little bookcase of Law Practice and Law Reports ... {Our Mutual Friend 1-8}
2. Position or job.
... he had with pains gradually worked the boy into his own school, and procured him some offices to discharge there, which were repaid with food and lodging. {Our Mutual Friend 2-1}
3. Duties, work.

office-candle *So they both stood at the stair-head with a pair of office-candles watching him down.* {The Battle of Life 2}
The candles kept in the office, apparently not of any special kind.

oil-cake *... and a thick crust upon the pavement like oil-cake* ... {Martin Chuzzlewit 8}
The thick mass of compressed seeds (linseeds, cottonseeds) remaining after the oil has been extracted by pressing them.

oil-skin *... his whole apparel shone so with the wet that it might have been mistaken for a full suit of prepared oil-skin.* {Pickwick Papers 51}
Cloth made waterproof by treating it with oil.

old Brown *He ordered a bottle of old Brown. I likewise ordered a bottle of old Brown.* {Somebody's Luggage 4}
Old porter, beer.

Old Clem *There was a song Joe used to hum fragments of at the forge, of which the burden was Old Clem. This was not a very ceremonious way of rendering homage to a patron saint, but I believe Old Clem stood in that relation towards smiths.* {Great Expectations 12}
As the context indicates, Old Clem (St. Clemens) is the patron saint of

blacksmiths. Many chants that invoked the saint were sung by black-smiths at their work.

Old Parr ... *Mr. Toots saying aloud to Mr. Feeder, B.A., "How are you, Feeder?" and asking him to come and dine with him to-day at the Bedford, in right of which feats he might set up as Old Parr if he chose, unquestioned.* {Dombey & Son 41}
Thomas Parr was supposed to have lived from 1483 to 1635, making him the longest lived Englishman ever. Modern medical knowledge makes the story highly unlikely. Nevertheless, Mr. Toots seemed of very great age to be able to address Mr. Feeder so informally.

old-story *Come, come! You alarm yourself with old-story fears, mother.* {Bleak House 58}
Folk tales.

omnibus ... *meeting from the window the eyes of turnpike-men, omnibus-drivers, and others* ... {Old Curiosity Shop 47}
A horse-drawn bus, often having seats on the roof.

once in a way *If the old girl fires wide--once in a way--at the call of duty--look over it, George. For she's loyal!* {Bleak House 34}
Rarely, exceptionally, once in a while.

one-pair ... *a married daughter who had bestowed her hand upon a non-resident waiter, who occupied the one-pair of some number in some street closely adjoining to some brewery somewhere* ... {Pickwick Papers 47}
Up one flight of stairs, i.e., in Great Britain on the first floor, in the United States on the second floor.

opposite ... *the thoroughfares about the market-place being filled with* ... *huckster's wares of every opposite description and possible variety of character.* {Martin Chuzzlewit 5}
Contrasting.

opposition ... *he would deduct this half-holiday from his weekly charge, or of course he would naturally expect to have an opposition started against him* ... {Old Curiosity Shop 25}

1. Inquisition or inquiry.

. . . the place for dancing ready chalked for the company's feet--and a Moorish band playing at one end of the gardens--and an opposition military band playing away at the other. {Sketches, Miss Evans and the Eagle}

2. Competing or contrasting, used by Dickens in both senses.

opposition coach *"The opposition coach contracts for these two; and takes them cheap," said Mr. Bumble. "They are both in a very low state, and we find it would come two pound cheaper to move 'em than to bury 'em . . .* {Oliver Twist 17}

Apparently a coach line. Hayward's *Dickens Encyclopedia* has a drawing of a race between the Oxford and Opposition coaches.

oppressed *. . . tall steeples looming in the air, and piles of unequal roofs oppressed by chimneys . . .* {Barnaby Rudge 3}

Weighed down.

orchestrina *By day, are there no Punches, Fantoccinis, Dancing-dogs, Jugglers, Conjurers, Orchestrinas, or even Barrel-organs?* {American Notes, 6}

A musical instrument designed to imitate the sounds of a variety of instruments and thus sound like a whole orchestra.

order of the garter *Shall I be a convict in a felt hat and a grey suit, trotting about a dockyard with my number neatly embroidered on my uniform, and the order of the garter on my leg . . .* {Old Curiosity Shop 34}

An iron shackle around the ankle. A wry analogy with the insignia of *The Most Noble Order of the Garter*, a club for the king and a limited number of noble knights who wore a garter on the calf as a sign of honor. The garter is a band of cloth originally worn around the upper calf or thigh to hold up a stocking.

orders *. . . how he well remembered that they had been to the play with orders on the very night previous, and had seen Romeo and Juliet, and the pantomime . . .* {Sketches, The Very Friendly Young Gentleman}

An admission pass to a theater, either free or at reduced price. The word is used in the same sense in chapter 2 of *Nicholas Nickleby*.

ordinary ... *dressed in the newest fashion, and damning the ordinary with unspeakable gallantry and grace* ... {Barnaby Rudge 16}
1. The local ordinary is that church official who has local jurisdiction. Here Dickens is referring to the church official in charge of the New-gate prison, the Chaplain.
It is the long vacation in the regions of Chancery Lane. The good Ships Law and Equity, those teak-built, copper-bottomed, iron-fastened, bra-zen-faced, and not by any means fast-sailing clippers are laid up in ordinary. {Bleak House 19}
2. The phrase 'in ordinary', applied to a ship, means 'out of commission'.
The ladies had a smaller ordinary of their own, to which their husbands and brothers were admitted if they chose ... {Martin Chuzzlewit 21}
3. A dining room, especially in an inn or tavern. Early British and American restaurants could be called 'ordinaries'.

ordinary room *There was a little cloister outside, and from that shel-tered place he knew he could look in at the window of their ordinary room, and see who was within.* {The Haunted Man 2}
The dining hall of the college (see definition 3 in the entry above).

organ *"I generally do it on gin and water." "Keeps the organ moist, does it, Wegg?"* {Our Mutual Friend 1-5}
The human organs of speech or voice.

organ of benevolence ... *[he] laughed all over himself, from his shoes to his organ of benevolence; and called out in a comfortable, oily, rich, fat, jovial voice* ... {A Christmas Carol 2}
From phrenology, a pseudoscience that associated bumps on the skull with functions of the brain beneath and assumed that part of the brain was an organ of thieving, an organ of representation, and so on. This spirit would have had a very well-developed organ of benevolence.

organ, mouth organ ... *whistling as he went along several of the most popular airs of the day, as arranged with entirely new movements for that noble instrument the organ, either mouth or barrel.* {Pickwick Papers 35}
The mouth organ is a harmonica. A barrel organ is operated by a crank

that turns a cylinder, or barrel, having projecting plugs to perform the function of keys.

oriel window ... *remains of oriel windows, and fragments of blackened walls, were yet standing* ... {Old Curiosity Shop 46}
Here it means stained-glass windows. It can refer to the window of the oriel, a recess on an upper story, projecting from the wall of a building.

originate *But I don't know how to originate, in such a case.* {Tale of Two Cities 2-19}
Begin.

ormolu clock *She also benignantly intimated to him, aloud, the nature of the objects upon which he looked ... "An aviary, George," "An ormolu clock, George," and the like.* {Our Mutual Friend 4-16}
A clock made of gilded bronze, or a bronze alloy with a color resembling gold.

ornamental painter *A friend of Miss Martin's who had long been keeping company with an ornamental painter and decorator's journeyman, at last consented ... to name the day* ... {Sketches, The Mistaken Milliner}
One who paints decorations on carriages, furniture, moldings, and the like.

ornamental stationer ... *Miss Knag's brother, who was an ornamental stationer and small circulating library keeper* ... {Nicholas Nickleby 18}
A stationer who sold fancy writing paper and writing materials. This occupation apparently often coincided with that of bookseller.

osier ... *ashore among the osiers, or tramping amidst mud and stakes and jagged stones in low-lying places* ... {Edwin Drood 15}
Osier is a kind of willow, grown to be used in basket making.

ostler ... *at a public house where some of Rouncewell's hands are dining, as the ostler tells him.* {Bleak House 63}
A man who attends to the horses at an inn, a hostler.

ottoman *Mrs. Boffin seated Bella on the large ottoman* ... {Our Mutual Friend 4-13}
A cushion seat without arms, sides, or back.

otto of roses *There was a shop to the house, but it was let off to an importer of otto of roses* ... {Nicholas Nickleby 10}
Attar of roses, the fragrant essence of roses.

ought *Two times ought's an ought, and twice five ten, and there's a hundred of 'em.* {The Haunted Man 1}
Naught, or zero.

out-at-elbows ... *Mr. Tapley, who entertained a constitutional dislike to gentlemen out-at-elbows who flourished on false pretences* ... {Martin Chuzzlewit 7}
With the elbows showing through worn-out clothing. The implication is that of one who had descended to poverty.

out of countenance *Even Dolly* ... *was put quite out of countenance* ... {Barnaby Rudge 27}
Out of sorts, annoyed.

out of drawing ... *though the proportions of St. Paul's Cathedral are very beautiful, it had an air of being somewhat out of drawing, in my eyes.* {The Uncommercial Traveller, On an Amateur Beat}
Incorrectly drawn, especially with incorrect perspective.

out of hand ... *time was beginning to press now, and it really must be got out of hand.* {David Copperfield 17}
No longer in process, done with.

out of my time *I was born nigh London, but have worked in a shop at Birmingham* ... *almost ever since I was out of my time.* {Reprinted Pieces, A Poor Man's Tale of a Patent}
Having completed an apprenticeship, having put in the required time as an apprentice.

out of number ... *the study with its pictures and easy chairs, and odd cabinets, and queer tables, and books out of number* ... {Pickwick

Papers 57}
Out in the sense of beyond the limits, hence beyond the limits of numbers, innumerable, uncountable.

out of place *It was a clumsy specimen [of boxing] (executed by two English grooms out of place)* {The Uncommercial Traveller, Travelling Abroad}
Without a job, said of servants.

out of temper *You're not out of temper, I hope?* {Martin Chuzzlewit 7}
Angry.

out-door apprentice ... *when the out-door apprentices ring us up in the morning* ... *and I see them standing on the door-step with their little pumps under their arms, I am actually reminded of the Sweeps.* {Bleak House 38}
An apprentice who lived at home and came to the workplace during the day.

out upon *Out upon merry Christmas! What's Christmas time to you but a time for paying bills without money* ... {A Christmas Carol 1}
Expresses abhorrence or reproach, as does 'fie upon'.

out-dacious, outdacity *That out-dacious Oliver has demogalized them all!* {Oliver Twist 17}
... *in case he offered any outdacity of that description, we could express our sentiments in the English language* ... {Martin Chuzzlewit 43}
Corruption of audacious, audacity.

out-pensioner ... *and as he made it a preliminary condition that Mrs. Jiniwin should be thenceforth an out-pensioner, they lived together after marriage with no more than the average amount of quarreling* ... {Old Curiosity Shop 73}
Someone given a pension but who resides elsewhere.

outhouse ... *in the rough outhouses of some tillers of the heavy lands adjacent to Paris, there were sheltered from the weather that very day, rude carts, bespattered with rustic mire* ... {Tale of Two Cities 1-1}

A house or building near the main house, used for some special purpose. Includes barns, stables, wash-houses, and the like. Does not specifically mean a toilet facility.

outsides *The outsides did as outsides always do. They were very cheerful and talkative at the beginning of every stage, and very dismal and sleepy in the middle* . . . {Pickwick Papers 35}
The outside passengers on a coach, those who rode on the open seats.

overalls . . . *a hairy cap and fustian overalls* . . . {Pickwick Papers 33}
Loose-fitting trousers worn over regular ones to protect against dirt. Fustian is a kind of coarse cloth.

overing *Playing at leapfrog with the tombstones:* . . . *'overing' the highest among them* . . . {Pickwick Papers 29}
To clear, in jumping over something.

overlook *He saw many visitors, overlooked a number of documents; went in and out, to and from, sundry places of mercantile resort* . . . {Dombey & Son 46}
1. Peruse or read, look over.
. . . *Miss Sally put the meat away and locked the safe, and then drawing near to the small servant, overlooked her while she finished the potatoes.* {Old Curiosity Shop 36}
2. Oversee, supervise.

overlooker . . . *defining the duties he sought to undertake as those of a general superintendent, or manager, or overlooker* . . . {Our Mutual Friend 1-15}
One who superintends or watches over.

overnight *He had played very well, and sung very well, overnight.* {No Thoroughfare 6}
On the preceding evening.

over-proof *Show us the best--the very best--the over-proof that you keep for your own drinking, Jack!* {Barnaby Rudge 54}
Liquor containing a higher percentage of alcohol than usual.

over-reach *Old Arthur, however, was so intent upon his own designs, that he suffered himself to be over-reached, and had no suspicion but that his good friend was in earnest.* {Nicholas Nickleby 47}
To outwit, even to cheat.

overset *A very small measure will overset him; he may be bowled off his unsteady legs with a half-pint pot.* {Little Dorrit 1-31}
Overturn, upset. When said of a boat or raft it means 'capsize'.

over-swinging lamp *The postilion cracked his whip, and they clattered away under the feeble over-swinging lamps.* {Tale of Two Cities 1-6}
Street lamps, hung from a projecting iron bar, which swung from their attachments overhead in the streets.

over the left *... and then each gentleman pointed with his right thumb over his left shoulder. This action, imperfectly described by the very feeble term of 'over the left'... has a very graceful and airy effect...* {Pickwick Papers 42}
A gesture indicating disbelief or incredulity.

over-top *Bar's interest in apples was so over-topped by the rapt suspense with which he pursued the changes of these pears...* {Little Dorrit 2-12}
To exceed.

own *She said you never tired; or never owned that you tired.* {The Chimes 3}
To admit that something is true.

Oxford mixture *... I am not at all shabby, having always a very good suit of black on (or rather Oxford mixture, which has the appearance of black and wears much better)...* {The Poor Relation's Story}
A dark-grey wool cloth, also called Oxford grey or pepper and salt.

packet, packet ship *Murdstone and Grinby's trade was among a good many kinds of people, but an important branch of it was the supply of wines and spirits to certain packet ships* . . . {David Copperfield 11}
A ship that sails between ports on a regular schedule to carry goods, passengers, and mail. Before the packets, ships would wait before sailing for days or weeks until they had acquired a full load of cargo.

packthread *His shoes were newly greased, and ornamented with a pair of rusty buckles; the packthread at his knees had been renewed; and where he wanted buttons he wore pins.* {Barnaby Rudge 69}
A stout thread or twine used for sewing up or tying packs or bundles.

paddle-box . . . *buttoning my pea-coat, and standing in the shadow of the paddle-box, stood as upright as I could, and made the best of it.* {Reprinted Pieces, The Ghost of Art}
The structure enclosing the upper part of the paddle wheel of an early steamboat.

pad the hoof *Charley Bates expressed his opinion that it was time to pad the hoof.* {Oliver Twist 9}
Slang for to go on foot.

paddles . . . *a great steam ship, beating the water in short impatient strokes with her heavy paddles* . . . {Old Curiosity Shop 5}
The paddle wheel of an early steam ship.

paid . . . *your tropical hat, strongly paid outside and paper-lined inside* . . . {Message From the Sea 1}
A nautical term meaning made waterproof by being smeared with pitch, tar, tallow, or the like.

painted tops *Mr. Samuel Weller happened to be at that moment engaged in burnishing a pair of painted tops, the personal property of a farmer*... {Pickwick Papers 10}
Top boots. It is not clear whether they were painted as decoration or only to color them.

paint *Nothing... can paint my misery. It is well deserved, but nothing can paint it.* {Martin Chuzzlewit 48}
Describe in words. It does not have the meaning here of making a picture.

pair (see **two-pair, chariot and pair**)

pal *"Who's t'other one?" "A new pal,"replied Jack Dawkins, pulling Oliver forward.* {Oliver Twist 8}
Slang for accomplice.

palanquin ...*teeming with... tigers, elephants, howdahs, hookahs, umbrellas, palm trees, palanquins, and gorgeous princes of a brown complexion*... {Dombey & Son 4}
A covered conveyance for one person, consisting of a box with slats for sides and carried by two or more men.

pale ... *I do not believe any mortal (unless he had put himself without the pale of hope) would deliberately drain a goblet of the waters of Lethe, if he had it in his power.* {Nicholas Nickleby 6}
The limit or boundary.

paling ... *staves roughly plucked from fence and paling*... {Barnaby Rudge 63}
A fence made of pales, vertical slats of wood. Also, the pales themselves.

pall *His legs, too, were encased in coffin plates as though in armour; and over his left shoulder he wore a short dusky cloak which seemed made of a remnant of some pall.* {Nicholas Nickleby 6}
The cloth spread over a coffin.

palladium *Other dispersed fragments of the same great palladium are*

the baths of Germany, and sprinkled on the sea-sand all over the
English coast. {Bleak House 19}
Anything which gives protection to a nation or group. Here it refers to
judges and lawyers, with at least a hint of sarcasm.

pallet bed ... *there was nothing else in the garret but a pallet bed...* {Tale
of Two Cities 1-6}
A straw bed or mattress.

palsy *His limbs were shaking with disease, and the palsy had fastened on*
his mind. {Pickwick Papers 42}
Palsy refers to neurological diseases in which there is impairment of
motor activity and usually tremors. Here the meaning is figuratively
applied to the mind in the sense of impairment and powerlessness.

pannier ... *Mrs. Gamp transferred them to her own pocket, which was*
a species of nankeen pannier. {Martin Chuzzlewit 29}
A large basket, usually carried in pairs by a beast of burden.

pannikin ... *the bright tin pots and pannikins upon the dresser shelves...*
{Bleak House 27}
A small metal drinking vessel.

pantaloon ... *Let us at once confess to a fondness for pantomimes--to a*
gentle sympathy with clowns and pantaloons--to an unqualified admira-
tion of harlequins and columbines--to a chaste delight in every action of
their brief existence ... {Sketches, The Pantomime of Life}
1. A character in the Harlequinade depicting an old man wearing
glasses, long trousers, and slippers. He was the butt of the clown's
jokes.
... *Mr. Crummles, after pretending that he thought he must have lost it,*
produced a square inch of newspaper from the pocket of the panta-
loons he wore in private life ... {Nicholas Nickleby 48}
2. Tight-fitting trousers with a strap which went under the boot. The
name is derived from the trousers worn by the character Pantaloon.

Pantechnicon (see **London Pantechnicon**)

pantomime-light ... *I saw her look towards his infernal red lamp with the pantomime-light.* {Oliver Twist 14}
A red light at night indicated a surgeon's establishment. Pantomimes were extravagant theatrical performances. Impressive lighting effects were part of the performance, and a wide variety of lamps and light sources were used. The reference here may be to the surgeon's light being unusually bright or in some way resembling the lights of a pantomime.

pap-boat ... *a pair of pattens, a toasting-fork, a kettle, a pap-boat, a spoon for the administration of medicine to the refractory* ... {Martin Chuzzlewit 49}
A boat-shaped dish for holding pap, the semiliquid food fed to infants.

paper cigar *He lighted another of his paper cigars* ... {Little Dorrit 1-1}
A cigarette.

paper of *After supper, another jug of punch was put upon the table, together with a paper of cigars and a couple of bottles of spirits.* {Pickwick Papers 32}
A packet of objects wrapped in paper.

papers *It was such a stupendous thing to know for certain that she put her hair in papers.* {David Copperfield 44}
Curl papers, pieces of paper around which the hair was rolled to form curls.

parachute *The balloon ascents of last season. Let me reckon them up. There were the horse, the bull, the parachute, and the tumbler hanging on--chiefly by his toes, I believe--below the car.* {Reprinted Pieces, Lying Awake}
Exhibitions of hot air balloons often included aerial acrobatics, taking animals aloft, and parachute jumping.

parapet ... *looking up he could just discern the face of Gride himself, cautiously peering over the house parapet from the window of the garret.* {Nicholas Nickleby 59}
A low wall at the edge of the roof.

parasol-head_ ... *and in a corner little Mellows's perambulator, with even its parasol-head turned despondently to the wall.* {The Uncommercial Traveller, An Old Stage-coaching House}
A folding top shaped like a parasol or umbrella. A perambulator is a baby carriage.

parchment-grease *The confined room, strong of parchment-grease, is warehouse, counting-house, and copying-office.* {Bleak House 10}
Parchment is actually the skin of sheep and, when new, smells of sheep fat.

parish dress *The scanty parish dress: the livery of his misery: hung loosely on his feeble body* ... {Oliver Twist 17}
The clothing issued to paupers as a form of charity by the parish.

park *[The old red brick house] that fifteen or twenty years ago stood in a park five times as broad* ... {Barnaby Rudge 1}
A large piece of ground attached to and surrounding a country house.

park-fence *He would on the whole admit nature to be a good idea (a little low, perhaps, when not enclosed with a park-fence)* ... {Bleak House 2}
The fence around the park when the park is small enough to be enclosed (see **park**).

Parliamentary *I came forty mile by Parliamentary this morning, and I'm going back the same forty mile this afternoon.* {Hard Times 1-12}
An act of Parliament required that every railroad company daily run one train both ways on its track at a price not to exceed one penny a mile. Poorer people took advantage of that once-a-day run of the Parliamentary train.

parliamentary return ... *if he had been required* ... *to tick her off into columns in a parliamentary return, he would have quite known how to divide her.* {Hard Times 1-14}
The official report and tabulation of the results of a parliamentary election, the election return.

parlour-boarder *We remember an idiotic goggle-eyed boy... who suddenly appeared as a parlour-boarder, and was rumoured to have come by sea from some mysterious part of the earth where his parents rolled in gold.* {Reprinted Pieces, Our School}
A privileged pupil in a boarding school who lived with the headmaster's family.

part *Her friend parted his breakfast--a scanty mess of coffee and some coarse bread--with the child and her grandfather...* {Old Curiosity Shop 44}
To share.

particular *"Oh, dear no, miss," he said. "This is a London particular." I had never heard of such a thing. "A fog, miss," said the young gentleman.* {Bleak House 3}
Belonging to a specified person or thing, not general. Here it has the sense of something specific to London.

particularize *"Would eight at a friendly dinner at all put you out, Ma?" "Nine would... " "My dear Ma, I particularize eight."* {Edwin Drood 6}
To speak specifically of something.

party-wall *... there's an excellent party-wall between this house and the next...* {Dombey & Son 3}
A shared wall, shared by two buildings or two plots of land.

passenger *The streets were as yet nearly free from passengers, the houses and shops were closed, and the healthful air of morning fell like breath from angels, on the sleeping town.* {Old Curiosity Shop 12}
1. Short for foot passenger, a person walking.
... the night coach changing horses--the passengers cheerless, cold, ugly, and discontented, with three months' growth of hair in one night... {Old Curiosity Shop 46}
2. Someone riding in a vehicle.

paste *... on all great holiday occasions it was his habit to exchange his plain steel knee-buckles for a pair of glittering paste...* {Barnaby Rudge 4}
A glass used in making imitations of precious stones.

pasteboard ... *a fusty castle made of pasteboard* ... {David Copperfield 5}
A cheaper form of cardboard, made by pasting together sheets of paper of lower quality.

pastile *He took the shovel from the grate, sprinkled a few live ashes on it, and from a box on the chimney-piece took a few pastiles, which he set upon them* ... {Our Mutual Friend 3-10}
A lozenge of aromatic material meant to be burned for fumigation.

pat *"You're in spirits, Tugby my dear." "No. Not particular. I'm a little elewated. The muffins came so pat."* {The Chimes 4}
Exactly suited to a purpose.

patent-leather ... *and rearing like a horse in heraldry; the plated harness and the patent-leather glittered in the sun* ... {Martin Chuzzlewit 27}
An artificial leather made by a patented process, having a very glossy surface.

Patent place ... *so we have got him at home again; and we have bought him a little Patent place, which agrees with him much better.* {David Copperfield 36}
A position to which one is appointed by letters patent, a document issued by the sovereign conferring an office or privilege.

patent theatre *And why* ... *were they not engaged at one of the patent theatres?* {Sketches, The Mistaken Milliner}
A legitimate theater, authorized by letters patent, a document issued by the sovereign conferring an office or privilege.

patten ... *and carrying a basket like the Great Seal of England in plaited straw, a pair of pattens, a spare shawl, and an umbrella.* {Great Expectations 13}
A kind of overshoe, consisting of a wooden sole with a metal ring attached to the undersurface, held on with straps like sandal straps. Used for walking in muddy streets.

patten rings ... *the water being uncomfortably cold, and in that slippy, slushy, sleety sort of state wherein it seems to penetrate through every*

kind of substance, patten rings included . . . {Cricket on the Hearth 1}
The metal ring attached to the under surface of the wooden sole of a
patten, which elevated it above the ground (see **patten**).

pattern   *"A little formal," observes the elder brother, refolding [the
letter] with a puzzled face. "But nothing that might not be sent to a
pattern young lady?" asks the younger.* {Bleak House 63}
Model. The sense here is that of a person who is a model of behavior.

paunch trade   *What between the buryin' ground, the grocer's, the
stables, and the paunch trade, the Marshalsea flies get very large.*
{Little Dorrit 1-6}
To paunch is to eviscerate. The paunch trade refers to the butcher's
trade in internal organs, especially tripe.

pauper-nurse   *My breast is softer than the pauper-nurse's; death in my
arms is peacefuller than among the pauper-wards.* {Our Mutual
Friend 3-8}
One who acts as a nurse to paupers.

pauper-ward   *My breast is softer than the pauper-nurse's; death in my
arms is peacefuller than among the pauper-wards.* {Our Mutual
Friend 3-8}
The bedroom in a shelter for paupers, which contained a number of
beds. It was usually very much overcrowded.

paviour, paviour's rammer   *. . . in his grievous distress he utters enforced
sounds like a paviour's rammer.* {Bleak House 26}
A paviour is one who paves streets and roads. His rammer is a heavy
length of wood or log used to pound the earth or the paving stones.

pay-place   *. . . the ferocious growling of Mim down below in the
pay-place . . .* {Doctor Marigold 2}
The box office of a theater, where tickets were purchased. It can also
mean the place or office where payment of wages was made.

pea and thimble   *Here a little knot gathered round a pea and thimble
table to watch the plucking of some unhappy greenhorn . . .* {Nicholas
Nickleby 50}

A cheating, gambling game. The operator places a pea under one of three thimbles which he then quickly moves around. The player bets on where the pea is to be found, but the operator is able to move the pea from under the thimbles without it being seen.

pea-coat *The weather-beaten pea-coat, and a no less weather-beaten cap and comforter*... {Dombey & Son 56}
A pea jacket (described below).

peach *Staunch to the last!... Never peached upon old Fagin!* {Oliver Twist 9}
Slang for to turn informer.

pea-jacket ... *the young gentleman wore over his kilt a man's pea-jacket reaching to his ankles*... {Old Curiosity Shop 17}
A stout, short coat of heavy wool worn by sailors.

peal of bells ... *the miser who had disowned his only child and left a sum of money to the church to buy a peal of bells*... {Old Curiosity Shop 54}
A set of bells tuned to one another.

pease-pudding *Salt meat and new rum; pease-pudding and chaff-biscuits.* {Nicholas Nickleby 22}
Peas cooked in a crust, similar to a dumpling (see **pudding**).

peck ... *the serving of the 'peck' was the affair of a moment; it merely consisting in the handing down of a capacious baking dish with three-fourths of an immense meat pie in it*... {Our Mutual Friend 4-7}
Slang for food.

peculate ... *he had really risen with his opportunities; and peculating on a grander scale, had become a grander man, altogether.* {Martin Chuzzlewit 27}
To embezzle public money.

peculiar *Standing on one side of his own peculiar fire (for there are two)*... {Bleak House 28}
Belonging to one person.

peculiarly ... *reminding her of the necessity of being peculiarly smart on the occasion, so as to counterbalance Miss La Creevy* ... {Nicholas Nickleby 63}
Especially, more than usually.

pedestrian *Their legs are so hard* ... *that they must have devoted the greater part of their* ... *lives* ... *to pedestrian exercises and the walking of matches.* {Bleak House 49}
The current meaning may be a person who walks, but in the nineteenth century, both in the United States and England, pedestrianism meant running in foot races, and the racers were called pedestrians.

pedestrian excursions ... *in the summer vacations he used to take pedestrian excursions with a knapsack* ... {Reprinted Pieces, Our School}
Walking tours, hikes.

peep-bo ... *small restless eyes that kept winking and twinkling* ... *as if they were playing a perpetual game of peep-bo* ... {Pickwick Papers 10}
Variation of peek-bo, or peek-a-boo.

peg away *Why should a grandson and grandfather peg away at each other* ... {Old Curiosity Shop 2}
Continually argue and fight.

peg-top ... *a motley collection of peg-tops, balls, kites, fishing-lines, marbles, half-eaten apples* ... {Old Curiosity Shop 24}
A wooden top with a metal peg as a point. A child's toy.

pelerine ... *would you object to putting your arm round me under my pelerine?* {Little Dorrit 2-9}
A woman's cape, one which covered the shoulders and had long ends coming down to a point in front.

pelisse ... *the young lady too was muffled in an old cloth pelisse and had a handkerchief tied about her head.* {Old Curiosity Shop 17}
A woman's outer garment, of various materials, usually ankle length.

pell-mell ... *bearing down the dry twigs and boughs and withered leaves, and carrying them away pell-mell* ... {Old Curiosity Shop 69}
Mingled in disorder.

pembroke-table *Nicholas and the infant phenomenon opposed each other at the pembroke-table, and Smike and the master Crummleses dined on the sofa bedstead.* {Nicholas Nickleby 23}
A table having two wings which can be swung up and supported by rails that extend from beneath the top.

penknife *He has blunted the blade of his penknife and broken the point off by sticking that instrument into his desk in every direction.* {Bleak House 20}
A pocketknife used for shaping the points on quill pens.

penn'orth *Bring me three penn'orth of rum, my dear.* {Pickwick Papers 55}
A penny's worth.

pennyweight ... *poor Mercantile Jack is having his brain slowly knocked out by pennyweights, on board the brig Beelzebub, or the barque Bowie-knife* ... {The Uncommercial Traveller, Poor Mercantile Jack}
Originally, the actual weight of a penny; it came to mean a trivial weight, a small fraction of an ounce.

pennywinkle *I may be very fond of pennywinkles, Mrs. Richards, but it don't follow that I'm to have 'em for tea.* {Dombey & Son 3}
Dialect for periwinkle, an edible mollusk or shellfish.

penthouse ... *Joe* ... *was protecting himself and the horse from the rain under the shelter of an old penthouse roof.* {Barnaby Rudge 2}
A shed having a sloping roof. It does not refer to an apartment on top of a building.

people of condition (see **condition**)

pepper and salt ... *decent pantaloons of pepper and salt* ... {Our Mutual Friend 2-1}

A kind of cloth woven from dark and light wool and showing dots of dark and light color.

pepper-castor *I mean to blot it a good deal and shake some water over it out of the pepper-castor, to make it look penitent.* {Old Curiosity Shop 8}
Pepper shaker.

perambulator . . . *and in a corner little Mellows's perambulator, with even its parasol-head turned despondently to the wall.* {The Uncommercial Traveller, An Old Stage-coaching House}
A perambulator is a baby carriage. The parasol-head is a folding top shaped like a parasol or umbrella.

periwig . . . *his horse was as smooth and cool as his own iron-grey periwig and pigtail.* {Barnaby Rudge 10}
A wig. The word 'wig' is a shortening of the word 'periwig'.

perquisition . . . *heaps of flies, who were extending their inquisitive and adventurous perquisitions into all the glutinous little glasses* . . . {Tale of Two Cities 2-16}
A thorough or diligent search.

personate *This gentleman, who personated the bride's father...* {Nicholas Nickleby 25}
Personify, in the theatrical sense. To act a part.

perspective . . . *gazing into the blaze* . . . *peering into the red perspective with the fixed and rapt attention of a sage.* {Dombey & Son 8}
1. A scene or view.
There were the Smiths, the Gubbinses, the Nixons, the Dixons, the Hicksons, people with all sorts of names, two aldermen, a sheriff in perspective, Sir Thomas Glumper . . . {Sketches, Mrs. Joseph Porter}
2. 'In perspective' means 'in expectation', thus, in this example, 'one who expects to become a sheriff'.

perspective-glass *If a girl, doll or no doll, swoons within a yard or two of a man's nose, he can see it without a perspective-glass.* {Tale of Two Cities 2-5}

A lorgnette, a kind of eyeglass. Instead of having temple pieces to keep it on the face, it is held in front of the eyes with a short handle.

perspiration ... *and do not be so energetic, for it will only put you into a perspiration and do no good whatever*... {Pickwick Papers 47} Sweat.

persuader *"The persuaders?"* *"I've got em,"* *replied Sikes.* {Oliver Twist 22} Slang for club or cudgel.

pert *A pert crooked little chit, Mr. Headstone! I knew she would put herself in the way, if she could*... {Our Mutual Friend 2-15} Impudent, saucy, cheeky.

Petersham great-coat *The cab stopped, and out jumped a man in a coarse Petersham great-coat*... {Sketches, A Passage in the Life of Mr. Watkins Tottle} A kind of very heavy overcoat, named after Viscount Petersham, and popular about 1815.

petticoat trousers *Then they wear the noblest boots, with the hugest tops--flapping and bulging over anyhow; above which they encase themselves in such wonderful overalls and petticoat trousers, made to all appearance of tarry old sails* ... {Reprinted Pieces, Our French Watering-place} Trousers with legs so wide that they have the appearance of a skirt.

pettifogging ... *you are a well-matched pair of mean, rascally, pettifogging robbers.* {Pickwick Papers 53} The action of a pettifogger, legal trickery and chicanery.

pettitoes ... *a little warm supper of a couple of sets of pettitoes and some toasted cheese.* {Pickwick Papers 26} Pigs' feet, used as food.

petty-bag *There is the registrar below the judge, in wig and gown; and there are two or three maces, or petty-bags, or privy purses, or*

whatever they may be, in legal court suits. {Bleak House 1}
A kind of officer of the Court of Chancery.

pew-opener ... *when they entered the church, the sobs of the affectionate parent were so heartrending that the pew-opener suggested the propriety of his retiring to the vestry* ... {Nicholas Nickleby 25}
The usher who opened the half door of the pew and was usually given a tip.

pewter measure ... *brooding over a little pewter measure and a small glass, strongly impregnated with the smell of liquor* ... {Oliver Twist 15}
A measuring cup made of pewter.

phaeton ... *he handed us into the little phaeton with the utmost gentleness and was all smiles* ... {Bleak House 18}
A one-horse, four-wheeled carriage with a folding top, seats for two passengers, and a box for the driver (see **box**).

phantasmagoria ... *approached again, again withdrew, and so on for half-a-dozen times, like a head in a phantasmagoria.* {Old Curiosity Shop 48}
A magic lantern (a kind of slide projector) that gave the illusion of movement.

phial ... *a well dusted row of spirit phials* ... {Pickwick Papers 27}
A small glass bottle, especially one for medicine.

philosophy *"What course of lectures are you attending now, ma'am?"* ... *"The Philosophy of the Soul--on Wednesdays." "On Mondays?" "The Philosophy of Crime." "On Fridays?" "The Philosophy of Vegetables."* {Martin Chuzzlewit 17}
Science, or the pursuit of wisdom.

phosphorous-box *Then, with the aid of a phosphorous-box and some matches, he procured a light* ... {Old Curiosity Shop 35}
A box containing phosphorous and chemically-tipped matches, which ignited when touched to the phosphorous.

phrenological *In respect of ideality, reverence, wonder, and other such phrenological attributes, it is now worse off than it used to be.* {Bleak House 21}
Phrenology is a pseudoscience which holds that the functions and abilities of the mind are revealed by the shape of the skull, especially the bumps on it.

physic *I've kept him here all day for pity's sake, and I've given him broth and physic . . .* {Bleak House 31}
1. Medicine of any kind.
I asked him what he wanted [the drugs] for? He said for no harm; to physic cats . . . {Martin Chuzzlewit 48}
2. To medicate, administer medicine.

physic bottle . . . *some giant load, which seemed to shake the house, and made the little physic bottles on the mantel-shelf ring again.* {Old Curiosity Shop 66}
Medicine bottle.

pianoforte *Eighteen of Mr. Tangles' friends, each armed with a little summary of eighteen hundred sheets, bob up like eighteen hammers in a pianoforte, make eighteen bows, and drop into their eighteen places of obscurity.* {Bleak House 1}
A piano.

picquet *The Major . . . had wheeled a little table up to Cleopatra, and was sitting down to play picquet with her.* {Dombey & Son 21}
1. The French card game called 'piquet'.
. . . he was marched to chapel by a picquet of teachers three times a day . . . {Little Dorrit 1-3}
2. Should be 'piquet' or 'picket'. A body of troops sent out to bring back men who have exceeded their leave.

piebald . . . *it's the neatest, pwettiest, gwacefullest thing that ever wan upon wheels. Painted wed, with a cweam piebald.* {Pickwick Papers 35}
Of two colors, usually white and a dark color, in large patches. Here it refers to a piebald horse.

pieman *I lodged in the same house vith a pieman once, sir, and a wery nice man he was . . .* {Pickwick Papers 19}
A vendor of pies, which could be made with fruit, vegetables, meat, etc.

pier-glass *The likeness passed away . . . like a breath along the surface of the gaunt pier-glass behind her . . .* {Tale of Two Cities 1-4}
A large, tall mirror originally designed to fit the pier, or space between two windows.

pig-tail *The same face; the very same. Marley in his pig-tail, usual waistcoat, tights, and boots . . .* {A Christmas Carol 1}
A single braid of hair hanging down from the back of the head. Worn especially by sailors through the beginning of the nineteenth century.

pilot *. . . at the house of one Bulph, a pilot . . . who had the little finger of a drowned man on his parlour mantel-shelf, with other maritime and natural curiosities.* {Nicholas Nickleby 23}
A person especially qualified to steer ships in and out of a harbor.

pinafore *. . . saying in reference to the state of his pinafore. "Oh, you naughty Peepy, what a shocking little pig you are!"* {Bleak House 30}
A washable cover worn over the clothing. So-called because it was originally pinned a'fore, that is, pinned to the front of the dress.

pinched bonnet *. . . Miss Flite had not already run upstairs to put on her pinched bonnet and her poor little shawl and to arm herself with her reticule of documents.* {Bleak House 47}
Shaped as though squeezed. 'Pinched' also has the earlier meaning 'fluted'.

pinched-up *His long black hair escaped in negligent waves from beneath each side of his old pinched-up hat . . .* {Pickwick Papers 2}
Small, scanty.

pink *. . . he got quite desperate, and had half a mind last night to play Tybalt with a real sword, and pink you--not dangerously, but just*

enough to lay you up for a month or two. {Nicholas Nickleby 29}
1. Stab.
It was our Vestry--pink of Vestries . . . {Reprinted Pieces, Our Vestry}
2. Paragon, the best.

Pinnock (see **globes**)

pins *Up with you on your pins. There!* {Oliver Twist 8}
1. Slang for legs.
[The wine makers helper's] present occupation consisted of poking his head into the pins, making measurements and mental calculations, and entering them in a . . . note-book . . . {No Thoroughfare 5}
2. Small casks or kegs holding 4½ gallons.

pioneer *Many of the rioters made belts of cord, of handkerchiefs, or any material they found at hand, and wore these weapons as openly as pioneers upon a field-day.* {Barnaby Rudge 53}
Pioneers were soldiers, detailed from military units, whose job was to clear roads and obstructions and to do military construction work. They carried axes, spades, billhooks, and other tools.

pipe *Mr. Linkinwater had only been here twenty years, sir, when that pipe of double-diamond was laid down.* {Nicholas Nickleby 37}
A large cask of about 100 gallons.

pipe-clayed *. . . everything, down to the stand of muskets before the guard-house, and the drum with a pipe-clayed belt attached, in one corner, impressed itself upon his observation . . .* {Barnaby Rudge 1}
1. The white clay from which tobacco pipes were made was used to whiten articles of clothing.
You never heard them called the young gentlemen, my dears, and probably would not understand allusions to their pipe-claying their weekly accounts . . . {Bleak House 17}
2. Put into spick-and-span order.

pipe-light *. . . the beery atmosphere, sawdust, pipe-lights, spittoons . . .* {Little Dorrit 1-8}
A twisted piece of paper, also called a spill, for lighting a pipe. When

gaslight was introduced a small gas flame was kept alight on the bar for lighting pipes and cigars.

piping *No fog, no mist; clear, bright, jovial, stirring, cold; cold, piping for the blood to dance to; . . .* {A Christmas Carol 5}
1. Playing or whistling a tune.
[He] had been made groggy, and had come up piping . . . {Dombey & Son 44}
2. Weeping.

pipkin *The water in the professional pipkin having been made to boil . . .* {Pickwick Papers 38}
A small earthenware pot or pan.

piquet *"Here, draw the table nearer, and let us have the cards again,"* said Sir Mulberry. *"More piquet. Come."* {Nicholas Nickleby 38}
A card game for two persons, played with a deck from which the cards numbered from two to six have been removed.

pitch *. . . and smelt the fish, and pitch, and oakum, and tar, and saw the sailors walking about . . .* {David Copperfield 3}
1. A black, resinous material obtained by boiling tar. It was much used on sailing ships, usually applied after softening by heating in a kettle.
Mr. Magsman was looking about for a good pitch, and he see that house . . . {Going Into Society}
2. A place selected for any business or occupation. It often means a place where a street performer sets up his act.

pitch-and-toss *Gentlemen . . . who express the wide range of their capacity for adventure by observing that they are good for anything from pitch-and-toss to manslaughter . . .* {A Christmas Carol 3}
A game in which coins are pitched at a mark. The person whose coin comes nearest the mark then tosses all the coins and gets to keep those that come up 'heads'.

pitched *Mr. Luffey, the highest ornament of Dingley Dell, was pitched to bowl against the redoubtable Dumkins . . .* {Pickwick Papers 7}
1. Determined, resolved, set.
The wickets were pitched, and so were a couple of marquees for the

rest and refreshment of the contending parties. {Pickwick Papers 7}
2. Set up, erected.

plaguy *There were . . . some plaguy ill-looking characters among them.*
{Barnaby Rudge 35}
Literally infected with the plague, but here it means pestilential, scruffy,
and ill-looking.

plait *No one looks at us as we plait and weave these words.* {The
Uncommercial Traveller, Tramps}
Braid.

plan *. . . she hopes you'll excuse her, because she's correcting proofs of
the plan.* {Bleak House 14}
Blueprint, if a structure; map, if geographical.

plane-tree *. . . Lucie proposed that the wine should be carried out
under the plane-tree, and they should sit there in the air.* {Tale of
Two Cities 2-6}
A tall, spreading tree commonly planted in Britain as an ornamental
tree.

plant *. . . they warn't of no more use than the other plant.* {Oliver
Twist 19}
An elaborately planned theft or crime.

plantation-fence *. . . we ran out of the wood, and up and down the moss-
grown steps which crossed the plantation-fence like two broad-staved
ladders placed back to back . . .* {Bleak House 18}
A plantation is a wood of planted trees.

plash *. . . and Mr. Brass, with the rain plashing down into his teacup,
made a dismal attempt to pluck up his spirits . . .* {Old Curiosity Shop 51}
Splash.

plaster *Then she took some butter (not too much) on a knife and spread
it on the loaf, in an apothecary way, as if she were making a
plaster--using both sides of the knife with a slapping dexterity . . .* {Great

Expectations 2}
A medication spread on a cloth and applied to the body.

plate *"I have parted with the plate myself," said Mrs. Micawber. "Six tea, two salt, and a pair of sugars, I have at different times borrowed money on, in secret, with my own hands."* {David Copperfield 11}
Tableware, usually valuable and made of silver or silver-plated.

plate-basket *I . . . seized the loaded pistol that always goes up-stairs with the plate-basket.* {Oliver Twist 28}
A basket lined with baize for silver tableware.

plate-chest *. . . in the form of a hollow square with the women and children and the regimental plate-chest in the center . . .* {Martin Chuzzlewit 7}
A strongbox for plate and other valuable items.

play *"Ever live by cheating at play?" "Never." "Ever live by play?" "No more than other gentlemen do."* {Tale of Two Cities 2-3}
Gambling, usually at cards.

play old Gooseberry *She took to drinking, left off working, sold the furniture, pawned the clothes, and played old Gooseberry.* {Hard Times 1-11}
Old Gooseberry is the Devil, hence to 'play old Gooseberry' is to play the Devil, or to create havoc.

play-table *. . . he supposed him to live by his wits at play-tables and the like . . .* {Little Dorrit 2-6}
Gambling table.

pledge *Hugh readily complied--pouring no liquor on the floor when he drank this toast--and they pledged the secretary as a man after their own hearts, in a bumper.* {Barnaby Rudge 44}
Toast.

plighted *Your niece has plighted her faith to me, and I have plighted mine to her.* {Barnaby Rudge 14}
Pledged or engaged, in relation to love and marriage.

plovers' eggs *A single basket made of moss, once containing plovers' eggs* . . . {Little Dorrit 1-27}
Eggs of the lapwing (a bird which is not really one of the plovers) eaten like hen's eggs.

plug *The plug of life is dry, sir, and but the mud is left.* {Nicholas Nickleby 52}
A plug is a draught of beer, and mud is the dregs or dirty remainder of anything. He might have said, 'The wine of life is dry and but the dregs are left'.

plume *Gentlemen of the free-and-easy sort, who plume themselves on being acquainted with a move or two* . . . {A Christmas Carol 3}
Take pride in, pride oneself, show self-satisfaction.

plummet-line *Each long black hair upon his head hung down as straight as any plummet-line* . . . {Martin Chuzzlewit 21}
Plumb line, a weighted piece of cord used to determine a vertical line.

plummy and slam *"Now then," cried a voice from below . . . "Plummy and slam," was the reply.* {Oliver Twist 8}
Plummy means 'rich', very good, desirable. Slam is a 'trick'. The words are used here as passwords and are therefore out of context.

plunging-bath . . . *dived in head-first, as into a plunging-bath.* {Martin Chuzzlewit 3}
A swimming pool large and deep enough to be used for diving. One for just swimming would be called a swimming-bath.

pochayses . . . *and all of them going twenty or thirty miles in three hours or so, and then coming back in pochayses?* {Sketches, Vauxhall-gardens by Day}
Dialect for post-chaises (see **post-chaise**).

pocket-book *Mr. Bumble produced some silver money rolled up in paper, from his pocket-book* . . . {Oliver Twist 17}
1. A booklike case of leather having compartments for papers, money, etc.
. . . *I wrote out our two addresses on a leaf of my pocket-book, which I*

tore out and gave to her . . . {David Copperfield 47}
2. A pocket-sized notebook.

pocket-glass . . . *the spectacles and pocket-glass were again adjusted--and the evolutions of the military recommenced.* {Pickwick Papers 4}
A telescope that collapses and can be carried in a pocket.

pocket-pistol . . . *Newman slowly brought forth from his desk one of those portable bottles, currently known as pocket-pistols . . .* {Nicholas Nickleby 47}
1. Pocket flask.
I had the water dragged by moonlight, in presence of a couple of our men, and the pocket-pistol was brought up before it had been there half-a-dozen hours. {Bleak House 54}
2. A real pistol small enough to fit into a pocket.

pocket-staff *He is no great scribe, rather handling his pen like the pocket-staff he carries about with him always convenient to his grasp . . .* {Bleak House 53}
A staff of authority, small enough to fit into a pocket. It was displayed when needed, like a detective's badge.

pointer . . . *a tall, raw-boned gamekeeper . . . bearing a bag of capacious dimensions, and accompanied by a brace of pointers.* {Pickwick Papers 19}
A kind of hunting dog that points to the game.

pokey *Attendant unknowns; pokey.* {Our Mutual Friend 1-10}
Shabby, dowdy.

poled *And with a footman up behind, with a bar across, to keep his legs from being poled!* {Our Mutual Friend 1-9}
Struck by the carriage pole (the shaft that extended forward between the horses). This could happen to a footman standing on the back of the carriage when another carriage behind it was moved.

polished heart . . . *While the Grocer and his people were so frank and fresh that the polished hearts with which they fastened their aprons*

behind might have been their own ... {A Christmas Carol 3}
From context, this must be a heart-shaped clasp, possibly made of
brass, and for some reason, commonly used by grocers.

poll ... *footmen with bright parti-colored plumage and white polls, like
an extinct race of monstrous birds* ... {Little Dorrit 1-27}
The head. White polls refer to white hair or wigs.

pollard *I pointed to where our village lay, on the flat in-shore among
the alder-trees and pollards, a mile or more from the church* ...
{Great Expectations 1}
1. A tree cut back to form a round head of growth.
... *his flat vista of pollard old men* ... {Little Dorrit 1-31}
2. Bald-headed.

poll-parrot ... *you jade of a magpie, jackdaw, and poll-parrot, what do
you mean* ... {Bleak House 21}
A parrot, but figuratively refers to the parrot's unintelligent repetition of
words.

Polonies ... *said Toby [smelling the dinner basket]. "It an't--I suppose it
an't Polonies?"* {The Chimes 1}
Polony sausage, a sausage made of partially cooked pork.

poltroon *"You--you're a shuffler, sir!" gasped the furious doctor. "A
poltroon--a coward--a liar--a--a--will nothing induce you to give me
your card, sir!"* {Pickwick Papers 2}
A spiritless coward; a mean-spirited, worthless wretch.

pomatum *It was a ragged head, the sandy hair of which, scrupulously
parted on one side and flattened down with pomatum, was twisted into
little semi-circular tails* ... {Pickwick Papers 20}
Pomade, a scented ointment for dressing hair.

pomp ... *the favourite undertaker (who turned a handsome sum out of
the one poor ghastly pomp of the neighborhood)* {Hard Times 1-10}
The ceremonial procession and display, here of funerals.

pompeyed *"It's only to be hoped," said my sister, "that he won't be pompeyed. But I have my fears."* {Great Expectations 7}
Pampered. Either dialect or a word made up by Dickens.

pony-chaise *. . . at the same time there came out of the yard a rusty pony-chaise, and a cart, driven by two labouring men.* {Nicholas Nickleby 7}
A small chaise, a kind of two-wheeled carriage, suitable in size and weight to be drawn by a pony.

Pony-nightmare *Anything suggestive of a Pony-nightmare was delicious to him.* {Cricket on the Hearth 1}
A nightmare is a creature who causes bad dreams (including the frightening toys sold by Mr. Tackleton) not the bad dream itself. The word 'pony' was often used as a diminutive and is especially appropriate here because it harmonizes with mare.

poorly *. . . I am expected not to be at home in the day-time, unless poorly; . . .* {The Poor Relation's Story}
Ill, in a poor state of health.

poor's-rates *. . . being untroubled with the vulgar inconveniences of hunger and thirst, being chargeable neither to the poor's-rates nor the assessed taxes, and having no young family to provide for.* {The Haunted Man 2}
A tax for the relief of the poor. A rate is a tax.

poor-surgeon's-friend *. . . I can't call at a man's house but I find a piece of this poor-surgeon's-friend on the staircase? I've been lamed with orange-peel once, and I know orange-peel will be my death at last.* {Oliver Twist 14}
Dickens several times accuses surgeons of strewing orange peel about, in the hope of causing someone to slip and fall so as to require medical services. Here he calls the orange peel 'the poor-surgeon's-friend'.

Pope Joan *[He] set out two card-tables; the one for Pope Joan and the other for whist.* {Pickwick Papers 6}
A card game for three or more players, played without the eight of diamonds.

popolorum tibby *"It knows it is talking demd charming sweetness, but naughty fibs,"* returned Mr. Mantalini. *"It knows it is not ashamed of its own popolorum tibby."* {Nicholas Nickleby 34}
A tender, tiny child.

porch ... *he saw no likeness of himself among the multitudes that poured in through the Porch.* {A Christmas Carol 4}
... *we pursued a pleasant footpath winding among the verdant turf and the beautiful trees until it brought us to the church-porch.* {Bleak House 18}
A covered approach to the entrance of a building, or a large vestibule.

porringer *When he had given him this information, and a tin porringer containing his breakfast, the man locked him up again* ... {Old Curiosity Shop 61}
A small bowl, usually with a flat handle, used for soup or cereal.

porter ... *there was a porter on the premises--a wonderful creature in a vast red waistcoat and a short-tailed pepper-and-salt coat* ... {Martin Chuzzlewit 27}
1. A person in charge of a door or gate.
A porter, carrying off his baggage on a trunk for shipment at the docks on board the Son and Heir *had got possession of them, and wheeled them away* ... {Dombey & Son 19}
2. One who carries burdens for pay.
... *I saw a ticket-porter coming up-stairs, with a letter in his hand.* {David Copperfield 25}
3. A ticket porter is a licensed street porter. He would carry letters and messages and deliver small packages.
... *against the door of which strong chamber the light-porter laid his head every night* ... {Hard Times 2-1}
4. A porter or watchman hired for light work.
... *he borrowed a shilling of me for porter* ... {David Copperfield 11}
5. Porter beer, a dark-brown, bitter beer.

porter-pot ... *in a few hours the house was emptied of everything, but pieces of matting, empty porter-pots, and scattered fragments of straw.* {Old Curiosity Shop 13}
A vessel for drinking porter beer.

porter's knot ... *preceded by a man who carried the immense petition on a porter's knot through the lobby* ... {Barnaby Rudge 49}
A pad worn on the shoulder by porters when carrying a heavy load. It often consisted of two pads connected by a band that went over the forehead, making it resemble a horse collar.

Porter's Lodge ... *outer doors of chambers are shut up by the score, messages and parcels are to be left at the Porter's Lodge by the bushel.* {Bleak House 19}
The shed or small room at the front of the building where the porter or doorman stayed.

portico *A great square house, with a heavy portico darkening the principal windows* ... {Hard Times 1-3}
A roof supported by columns at intervals and forming a kind of covered walkway.

portion ... *that I, a friendless, portionless girl, with a blight upon my name* ... {Oliver Twist 35}
1. A dowry, the money and property a woman was obliged to transfer to her husband when she married.
... *when I marry with their consent they will portion me most handsomely.* {Our Mutual Friend 3-4}
2. Provide a dowry.

portmanteau ... *grinning assent from under a leathern portmanteau* ... *hobbled down the stairs with his portion of their worldly goods* ... {Martin Chuzzlewit 17}
A piece of stiff luggage with hinges at the back that opens like a book.

pose ... *as if he had, that moment, posed a boy, and were waiting to convict him from his own lips.* {Dombey & Son 11}
To place someone in difficulty by a question, to puzzle them.

post-boy, postboy *The post-boy was driving briskly through the open streets* ... {Pickwick Papers 50}
The postilion of a coach or carriage. He rode one of the horses immediately in front of the carriage and was either the sole driver or rode with a coachman on the driver's box.

post-captain ... *to have come back an admiral ... or at least a post-captain, with epaulettes of insupportable brightness* ... {Dombey & Son 9}
A naval officer having the official rank of Captain, so-called to distinguish him from someone of lower rank called a Captain because he commanded a small ship.

post-chaise *Looking around, he saw that it was a post-chaise, driven at great speed* ... {Oliver Twist 34}
A fast, hired carriage for traveling, seating up to three, with the driver seated on one of the horses.

postern ... *he reached a small postern in the wall of the sister's orchard, through which he passed, closing it behind him.* {Nicholas Nickleby 6}
A back or side door.

post-horse *An old gentleman and a young lady, travelling, unattended, in a rusty old chariot with post-horses* ... {Martin Chuzzlewit 3}
Horses used for travel in stages, usually hired at each stage.

postilion *The postilion cracked his whip, and they clattered away* ... {Tale of Two Cities 1-6}
A person who rides one of the horses pulling a coach or carriage. He may be there in addition to or in place of a driver.

posting-house *He had heard of Monseigneur, at the posting-houses, as being before him.* {Tale of Two Cities 2-9}
An inn or other house where horses are kept for the use of travelers.

post-obit *The very day I put [this suit] on, old Lord Mallowford was burnt to death in his bed, and all the post-obits fell in.* {Nicholas Nickleby 51}
A bond given by a borrower, to be paid from the money inherited by the borrower on the death of someone else.

post octavo ... *another book, in three volumes post octavo.* {Nicholas Nickleby 18}
Post paper is the size of a sheet of paper. Octavo meant that it was folded three times, to make eight pages.

pot . . . *their nightly pipes and pots* . . . {Barnaby Rudge 30}
A drinking vessel, usually of metal. Here it refers to pots of liquor or beer.

potation *Mr. Riderhood got out his bottle, and fetched his jug-full of water, and administered a potation.* {Our Mutual Friend 4-7}
A drink.

pot-boy, potman *By this time the pot-boy of the Sol's Arms appearing with her supper-pint well frothed, Mrs. Piper accepts that tankard and retires indoors* . . . {Bleak House 32}
. . . *a potman was going his rounds with beer, and the prisoners, behind bars in yards, were buying beer* . . . {Great Expectations 32}
A man or boy employed at a tavern to serve beer or deliver beer to outside customers.

pot companions . . . *old John was so red in the face with perpetually shaking his head in contradiction of his three ancient cronies and pot companions, that he was quite a phenomenon to behold* . . . {Barnaby Rudge 54}
Drinking companions.

pot-shop *Mr. Ben Allen and Mr. Bob Sawyer betaking themselves to a sequestered pot-shop on the remotest confines of the borough* . . . {Pickwick Papers 52}
A small public house or tavern.

poulterer *"Do you know the Poulterer's, in the next street but one, at the corner?" Scrooge inquired.* {A Christmas Carol 5}
A dealer in poultry, rabbits, and other game.

pounce . . . *office quills, pens, ink, India-rubber, pounce, pins, pencils, sealing-wax* . . . {Bleak House 10}
Pumice powder for preparing greasy parchment to be written upon.

pounce box . . . *two or three common books of practice; a jar of ink, a pounce box* . . . {Old Curiosity Shop 33}
A shaker-top box containing pounce.

pouncing ... *[She could] transact any ordinary duty of the office down to pouncing a skin of parchment or mending a pen.* {Old Curiosity Shop 33}
Powdering the parchment with pounce (see **pounce**).

pound *I'll pound it, that Barney's managing properly.* {Oliver Twist 26}
1. Slang for to be certain.
... *then there were a few more cottages; then the cage and pound, and not unfrequently, on a bank by the way-side, a deep old dusty well.* {Old Curiosity Shop 15}
2. An enclosure for stray animals.

poundage ... *about a thirtieth part of the annual revenue was now expended* ... *the rest being handsomely laid out in Chancery, law expenses, collectorship, receivership, poundage, and other appendages of management* ... {Seven Poor Travellers 1}
A commission fee of so much per pound sterling

pounder, eight and forty pounder *You could as soon take up and shoulder an eight and forty pounder by your own strength as turn that man when he has got a thing into his head and fixed it there.* {Bleak House 52}
An 'eight and forty pounder' is a cannon that fires a ball weighing 48 pounds.

poussette ... *picturing the locksmith's daughter going down long country-dances, and poussetting dreadfully with bold strangers* ... {Barnaby Rudge 14}
A dance step done by a couple who hold hands and dance round and round.

pouter *The wheeling and circling flights of runts, fantails, tumblers, and pouters* ... {Barnaby Rudge 1}
A kind of pigeon, as are runts, fantails, and tumblers.

powder *He had been wondering, with his eyes fixed on the magistrates' powder, whether all boards were born with that white stuff on their heads* ... {Oliver Twist 3}
1. Wigs and hair were powdered with flour, or other white material, as a matter of fashion.
A bitter powder was administered to me next morning, and I was wretched. {The Uncommercial Traveller, Birthday Celebrations}

2. Many medications were ground into a powder and wrapped in a folded piece of paper. They were administered by putting the powder into a spoon or directly into the mouth. The unpleasant flavor of most medications was thus left undisguised.

powder-magazine *[Architects drawings of a] jail. A church. A powder-magazine. A wine-cellar. A portico. A summer-house.* {Martin Chuzzlewit 5}
A place where gunpowder is stored.

powder-mill *As he wanted the candles close to him, and as he was always on the verge of putting either his head or the newspaper into them, he required as much watching as a powder-mill.* {Great Expectations 37}
A mill for grinding gunpowder, a dangerous process often subject to accidental fire and explosion.

power of feature ... *the overwhelming politeness with which he endeavoured to hide his confusion . . . exercised the utmost power of feature that even Martin Chuzzlewit the elder possessed.* {Martin Chuzzlewit 52}
Control over facial expression.

practised *Sammy has been practised upon, and has broken confidence. It has all come out.* {Old Curiosity Shop 67}
Worked on to persuade to some course of action.

prad *He's in the gig, a-minding the prad.* {Oliver Twist 31}
Slang for horse.

pray *"If such an idea has ever presented itself to you," faultered Tom, "pray dismiss it."* {Martin Chuzzlewit 31}
An expression, like 'please', which adds deference to a request.

Precentor ... *being so much respected as Lay Precentor, or Lay Clerk, or whatever you call it* ... {Edwin Drood 2}
One who leads the singing of a church choir or congregation.

prefigure *But no romancer that I know of has had the boldness to prefigure the life and home of this young husband and young wife in the*

Children's Hospital in the east of London. {The Uncommercial Traveller, A Small Star in the East}
To picture or imagine beforehand.

prentice *Some of the small tradesmen's houses . . . had a Cyclops window in the middle of the gable, within an inch or two of its apex, suggesting that some forlorn rural Prentice must wriggle himself into that apartment horizontally, when he retired to rest, after the manner of the worm.* {Tom Tiddler's Ground 1}
Apprentice.

preparation *The centaur would make a very handsome preparation in Surgeon's Hall, and would benefit science extremely.* {Barnaby Rudge 75}
An anatomical preparation, a display of dissected material.

prepossessed *. . . seeing that you have been prepossessed and set against me . . .* {Martin Chuzzlewit 54}
Prejudiced.

prepossession *We all conceived a prepossession in his favour, for there was a sterling quality in this laugh, and in his vigorous, healthy voice . . .* {Bleak House 9}
A prejudice or predisposition.

prescription *There is an air of prescription about him which is always agreeable to Sir Leicester; he receives it as a kind of tribute.* {Bleak House 2}
Ancient and authoritative custom.

presentation *"I don't know whether you are aware," my lady proceeded, "that we have a presentation to a living? I say we have; but, in point of fact, I have.* {Reprinted Pieces, George Silverman's Explanation 7}
A presentation is the privilege of appointing someone to a living. A living is a job for a church official that provides a fixed income, a benefice.

press *After breakfast, Joe brought my indentures from the press in the best parlour, and we put them in the fire, and I felt that I was free.*

{Great Expectations 19}
A cupboard with shelves, often placed in a recess in the wall.

pressed ... *in consequence of her husband having been pressed three weeks previous, and she being left to beg, with two young children* ...
{Barnaby Rudge 37}
Impressed into the navy, forced into service in the navy.

pretend ... *On his return he told us, more than once, that Vholes was a good fellow, a safe fellow, a man who did what he pretended to do, a very good fellow indeed!* {Bleak House 60}
To intend or plan or claim. Here, 'he did what he said he would do'.

Preventive ... *Mr. Toots ... said "Smugglers". But with an impartial remembrance of there being two sides to every question, he added, "or Preventive."* {Dombey & Son 12}
The department of the Customs concerned with the prevention of smuggling. It later became the Coast Blockade, then the Coast Guard.

prig *"What lay are you upon?" asked the tinker. "Are you a prig?"* {David Copperfield 13}
1. Slang for pickpocket or thief.
If father was determined to make me either a Prig or a Mule, and I am not a Prig ... I must be a Mule. {Hard Times 1-8}
2. A conceited, didactical, boring person.

prime ... *he was a sensible practical good-hearted prime fellow.* {Great Expectations 19}
1. Best, choicest, most desirable, first-rate.
The officer then gave the command to prime and load. The heavy ringing of the musket-stocks upon the ground, and the sharp rapid rattling of the ramrods in their barrels, were a kind of relief to Barnaby ...
{Barnaby Rudge 57}
2. Place the priming charge, which will be ignited by the flint of the flintlock, in the priming pan of a firearm.

prime plant *"The old gentleman over the way?" said Oliver. "Yes, I see him." "He'll do," said the Dodger. "A prime plant," observed Master*

Charley Bates. {Oliver Twist 10}
Slang for a good subject for plunder or robbery.

priory . . . *and the rooks, as they hovered about the grey tower and swung in the bare high trees of the priory-garden, seemed to call to me that the place was changed* . . . {Great Expectations 49}
A monastery or nunnery governed by a prior or prioress.

prison-lock *His father . . . had from his early youth familiarised him with the duties of his office, and with an ambition to retain the prison-lock in the family.* {Little Dorrit 1-18}
The doorkeeper of the prison, the one who locks and unlocks the gate.

Private Bill *Mr. Bailey, Junior . . . had now regularly set up in life under that name without troubling himself to obtain from the legislature a direct license in the form of a Private Bill* . . . {Martin Chuzzlewit 27}
A parliamentary act which concerns the interests of an individual or an individual corporation.

privateersman . . . *had been a pilot, or a skipper, or a privateersman, or all three perhaps* . . . {Dombey & Son 4}
An officer or crew member of a privateer, a private ship authorized by the government to engage in war activities.

privity . . . *so his mental faculties, without his privity or concurrence, set all these springs in motion, with a thousand others* . . . {The Chimes 1}
Private knowledge of something, implying consent.

privy purse *There is the registrar below the judge, in wig and gown; and there are two or three maces, or petty-bags, or privy purses, or whatever they may he, in legal court suits.* {Bleak House 1}
A financial officer of the royal household.

prize . . . *though many men, a dozen times their match, had tried in vain to do so, and were seen, in--yes, in--the fire, striving to prize it down, with crowbars.* {Barnaby Rudge 64}
Pry, as with a prybar or crowbar.

proctor ... *Six poor Travelers, who not being Rogues, or Proctors, May receive gratis for one Night, Lodging and Entertainment, and Fourpence each.* {Seven Poor Travellers 1}
In the sixteenth and seventeenth centuries, a person licensed to beg or collect alms for lepers and others. Proctors were not supposed to keep any of the collected money for themselves. Unfortunately they often stole the funds, and consequently had a bad reputation. The word also appears with a different meaning in *David Copperfield*, where the context defines it, in some detail, as a type of lawyer who worked in Doctors Commons.

Professor Owen ... *dancers with such astonishingly loose legs, furnished with so many joints in the wrong places, utterly unknown to Professor Owen*... {Reprinted Pieces, Our French Watering-place}
Famous English comparative anatomist of Dickens' time.

projector *Projectors who had discovered every kind of remedy for the little evils with which the state was touched*... {Tale of Two Cities 2-7}
One who forms a project, who plans an enterprise.

proof, steel of proof ... *being clad from head to heel in steel of proof, they did on many occasions lead their leather-jerkined soldiers to the death*... {Martin Chuzzlewit 1}
Steel armor which had been tested and found impervious to lead bullets. Since early firearms had relatively little force, armor of that strength could be made.

prop ... *and in his shirt-front there's a beautiful diamond prop, cost him fifteen or twenty pound--a very handsome pin indeed.* {Reprinted Pieces, Three "Detective" Anecdotes}
Slang for a scarf pin or brooch.

prose *He was only sauntering by and stopped to prose.* {Bleak House 32}
1. Chat.
... *you have said that fifty thousand times, in my hearing. What a Prose you are!* {Martin Chuzzlewit 37}
2. Dull, commonplace, boring person.

prosody ... *etymology, syntax, and prosody* ... {Hard Times 1-2}
The correct pronunciation of words.

prospect *We were glad to change the subject, and going to the window, pointed out the beauties of the prospect* ... {Bleak House 8}
The view, the landscape.

prosper ... *God knows that this one child is the thought and object of my life, and yet He never prospers me* ... {Old Curiosity Shop 1}
To cause to prosper. Here the sense is, 'He never makes me prosperous'.

prosy *"My dear boy," returned his father, "confide in me, I beg. But you know my constitution--don't be prosy, Ned."* {Barnaby Rudge 15}
Dull and tedious.

prove *"I will prove you," whispers mademoiselle, stretching out her hand, "I will try if you dare to do it!"* {Bleak House 42}
Test.

provender ... *Monsieur Defarge had made all ready for the journey, and had brought with them* ... *bread, meat, wine, and hot coffee. Monsieur Defarge put his provender, and the lamp he carried, on the shoemaker's bench* ... {Tale of Two Cities 1-6}
Food and provisions.

prove to demonstration *The oldest heaver present proved to demonstration, that the moment the piers were removed all the water in the Thames would run clean off* ... {Sketches, Scotland Yard}
Use a geometrical or mathematical proof, as in the proof of a mathematical theorem.

pshaw *Pshaw! match-making mothers do the same thing every day.* {Nicholas Nickleby 26}
An exclamation of contempt or disgust.

psychological *It was understood that nothing of a tender nature could possibly be confided to Old Barley, by reason of his being totally unequal to the consideration of any subject more psychological than gout,*

rum, and purser's stories. {Great Expectations 46}
Pertaining to the mind. The sense here is 'intellectual'.

public vehicle *The Defarges, husband and wife, came lumbering under the starlight, in their public vehicle . . .* {Tale of Two Cities 2-16}
A hired carriage.

public-house *We went arm-in-arm to the public-house where the carrier put up . . .* {David Copperfield 3}
An inn or hostelry providing rooms, meals, and drink. Also a tavern.

pudding *. . . ring the bell for the waiter, and bespeak a hot kidney-pudding and a plate of shrimps for breakfast in the morning.* {Oliver Twist 34}
Almost any kind of food cooked in a crust of dough, similar to a large dumpling. It could be made with meats or vegetables. Does not have the limited, current meaning of a sweet desert (e.g., chocolate pudding) as it does in the United States.

pug-dog *"Husbands die every day, ma'am, and wives too." "And brothers also, sir," said Nicholas, with a glance of indignation. "Yes, sir, and puppies, and pug-dogs likewise," replied his uncle . . .* {Nicholas Nickleby 3}
A breed of dog resembling a miniature bulldog.

puling *. . . well knowing that her heart was given to that puling boy.* {Pickwick Papers 11}
Crying, whining like a child.

pull one's hair *The brandy was brought; and Mr. Weller, after pulling his hair to Mr. Pickwick and nodding to Sam, jerked it down his capacious throat as if it had been a small thimbleful.* {Pickwick Papers 20}
A kind of salute done by tugging at the hair of the front of the head.

pumping engines *He would have been invaluable to a fire-office; never was a man with such a natural taste for pumping engines, running up ladders, and throwing furniture out of two-pair-of-stairs' windows . . .* {The Public Life of Mr. Tulrumble}

The engine was a hand-operated mechanical pump used to throw water on fires (until steam-powered engines were invented). We still speak of fire engines.

pumps . . . *when the out-door apprentices ring us up in the morning . . . and I see them standing on the door-step with their little pumps under their arms, I am actually reminded of the Sweeps.*
{Bleak House 38}
A light, low-heeled shoe for dancing.

Punch *The single gentleman among his other peculiarities . . . took a most extraordinary and remarkable interest in the exhibition of Punch.*
{Old Curiosity Shop 37}
The main character in Punch and Judy, a children's hand-puppet show, hence the puppet show itself.

puncheon *If I lend him a helping hand, the only difference is, that he may, upon the whole, possibly drink a few gallons, or puncheons, or hogsheads, less in this life then he otherwise would.* {Barnaby Rudge 40}
A large cask for liquids

pupil dresser *I find him making his round of the beds, like a house surgeon, attended by another dog,--a friend,--who appears to trot about with him in the character of his pupil dresser.* {The Uncommercial Traveller,On an Amateur Beat}
Student dresser. A dresser is the surgeon's assistant who applies bandages or dressings.

pupil-teacher *You come to be a pupil-teacher, and you still go on better and better, and you rise to be a master full of learning and respect.*
{Our Mutual Friend 1-3}
A student teacher, one who is preparing for the teaching profession and is doing practice teaching.

purblind *The purblind day was feebly struggling with the fog when I opened my eyes to encounter those of a dirty-faced little spectre fixed upon me.* {Bleak House 5}
Having impaired vision, being partially blind.

purchase ... *and the last screw of the rack having been turned so often that its purchase crumbled, and now it turned ... with nothing to bite.* {Tale of Two Cities 2-23}
Hold or grip. Here, that portion of the wood into which the thread of the screw penetrated.

purchase-money *His name was entered at the Horse Guards as an applicant for an ensign's commission; the purchase-money was deposited at an agents; and Richard, in his usual characteristic way, plunged into a violent course of military study ...* {Bleak House 24}
Officer's commissions were bought, and the purchase money was the cost of the commission.

purl ... *a great pot, filled with some very fragrant compound, which sent forth a grateful steam, and was indeed choice purl, made after a particular recipe which Mr. Swiveller had imparted to the landlord ...* {Old Curiosity Shop 57}
Hot beer or ale with gin, sugar, and ginger. It also contained an extract of a wormwood plant related to absinthe.

purpose *Do you purpose calling witnesses?* {Pickwick Papers 31}
Intend to or mean to.

pursy *[Mr. Sleary was] rendered more pursy than ever by so much talking ...* {Hard Times 1-6}
Short of breath.

put someone's pipe out ... *I knew I should get into scrapes there if she put old Bounderby's pipe out ...* {Hard Times 2-3}
To put a stop to someone's success, to take the wind out of his sails.

put to *The horses were put to, punctually at a quarter before nine next morning, and ... the postilion was duly directed to repair in the first instance to Mr. Bob Sawyer's house ...* {Pickwick Papers 50}
Attach horses to a vehicle, hitch up the horses.

put to the blush *Take care, when we are growing old and foolish, Barnaby doesn't put us to the blush, that's all.* {Barnaby Rudge 5}
Outstrip. The sense is 'make us eat our words'.

put-up job *At least it can't be a put-up job, as we expected.* {Oliver Twist 19}
An inside job, a burglary with a servant in on it.

quadrille ... *Mr. Swiveller had Miss Sophy's hand for the first quadrille* ... {Old Curiosity Shop 8}
1. A French square dance.
... *incidents like these, arising out of drums and masquerades and parties at quadrille* ... {Barnaby Rudge 16}
2. A card game played by four people.

Quality ... *violence and vagabondism* ... *were at once the ennobling pursuit and the healthful recreation of the Quality of this land.* {Martin Chuzzlewit 1}
Persons of quality, high-ranking nobility.

quantum ... *Mr. Gabriel Parsons* ... *had been coughing and frowning at his wife, for half-an-hour previously--signals which Mrs. Parsons never happened to observe, until she had been pressed to take her ordinary quantum [of wine]* ... {Sketches, A Passage in the Life of Mr. Watkins Tottle}
A share or portion, also an amount or quantity.

quarter *Only a quarter, and a month or so* ... {Pickwick Papers 32}
A fourth of a year, three months. The quarters are marked by the quarter days.

quarter-day *The population is migratory, usually disappearing on the verge of quarter-day, and generally by night.* {Pickwick Papers 32}
One of four days which marked the quarters of the year: 25 March, 24 June, 29 September, and 25 December. Rents and interest usually became due on quarter days.

quartern ... *the pudding, like a speckled cannon-ball, so hard and firm, blazing in half-a-quartern of ignited brandy* ... {A Christmas Carol 3}
A quartern is a quarter of anything. Here it refers to a quarter of a pint.

quartern loaf *Mr. Tappertit looked immensely big at a quartern loaf on the table, and breathed hard.* {Barnaby Rudge 4}
A loaf of bread made from a quartern, a quarter pound of flour.

quarter-sessions *... the court has appointed me ... to depose a matter before the quarter-sessions at Clerkinwell.* {Oliver Twist 17}
A court of limited criminal and civil jurisdiction, held in the counties.

quarter-staff *One bear ... had essayed to wield his quarter-staff for the amusement of the multitude ...* {Sketches, Full Report of the Second Meeting of the Mudfog Association}
A six to eight foot long stout pole, often tipped with iron, used as a weapon. Fighting with the quarterstaff had its own techniques of offense and defense. It was a deadly weapon in the hands of an expert. It may have been so-named because it was made from a quarter of a properly sized tree.

queer *Some of the queer frequenters of the house were a little suspicious of me at first, and I was obliged to be very cautious indeed ...* {Reprinted Pieces, The Detective Police}
Questionable, suspicious.

queer bill *I want to go a little more into buying-up queer bills.* {Our Mutual Friend 2-5}
Queer is slang for worthless. Queer bills were promissory notes or commercial paper that were considered worthless by the owner and therefore could be bought very cheaply.

Queer Street *If you had gone to any low member of my profession, it's my firm conviction, and I assure you of it as a fact, that you would have found yourselves in Queer Street before this.* {Pickwick Papers 55}
An imaginary street where people in difficulty were supposed to live. It refers here simply to being in trouble or difficulty.

quicken *... a fire ... quickening nothing, lighting nothing, doing no service, idly burning away.* {Tale of Two Cities 2-13}
Animate, excite, inspire.

quick-lime *"I see it. What is it?" "Lime."... "What you call quick-lime?" "Ay!" says Durdles; "quick enough to eat your boots...."* {Edwin Drood 12}
Calcium oxide, limestone which has been roasted. It reacts vigorously with water and was used to consume dead bodies.

quicksilver ... *by heaven, they ought to be worked in quicksilver mines for the short remainder of their miserable existences ...* {Bleak House 13}
Mercury. Because the compounds of mercury are poisonous and are absorbed through the skin, mercury mining is not a healthful occupation.

quiz *Oh, you quiz--I know what you are going to say.* {Pickwick Papers 4}
An odd or eccentric person.

quizzing-glass *They didn't behave at all well. Some of them looked through quizzing-glasses at others, and said, "Who are those? Don't know them."* {Reprinted Pieces, Holiday Romance 4}
A small, single eyeglass, similar to a monocle, with a handle.

quod *"Gaffer has never been where you have been." "Signifying in Quod, Miss? Perhaps not. But he may have merited it."* {Our Mutual Friend 1-6}
Prison, usually meaning debtor's prison.

rack *Protestants in anything but the name, were no more to be considered as abettor of these disgraceful occurrences, than they themselves were chargeable with the uses of the block, the rack, the gibbet, and the stake in cruel Mary's reign.* {Barnaby Rudge 51}
An instrument of torture on which the victim was stretched until his joints tore.

racket-court, racket-ground ... *a centre of attraction to indifferent foreign hotels and indifferent foreigners, racket-courts, fighting-men, swordsman, footguards, old china, gaming-houses* ... {Bleak House 21}
This area, it appeared from Mr. Roker's statement, was the racket-ground [of Fleet prison] ... {Pickwick Papers 41}
The open court on which the game of rackets was played.

rackets ... *[He] wos alvays a-bustlin' about for somebody or playin' at rackets and never vinnin* ... {Pickwick Papers 41}
A game played by hitting a ball with a racket, usually against a wall. In the prison courtyard it was played with a racket somewhat resembling a lacrosse racket.

railway-navigator *There are disorderly classes of men who are not thieves; as railway-navigators, brickmakers, wood-sawyers, coster-mongers.* {The Uncommercial Traveller, The Ruffian}
A workman who dug canals was called a navigator, often shortened to navvy. The name then became applied to laborers who dug ditches or worked on the railroad tracks.

railway wrapper ... *no pigeon-pie is especially made for me, no hotel-advertisement is personally addressed to me, no hotel-room tapestried with great-coats and railway wrappers is set apart for me* ...
{The Uncommercial Traveller, His General Line of Business}
Traveling cloak.

raised-pie ... *the Baby ... was invested, by the united efforts of Mrs. Peery-bingle and Miss Slowboy, with a cream-coloured mantle for its body, and a sort of nankeen raised-pie for its head* ... {Cricket on the Hearth 2}
A pie with a raised crust, one which is made of flour stiffened enough to stand by itself. Dickens is, of course, describing the baby's hat.

rake ... *to think that the man about town, the rake, the* roué, *the rook of twenty seasons, should be brought to this pass by a mere boy!* {Nicholas Nickleby 38}
A loose, immoral person.

rally ... *the Captain, when he reached the outer office, could not refrain from rallying Mr. Perch a little, and asking him whether he thought everybody was still engaged.* {Dombey & Son 17}
To make fun of, gently ridicule.

rampacious ... *a stone statue of some rampacious animal with flowing mane and tail, distantly resembling an insane cart-horse* ... {Pickwick Papers 22}
Should be 'rampagious', meaning violent, unruly, or boisterous. 'Rampacious' was apparently often used in error.

ranger ... *short Tom Cobb the general chandler and post-office keeper, and long Phil Parkes the ranger* ... {Barnaby Rudge 1}
A gamekeeper.

rappee *I carried coffee, sir, for a long time. It looks like rappee, sir.* {Pickwick Papers 35}
A coarse, dark kind of snuff.

rare ... *the raisins were so plentiful and rare, the almonds so extremely white, the sticks of cinnamon so long and straight* ... {A Christmas Carol 3}
Splendid, excellent, fine. It does not mean 'infrequent' or 'few'.

rarullarulling ... *Veneering thanking his devoted friends one and all, with great emotion, for rarullarulling round him.* {Our Mutual

Friend 2-3}
Rallying, but said in Mr. Veneering's pompous way, something like 'Ra--ra--rall--a--rallying'. At the beginning of the chapter he wants to know 'whether his friends will rally round him'.

rasher *It is not necessarily a lengthened preparation, being limited to the setting forth of very simple breakfast requisites for two and the broiling of a rasher of bacon at the fire in the rusty grate* . . . {Bleak House 26}
A thin slice, meant to be broiled or fried.

rasped roll . . . *having breakfasted . . . on her customary viands; to wit, one French roll rasped, one egg new laid (or warranted to be), and one little pot of tea* . . . {Dombey & Son 29}
A roll crumbled, reduced to crumbs. In the eighteenth century raspings of bread could be purchased from the bakers.

rasper . . . *he was a long-headed man, a dry one, a salt fish, a deep file, a rasper* . . . {Martin Chuzzlewit 38}
Slang for a harsh or unpleasant person.

rate . . . *the lady* . . . *rated him in good round terms, signifying that she would be glad to know what he meant by terrifying delicate females* . . . {Martin Chuzzlewit 19}
1. Scold angrily.
. . . *being untroubled with the vulgar inconveniences of hunger and thirst, being chargeable neither to the poor's-rates nor the assessed taxes, and having no young family to provide for.* {The Haunted Man 2}
2. A tax.
. . . *in the midst of a vast fleet of ships of all rates, and boats of all sizes* . . . {Little Dorrit 2-26}
3. British naval vessels were divided into six rates according to the number of guns carried. A first-rate ship carried 74 to 120 guns.

rattler *I should have given him a rattler for himself, if Mrs. Boffin hadn't thrown herself betwixt us* . . . {Our Mutual Friend 1-8}
A sharp blow.

ready-reckoner *Nor did he trouble his borrowers with abstract calcu-lations of figures, or references to ready-reckoners; his simple rule of interest being all comprised in the one golden sentence "two-pence for every half-penny"* . . . {Nicholas Nickleby 1}
Tables of business calculations.

reassume *After some minutes, however, during which he had reas-sumed his pen, he appeared to be again aware of the presence of his clients* . . . {Pickwick Papers 31}
To take up again a material thing that was laid down or handed to another.

receiver . . . *whether he is a smuggler, or a receiver, or an unlicensed pawnbroker, or a money-lender* . . . {Bleak House 20}
1. Someone who knowingly receives stolen goods.
The receiver in the cause has acquired a goodly sum of money by it but has acquired too a distrust of his own mother, and a contempt for his own kind. {Bleak House 1}
2. A person appointed by the court to administer the property of a bank-rupt or an estate in litigation.
As a professional Receiver of rents, so very few people do wish to see me . . . {Edwin Drood 9}
3. Someone appointed to collect money due.
I cannot dine on a sandwich that has long been pining under an exhaust-ed receiver. {The Uncommercial Traveller, Refreshments for Travel-lers}
4. Any kind of basin or receptacle, usually metal.

reckoning . . . *the young man beckoned to Joe, and handing him a piece of money in payment of his reckoning, hurried out* . . . {Barnaby Rudge 1}
The bill, as in a restaurant or tavern.

recover . . . *he turns towards the voice, and in trying to answer, falls down insensible. They recover him again, and tell him he must be composed, and bear this like a man.* {Old Curiosity Shop 68}
To restore someone to life or consciousness.

recreant . . . *what I ask you will you say of that working-man* . . . *who, at such a time, turns a traitor and a craven and a recreant* . . .

{Hard Times 2-4}
One who surrenders, is cowardly or afraid.

recruited *Feeling their strength recruited and their spirits roused, now that there was a new necessity for action, they hurried away, quite forgetful of the fatigue under which they had been sinking but a few minutes before* . . . {Barnaby Rudge 60}
Restored.

red lamp . . . *I saw her look toward [the surgeon's] infernal red lamp* . . . {Oliver Twist 14}
A lamp with red glass was used as a sign of a doctor's office.

redpoll *You'll never want to buy any more redpolls now, to hang up over the sink, will you?* {Martin Chuzzlewit 26}
A kind of bird, commonly kept as a caged bird in England.

reduced *I put it on, I remember, for the first time, to attend the inquest on that reduced tradesman, who died in the doorway at midnight.* {Oliver Twist 4}
Impoverished, brought to a lower condition in life.

reek . . . *and the reek of the labouring horses* . . . {Tale of Two Cities 1-2}
The fumes and odor emanating from some body, here that of the horses.

refection *The solitary little table for purposes of refection and social enjoyment* . . . {Martin Chuzzlewit 11}
The partaking of food or refreshment.

refer . . . *to what would you refer this attack.* {Tale of Two Cities 2-19}
Attribute, in the sense of 'the cause'.

refulgent . . . *and bestowing upon the locksmith a most refulgent smile, he left them.* {Barnaby Rudge 27}
Shining brightly with reflected light, gleaming.

register *The scene is the Vestry-room of St. James's Church, with a number of leathery old registers on shelves* ... {Our Mutual Friend 1-10}
The parish book recording births, deaths, marriages, etc.

register stove ... *Mr. Gamfield [the chimney-sweeper], knowing what the dietary of the workhouse was, well knew that [Oliver] would be a nice small pattern, just the thing for register stoves.* {Oliver Twist 3}
A stove in which the flow of air is controlled by a register, a set of movable metal slats partly closing an opening. The chimney-sweep's boy would have to climb inside to clean both stove and chimney (see **stove**).

relict *His landlady, Mrs. Bardell--the relict and sole executrix of a deceased custom-house officer* ... {Pickwick Papers 12}
A widow. Also, a surviving partner.

relish *He was very fond of pickled walnuts, gentlemen. He said he always found that, taken without vinegar, they relished the beer.* {Pickwick Papers 49}
Impart an improved flavor.

remainder ... *when an advantageous place cannot be obtained, either in possession, reversion, or remainder, or expectancy, for the young man who is growing up* ... {Oliver Twist 4}
A right to succeed to a title or position.

remonstrance ... *the parishioners would rebelliously affix their signatures to a remonstrance.* {Oliver Twist 2}
A formal statement of grievances.

rent *I have looked at her, speculating thousands of times upon the unborn child from whom I had been rent.* {Tale of Two Cities 2-17}
Torn. Also a tear, as a rent in an article of clothing.

repair ... *she withdrew at once, and repairing straightaway to her own little parlour below stairs, sat down in her easy chair* ... {Martin Chuzzlewit 3}
To go to, or take oneself to, a place.

repeater *He touched the spring of his repeater, to correct this most preposterous clock. Its rapid little pulse beat twelve, and stopped.* {A Christmas Carol 2}
A watch that chimes the hours and the quarter hours whenever a button is pressed.

repine *No one will repine if I take cold or fever. Let John Grueby pass the night beneath the open sky--no one will repine for him.* {Barnaby Rudge 35}
To feel dissatisfaction or discontent, to complain.

requisition *Telescopes, sandwiches, and glasses of brandy-and-water cold without, begin to be in great requisition . . .* {Sketches, The River}
Demand.

rest, set up one's rest *But the uncertain temper of Mrs. MacStinger, and the possibility of her setting up her rest in the passage during such an entertainment . . . operated as a check on the Captain's hospitable thoughts . . .* {Dombey & Son 17}
To take up an abode, a permanent place.

resurrection-man *"Father," said Young Jerry, as they walked along: taking care to keep at arm's length and to have the stool well between them: "what's a Resurrection-Man?"* {Tale of Two Cities 2-14}
An exhumer and stealer of corpses, in the seventeenth and eighteenth centuries, which were then sold to medical schools for dissection.

retainer *Four pigeon-breasted retainers in plain clothes stand in line in the hall. A fifth retainer, proceeding up the staircase with a mournful air . . .* {Our Mutual Friend 1-2}
Someone attached to a house or manor, owing service. Not a menial servant.

reticle *. . . some half dozen reticles and work-bags "containing documents," as she informed us.* {Bleak House 5}
Alternate form of reticule (see next entry).

reticule *"Dear me!" said she, putting her hand into her reticule, "I have nothing here but documents, my dear Fitz Jarndyce; I must borrow a*

handkerchief." {Bleak House 35}
A small bag of woven or netted material, carried by women as a hand-bag or work bag.

retired ... *undecided whether to pursue the footpath which was lonely and retired, or to go back by the road.* {Martin Chuzzlewit 47}
Secluded.

retort *But, now that fortune had cast in his way a nameless orphan, at whom even the meanest could point the finger of scorn, he retorted on him with interest.* {Oliver Twist 5}
To pay back, retaliate.

returned ... *each had it in his power to state with the utmost confidence that he was the man who would eventually be returned.* {Pickwick Papers 14}
Returned to parliament, i.e., elected or re-elected.

return post-chaise ... *bribed the driver of a return post-chaise to take him on with him* ... {Martin Chuzzlewit 47}
A post chaise returning from a one-way trip for which it was hired.

reversion, reversionary interest ... *Fledgeby's mother had raised money ... on a certain reversionary interest. The reversion falling in soon after they were married, Fledgeby's father laid hold of the cash for his separate use and benefit.* {Our Mutual Friend 2-5}
An inheritance, based on the return of an estate to the heirs of the original grantor.

revived coat *The boy ... now appeared for the first time, in a revived black coat of his masters.* {Sketches, The Boarding-house}
A reviver was a black liquid dye that could be rubbed on a worn or threadbare article of black clothing, improving its appearance tempo-rarily.

revoke *Another game, with a similar result, was followed by a revoke from the unlucky Miller; on which the fat gentleman burst into a state of high personal excitement* ... {Pickwick Papers 6}

In the game of whist, failure to follow suit when a proper card can be played.

riband ... *and, opening a double eye-glass, which he wore attached to a broad black riband, took a view of Oliver* ... {Oliver Twist 14}
1. A ribbon.
... *the coachman, undoing the buckle which keeps his ribands together, prepares to throw them off the moment he stops.* {Pickwick Papers 28}
2. The reins of the horse, which were flat leather straps resembling ribbons.

Ribston pippin ... *the officiating clerk peeled and ate three Ribston pippins* ... {Pickwick Papers 55}
A variety of dessert apple.

rick ... *and crouch for warmth beneath the lee of some old barn or rick, or in the hollow of a tree* ... {Barnaby Rudge 18}
A stack of hay, wheat, or other farm material but usually a haystack.

rick-yard ... *and at last we got into a real country road again, with windmills, rick-yards, milestones, farmers' waggons, scents of old hay, swinging signs, and horse troughs.* {Bleak House 6}
A farmyard containing ricks (see **rick**).

ride *In the public rides there were no carriages, no horses, no animated existence, but a few sleepy policemen* ... {Reprinted Pieces, Out of Town}
A road or path suitable for riding in a carriage or on horseback.

ridicules *"... there's more things besides tills to be emptied." "What do you mean?"* ... *"Pockets, women's ridicules, houses, Mail-coaches, banks!"* ... {Oliver Twist 42}
Mr. Claypole, who is speaking here, means 'reticules' (see **reticule**).

riding-rod ... *certain heavy riding-rods and riding-whips, of which mar y a peasant* ... *had felt the weight when his lord was angry.* {Tale of Two Cities 2-9}
A short rod or switch used in horseback riding.

rifle-distance *The trooper, after taking a turn or two in the rifle-distance and looking up at the moon now shining through the skylights, strides to his own mattress by a shorter route and goes to bed too.* {Bleak House 21}
Rifle range.

rigger, pea and thimble rigger *Tom's evil genius did not... mark him out as the prey of ring-droppers, pea and thimble riggers, duffers, touters, or any of those bloodless sharpers* ... {Martin Chuzzlewit 37}
The pea and thimble rig is a game in which the operator hides a pea under one of three thimbles and bets bystanders that they cannot guess under which one the pea is to be found. He cheats, being able to conceal the movements of the pea.

rime, rimy *A frosty rime was on his head, and on his eyebrows, and his wiry chin.* {A Christmas Carol 1}
It was a rimy morning, and very damp. {Great Expectations 3}
Hoarfrost, white or gray frozen mist.

ring dropper *Tom's evil genius did not* ... *mark him out as the prey of ring-droppers, pea and thimble riggers, duffers, touters, or any of those bloodless sharpers* ... {Martin Chuzzlewit 37}
A cheat who pretends to find a valuable 'dropped' ring and offers to sell it.

ring the bull ... *a wide circle of people assembled round some itinerant juggler, opposed, in his turn, by a noisy band of music, or the classic game of 'Ring the Bull'* ... {Nicholas Nickleby 50}
A game in which the player attempts to throw a ring so that it encircles a hook mounted on a wall.

ring up *Ring up, Mrs. G* ... {Nicholas Nickleby 30}
A theatrical expression meaning 'raise the curtain'.

rip ... *it was a blessing he went mad at last, through evil tempers, and covetousness, and selfishness, and guzzling, and drinking, or he'd have drove many others so. Hope for him an old rip!* {Nicholas Nickleby 41}
A worthless, dissolute man.

riving ... *at his elbow passed an errand-lad, swinging his basket round and round, and with his shrill whistle riving the very timbers of the roof;* ... {Barnaby Rudge 43}
Cleaving, dividing, cutting through.

roasting jack ... *and hanging the wig upon the weathercock, sent it twirling round like a roasting jack.* {Barnaby Rudge 29}
A device for turning meat while it roasts, a rotisserie.

robing-room *Mr. Stryver had left then in the passages, to shoulder his way back to the robing-room.* {Tale of Two Cities 2-4}
A room for putting on official robes, as for example, the one for lawyers at a court.

Roebuck *So he called to him a Roebuck who had the gift of speech, and he said, "Good Roebuck, tell them they must go."* {Reprinted Pieces, Prince Bull. A Fairy Tale}
A male roe deer, a species of small deer found in Europe and Asia.

roll ... *if every one of your clients is to force us to keep a clerk, whether we want to or not, you had better leave off business, strike yourself off the roll, and get taken in execution as soon as you can.* {Old Curiosity Shop 33}
The official list of lawyers eligible to practice.

roller ... *the gardeners to sweep the dewy turf and unfold emerald velvet where the roller passes* ... {Bleak House 41}
A very heavy, wide wheel used to flatten the lawn.

romps ... *Berry played with them there, and seemed to enjoy a game at romps as much as they did* ... {Dombey & Son 8}
Lively boisterous play.

roof *"Up with you," said the stranger, assisting Mr. Pickwick on to the roof with so much precipitation as to impair the gravity of that gentleman's deportment very materially.* {Pickwick Papers 2}
The roof of the coach, where the outside passenger's found their seats.

roof-tree *No two houses in the village were alike, in chimney, size, shape, door, window, gable, roof-tree, anything.* {Message From the Sea 1}
The ridge pole, the main timber of a roof.

rook . . . *to think that the man about town, the rake, the* rou?*, the rook of twenty seasons, should be brought to this pass by a mere boy!* {Nicholas Nickleby 38}
1. A cheat at gambling.
When he bought the house, he liked to think that there were rooks about it. {David Copperfield 1}
2. A crow.

rookery . . . *it was quite a large rookery; but the nests were very old ones, and the birds have deserted them* . . . {David Copperfield 1}
A place where rooks congregate (see **rook**).

Rope-dancing *There was no rope-dancing for me* . . . {Hard Times 1-5}
Dancing on a tightrope.

rosy . . . *whom I shall never more pledge in the rosy* . . . {Old Curiosity Shop 56}
Slang for wine.

rot . . . *and have been carried out dead and dying "like sheep with the rot."* {Bleak House 22}
A disease of sheep caused by a fluke, a kind of worm that invades the liver.

rotten reed . . . *he has been induced to trust in that rotten reed, and it communicates some portion of its rottenness to everything around him.* {Bleak House 35}
An unreliable person or thing (see **bruised reed**).

rouge-et-noir *There were* . . . *half-a-mile of club-houses to play in; and there were* rouge-et-noir, *French hazard, and other games to play* at. {Nicholas Nickleby 50}
A version of roulette.

rouleau *He now gave me a rouleau of gold.* {Tale of Two Cities 3-10}
A roll of coins.

roundabout ... *on roundabouts and swings, from fairs* ... {The Haunted House 2}
Merry-go-round.

round-game *The round-game table, on the other hand, was ... boisterously merry* ... {Pickwick Papers 6}
Any card game in which the players act as individuals and not partners.

round-house *Mr. Denis, having been made prisoner late in the evening, was removed to a neighboring round-house for that night, and carried before a justice for examination on the next day, Saturday.* {Barnaby Rudge 74}
A lockup, place of detention.

round jackets ... *and made appointments on 'Change with men in glazed hats and round jackets pretty well every day.* {Old Curiosity Shop 4}
A jacket having no skirt. The morning jacket, or morning coat, was designed by cutting the front half of the skirt off, leaving the skirts on the back of the jacket. The next step was to remove the entire skirt, making the round jacket. It was apparently the kind of suit jacket worn by middle-class businessmen.

round trot ... *as if he had just remembered an appointment, and was off, at a round trot, to keep it.* {Cricket on the Hearth 1}
A quick, brisk trot.

rout ... *and every day made such a rout in renewing his investigations into the robbery that the officers who had it in hand almost wished it had never been committed.* {Hard Times 3-4}
1. Riot, disturbance, uproar.
If the company at a rout, or drawing-room at court, could only for one moment be as unconscious of the eyes upon them as blind men and women are... {American Notes, 3}
2. A large evening party or reception (see also **rout cakes** and **rout seat**).

rout-cakes ... *they waited for an hour with the utmost patience, being enlivened by an interlude of rout-cakes and lemonade.* {Sketches, Mrs. Joseph Porter}
A rout is a large evening party or reception, and a specially made rich cake was known as a rout cake.

rout seat ... *a heterogeneous litter of pastrycook's trays, lamps, waiters full of glasses, and piles of rout seats which were strewn about the hall* ... {Nicholas Nickleby 17}
A rout is a large evening party or reception for which tables, chairs, etc. would have to be temporarily obtained. These were used as folding or stacking chairs are used now.

row, what's the row *Hullo! my covey, what's the row?* {Oliver Twist 8}
Slang for what's the matter.

Rowland's Macassar Oil ... *she turned to a walking advertisement of Rowland's Macassar Oil, who stood next to her* ... {Sketches, The Tuggs's at Ramsgate}
(see **Macassar**)

roystering *Never were such jolly, roystering, rollicking, merry-making blades, as the jovial crew of Grogzwig.* {Nicholas Nickleby 6}
Roistering. A roister is a noisy reveler.

rubber *Mr. Pecksniff, after playing a pretty long game of bowls ... seemed to be at last in a very fair way of coming in for a rubber or two.* {Martin Chuzzlewit 52}
1. A source of annoyance, or an obstacle.
The rubber was conducted with all that gravity of deportment and se-dateness which befit the pursuit entitled "whist" ... {Pickwick Papers 6}
2. A set of games, usually three or five, here of the card game whist.

rue ... *amazing infusions of gentian, peppermint, gilliflower, sage, pars-ley, thyme, rue, rosemary, and dandelion* ... {Edwin Drood 10}
An evergreen having bitter leaves, formerly used in medicines.

ruff ... *the collar was cut into curious peaks, which served the goblin in lieu of ruff or neckerchief* ... {Pickwick Papers 29}

A piece of neckwear made of fluted cloth standing out from the neck, worn especially in Elizabethan times.

ruffles *He had been seen . . . to pull off ruffles of the finest quality at the corner of the street on Sunday nights, and to put them carefully in his pocket before returning home . . .* {Barnaby Rudge 4}
A strip of lace gathered at one edge, commonly worn at the wrists by men in the eighteenth century.

Rules *Cross over to the Surrey side, and look at such shops of this description as are to be found near the King's Bench prison, and in "the Rules."* {Sketches, Broker's and Marine-store Shops}
An area in the neighborhood of some prisons, including King's Bench, where some prisoners were allowed to live. This was done with debtors who could give proper security, ensuring that they would not run away.

rullock *. . . to muffle the rullocks of the boats . . .* {English Prisoners 1}
Rowlock, or oarlock.

rum *Rum creeturs is women . . .* {Pickwick Papers 14}
Slang for good, great, wonderful.

rumble *. . . Kit, well wrapped and muffled up, was in the rumble behind . . .* {Old Curiosity Shop 69}
A seat behind the coach to accommodate servants.

runt *The wheeling and circling flights of runts, fantails, tumblers, and pouters . . .* {Barnaby Rudge 1}
A kind of fancy pigeon, as are fantails, tumblers, and pouters.

rush-candle, rushlight *. . . a feeble rush-candle which was to burn all night.* {Old Curiosity Shop 9}
As I had asked for a night-light, the chamberlain had brought me in, before he left me, the good old constitutional rushlight of those virtuous days . . . {Great Expectations 45}
A candle made by dipping the pith of the stems of rush plants in tallow. It gave a weak light compared with a wax candle.

rusk . . . *disgorged such treasures of tea, and coffee, and wine, and rusks, and oranges, and grapes, and fowls ready trussed* . . . {Old Curiosity Shop 66}
Pieces of bread baked a second time to make them hard and longer lasting.

russia leather *That whiff of russia leather, too, and all those rows on rows of volumes, neatly ranged within--what happiness did they suggest!* {Martin Chuzzlewit 5}
A kind of durable leather used in bookbinding, treated with the oil from birch bark.

rusty *Some rusty gowns and other articles of that lady's wardrobe depended from the posts* . . . {Martin Chuzzlewit 49}
Shabby and worn out.

sable *Another sable warder (a carpenter who had once eaten two geese for a wager) opened the door...* {Great Expectations 35}
Sable means a suit of black mourning garments. The warder here was dressed in black because of the death of Pip's sister.

sackcloth coat *... a strange specimen of the human race in a sackcloth coat and apron of the same...* {Pickwick Papers 2}
A coarse and cheap material used for making sacks, but when used for clothing was often lined with expensive fabrics.

sacristan *... and sent word to the sacristan who kept the keys of the church, that there might be need to ring the tocsin by-and-by.* {Tale of Two Cities 2-23}
The sexton of a parish church.

saddle-donkey *... in whose hand every pen appeared to become perversely animated, and to go wrong and crooked, and to stop, and splash, and sidle into corners like a saddle-donkey.* {Bleak House 31}
A donkey used for riding, a mount less manageable than a horse.

saddle-girth *You shall see him... bound hand and foot, and brought to London at a saddle-girth, and you shall hear of him at Tyburn Tree if we have luck.* {Barnaby Rudge 17}
The band which runs under the belly of a horse from one side of the saddle to the other.

saddler *[His eyes] suddenly rested on the blooming countenance of Maria Lobbs, the only daughter of old Lobbs, the great saddler over the way.* {Pickwick Papers 17}
A person who makes or who sells saddles.

safety-lamp *"Are they all brothers, sir?" inquired the lady who had carried the "Davy" or safety-lamp.* {Nicholas Nickleby 6}
A miner's lamp, invented by Sir Humphry Davy, which could be carried safely while lit in the presence of inflammable gases.

sage-cheese *. . . whose countenance it greenly mottles in the manner of sage-cheese . . .* {Bleak House 12}
Cheese made by mixing it with a decoctation of the herb sage.

sago *. . . and calves'-foot jelly, and arrow-root, and sago, and other delicate restoratives . . .* {Old Curiosity Shop 66}
A starch obtained from certain kinds of palm trees.

sail-loft *. . . among the riggers, and the mast, oar and block makers, and the boat-builders, and the sail-lofts . . .* {Our Mutual Friend 2-12}
A large room, usually on an upper floor, in which sails are made.

Saint Anthony's fire *. . . our last servant went to the hospital a week ago with Saint Anthony's fire in her face . . .* {Nicholas Nickleby 18}
Erysipelas, an infection of the skin marked by a red color and severe constitutional symptoms.

salamander *. . . There was no rolling-pin, there was no salamander . . . , there was nothing in the house . . .* {The Haunted House 1}
A circular plate of iron. When heated red hot, it was placed over a dish of food to brown the surface.

sale-board *On the front of his sale-board hung a little placard, like a kettle holder, bearing the inscription in his own small text . . .* {Our Mutual Friend 1-5}
Mr. Wegg's place of business was a wooden board, set up on trestles on the sidewalk, on which items for sale were displayed. That board was called a sale-board.

Salisbury carriage *"And a Salisbury carriage, eh!" said Mr. Tapley. "That's what he came in, depend on it . . ."* {Martin Chuzzlewit 43}
There was no carriage called a Salisbury carriage. This may refer to a carriage with a Salisbury boot. The stowage box, under the driver's seat, was a plain rectangular box. A fashion grew, begun by a coachmaker in

Salisbury, of making boots with rounded surfaces which then took their name from the town.

Sally Lunn *It's a sort of night that's meant for muffins. Likewise crumpets. Also Sally Lunns.* {The Chimes 4}
A sweet, light tea cake.

salt fish ... *he was a long-headed man, a dry one, a salt fish, a deep file, a rasper*... {Martin Chuzzlewit 38}
Slang for a wise, silent man.

salve ... *in the doorway stood the missing Blandois, the cause of many anxieties. "Salve, fellow jail-bird!" said he.* {Little Dorrit 2-28}
Latin for 'hail'. Used as a greeting.

sal volatile *Raymond is a witness what ginger and sal volatile I am obliged to take in the night.* {Great Expectations 11}
Smelling salts, salt-like chemicals with a pungent odor, usually of ammonia. They were found in every home and were used to awaken someone who had fainted.

sallyport *All eyes were turned in the direction of the sallyport.* {Pickwick Papers 4}
An opening in a fortification through which troops may suddenly emerge, thus performing a sally.

saloon *I had believed in the best parlour as a most elegant saloon* ... {Great Expectations 14}
A large hall, from the French word *salon*, and not a low-class tavern. It can also mean a hall or apartment used for professional entertainment.

salver *This young gentleman took the card up-stairs on a salver*... {Nicholas Nickleby 21}
A tray.

sandals *Just then, the door opened, and in came a young lady, with her hair curled in a crop all over her head, and her shoes tied in sandals all over her ankles.* {Sketches, The Dancing Academy}
The straps around the ankles and instep that hold on any low shoe.

Here it does not mean a shoe consisting of a sole held on by straps or thongs.

sand-box ... *the inkstand top, the other inkstand top, the little sand-box.* {Bleak House 10}
A shaker-top box containing sand, which was sprinkled over the ink on freshly written pages to dry them.

sandboy ... *a small road-side inn of pretty ancient date, with a sign, representing three Sandboys increasing their jollity with as many mugs of ale and bags of gold* ... {Old Curiosity Shop 18}
A seller of sand for use on tavern floors, before sawdust replaced sand.

sanded floor ... *one public room with a sanded floor, and a chair or two.* {Nicholas Nickleby 6}
A floor with sand spread on it, to absorb dust and spilled materials.

sanding ... *I found the landlord of the little inn, sanding his door-step.* {The Haunted House 1}
1. Sprinkling sand to absorb the dirt, not sandpapering.
Reams--of forms illegibly printed on whitey-brown paper were filled up about the Bottle, and it was the subject of more stamping and sanding than I had ever seen before. {The Uncommercial Traveller, The Italian Prisoner}
2. Before blotting paper, the ink on freshly written paper was dried by sprinkling fine sand over it.

sarcenet ... *a particularly tall lady in a blue sarcenet pelisse and bonnet of the same* ... {Sketches, Vauxhall-gardens by Day}
A fine, soft silk cloth. The name may be a diminutive of Saracen.

sash window ... *a barmaid who was looking on from behind an open sash window* ... {Nicholas Nickleby 43}
An ordinary window with sections that slide up and down, as distinguished from a casement window.

sate *So there Casby sate, twirling and twirling* ... {Little Dorrit 2-9}
An old form of the past tense of sit.

saunter ... *he sauntered away his time in the fields or sotted in the ale-house* ... {Pickwick Papers 6}
To stroll.

saveloy *... regaling himself... with a cold collation of an Abernethy biscuit and a saveloy.* {Pickwick Papers 55}
A highly seasoned, cooked, and dried sausage.

savoury ... *here is a devilled grill, a savoury pie, a dish of kidneys, and so forth. Pray sit down.* {Dombey & Son 20}
... savoury puddings, compounded of such scraps as were to be bought in a heap for the least money at Fleet Market ... {Barnaby Rudge 8}
Spiced.

saw out (see **see out**)

saw-pit ... *it charged small parties of [fallen leaves] and hunted them into the wheelwright's saw-pit, and below the planks and timbers in the yard* ... {Martin Chuzzlewit 2}
A large hole or trench dug in the ground so that one of the people sawing a log into boards could work from below.

sawyer *And her brother's the sawyer that was put in the cage, Miss, and they expect he'll drink himself to death entirely on beer* ... {Bleak House 37}
One who saws timber.

saxony dress coat *He wore a white favor in his button-hole, and a bran new extra super double-milled blue saxony dress coat (that was its description in the bill)* ... {Martin Chuzzlewit 54}
Saxony is a fine kind of wool, often dyed blue with indigo.

scandalise ... *the company being accustomed to scandalise each other in pairs were deprived of their usual subject of conversation now that they were all assembled in friendship* ... {Old Curiosity Shop 4}
To tell false or malicious things about someone.

'scapegallows *"... and remember this, 'scapegallows," said Ralph, menacing him with his hand, "that if we meet again, and you so much as notice*

me by one begging gesture, you shall see the inside of a jail once more ... "
{Nicholas Nickleby 44}
Someone who has escaped the gallows, although he deserves it.

scapegrace *He is sorely taken aback, too, by the dutiful behaviour of his nephew and has a woeful consciousness upon him of being a scapegrace.* {Bleak House 63}
In five minutes time the chaise was ready, and this good scapegrace in his saddle. {Barnaby Rudge 61}
A person somewhat reckless or disorderly, a scamp. In the second example it is meant affectionately.

scarlatina ... *all of them flushed with breakfast, as having taken scarlatina sociably* ... {Our Mutual Friend 1-10}
Scarlet fever, a bacterial disease in which a bright-red rash appears.

scavenger ... *a scavenger's cart happening to stand unattended at the corner, with its little ladder planted against the wheel* ... {Our Mutual Friend 4-14}
A street cleaner.

Schiedam ... *there is a house by the waterside where they have some of the noblest Schiedam--reputed to be smuggled, but that's between ourselves* ... {Old Curiosity Shop 21}
Schiedam gin, from that city in Holland.

sconce *The candles that lighted that room of hers were placed in sconces on the wall.* {Great Expectations 38}
A wall bracket for holding candles often with a mirror behind it.

score *Why there's a score between him and [the inn keeper] Mrs. Lupin. And I think Mrs. Lupin lets him and his friend off very easy in not chargin 'em double* ... {Martin Chuzzlewit 7}
Unpaid charges, a bill or tab (see other entries below).

score, go off at score *Caleb no sooner sees [the others dancing] than he clutches Tilly Slowboy by both hands and goes off at score;* ...

{Cricket on the Hearth 3}
To make a sudden dash at full speed.

score it under *"Put down that, Mr. Jinks" said the magistrate, who was fast rising into a rage. "Score it under," said Sam.* {Pickwick Papers 25}
Underscore it, underline it.

score, start off at score *She started off at score, tossing her head, sighing in the most demonstrative manner...* {Little Dorrit 1-24}
To suddenly break into impetuous speech.

scot and lot *... but I'll pay you off scot and lot bye and bye.* {Martin Chuzzlewit 24}
To contribute equally to some cost or charge, though here it seems to mean fully or completely.

scout *... Toby scouted with indignation a certain rumour that the Chimes were haunted...* {The Chimes 1}
Treat as absurd.

scrag *... remnants of loaves, and pieces of cheese, and damp towels, and scrags of meat...* {Pickwick Papers 42}
1. The poor quality end of the neck of mutton or veal.
"It's naughty, ain't it, Oliver?" inquired Charley Bates. "He'll come to be scragged, won't he?" {Oliver Twist 18}
2. Slang for to hang.

scraper *... a straggling and solitary young lady of tender-years standing on the scraper on the tips of her toes and making futile attempts to reach the knocker with a spelling-book.* {Old Curiosity Shop 8}
A strip of metal, affixed near the entrance to a house, used to scrape mud from the shoes before entering.

scratch *... he had a genius for coming up to the scratch... and proving himself an ugly customer.* {Hard Times 1-2}
The line in a boxing ring at which the boxers stood to start a round. It was originally a line scratched on the ground.

scratchers *The noise of these various instruments, the orchestra, the shouting, the "scratchers," and the dancing, is perfectly bewildering.* {Sketches, Greenwich Fair}
A scratch-back. A toy, working somewhat like a rattle, which produces the sound of tearing cloth when rubbed on someone's back.

screen, hand-screen *My Lady, with a careless toss of her screen, turns herself toward the fire again, sitting almost with her back to the young man of the name of Guppy.* {Bleak House 29}
A device resembling a hand fan, used to screen the face from the heat of the fireplace.

screw *" . . . a wicked old screw", pursued the woman. "Why wasn't he natural in his lifetime? . . . "* {A Christmas Carol 4}
1. A stingy person, a miser.
I have him periodically in a vice. I'll twist him, sir. I'll screw him, sir. If he won't do it with a good grace, I'll make him do it with a bad one, sir! {Bleak House 27}
2. To apply pressure or to coerce.
. . . running up to him with a kind of screw in her face and carriage, expressive of suppressed emotion . . . {Dombey & Son 1}
3. A contorted expression.
. . . a knife, some butter, a screw of salt, and a bottle of sherry. {Martin Chuzzlewit 36}
4. Something wrapped in a twisted bit of paper.

screw collier *. . . a rather nautical and Screw-Collier like appearance . . .* {The Uncommercial Traveller, Chambers}
A coal-carrying steamship driven by a propeller (at first called a water-screw, or screw) instead of paddlewheels.

scrip *He wore, hanging with a long strap round his neck, a kind of scrip or wallet, in which to carry food.* {Barnaby Rudge 45}
A small bag or satchel carried by pilgrims or beggars.

Scrip-Church *. . . Lady Tippins is eminently facetious on the subject of these Fathers of this Scrip-Church . . .* {Our Mutual Friend 3-17}
Scrip refers to stock certificates or commercial documents exchange-

able for stock certificates. The made-up word 'Scrip-Church' is used here sarcastically.

scrivener . . . *made a clerk in a sharp scrivener's office at twelve years old.* {Bleak House 21}
A professional scribe or copyist.

scrub *No scrubs would do for no such purpose. Nothing less would satisfy our Directors than our member in the House of Commons* . . .
{Martin Chuzzlewit 35}
A person of poor appearance, an insignificant person.

scudded . . . *the Dodger scudded at a rapid pace: directing Oliver to follow close at his heels.* {Oliver Twist 8}
Moved briskly.

scull . . . *he promptly set to work to haul up his boat, and make her fast, and take the sculls and rudder and rope out of her.* {Our Mutual Friend 1-6}
A kind of oar.

scullery *It was a little lattice-window* . . . *which belonged to a scullery, or small brewing place, at the end of the passage.* {Oliver Twist 22}
A small room off the kitchen where the dishes are washed, or other dirty work is done.

scullion *To these young scullions Mrs. Bagnet occasionally imparts a wink, or a shake of the head, or a crooked face, as they made mistakes.*
{Bleak House 49}
The lowest servant who did the most menial work.

sea-coal *You will find a fine sea-coal fire, sir.* {Tale of Two Cities 1-4}
Ordinary coal, as distinguished from charcoal. Possibly so-called because it was first found in seams exposed at the seashore by action of the waves.

sea-jacket . . . *a torn and darned rough-weather sea-jacket, out at elbows* . . . {Little Dorrit 1-6}
A sailors jacket, a pea jacket.

seal, on a watch chain ... *his clothes of the blackest and sleekest, his gold watch-chain of the heaviest, and his seals of the largest.* {Martin Chuzzlewit 27}
A trinket of engraved or flat stone or glass hung from a watch chain as decoration.

sealing-wax *Paper, pens, ink, ruler, sealing-wax, wafers, pounce-box, string-box, fire-box, Tim's hat, Tim's scrupulously-folded gloves, Tim's other coat* ... {Nicholas Nickleby 37}
A material which becomes soft when heated, so that it will take the impression of a seal, but hard and adhesive to paper when cooled. Used for fastening documents or letters, and for affixing seals to paper. It is not made of wax, which is too soft and fragile for that use.

sealing-waxed end ... *fill your pipe again and smoke it fast, down to the last whiff, or I'll put the sealing-waxed end of it in the fire and rub it red-hot upon your tongue.* {Old Curiosity Shop 11}
Clay pipes had sealing wax on the stem to make them smooth.

seal-ring *A portly, important-looking gentlemen, dressed all in black, with a white cravat, large gold watch seals, a pair of gold eye-glasses, and a large seal-ring upon his little finger.* {Bleak House 3}
A finger ring bearing a seal, an engraving that could be used to leave an impression on warm sealing wax.

sear ... *a face that even the rose-coloured curtains could not make otherwise than sear and wild.* {Dombey & Son 37}
... *I am falling into the sear and yellow leaf.* {Bleak House 23}
Withered. The phrase in the second example implies, 'I am aging and will die soon'.

seeds-man *Mr. Pumblechook's premises ... were of a peppercorny and farinaceous character, as the premises of a corn-chandler and seeds-man should be.* {Great Expectations 8}
A dealer in seeds.

see out, saw out *We saw out all the drink that was produced, like good men and true* ... {English Prisoners 1}

To outlast, in a drinking contest. Here the sense is to be able to drink everything that was available and still be able to walk home.

seise, seize ... *that gentleman may have been led to consider himself as specially licensed to bag sparrows, and as being specially seised and possessed of all the birds he had got together.* {Martin Chuzzlewit 20} *It involved the only idea of which he did not stand seized and possessed in equal moieties with Snitchey* ... {The Battle of Life 1} To be put into legal possession of something.

self-love *"Again, not very flattering to my self-love," said Eugene* ... {Our Mutual Friend 4-6} Regard for oneself, self-centerdness, selfishness. Here it has the sense of 'pride'.

sell ... *what a time this would be for a sell! I've got Phil Barker here: so drunk, that a boy might take him.* {Oliver Twist 26} Slang for a betrayal.

sempstress ... *Susan Nipper worked away at her side, all day, with the concentrated zeal of fifty sempstresses.* {Dombey & Son 56} Seamstress, a person who does plain sewing.

seneschal *[On the stage] a grey-headed seneschal sings a funny chorus with a funnier body of vassals* ... {Oliver Twist 17} An official, serving a king or high noble, who controlled all household functions and the administration of justice.

se'nnight *On the Thursday, both Houses had adjourned until the following Monday se'nnight* ... {Barnaby Rudge 73} Seven days and nights, a week. The adjournment was until a week from the next Monday.

sensible *And Pa said ... that he was sensible the best thing that could happen to them was their being all tomahawked together.* {Bleak House 30} Conscious of, or aware of, something.

serious, serious family *I must look for a private service I suppose, sir. I might come out strong, perhaps, in a serious family* . . . {Martin Chuzzlewit 7}
Devoutly religious.

serjeant . . . *Mr. Serjeant Snubbin appeared, followed by Mr. Mallard, who half hid the serjeant behind a large crimson bag* . . . {Pickwick Papers 34}
A member of a particular order of lawyers, abolished in 1880.

serve you out *He faintly moaned, "I am done for," as the victim, and he barbarously bellowed, "I'll serve you out," as the murderer.* {Great Expectations 18}
To administer corporal punishment.

service *Your granddaughter I have had the honor of seeing before; my service to you, Miss.* {Bleak House 21}
A polite expression similar to 'at your service,' or 'your servant'.

servitor *With these instructions, Mr. Pickwick placed a sum of money in the hands of his faithful servitor and ordered him to start for Bristol immediately* . . . {Pickwick Papers 37}
A servant, but sometimes with the implication of one who serves in war.

set, top set *Tenant of a top set--bad character--shut himself up in his bedroom closet and took a dose of arsenic.* {Pickwick Papers 21}
A suite of rooms, the top set being on the top floor.

set against . . . *all courageous fellows were invited to come forward and enroll themselves in a Society for making a set against [Old Cheeseman].* {The Schoolboy's Story}
To place in a position of hostility or opposition.

set-off *If as a set-off (excuse the legal phrase from a barrister-at-law) you would like to ask Tippins to tea* . . . {Our Mutual Friend 2-6}
A claim which counterbalances another claim, the debt of one party being balanced by the debt of the second party.

set one's cap *I think it might be a good speculation if I were to set my cap at Michael Warden . . .* {The Battle of Life 3}
To seek to marry, to decide to court. The expression comes from the French word *cap*, which is the bow of a boat. To set the *cap* on a place (*mettre le cap sur*) is to set a course for that place, to steer for that place.

set-out *Did you ever see such a set-out as that?* {Nicholas Nickleby 23}
1. A person's costume or manner of dress.
She must just hate and detest the whole set-out of us. {Hard Times 1-8}
2. By analogy with equipage, the group and the way they are dressed.

settee *Miss Havisham seated on a settee near the fire, and Estella on a cushion at her feet.* {Great Expectations 44}
A seat with arms, usually for two people.

settens *It'll come on in the settens after term; fourteenth of Febooary, we expect . . .* {Pickwick Papers 31}
A dialect pronunciation of 'sittings' (of the court).

settle *So, I nodded, and then he nodded again, and made room on the settle beside him that I might sit down there.* {Great Expectations 10}
A wooden bench with arms, a high back, and a box under the seat.

settlement *. . . we have never been able to discover who is his father, or what was his mother's settlement, name, or condition.* {Oliver Twist 2}
1. The establishment of a person in life, marriage, or employment.
. . . a paved Quaker settlement, in color and general conformation very like a Quakeress's bonnet . . . {Edwin Drood 3}
2. A place where a religious community is established.

sexton *It by no means follows that because a man is a sexton, and constantly surrounded by the emblems of mortality, therefore he should be a morose and melancholy man . . .* {Pickwick Papers 29}
A church officer concerned with the digging of graves and the ringing of bells.

shake *. . . both gentlemen, in compliance with a solemn custom of the ancient Brotherhood to which they belonged, joined in a fragment of*

the popular duet of 'All's Well', with a long shake at the end. {Old Curiosity Shop 56}
1. A rapid repetition of two notes.
I heard the children crying out your name, and the shake passed from me at the very sound of it. {The Haunted Man 3}
2. Shiver, chill.

shake-down *"He'll take a meal with us to-night," said Squeers, "and go among the boys to-morrow morning. You can give him a shake-down here to-night, can't you?"* {Nicholas Nickleby 7}
A makeshift bed made up on the floor, originally one made of a pile of hay shaken down from the overhead hayloft.

shambling *... speaking aloud for the first time, and speaking very sulkily; shambling with his legs the while.* {Martin Chuzzlewit 4}
Making irregular and awkward motions.

shares *He goes ... into the City, attends meetings of Directors, and has to do with traffic in Shares.* {Our Mutual Friend 1-10}
Stocks, shares in a company.

shark-headed screw *... a gross or two of shark-headed screws for general use ...* {Great Expectations 15}
A shark is a notch, in Gloucestershire dialect. These screws have a notched or slotted head.

shaving-glass *... in little black frames like common shaving-glasses ...* {Martin Chuzzlewit 13}
A small mirror used while shaving.

shaving paper *Would he like his debts paid and his house furnished, and a few bank-notes for shaving paper--if he shaves at all!* {Nicholas Nickleby 54}
Pieces of scrap paper used to wipe the soap and hair from a straight razor after each stroke.

shaving-shop *... more unwashed skins and grizzly beards than all the pumps and shaving-shops between Tyburn and Whitechapel could*

render decent between sunrise and sunset. {Pickwick Papers 43}
A shop in which customers were shaved, as in a barbershop.

shawl-pattern . . . *a coarse, staring, shawl-pattern waistcoat; and drab breeches.* {Oliver Twist 22}
A pattern resembling that of an Oriental shawl.

shay-cart *Master sent me over with the shay-cart to carry your luggage up to the house.* {Pickwick Papers 28}
Chaise-cart, a two-wheeled, one-horse cart similar to the light vehicle called a chaise.

shears *For all that, however, the Yard made no display,* . . . *its great chimneys smoking with a quiet--almost a lazy--air* . . . *the great Shears moored off it, looking meekly and inoffensively out of proportion* . . .
{The Uncommercial Traveller, Chatham Dockyard}
A kind of crane made of two tall timbers set wide apart at the bottom and crossed near the top, similar in appearance to a pair of scissors or shears.

sheep-skin *In dirty upper casements, here and there, hazy little patches of candlelight reveal where some wise draughtsman and conveyancer yet toils for the entanglement of real estate in meshes of sheep-skin, in the average ration of about a dozen of sheep to an acre of land.* {Bleak House 32}
The parchment on which legal documents were written.

sheet-anchor *Since his sheet-anchor had come home, Mr. Gradgrind had been sparing of speech.* {Hard Times 3-4}
The largest anchor carried by a ship, usually used in extreme conditions. Hence, figuratively, someone depended upon in difficult situations.

shelving *It had a shelving roof; high in one part, and at another descending almost to the floor.* {Nicholas Nickleby 62}
Sloping. It has nothing to do with shelves or the wood from which shelves are made.

shelving-trap *So, when they had crawled through the passage indicated by the vintner (which was a mere shelving-trap for the admission of*

casks), and had ranged with some difficulty to unchain and raise the door at the upper end, they emerged into the street . . . {Barnaby Rudge 67}
A trap is a ladder with broad flat rungs. In this case the trap is shelving (sloping) and leads to a trap door. A trap door may also be called a trap.

shepherd's-plaid   *. . . a genteel female, in shepherd's-plaid boots, who appeared to be the client.* {Nicholas Nickleby 16}
A black and white checked pattern.

Sheppard, Jack *Then, why are my poor child's limbs fettered and tied up? Am I to be told that there is any analogy between [him] and Jack Sheppard?* {Reprinted Pieces, "Births. Mrs. Meek, of a Son"}
A notorious eighteenth-century robber condemned to death who several times escaped from prison.

shew *. . . with an ease and expedition that shewed he was well acquainted with them.* {Oliver Twist 8}
Show.

shifts *. . . gentlemen who . . . live upon their wits . . . are occasionally reduced to very narrow shifts and straits . . .* {Nicholas Nickleby 27}
A stratagem or expedient, often forced by circumstances.

shiner *. . . is it worth fifty shiners extra, if it's safely done from the outside?* {Oliver Twist 19}
Slang for a guinea coin, worth a pound plus a shilling.

shingle *. . . an unsuccessful attempt to smoke a very blunt cigar . . . which that young gentleman had covertly purchased on the shingle from a most desperate smuggler . . .* {Dombey & Son 14}
A beach covered with small rounded stones.

ship-breaker *. . . Daniel Quilp was a ship-breaker, yet to judge from these appearances he must have either been a ship-breaker on a very small scale, or have broken up his ships very small indeed.* {Old Curiosity Shop 4}
A person who buys old ships to disassemble them and sell the parts.

shipping-broker ... *we found a worthy young merchant or shipping-broker, not long established in business* ... {Great Expectations 37}
An agent who transacts the business of a ship when it is in port.

shirt-frill ... *and grandpapa with a beautifully plaited shirt-frill, and white neckerchief* ... {Sketches, A Christmas Dinner}
A frilled decorative cloth worn on the shirt front and wristbands.

shiver *The upshot of which was to smash this witness like a crockery vessel, and shiver his part of the case to useless lumber.* {Tale of Two Cities 2-3}
Shatter into pieces.

shoe *Pardon, Monseigneur; he swung by the chain of the shoe--the drag.* {Tale of Two Cities 2-8}
A metal plate placed under the wheel of a carriage to slow its descent when going downhill by preventing the wheel from turning. It was attached to the frame of the carriage by a chain.

shoe-binding *Miss Evans* ... *had adopted in early life the useful pursuit of shoe-binding, to which she had afterwards superadded the occupation of a straw-bonnet maker.* {Sketches, Miss Evans and the Eagle}
Attaching a leather or ribbon binding, used to cover the raw, cut edges of the leather from which the shoe is made.

shoe-buckles ... *the light of the fire, which shone too in his bright shoe-buckles* ... {Barnaby Rudge 1}
Decorative buckles worn on the instep of the shoes.

shoe-vamper *Here the clothesman, the shoe-vamper, and the rag-merchant, display their goods.* {Oliver Twist 26}
A person who repairs the vamps of shoes, that is, the front of the shoe. A shoe repairman.

shoeblack ... *he was established in business as a shoeblack, and opened a shop under the archway near the Horse Guards* ... {Barnaby Rudge 82}
A shoeshine man.

shoot ... *he was standing by at the shoot of the Cunard steamer, off tomorrow, as the stocks in trade of several butchers, poulterers, and fish-mongers, poured down into the icehouse* ... {The Uncommercial Traveller, Poor Mercantile Jack}
Chute, a steep ramp down which the goods mentioned were slid.

shoot rubbish, shot ... *where tiles and bricks were burnt, bones were boiled, carpets were beat, rubbish was shot, dogs were fought, and dust was heaped by contractors.* {Our Mutual Friend 1-4}
Chute. The rubbish shoot is a place where rubbish is dumped down a steep incline, as if in a chute.

shooting-coat ... *a new green shooting-coat, plaid neckerchief, and closely fitted drabs.* {Pickwick Papers 1}
A coat worn for shooting, styled with appropriate numbers and placement of pockets.

shoots ... *he watches the spasmodic shoots and darts that break out of her face and limbs* ... {Edwin Drood 1}
A sudden involuntary movement.

shop *It was Bartlemy time when I was shopped* ... {Oliver Twist 16}
To be shopped is to be put in prison.

shop-board ... *and we have detected his assistants (for he has assistants now) in the act of sitting on the shop-board in the same uniform.* {Sketches, Scotland-yard}
The counter or table on which goods to be sold are displayed.

short *If you'll order the waiter to deliver him anything short he won't drink it off at once, won't he!* {Pickwick Papers 46}
A drink of undiluted spirits, a straight drink.

short commons ... *the gruel was served out; and a long grace was said over the short commons.* {Oliver Twist 2}
Commons is the share of provisions to which each member of a company is entitled. Short commons is a very small share.

short-sixes ... *[a] general illumination of very bright short-sixes* ... {Martin Chuzzlewit 2}
A kind of candle, referred to by the number required to make a pound in weight.

shorts, knee-shorts ... *the gentleman ... in plush shorts and cottons* ... {Pickwick Papers 47}
Forced the lock; and a very dusty skeleton, in a blue coat, black knee-shorts, and silks, fell forward in the arms of the porter who opened the door. {Pickwick Papers 21}
Knee breeches, small clothes.

short-stepped ... *the cheery good-nights of passing travellers jogging past on little short-stepped horses* ... {Old Curiosity Shop 46}
A horse equally lame in all its legs.

shoulder-belt ... *no coat; a red shoulder-belt; and a demi-semi-military scarlet hat* ... {The Uncommercial Traveller, A Plea for Total Abstinence}
A belt passing over the right shoulder and around the waist. A Sam Browne belt.

shovel-hat ... *in a shovel hat and gaberdine.* {Our Mutual Friend 3-10}
A stiff-brimmed hat with the brim turned up at the sides so that at front and rear it resembles the blade of a shovel.

show saloon ... *ushered them, through a handsome hall and up a spacious staircase, into the show saloon, which comprised two spacious drawing-rooms* ... {Nicholas Nickleby 10}
Showroom.

show-tramp *So, all the tramps with carts or caravans--the Gipsy-tramp, the Show-tramp, the Cheap-Jack--find it impossible to resist the temptations of the place* ... {The Uncommercial Traveller, Tramps}
The itinerant Punch-and-Judy showman carrying his stage and puppets with him.

shrub ... *there to make merry upon a cold collation, bottled-beer, shrub, and shrimps* ... {Nicholas Nickleby 52}

A drink made, according to one recipe, of orange or lemon, sugar, water, and rum. In another recipe it is made of brandy, white wine, lemon juice and peel, and sugar.

shuffler *"You--you're a shuffler, sir!" gasped the furious doctor.* {Pickwick Papers 2}
A slippery, shifty person.

sick bay *"Then you have not been to sea lately?" "No. Been in the sick bay since then, and been employed ashore."* {Our Mutual Friend 2-12}
A place on a ship where sick and wounded were kept and cared for. A seaman might refer to an onshore hospital as a sick bay, or might say that he had been in sick bay if he were sick and confined to home.

sick couch *They sent the sick couch for the old 'ooman, and Simmons took the children away at night.* {Sketches, The Broker's Man}
Usually means a sickbed, but here it appears to mean some sort of stretcher or, perhaps, wheelchair used to convey the sick old woman to the workhouse infirmary.

sides *Poor Kate was well nigh distracted on the receipt of four closely-written and closely-crossed sides of congratulations on the very subject which had prevented her closing her eyes all night . . .* {Nicholas Nickleby 28}
Pages.

side-face *. . . [she] treated Mr. Moddle that very evening with increased consideration, and presented her side-face to him as much as possible.* {Martin Chuzzlewit 32}
The face in profile.

side-wind *I am a straightforward man, I believe. I don't go beating about for side-winds.* {Hard Times 2-9}
An indirect or devious method or manner.

sifter *. . . a little, pale, wall-eyed, woebegone inn like a large dust-binn of two compartments and a sifter.* {Bleak House 39}
A sieve.

sight (see **taking a sight**)

signalize ... *to repair to the arbour in which Mr. Tupman had already signalized himself* ... {Pickwick Papers 8}
Draw attention to.

signify ... *it don't signify.* {Barnaby Rudge 56}
To be of importance; hence, this example means 'it is not important'.

sign-manual *The chairman of the Board employed the rest of the morning in affixing his sign-manual of gracious acceptance to various new proposals* ... {Martin Chuzzlewit 28}
An autograph, usually that of a sovereign.

silks ... *and Ralph himself, divested of his boots, and ceremoniously embellished with black silks and shoes, presented his crafty face.* {Nicholas Nickleby 19}
Silk stockings.

siller *And she shall walk in silk attire, and siller have to spare, or may I never rise fro this bed again.* {Old Curiosity Shop 66}
An old form of the word 'silver'. Here Dickens quotes an eighteenth-century poem *The Siller Crown.*

silver-chaser *Yes, Miss, she is alive ... and married to a silver-chaser.* {Dombey & Son 8}
Someone who engraves or embosses silver.

simoom ... *the ham (though it was good enough of itself) seemed to blow a faint simoom of ham through the whole Marshalsea.* {Little Dorrit 2-27}
The hot, dry, suffocating wind of the African desert.

single harness ... *while playing with Florence, or driving Miss Tox in single harness.* {Dombey & Son 8}
The harness arrangement used for a carriage drawn by a single horse.

single-stick *"Did you ever try a fall with a man when you were young, master?" said Hugh. "Can you make any play at single-stick?"* {Barnaby

Rudge 35}
Fencing with a stick having a hand guard, and used one-handed, like a
sword. A fall, as used here, means a bout, or round, in wrestling.

situate ... *a low public-house, situate in the filthiest part of Little Saffron-
Hill* ... {Oliver Twist 15}
Situated, located.

situation *"Let me hear another sound from* you*" said Scrooge, "and
you'll keep your Christmas by losing your situation."* {A Christmas
Carol 1}
Job, position.

six-in-hand ... *one of them, alone in a Greek chariot, drove six-in-hand
into every town they came to.* {Hard Times 1-6}
Driving a carriage drawn by six horses, so-named because the reins for
all six horses are held in the hand at one time.

sixpence'orth ... *as near the real thing as sixpence'orth of halfpence is to
sixpence.* {Cricket on the Hearth 2}
Worth six pennies..

sizar ... *Little Dorrit, as an enforced sizar of that college, was obliged to
submit herself humbly to its ordinances.* {Little Dorrit 2-7}
One who receives a sort of scholarship at a university.

size *A brandnew tavern, redolent of fresh mortar and size, and
fronting nothing at all* ... {Dombey & Son 6}
A glutinous material applied to surfaces to prepare them for gilding or
painting.

skaiter *"Cold, isn't it?" "Seasonable for Christmas time. You're not a
skaiter, I suppose?"* {A Christmas Carol 4}
Ice skater.

skeleton suit *Although he could not have been less than eighteen or nine-
teen years old, and was tall for that age, he wore a skeleton suit, such
as is usually put upon very little boys* ... {Nicholas Nickleby 7}
A straight, blue-cloth suit usually worn by small boys.

skewer *For, Mr. Mopes, by suffering everything about him to go to ruin, and by dressing himself in a blanket and skewer, and by steeping himself in soot and grease and other nastiness, had acquired great renown in all that country-side . . .* {Tom Tiddler's Ground 1}
A metal pin used to hold clothing together.

skid the wheel *. . . the guard got down to skid the wheel for the descent, and open the coach-door to let the passengers in.* {Tale of Two Cities 1-2}
The skid is the iron plate, or drag, used under the wheel to prevent it from turning, thus slowing the vehicle when going downhill.

skiff *. . . and we went ahead among many skiffs and wherries briskly.* {Great Expectations 54}
A small, light boat which could be rowed.

skirting-board *And there she was sitting down on the ground handcuffed, taking breath against the skirting-board . . .* {Mrs. Lirriper's Lodgings 1}
A baseboard, a narrow board set close to the floor and bordering the walls of a room.

skirt-pocket *Finally, he raised his hat an inch or two from his head, . . . stuck his hands in his skirt-pockets and swaggered round the corner.* {Martin Chuzzlewit 13}
A pocket in the skirt of a coat or jacket.

skittle *So he sat for half an hour, quite motionless, and looking all the while like nothing so much as a great Dutch Pin or Skittle.* {Barnaby Rudge 78}
One of the ninepins used in the game of skittles (see **skittles**).

skittle-ground *With these hasty words, Daniel Quilp withdrew into a dismantled skittle-ground behind the public-house . . .* {Old Curiosity Shop 21}
A flat piece of ground on which the game of skittles is played.

skittles *"Playing skittles!" said the captain moodily. "Light-hearted revellers!"* {Barnaby Rudge 8}

A bowling game of ninepins, in which a thick disk is thrown at the pins instead of a ball.

skreek *How it skreeks! There ain't such a rusty bit of metal in the place* ... {A Christmas Carol 4}
To creak. A Cockney word.

skull-cap *The excellent old gentleman being at these times a mere clothes-bag with a black skull-cap on top of it, does not present a very animated appearance* ... {Bleak House 21}
A small, light, close-fitting cap without a brim, worn on top of the head.

slab ... *they made the gruel thick and slab* ... {Martin Chuzzlewit 16}
1. Another word for thick.
Two dozen extra tumblers, and four ditto wine-glasses--looking anything but transparent, with little bits of straw on them--were on the slab in the passage, just arrived. {Sketches, The Bloomsbury Christening}
2. A small table hinged to the wall in the hall of a house, or a shelf mounted on that wall.

slack-baked *[The mug] Toby looked on from a tall bench hard by; one beaming smile, from his broad nut-brown face down to the slack-baked buckles in his shoes.* {Barnaby Rudge 41}
Insufficiently baked.

slam *"Plummy and slam!" was the reply. This seemed to be some watch-word or signal that all was right* ... {Oliver Twist 8}
Slang for trick.

slang song, slang dance *Immediately after singing a slang song and dancing a slang dance, this engaging figure approached the fatal lamps, and, bending over them, delivered a random eulogium* ... {The Uncommercial Traveller, Mr. Barlow}
A slang is a travelling show or performance, hence a somewhat coarser kind of song and dance than would be expected in a theater.

slantindicularly ... *I might venture to con-clude with a sentiment, glancing--however slantindicularly--at the subject in hand* ... {Martin Chuz-

zlewit 21}
Slantingly or slopingly.

slap-bang *they lived in the same street, walked into town every morning at the same hour, dined at the same slap-bang every day, and revelled in each other's company every night.* {Making a Night of it}
A low-class restaurant in which no credit is given. So-named because payment was often made by slapping coins onto the counter.

slate *The old battery out on the marshes was our place of study, and a broken slate and a short piece of slate pencil were our educational implements* . . . {Great Expectations 15}
A tablet made of a piece of slate upon which one could write or keep accounts, using a pencil-shaped piece of slate or soapstone. The writing could also be erased.

slate pencil *The principal currency of Our School was slate pencil. It had some inexplicable value, that was never ascertained, never reduced to a standard.* {Reprinted Pieces, Our School}
A pencil made of soft slate or soapstone and used for writing on slates.

slattern *A slatternly full-blown girl who seemed to be bursting out at the rents in her gown and the cracks in her shoes* . . . {Bleak House 43}
There were children of all ages; from the baby at the breast, to the slattern-girl who was as much a grown woman as her mother. {Martin Chuzzlewit 15}
Untidy, slovenly.

slavey *Two distinct knocks, sir, will produce the slavey at any time.* {Old Curiosity Shop 13}
Maid of all work, usually the only servant in the house.

sleeping-closet *Mr. Quilp caught up the poker, and hurrying to the door of the good lady's sleeping-closet beat upon it therewith* . . . {Old Curiosity Shop 50}
A small bedroom.

slime draught *He took his last slime draught at seven.* {Martin Chuzzlewit 25}

Lime water (*Aqua Calcis*), a solution of lime in water, was used as a medication. By saying 'slime draught' Mrs. Prig has converted an ordinary medication into a disgusting one (see **draught**).

slip-room *Mr. Pickwick at length yielded a reluctant consent to his taking lodgings by the week of a bald-headed cobbler who rented a small slip-room in one of the upper galleries.* {Pickwick Papers 44}
A long, narrow room.

slipshod *. . . listening to the footsteps . . . to detect the child's step from the man's, the slipshod beggar from the booted exquisite, the lounging from the busy . . .* {Old Curiosity Shop 1}
Shoes that are loose and worn down or shabby.

slope *. . . like the lines they used to rule in the copy-books at school to make the boys slope well.* {Pickwick Papers 14}
To write with the letters sloping at the angle prescribed for good penmanship.

slop, slops *"Good boy", said Mr. Brownlow, stoutly. "Have you given him any nourishment, Bedwin? Any slops, eh?"* {Oliver Twist 12}
1. Soft food such as is served to an invalid.
. . . he was at present dressed in a seafaring slop suit, in which he looked as if he had some parrots and cigars to dispose of . . . {Great Expectations 40}
2. Readymade clothing, especially sailors' clothing, but also refers to cheap clothing of any kind.

slop-basin *[The potter] caught up more clay and made a saucer-- . . . coaxed a middle-sized dab for two seconds . . . and made a milkpot--laughed, and turned out a slop-basin* {Reprinted Pieces, A Plated Article}
A bowl used on the table to receive the dregs of teacups and coffee cups.

slopseller *. . . Nicholas hurried into a slopseller's hard by, and bought Smike a great-coat.* {Nicholas Nickleby 30}
A seller of slops, readymade cheap clothing.

slop-work ... *the waistcoat of sprigs--mere slop-work, if the truth must be known* ... {Little Dorrit 1-19}
Work cheaply and poorly done, usually with reference to clothing.

slouched hat *Lying upon the table beside him ... were a heavy riding-whip and a slouched hat, the latter worn no doubt as being best suited to the inclemency of the weather.* {Barnaby Rudge 1}
A hat with a soft, wide brim that hangs down over the face.

slued *He came into our place one night to take Her home; rather slued, but not much* ... {Martin Chuzzlewit 28}
Slewed, slang for drunk.

sluice-house ... *the appointed place was the little sluice-house by the lime-kiln on the marshes* ... {Great Expectations 52}
A sluice is a kind of dam with a gate for controlling the flow of water. A sluice house is the shed containing the gate controls.

sluice-keeper *He lodged at a sluice-keeper's out on the marshes* ...
{Great Expectations 15}
The person who controlled the gate of the sluice.

smack *"Ah - h!" cried Mr. Inspector. "That's the smack!"* {Our Mutual Friend 4-12}
A characteristic odor or taste.

small-clothes ... *red worsted stockings; and very strong leather small-clothes.* {Dombey & Son 5}
Knee breeches.

Small Germans ... *when circumstances over which you have no control, interpose obstacles between yourself and Small Germans, you can't do better than bring a contented mind to bear on ... Saveloys!* {Our Mutual Friend 2-8}
A kind of sausage, obviously more highly thought of than Saveloys, which is another kind of sausage.

small-hand ... *he would be expected to inform Doctor and Mrs. Blimber, in superfine small-hand, that Mr. P. Dombey would be happy to*

have the honour of waiting on them . . . {Dombey & Son 14}
Handwriting used in ordinary correspondence, as distinguished from
'text,' or 'large hand'.

small-sword . . . *two preserved frogs fighting a small-sword duel.* {Our
Mutual Friend 1-7}
A kind of light sword used in fencing.

small text *On the front of his sale-board hung a little placard, like a
kettle holder, bearing the inscription in his own small text . . .* {Our
Mutual Friend 1-5}
Ordinary cursive handwriting, as distinguished from such things as
church text and german text, which are large and ornamental.

smashing *"I hope, Tom," lowering his voice in a friendly way, "[your
secret activity] isn't coining or smashing?"* {Somebody's Luggage 3}
Passing counterfeit money.

smoke-jack . . . *struck his iron heel on the top of the coal-cellar with a
noise resembling the click of a smoke-jack.* {Sketches, Mr. Minns and
his Cousin}
A device for turning a roasting-spit, powered by the movement of hot
air rushing up the fireplace chimney.

sneeze-box *To think of Jack Dawkins--lummy Jack--the Dodger--The
Artful Dodger--going abroad for a common twopenny-halfpenny
sneeze-box!* {Oliver Twist 43}
Slang for snuffbox. When snuff is inhaled it often makes the user
sneeze.

snowed up *In the morning I found that it was snowing still, that it had
snowed all night, and that I was snowed up.* {The Holly-Tree 1}
Snowed in, blocked by large amounts of snow.

snuff . . . *a kitchen-candle, with a very long snuff, burnt cheerfully on the
ledge of the staircase window . . .* {Pickwick Papers 32}
The part of the wick of a candle that has been burned. Not the snuff
made from tobacco.

snuff-coloured ... *and was dressed in a snuff-coloured suit, of an uncouth make at the best* ... {Martin Chuzzlewit 2}
Brown, the color of the tobacco used as snuff.

snuffers *I don't see any snuffers in that candlestick. Will you oblige me by going down, and asking for a pair?* {Martin Chuzzlewit 5}
A scissor-like instrument for snuffing candles. To snuff a candle is to cut off the snuff, the burned part of the wick, not to extinguish it. The phrase 'snuff out' means to extinguish a candle.

Snuffles ... *the nose afflicted with that disordered action of its functions which is generally termed The Snuffles* ... {The Chimes 4}
A stopped-up nose, as one caused by a cold.

snuff out ... *putting on his great-coat (for the weather was very cold), drawing on his gloves, and snuffing out one candle* ... {The Battle of Life 2}
To put out a candle.

snuffy *She was neatly, but not gaudily attired,* ... *and was perhaps the turning of a scale more snuffy.* {Martin Chuzzlewit 25}
Ready to take offense.

sociable *Cabs, hackney-coaches, "shay" carts, coal-wagons, stages, omnibuses, sociables, gigs, donkey-chaises* ... {Sketches, Greenwich Fair}
A privately owned carriage drawn by two horses (a kind of Landau, a four-wheeled carriage with a long body). It seated two couples, facing one another, and was driven by a coachman. It had a folding top over each pair of seats. Used for afternoon drives, it could stop alongside another carriage while the occupants chatted.

soda ... *a remarkable manuscript volume entitled "Mr. Sweeney's Book," from which much curious statistical information may be gathered respecting the high prices and small uses of soda, soap, sand, firewood, and other such articles.* {The Uncommercial Traveller, Chambers}
A variety of compounds of sodium used, among other things, in baking and soap making were referred to as soda.

sold up *Miss Wozenham's sold up!* {Mrs. Lirriper's Legacy 1}
Having the goods of a bankrupt person seized and sold.

solus ... *I don't know what I am saying Mr. Clennam solus -* ... {Little
Dorrit 2-17}
Latin word for alone, by oneself (feminine, *sola*).

something to say to someone (see **nothing to say to someone**)

sooth *In good sooth they were big enough* ... {Martin Chuzzlewit 5}
Truth.

sop *As wet as a sop. A foot of water in it* ... {Hard Times 1-4}
Any accumulation of liquid.

soused *The wind blew keenly* ... *stopping his breath as though he had been
soused in a cold bath* ... {Martin Chuzzlewit 12}
Soaked.

sovereign *There was a man who came to ask for change for a sovereign* ... {Dombey & Son 4}
1. A gold coin worth twenty shillings.
[It] was not a sovereign remedy ... {Dombey & Son 11}
2. Extremely effective.

spanker *Mr. Sownds the beadle, who, though orthodox and corpulent,
is still an admirer of female beauty, observes, with unction, yes, he
hears she is a spanker* ... {Dombey & Son 31}
Anything of exceptionally fine quality.

spanking *A very spanking grey in that cab, sir, if you're a judge of
horseflesh.* {Old Curiosity Shop 40}
A smart, fast horse.

speaking-trumpet ... *the screams of women, the shouts of boys, the
clanging of gongs, the firing of pistols, the ringing of bells, the bellowings
of speaking-trumpets, the squeaking of penny dittoes* ... {Sketches,
Greenwich Fair}

A megaphone. A cone of leather or cardboard into the narrow end of which one speaks or shouts, thus concentrating the sound so that it can be heard at a greater distance.

spectacles ... *the Captain trimmed the candle, put on his spectacles--he had felt it appropriate to take to spectacles on entering the instrument trade, though his eyes were like a hawk's* ... {Dombey & Son 32}
Eyeglasses.

sperm-oil ... *delivered a lecture* ... *on the qualities of sperm-oil, with a glance at the whale fisheries.* {The Uncommercial Traveller, Mr. Barlow}
Oil from the spermaceti whale.

spike *Mr. Toodle himself preferred to ride behind among the spikes [of the hackney-coach], as being the mode of conveyance to which he was best accustomed.* {Dombey & Son 2}
Many carriages had a spiked bar at the rear to prevent anyone from jumping on and getting a free ride. A legitimate ride could be had if one had permission and got on while the carriage was not moving.

spill ... *he sent in a piece of paper twisted more like one of those spills for lighting candles than a note* ... {Mrs Lirriper's Legacy 1}
As the context implies, a twisted piece of paper usually set alight at the fireplace, then used to light candles, cigars, or another fire.

spittoon *The monotonous appearance of the sanded boards was relieved by an occasional spittoon; and a triangular pile of those useful articles adorned the two upper corners of the apartment.* {Sketches, The Parlor Orator}
A receptacle, usually made of brass, for spit. Not used in England as commonly as it was in the United States where most men chewed tobacco.

spleen ... *it might have been the death of Mrs. Sparsit in spleen and grief.* {Hard Times 2-10}
Depression, melancholy.

spoken *The* Son and Heir *has not been spoken, I find by the list, sir* . . . {Dombey & Son 22}
To 'speak a ship' at sea is to communicate with her from another ship. The ships would then carry information about each other's location and condition to the port where they were bound.

spoon-meat . . . *words were but spoon-meat for babes and sucklings, and that oaths were the food for strong men.* {Old Curiosity Shop 60}
Soft or liquid food for which a spoon is needed.

spout *"You have forgotten your coat," said Mr. Pickwick* . . . *"Eh?" said Jingle. "Spout--* . . . *couldn't help it--must eat, you know* . . . *"* {Pickwick Papers 42}
1. The pawn shop. Jingle has had to pawn his coat to get money for food.
I wish I'd got the gift of the gab like you; see if I'd be up the spout so often then! {Sketches, The Pawnbroker's Shop}
2. Up the spout means in a bad way, in a hopeless condition. To shove something up the spout also means to pawn it.

sprats . . . *Mr. Jonas said, whenever such a thing was practicable, to kill two birds with one stone, and never to throw away sprats but as bait for whales.* {Martin Chuzzlewit 8}
A variety of small fish.

sprig *I shall be delighted to know the gay sprig.* {Martin Chuzzlewit 44}
A young fellow.

spring . . . *touched the spring of a little secret drawer, and took from it an ordinary ring-case* . . . {Edwin Drood 11}
1. The device which causes a drawer or door to open.
Nay, so intricate and subtle are the toils of the hunter that on the very next night after that, I was again entrapped, where no vestige of a spring could have been apprehended by the timidest. {The Uncommercial Traveller, Mr. Barlow}
2. A noose or snare, a trap.

spring cart . . . *he deems it a trying distance for the old lady to walk; she shall be fetched by niece in a spring-cart.* {The Uncommercial Travel-

ler, Poor Mercantile Jack}
A cart with the body suspended on springs instead of being attached
directly to the axles.

spring-gun *Man-traps and spring-guns are set here at all times of the
day and night.* {Bleak House 18}
A gun, with a string or wire led from the trigger, which will discharge
when someone touches it. A kind of booby trap.

spring knob ... *by merely touching the spring knob of a locker and the
handle of a drawer* ... {Edwin Drood 22}
(see **spring**)

spring-roller blinds *There were meat-safe-looking blinds in the par-
lour-windows, blue and gold curtains in the drawing-room, and
spring-roller blinds, as Mrs. Tibbs was wont in the pride of her
heart to boast, "all the way up."* {Sketches, The Boarding-house}
Most probably a blind which rolls up under the action of a spring, as
does the common cloth or paper window shade.

sprung-mine *There was a Sir Somebody Dedlock, with a battle, a
sprung-mine, volumes of smoke, flashes of lightning ... and a stormed
fort, all in full action between his horse's two hind legs* ... {Bleak
House 37}
A mine, or buried explosive charge, that has been exploded.

spring-van ... *a spring-van is delivering its load of green-house
plants at the door* ... {Our Mutual Friend 1-10}
A covered cart for carrying goods, with the body suspended on springs.

spunging-house *And the next time you're locked up in a spunging-house,
just wait there till I come and take you out, there's a good fellow.*
{Sketches, A Passage in the Life of Mr. Watkins Tottle}
A house kept by a bailiff or sheriff's officer in which debtors are temporarily confined. From 'sponge', in the sense of to squeeze someone for
money.

squab ... *there were Norfolk Biffins, squab and swarthy, setting off the
yellow of the oranges and lemons* ... {A Christmas Carol 3}

1. Squat and plump, though the word is usually used when speaking of a person.
Chairs, with turned legs and green chintz squabs to match the curtains.
{Nicholas Nickleby 10}
2. A thick cushion on the seat of a chair.

squally *After that, he sat . . . following Mrs. Joe about with his blue eyes, as his manner always was at squally times.* {Great Expectations 2}
Stormy. 'Squall' is the sailor's word for a storm.

squaring *My heart failed me when I saw him squaring at me with every demonstration of mechanical nicety, and eyeing my anatomy as if he were minutely choosing his bone.* {Great Expectations 11}
Getting into the position for boxing.

squeezed, squeezed bonnet *Miss Blimber came down soon after her mama, a little squeezed in appearance, but very charming.* {Dombey & Son 14}
1. Thin.
. . . a little mad old woman in a squeezed bonnet who is always in court, from its sitting to its rising . . . {Bleak House 1}
2. Compressed, looking as though it had been squeezed.

squib *. . . 'Farewell' on a transparency behind; and nine people at the wings with a squib in each hand--all the dozen and a half going off at once--it would be very grand . . .* {Nicholas Nickleby 30}
1. A kind of firework which sprays colored fire and ends with a small explosion.
. . . a gentleman of a debating turn, who was strong at speech-making; and a gentleman of a literary turn, who wrote squibs upon the rest, and knew the weak side of everybody's character but his own. {Martin Chuzzlewit 9}
2. A short written piece, usually humorous or satirical.

squint *. . . with a very ill-favoured face, and a most sinister and villainous squint.* {Old Curiosity Shop 29}
Strabismus. Both eyes do not point in the same direction.

srub ... *the gentleman in blue ... ordered 'cold srub and water'* ... {Pickwick Papers 37}
A variant spelling of 'shrub', a drink made of orange or lemon, sugar, and rum.

staff *The constable looked as wise as he could, and took up his staff of office; which had been reclining indolently in the chimney-corner.* {Oliver Twist 30}
A rod or wand carried as a sign of authority.

staff of rest ... *Mrs. Chopper, when her daughter was married, made the house of her son-in-law her home from that time henceforth, and set up her staff of rest with Mr. and Mrs. Merrywinkle.* {Sketches, The Couple Who Coddle Themselves}
To set up one's staff of rest is to settle down, take up one's abode.

stage ... *the chaise proceeded without any slackening of pace towards the conclusion of the stage.* {Pickwick Papers 9}
The distance between places to change horses, also the place where the horses are changed.

stage-coach-hire *I am on my way there now ... They allowed me the stage-coach-hire--outside stage-coach-hire all the way.* {Old Curiosity Shop 46}
The cost of the stagecoach ticket.

stage-waggon ... *a stage-waggon, which travelled for some distance on the same road as they must take, would stop at the inn to change horses* ... {Old Curiosity Shop 46}
A wagon belonging to an organized system for the transport of goods, traveling and changing horses in stages.

staid *It was a cool spot, staid but cheerful* ... {Tale of Two Cities 2-6}
Dignified.

stair-rod *The old man raked the fire together with an old stair-rod* ... {A Christmas Carol 4}
A metal rod, attached at the ends to the stair tread, used to hold down the carpeting on the stairs.

stair-wire ... *for the stair-carpets, besides being very deficient in stair-wires, were so torn as to be absolute traps.* {Bleak House 4}
A slender stair-rod (see **stair-rod**).

stake ... *and turn the pens of Smithfield market into stakes and cauldrons* ... {Barnaby Rudge 37}
The vertical post at which people were burned alive.

stamp-office ... *while Jack was up-stairs sorting papers, and you two were gone to the stamp-office.* {Pickwick Papers 20}
The office in which government revenue stamps are issued, not the post office.

stand-up man ... *but he was a queer subject altogether--a kind of gypsy--one of the finest, stand-up men, you ever see.* {Barnaby Rudge 39}
Someone who will stand up boldly, who is loyal.

stand and deliver ... *the Lord Mayor of London, was made to stand and deliver on Turnaham Green, by one highwayman* ... {Tale of Two Cities 1-1}
A highwayman's order to his victim to stand still and deliver his money.

stand out "... *I declare! I dine at five, gentlemen.*" "*So do I,*" *says everybody else except two men who ought to have dined at three, and seem more than half disposed to stand out in consequence.* {Pickwick Papers 34}
Not to participate, not to join in.

standish *He wanted pen, ink, and paper. There was an old standish on the mantelshelf containing a dusty apology for all three.* {Barnaby Rudge 10}
An inkstand, a kind of small tray with a container of ink, several pens, and often a shaker of sand or pounce.

stanhope *The vehicle was not exactly a gig, neither was it a stanhope.* {Pickwick Papers 40}
A Stanhope gig is a light two-wheeled carriage designed to carry only one person.

star ... *for the sake of a ribbon, star, or garter* ... {Martin Chuzzlewit 10}
A star-shaped ornament worn as part of the insignia of an order of knighthood.

stare out of countenance ... *Mr. Quilp first stared her out of countenance and then drank her health ceremoniously.* {Old Curiosity Shop 23}
Stare at someone until he is disconcerted.

start, have the start of someone ... *she saw her father come out in his morning-gown, and start when he was told his wife had not come home.* {Dombey & Son 47}
1. A startle, a fright.
... *they'll have had all the advantage of the moonlight to get the start of us* ... {Pickwick Papers 9}
2. To get ahead of someone, to get a head start.
A dingy handkerchief twisted like a cord about his neck, left its great veins exposed to view, and they were swollen and starting ... {Barnaby Rudge 37}
3. Project, protrude.

state ... *John ushered them into the state apartment, which, like many other things of state, was cold and comfortless.* {Barnaby Rudge 35}
Usually means costly and imposing, but often is used to mean the best or finest available.

station-house *Not a station-house or bone-house, or workhouse in the metropolis escaped a visit from the hard glazed hat.* {Dombey & Son 25}
Part of the police station in which prisoners were locked up temporarily.

statuary *The statuary gives him back the paper, and points out, with his pocket rule, the words, "beloved and only child."* {Dombey & Son 18}
A sculptor, here a carver of tombstones.

stave ... *Mr. Stryver had begun cautiously to hew away the lower staves of the ladder on which he mounted.* {Tale of Two Cities 2-5}
1. A rung of a ladder, the wooden rod or slat that makes up a step of a ladder.

. . . gardens paled with staves of old casks, or timber pillaged form
houses burnt down . . . {Old Curiosity Shop 15}
2. The curved pieces of wood from which barrels are made.
There were bodies of constables with staves . . . {Pickwick Papers 13}
3. Staffs.

stays *. . . the landlady, assisted by a chambermaid, proceeded to*
vinegar the forehead, beat the hands, . . . and unlace the stays of the
spinster aunt . . . {Pickwick Papers 10}
A kind of corset made from two sections of fabric laced together.

stay-lace *. . . her dress didn't nearly meet up the back and that the open*
space was railed across with a lattice-work of stay-lace--like a sum-
mer-house. {Bleak House 4}
The lacing or cord used on stays (see **stays**).

steam-gun *. . . a greater number . . . than the steam-gun can discharge balls*
in a minute. {Martin Chuzzlewit 11}
A kind of machine gun operated by steam.

steam-hammer *. . . he holds his steam-hammer beating head and heart,*
and staggers away. {Edwin Drood 8}
A kind of trip hammer operated by a steam engine.

steam-packet *. . . the shipping-announcements and steam-packet lists which*
decorated the counting-house walls . . . {Nicholas Nickleby 37}
A steamship used as a packet, a ship that carries goods and passengers
on a regular schedule.

steel drops *. . . the small squat measuring glass in which little Rickitts*
(a junior of weakly constitution), took her steel drops daily. {Edwin
Drood 13}
A liquid medication containing iron.

stew *. . . a costly police-system . . . has left in London, in the days of*
steam and gas and photography of thieves, the sanctuaries and stews of
the Stuarts! {The Uncommercial Traveller, On an Amateur Beat}
Brothel, house of prostitution.

stick *There is an immensity of promenading, on crutches and off, with sticks and without* . . . {Pickwick Papers 36}
A walking stick.

sticking-plaster, sticking-plaister . . . *and put their sticking-plaster patches on to terrify commoners as the chiefs of some other tribes put on their war-paint.* {Bleak House 37}
. . . *he was fixing a very small patch of sticking-plaster on a very small pimple near the corner of his mouth* {Barnaby Rudge 23}
Adhesive tape. In the first example it is being used decoratively.

stickle . . . *may God reward the worthy gentlemen who stickle for the Plague as part and parcel of the wisdom of our ancestors* . . . {Dombey & Son 29}
To contend for (an object or principle).

stick up . . . *the President stuck up, and said that they must stand or fall together* . . . {The Schoolboy's Story}
To resist, offer resistance or opposition.

stile . . . *Mr. Pickwick was joking with the young ladies who wouldn't come over the stile while he looked* . . . *although it was full three feet high and had only a couple of stepping-stones* . . . {Pickwick Papers 28}
A set of steps arranged to allow crossing a fence.

still-room . . . *that floors are rubbed bright, carpets spread, curtains shaken out, beds puffed and patted, still-room and kitchen cleared for action--all things prepared as beseems the Dedlock dignity.* {Bleak House 40}
A room in which coffee and tea are prepared and cakes and liqueurs kept.

stilts . . . *he had taken the air, in the first instance, behind a hackney-coach that went to Camberwell, and had followed two Punches afterwards, and had seen the stilts home to their own door.* {Nicholas Nickleby 37}
Someone walking on stilts, possibly someone who was part of a street show or, perhaps, some children playing on stilts.

stipendiary ... *my very carpet-bag was an object of veneration to the stipendiary clerks* ... {David Copperfield 26}
A salaried person.

stir-about ... *the boys, having previously had their appetites thoroughly taken away by stir-about and potatoes, sat down in the kitchen to some hard salt beef* ... {Nicholas Nickleby 8}
Porridge or oatmeal, so-called because it is made by stirring the oatmeal in hot water as it cooks. Because it was stirred for a long time it was often overcooked and not very tasty.

stirrup-cup *[They] were taking a copious stirrup-cup, preparatory to issuing forth after a boar or two.* {Nicholas Nickleby 6}
A drink given to someone on horseback, usually when about to set out or when just returned.

stirrup-iron *A busy little man he always is, in the polishing at harness-house doors, of stirrup-irons, bits, curb-chains, harness bosses, anything in the way of a stable-yard that will take a polish* ... {Bleak House 66}
The metal part of a stirrup.

stock *And then they stood about, as soldiers do; now with their hands loosely clasped before them; ... now easing a belt or pouch; now opening the door to spit stiffly over their high stocks, out into the yard.* {Great Expectations 5}
1. A stiff kind of neck cloth worn by men, and especially soldiers.
I've been carted here and carted there, and put out of this town and put out of that town, and stuck in the stocks and whipped and worried and drove. {Great Expectations 42}
2. A device for punishment, with the legs or head and wrists held in holes in a plank of wood.
... whether it wouldn't be better to wrench his blunderbuss from him ... [and] knock the rest of the company on the head with the stock ... {Pickwick Papers 49}
3. The wooden end of the weapon.
... so that the stocks and stones appeared infected with the common

fear ... {Barnaby Rudge 37}
4. A contemptuous reference to an idol. Here the phrase 'stocks and stones' means 'gods of wood and stone'.

stolen match ... *if any young lady made a stolen match, Mr. Percy Noakes gave her away* ... {Sketches, The Steam Excursion}
A marriage accomplished secretly, an elopement.

stomacher ... *a young lady* ... *attired in an old-fashioned green velvet dress with a long waist and stomacher.* {Pickwick Papers 49}
An ornamental covering for the chest worn under the lacing of the bodice of a dress.

stomach-warmer ... *and pass round a wine-glass, which is frequently replenished from a flat bottle like a stomach-warmer, with considerable glee* ... {Sketches, The River}
A flat metal vessel filled with hot water, for application to the stomach. The equivalent of the rubber hot-water bottle.

stone *The old girl's weight--is twelve stone six.* {Bleak House 34}
A measure of weight, usually 14 pounds. The 'old girl' probably weighed about 174 pounds.

stone-chaney "... *it's surprising how stone-chaney catches the heat this frosty weather, to be sure!*" *Here he turned the plate, and cooled his fingers.* {The Haunted Man 1}
Chaney is 'chiney', or chinaware, porcelain ware. Stoneware is earthenware of a grayish color, and that may be what is being referred to here.

stone fruits ... *in summer, when stone fruits flourish and stomach aches prevail, we have the ladies' dispensary, and the ladies' sick visitation committee* ... {Sketches, The Ladies' Societies}
Fruits with hard pits, such as plums and cherries.

Stone Jug ... *the mill as takes up so little room that it'll work inside a Stone Jug* ... {Oliver Twist 8}
Slang for the Newgate prison.

stones, off the stones ... *his house is a goodish way out of London, and they do say that the rioters won't go more than two miles, or three at the farthest, off the stones.* {Barnaby Rudge 54}
Refers to the paving stones that marked the limits of the town, so 'two miles off the stones' means 'two miles from the edge of town'.

stone yard *[He] appeared to me to be the most intolerably arrogant pauper ever relieved, and to show himself in absolute want and dire necessity of a course of Stone Yard.* {The Uncommercial Traveller, Two Views of a Cheap Theatre}
A yard where stones are broken by hard manual labor.

stop ... *he calls his 'prentice idle dog, and stops his beer unless he works to his liking.* {Barnaby Rudge 8}
1. Withhold part of someone's wages, in money or goods.
"We can stop in this house, I suppose," said Mr. Pickwick. {Pickwick Papers 13}
2. To stay, to remain. In this case, to stay overnight.
"You must be more careful, sir," said Jerry, walking coolly to the chair where he had placed the organ, and setting the stop. {Old Curiosity Shop 18}
3. The handle by which a set of organ pipes is turned on or off.
... and purchased a handsome silver mug for the infant Kitterbell, upon which he ordered the initials "F. C. W. K.," with the customary untrained grape-vine looking flourishes, and a large full stop, to be engraved forthwith. {Sketches, The Bloomsbury Christening}
4. A full stop is the period at the end of a sentence.

stoppage *There are also ladies and gentlemen of another fashion ... For whom everything must be languid and pretty. Who have found out the perpetual stoppage. Who are to rejoice at nothing and be sorry for nothing.* {Bleak House 12}
The action of causing something to stop or cease. Here it refers to stopping the perception of reality.

stout mug ... *half-emptied stout mugs in the supper boxes ...* {Sketches, Vauxhall-gardens by Day}
Mugs used to hold stout, a strong kind of beer.

stove *The kind of rostrum he occupied will be very well understood, if I liken it to a boarded-up fireplace turned towards the audience, with a gentleman in a black surtout standing in the stove and leaning forward over the mantelpiece.* {The Uncommercial Traveller, Two Views of a Cheap Theatre}
Not a stove at all, but the metal grate and shelves in the fireplace.

stow *"Stow that gammon," interposed the robber, impatiently...* {Oliver Twist 15}
Slang for leave off, stop.

strachino cheese *... he gets sausage of Lyons, veal in savory jelly, white bread, strachino cheese, and good wine ...* {Little Dorrit 1-1}
A kind of Italian cheese.

straight veskit *I'd come down wery handsome towards straight veskits for some people at home.* {Pickwick Papers 27}
Strait waistcoat, strait jacket. (The accent is Sam Weller's.)

strait *I hope I would have done at least as much for any man in such a strait, and most of all for you, sir ...* {Barnaby Rudge 6}
Privation, hardship. Also dilemma.

strait-waistcoat *... her course of pouncing upon the poor and applying benevolence to them like a strait-waistcoat ...* {Bleak House 30}
Strait jacket.

straw yard *I had scarcely had time to enjoy the coach and to think how like a straw yard it was, and yet how like a rag-shop, and to wonder why the horses nose-bags were kept inside ...* {Great Expectations 20}
A yard littered with straw for horses or cattle. Straw was put on the floor of stagecoaches for warmth and comfort.

street-crying *... the wall-chalking and the street-crying would come on directly ...* {Bleak House 41}
The shouting of a street seller of goods. Here it may refer to the selling of ballads made up about scandals.

street-door scraper ... *when the cottage had been, as she emphatically said, 'thoroughly got to rights, from the chimney-pots to the street-door scraper'*... {Nicholas Nickleby 38}
The boot scraper at the front door, a vertically mounted iron plate on which the boot soles could be cleaned of the mud, dirt, and horse manure present on every street and road.

street-keeper ... *the boy in grey, who, having handed over the fly to the care of the street-keeper, had come back to see what all the noise was about.* {Pickwick Papers 48}
A kind of porter who watched or held carriage horses in a given street.

street-post ... *while his friends were content to leap over the common-sized gravestones, the first one took the family vaults, iron railings and all, with as much ease as if they had been so many street-posts.* {Pickwick Papers 29}
Posts sunk into the pavement to prevent carriages from mounting the sidewalk and to which horses could be tied. They were often made from old cannons sunk into the ground muzzle uppermost, with a cannon ball cemented to the muzzle.

stretcher *I'll* ... *chop you over the fingers with the stretcher, or take a pick at your head with the boat-hook.* {Our Mutual Friend 1-1}
A removable crosspiece placed between the sides of a boat to keep them from bending toward each other when the boat is hoisted out of the water.

stripe ... *it was no sooner observed that he had become attached to Nicholas, than stripes and blows, stripes and blows, morning, noon, and night were his only portion.* {Nicholas Nickleby 12}
A stroke with a whip or lash.

stroller *I was separated from my father--he was only a stroller--and taken pity on by Mr. Gradgrind.* {Hard Times 3-2}
1. An itinerant actor, a strolling player.
... *vagabond groups assembled round the doors to see the stroller woman dance* ... {Old Curiosity Shop 19}
2. A vagabond, here a vagabond woman.

struck ... *these trees, the roots of which are struck in Men, not earth* ... {The Battle of Life 1}
Thrust into.

stud *The same authority observes that she is perfectly got up and remarks in commendation of her hair especially that she is the best-groomed woman in the whole stud.* {Bleak House 2}
A collection of female horses kept for breeding.

stuff ... *she is dressed in a plain, spare gown of brown stuff.* {Bleak House 21}
Fabric, cloth.

stump *The ball flew from his hand straight and swift towards the centre stump of the wicket.* {Pickwick Papers 7}
1. The upright sticks which form part of the wicket, in the game of cricket.
... *I'll fork out and stump.* {Oliver Twist 8}
2. Slang for to pay.

stump bedstead *It was a large, bare, desolate room, with a number of stump bedsteads made of iron, on one of which lay stretched the shadow of a man* ... {Pickwick Papers 44}
A bedstead without posts.

stump out ... *when Dumkins was caught out and Podder stumped out, All-Muggleton had notched some fifty-four while the score of the Dingley Dellers was as blank as their faces.* {Pickwick Papers 7}
In the game of cricket, to be put out by the wicket keeper when he knocks over a stump or bail at the appropriate time.

stump up ... *the hour is come for Boffin to stump up.* {Our Mutual Friend 4-14}
Pay up, come up with money.

stumpy ... *or, to adopt his own figurative expression in all its native beauty, "till they was rig'larly done over, and forked out the stumpy."* {Sketches, The Last Cab-driver and the First Omnibus-cad}
Slang for money.

succeed to a miracle ... *he bethought himself of the stratagem of sending Miss La Creevy on a few paces in advance, and urging the old gentleman to follow her. It succeeded to a miracle; and he went away in a rapture of admiration* ... {Nicholas Nickleby 49}
Succeed miraculously, succeed extremely well.

sugar-baker *He was a rich sugar-baker, who mistook rudeness for honesty, and abrupt bluntness for an open and candid manner* ... {Sketches, A Passage in the Life of Mr. Watkins Tottle}
A refiner of sugar. One who converts the crude material obtained by crushing sugar cane into common white sugar.

sugar-loaf hat *On his head he wore a broad-brimmed sugar-loaf hat, garnished with a single feather.* {Pickwick Papers 29}
A hat shaped like a sugar loaf, a blunt cone.

suit and service ... *he rendered suit and service to Stryver in that capacity.* {Tale of Two Cities 2-5}
Personal service, rendered at court, to a lord by his tenant.

summerset ... *leaving his delighted young friend in an ecstasy of summersets on the pavement.* {Old Curiosity Shop 49}
Somerset, somersault.

sunders *Me to the North, and you to the South!--Keep in sunders!* {Great Expectations 15}
In sunder, or asunder. Apart, separated.

sunset-gun *"There was a conwict off last night,"* said Joe, aloud, *"after the sunset-gun ... "* {Great Expectations 2}
A gun fired at sunset as a mark of the time, used in military settings.

superadded *It is difficult for a large-headed, small eyed youth ... to look dignified ... when superadded to these personal attractions are a red nose and yellow smalls.* {Oliver Twist 5}
Added over and above what was previously added.

supercargo ... *and now he's supercargo aboard another ship, same owners.* {Dombey & Son 56}

The officer on a merchant ship who takes care of commercial business and cargo.

supposititious ... *a church with hoarding and scaffolding about it, which had been under supposititious repair so long that the means of repair looked a hundred years old, and had themselves fallen into decay*... {Little Dorrit 2-6}
Pretended, spurious.

suppressing *"Thankee, mum," said Toodle, "since you* are *suppressing".* {Dombey & Son 2}
Overwhelming.

surface *If Miss Amy Dorrit will direct her own attention to, and will accept of my poor assistance in, the formation of a surface, Mr. Dorrit will have no further cause of anxiety.* {Little Dorrit 2-5}
Outward appearance, here in the sense of a social facade or aspect.

surtout *He wore a long black surtout reaching nearly to his ankles*... {Old Curiosity Shop 11}
A double-breasted, very full-skirted, close-bodied overcoat.

suverins ... *says old Fixem, grinning like mad, and shoving a couple of suverins into my hand*... {Sketches, The Broker's Man}
Dialect for 'sovereigns', British gold coins worth twenty shillings.

Sving *"A--what?" interrupted the boots. "Anonymous--he's not to know who it comes from." "Oh! I see...I see--bit o' Sving, eh?"*... {Sketches, The Great Winglebury Duel}
In the 1830's threatening letters signed by a fictitious Captain Swing were sent to farmers in the south of England. Because the Captain did not exist, the name came to represent an anonymous letter.

swab *A certain dark-complected swab*... {Great Expectations 47}
A mild term of contempt, from the swab (mop) used by sailors.

swag *It's all arranged about bringing off the swag, is it?* {Oliver Twist 19}
Booty, loot.

sward ... *Pickwick, who has choked up the well and thrown ashes on the sward* ... {Pickwick Papers 34}
The surface of soil covered by grass. Greensward.

swart ... *the trooper, swart with the dust of the coal, checks his horse* ...
{Bleak House 63}
Dark in color, swarthy.

swear *"Swear this person!" said Fang to the clerk. "I'll not hear another word. Swear him."* {Oliver Twist 11}
Swear in, administer the oath to a witness.

sweat a pound *You understand what sweating a pound means, don't you?*
{Our Mutual Friend 3-1}
Shaking silver coins in a cloth bag for a period of time would leave some silver on the cloth, which could then be removed. The coins would not be enough changed for this to be detected.

sweep *It was in the window of what seemed to be an old-fashioned house with three peaks in the roof in front and a circular sweep leading to the porch.* {Bleak House 6}
1. A curved, carriage drive leading to a house.
At intervals were heard the tread of slipshod feet, and the chilly cry of the poor sweep as he crept, shivering, to his early toil ... {Nicholas Nickleby 22}
2. A chimney sweep.
... when the out-door apprentices ring us up in the morning... and I see them standing on the door-step with their little pumps under their arms, I am actually reminded of the Sweeps. {Bleak House 38}
3. Nickname for a certain rifle brigade, from their dark-colored uniforms.

sweet-bread ... *Mrs. Pipchin's constitution wouldn't go to sleep without sweet-bread* ... {Dombey & Son 8}
Probably analogous to sweet-cake, a bread made with a high proportion of sugar. Not sweetbread, which is cooked pancreas or thymus.

sweetbriar ... *my mother and he had another stroll by the sweetbriar, while I was sent in to get my tea.* {David Copperfield 2}
A kind of rose.

sweetmeats ... *the young gentleman ... having to all appearance his faculties absorbed in the contemplation of the sweetmeats* ... {Barnaby Rudge 80}
Sweet or candied foods.

swell *And Mr. Crackit is a heavy swell; an't he Fagin?* {Oliver Twist 39}
Slang for a fashionable or showy man.

swing-bridge ... *neighborhood of narrow thoroughfares checquered by docks and basins, high piles of warehouses, swing-bridges, and masts of ships.* {Bleak House 57}
A pivot bridge, one that swings on a pivot to permit boats to pass. The pivot was usually on a pier in the middle of the river, providing a passage on either side of the pier when the bridge was turned.

swipes *"Anything been doing?" "Flat as ever so much swipes," says Phil.* {Bleak House 21}
Slang for small beer, beer that is weak or of poor quality.

swivel-bridge ... *the hackney coach, after encountering unheard of difficulties from swivel-bridges, soft roads, impassable canals ... stopped at the corner of Brig Place.* {Dombey & Son 23}
Probably a pivot bridge (see **swing-bridge**).

swivel eye ... *she found herself possessed of what is colloquially termed a swivel eye (derived from her father)* ... {Our Mutual Friend 2-12}
A squinting eye, one that points in a direction different from its partner.

swoln *Kit laughing so heartily, with his swoln and bruised face looking out of the towel, made little Jacob laugh* ... {Old Curiosity Shop 13}
Swollen.

swoon ... *the Doctor had covered his eyes with his hands, and swooned away in the midst of it.* {Tale of Two Cities 3-4}
To faint, pass out.

table-beer *Cheese, butter, firewood, soap, pickles, matches, bacon, table-beer, peg-tops, sweetmeats* ... {The Chimes 4}
Ordinary beer such as is drunk with a meal.

table-drawer ... *had engendered in him a holy determination to examine his master's table-drawers and pockets, and secrete his papers.* {Tale of Two Cities 2-3}
A drawer fitted into a table.

table-land ... *attired in a spangled robe and cap she might walk about the table-land on the top of a barrel-organ without exciting much remark* ... {Bleak House 21}
Flat land, a flat landscape. Here it refers to the large flat top of the barrel organ.

tables (see **globes**)

tablets ... *the count drew forth a set of tablets* ... {Pickwick Papers 15} ... *she took from her pocket a yellow set of ivory tablets, mounted in tarnished gold, and wrote upon them with a pencil* ... {Great Expectations 49}
A kind of notebook or note pad.

tags ... *a great footman appeared in due time at the great hall-door, with such great tags upon his liveried shoulder that he was perpetually entangling and hooking himself among the chairs and tables* ... {Martin Chuzzlewit 9}
The decorative knots on the footman's shoulders.

tagrag and bobtail *We don't take in no tagrag and bobtail at our house, sir* ... {Barnaby Rudge 35}
Contemptuous term for lower-class people, rabble.

take ... *I've put the rolling pin in your berth to take it* ... {Martin Chuzzlewit 34}
To reserve, to indicate that the berth is taken.

take care of ... *Take care of that man, and pray don't trust him* ... {Barnaby Rudge 22}
Be careful of, watch out for.

take-down ... *there was a belief among us that this was because he was too wealthy to be "taken down."* {Reprinted Pieces, Our School}
To humble or humiliate.

take in ... *you buried paving-stones ... in that coffin. Don't go and tell me that you buried Cly. It was a take in. Me and two more knows it.* {Tale of Two Cities 3-8}
A deceit or trick.

take leave *Lady Dedlock, there is nothing to be done. I will take leave to say a few words when you have finished.* {Bleak House 41}
Leave, in the sense of permission.

take (someone) up *Why see again there, how you take one up!* {Martin Chuzzlewit 3}
1. Interrupt someone sharply, with a rebuke or reprimand.
I now know Riderhood to have been previously taken up for being concerned in the robbery of an unlucky seaman, to whom some such poison had been given. {Our Mutual Friend 2-13}
2. To be arrested by the police.

taking a sight ... *Mr. Chuckster would sometimes condescend to give him a slight nod, or to honor him with that peculiar form of recognition which is sometimes called 'taking a sight'* ... {Old Curiosity Shop 38}
A gesture with thumb on nose, middle three fingers closed, and the little finger being wiggled.

take off ... *and invites the entering Durdles to take off that glass of wine (handing him the same)* ... {Edwin Drood 4}
To drink the glass to the bottom at one swallow.

tale *You must be Mr. Carton, if the tale of fifty-two is to be right.* {Tale of Two Cities 3-13}
Count or number.

talk-over *[He] passes me by, and puts a talking-over stranger above my head.* {Our Mutual Friend 2-7}
Overtalking, talking too much.

tallyman *Do you say ten shillings? Not you, for you owe more to the tallyman.* {Doctor Marigold 1}
Someone who supplies goods which are then paid for in small amounts over time. A version of the installment plan.

tally-shop *Down by the Docks they "board seamen" at the eating-houses, the public-houses, the slop-shops, the coffee-shops, the tally-shops, all kind of shops mentionable and unmentionable . . .* {Reprinted Pieces, Bound for the Great Salt Lake}
A shop where goods were sold on the installment plan.

tamarind *. . . preserved tamarinds and ginger.* {Edwin Drood 10}
The fruit pod of the tamarind tree, used as a relish and as a medicine.

tambour work *I and my sister worked at tambour work. Our father and our brother had a builder's business.* {Bleak House 35}
Embroidering, so-called from the tambour or hoop on which the material is stretched to facilitate the work.

tan *. . . I noticed the stifled sound of wheels on the straw or tan that was littered in the street . . .* {Doctor Marigold 3}
Crushed tree bark, either fresh or after it was used for tanning leather. It was used in gardening and on paths for horses.

tankard *. . . the room's as warm as any toast in a tankard.* {Barnaby Rudge 12}
A tall drinking mug, usually of pewter and often with a hinged lid.

tanner *"How much a-piece?" The Man in the Monument replied, "A Tanner."*
Slang for a sixpence coin.

tap *He sat softly whistling, and turning little drops of beer out of the tap upon the ground* . . . {The Chimes 4}
1. The valve through which the beer or wine was allowed to flow from a keg.
. . . *if it was the same tap as he had tasted before, he had rather not [drink it].* {A Christmas Carol 2}
2. The liquor from a particular batch.

tap-room . . . *the young gentleman turned into a small public-house; and led the way to a tap-room in the rear of the premises.* {Oliver Twist 8}
A barroom.

taper . . . *still there was Mr. Haredale, haggard and careworn, listening in the solitary house to every sound that stirred, with the taper shining through the chinks until the day should turn it pale and end his lonely watching.* {Barnaby Rudge 42}
A candle.

tapis *To be informed what the* Galaxy Gallery of British Beauty *is about, and means to be about, and what Gallery marriages are on the tapis, and what Galaxy rumors are in circulation, is to become acquainted with the most glorious destinies of mankind.* {Bleak House 20}
A tablecloth. Used here in the sense of 'on the tablecloth', or 'on the table', hence 'being talked about'.

Tare and Tret *We learned Tare and Tret together, at school.* {Martin Chuzzlewit 19}
Tare is the amount deducted from gross weight for the weight of the packaging material, and tret the allowance for wear and damage in transit.

tar-water . . . *some medical beast had revived tar-water in those days as a fine medicine, and Mrs. Joe always kept a supply of it in the cupboard* . . . {Great Expectations 2}
An infusion of tar in cold water.

tauto . . . *for, within a few minutes of the first alarm, we had wore ship and got her off, and were all a-tauto--which I felt very grateful for* . . . {The Uncommercial Traveller, The Short Timers}

'Taut' was a common nautical term of approbation meaning in good shape, in good condition.

taunto *She was a noble vessel. Trim, ship-shape, all a taunto, as Captain Swosser used to say. You must excuse me if I occasionally introduce a nautical expression; I was quite a sailor once.* {Bleak House 13}
The Captain probably said 'all a taut-o' (see **tauto**).

taxed-cart *It was not what is currently denominated a dog-cart, neither was it a taxed-cart, nor a chaise-cart, nor a guillotined cabriolet . . .* {Pickwick Papers 40}
A plain two-wheeled, one-horse cart with a simple board seat and no springs. It was cheap and was often used in trade. The words 'taxed cart' were written on the side, and it was taxed at a lower rate than more expensive vehicles.

tea-board *[She] took up her station on a low stool at his feet: thereby bringing her eyes on a level with the tea-board.* {Martin Chuzzlewit 2}
A wooden tea tray.

tea-caddy *. . . and thrusting a silver spoon . . . into the inmost recesses of a two-ounce tea-caddy, proceeded to make the tea.* {Oliver Twist 23}
A small box for holding tea leaves.

tea-garden *Afterwards there were tea-gardens, shrimps, ale, and other delicacies . . .* {Little Dorrit 1-7}
An open-air place next to an inn or restaurant where tea and refreshments were served.

Teetotal *It was a Teetotal procession, as I learnt from its banners, and was long enough to consume twenty minutes in passing.* {The Uncommercial Traveller, A Plea for Total Abstinence}
A movement advocating total abstinence from alcoholic beverages.

tee-totum *The town awakes; the great tee-totum is set up for its daily spin and whirl . . .* {Bleak House 16}
A four-sided top, spun in a gambling game.

tell `Jo attends closely while the words are being spoken; tells them off on his broom-handle, finding them rather hard . . .* {Bleak House 16}
1. Count, enumerate.
. . . I feel that Miss Manette will tell well in any station, and will always do me credit. {Tale of Two Cities 2-11}
This was a smart stab . . . It told immensely. {Martin Chuzzlewit 4}
2. To be effective, be of account.

tell off, told off *Four-and-twenty marines under command of a lieutenant . . . had been told off at Belize . . .* {English Prisoners 1}
To detach a number of soldiers for a particular duty.

Temple *I had a very particular engagement to breakfast in the Temple.* {Reprinted Pieces, Hunted Down}
A series of buildings on Fleet Street belonging to the Inns of Court, the institutions responsible for legal education and admission to the practice of law. The Temple was its named for the nearby tombs of the Knights Templars.

tender *But opening [his fist] immediately again, he spread it out . . . (for he was tender of her, even then) . . .* {Cricket on the Hearth 2}
Considerate of, thoughtful of, fond of, protective of someone.

tender string *I might have known it was a tender string.* {Martin Chuzzlewit 20}
A tender spot, a tender nerve.

ten-pound householder *What would your sabbath enthusiasts say to . . . a general hands-four-round of ten-pound householders, at the foot of the Obelisk in St. George's-Fields?* {Sketches, The First of May}
In 1832 the right to vote was extended to householders paying ten pounds or more in rent annually. The phrase then came to mean a reasonably well-off, middle-class male voter.

tent bedstead *In the other [room] stood an old tent bedstead, and a few scanty articles of chamber furniture.* {Nicholas Nickleby 1}
A bed having an arched canopy and covered sides.

tenter-hooks *Mr. Bumble, in his alarm, could not immediately think of the word 'tenter-hooks', so he said, 'broken bottles.'* {Oliver Twist 27}
The bent hooks on a tenter, the frame on which cloth is stretched to dry. To be on tenterhooks is to be in a state of painful suspense.

tergiversation *... he was tied fast under the axe; and ... in spite of his utmost tergiversation ... a word might bring it down upon him.* {Tale of Two Cities 3-8}
To turn the back on something that was previously of great interest. Desertion of a cause or political party.

term-time *The long vacation saunters on towards term-time like an idle river very leisurely strolling down a flat country to the sea.* {Bleak House 20}
The period when the law courts are in session.

terms, on terms *Mrs. Smallweed's brother, my dear friend--her only relation. We were not on terms, which is to be deplored now, but he never would be on terms. He was not fond of us.* {Bleak House 33}
To be 'on terms' is to be 'on friendly terms'.

terrific *And this was more terrific to her husband ... than any flow of eloquence with which she could have edified the company.* {Our Mutual Friend 3-16}
Terrifying.

text, large text *... he found that the more advanced pupils who were in large text and the letter M, had been set the copy, "Merdle, Millions."* {Little Dorrit 2-13}
A large handwriting taught in school with the lines a half inch apart.

thereat *... the matron was in no way overpowered by Mr. Bumble's scowl, but on the contrary treated it with great disdain, and even raised a laugh thereat ...* {Oliver Twist 37}
Thereupon.

thief-taker *... a body of thief-takers had been keeping watch in the house all night.* {Barnaby Rudge 61}
Detective.

this day twelvemonth *I make an agreement with my son Watt that on this day twelvemonth he shall marry as pretty and as good a girl as you have seen in all your travels.* {Bleak House 63}
One year from today.

this night week . . . *send Charley to me this night week . . .* {Bleak House 44}
One week from tonight.

three-cornered hat . . . *tied in a convenient crease of his double chin [the handkerchief] secured his three-cornered hat and bob-wig from blowing off his head . . .* {Barnaby Rudge 2}
A hat with the brim folded up on three sides.

three-out . . . *a little crowd has collected round a couple of ladies, who having imbibed the contents of various "three-outs" of gin and bitters in the course of the morning, have at length differed on some point of domestic arrangement . . .* {Sketches, Seven-dials}
A glass holding one-third of a quartern. When referring to liquor, a quartern is usually a quarter of a pint.

threshing *[He was in the coal cellar with] two other young gentlemen, who, after participating with him in a sound threshing, had been locked up therein for atrociously presuming to be hungry . . .* {Oliver Twist 2}
Thrashing, beating.

throttle . . . *invigorated himself with a bumper [of punch] for his throttle . . .* {Tale of Two Cities 2-5}
1. Throat.
Speak out or I'll throttle you! {Oliver Twist 13}
2. Strangle.

throw back *But the Princess Alicia . . . quietly called to them to be still, on account of not throwing back the queen upstairs, who was fast getting well . . .* {Reprinted Pieces, Holiday Romance 2}
To delay the progress of something, in this case the recovery of the queen from an illness.

throwing-off *Well; he certainly has a habit of throwing-off, but then--"* {Sketches, The "Throwing-Off" Young Gentleman}
Speaking sarcastically or boastfully while pretending to be pleasant.

throw up *"No!", returned the spy. "I throw up. I confess . . . "* {Tale of Two Cities 3-8}
Give up.

thrush . . . *he thought of measles, scarlet fever, thrush, hooping cough, and a good many other sources of consolation besides.* {Pickwick Papers 29}
A disease of the mouth and throat caused by a yeast-like fungus, most often attacking children.

thunder-and-lightening buttons *He wore a black velvet waistcoat with thunder-and-lightening buttons . . .* {Pickwick Papers 32}
Buttons made of two sharply contrasting colors.

ticker . . . *if you don't take fogles and tickers--* {Oliver Twist 18}
Slang for a watch.

ticket *The door was opened by a Porter. Such a Porter! Not of Toby's order. Quite another thing. His place was the ticket though; not Toby's.* {The Chimes 2}
Pun on 'ticket porter', which is Toby's occupation, and the sense of 'that's the ticket'.

ticketed linen-drapers . . . *the vehicle stopped before a dirty-looking ticketed linen-drapers shop . . .* {Sketches, Horatio Sparkins}
Having placards, labels, and tags on and in it. (A high-class shop would not be so undignified in appearance.)

ticket-porter *Mr. George sealed it at a coffee-house, that it might lead to no discovery, and we sent it off by a ticket-porter.* {Bleak House 24}
Porters licensed by the city of London wore a badge, or ticket, and a small white apron. They could carry, load, and ship goods as well as documents and messages. They could be hired on the street.

'tickler *"All right, Governors Both," returned the ghost carefully closing the room door; " 'tickler business."* {Our Mutual Friend 1-12}
Dialect for particular.

tide-boat ... *he may get to the Tower Stairs, and away by the Greavesend tide-boat, before any search is made for him.* {Barnaby Rudge 51}
A small boat that traveled on the tide.

tie-wig ... *for he wore an old tie-wig as bare and frowzy as a stunted hearth-broom* ... {Barnaby Rudge 8}
A wig with the hair gathered in a small pigtail at the rear, and tied with a ribbon. This was another of the many fashions in wigs.

tiger *[Lest any man] should doubt in tiger, cab, or person, Tigg Montague, Esquire* ... {Martin Chuzzlewit 27}
A miniature groom, a small man or boy who wore livery. He often rode in the little seat at the back of his master's cabriolet, ready to leap down to hold the horse or run an errand. No smart man-about-town would be without one, and the smaller the tiger the more fashionable he was. The name came from the striped waistcoats they often wore.

tights ... *his elevated position revealing those tights and gaiters which, had they clothed an ordinary man, might have passed without observation* ... {Pickwick Papers 1}
Breeches, knee breeches.

tile ... *wery smart--top-boots on--nose-gay in his button hole--broad-brimmed tile--green shawl--quite the gen'lman.* {Pickwick Papers 10}
Slang for hat.

till ... *took the money from the till* ... {Oliver Twist 42}
1. A money box or cashbox.
... *prompting her... to private researches in the day book and ledger, till, cash-box, and iron safe* ... {Bleak House 25}
2. The removable drawer in a cashbox, in which the day's cash or change is kept.

tilt *[He] was lying at full length upon a truss of straw, high and dry at the top of the van, with the tilt a little open in front for the convenience of talking to his new friend* . . . {Martin Chuzzlewit 13}
The canvas cover or awning of a cart or wagon.

tilted wagon *All sorts of vehicles are in attendance, from a tilted waggon to a wheelbarrow.* {Dombey & Son 59}
A wagon having a tilt, a canvas cover or awning.

timbrel *Mrs. Snagsby sounds no timbrel in anybody's ears, but holds her purpose quietly, and keeps her counsel.* {Bleak House 25}
A tambourine.

time being out *His time being out, he had 'worked in the shop' at weekly wages seven or eight years more* . . . {Little Dorrit 1-16}
The time of apprenticeship being completed.

time, what time . . . *Miss Tox directed her steps one evening, what time Mr. Toodle, cindery and swart, was refreshing himself with tea* . . . {Dombey & Son 38}
When, at the time that something was happening.

time of day *Oh! That's the time of day. Come on!* {Oliver Twist 20}
The right way. Slang, somewhat like rhyming slang.

time out of mind *It was, in fact, the twenty-fifth of March, which, as most people know to their cost, is, and has been time out of mind, one of those unpleasant epochs termed quarter-days.* {Barnaby Rudge 13}
From a time beyond human memory.

times, by times . . . *he contemplates Durdles* . . . *curiously, and Durdles is by times conscious of his watchful eyes.* {Edwin Drood 12}
From time to time.

time-serving *You ought to be above the base tale-bearing of a time-serving woman* . . . {Our Mutual Friend 3-15}
A time-server is a person who, for reasons of self-interest, behaves in ways that are in favor at the time. It does not mean a 'convict' as it does in the United States.

times out of number ... *me and Mrs. Boffin have stood out against the old man times out of number* ... {Our Mutual Friend 1-8}
Many times, innumerable times.

tin ... *an't it a pity that this state of things should continue, and how much better it would be for the old gentleman to hand over a reasonable amount of tin, and make it all right and comfortable?* {Old Curiosity Shop 2}
Slang for money.

tinder *[He would put the letters] in the fire, with such distrust and caution that he would bend down to watch the crumpled tinder while it floated upward* ... {Martin Chuzzlewit 38}
Partially burned material, in this case the letter paper. Tinder usually refers to partially burned linen used to start a fire from the sparks produced by striking flint on steel.

tinder-box ... *he took from his pocket a pipe, flint, steel, and tinder-box, and began to smoke.* {Barnaby Rudge 46}
The box in which flint, steel, and tinder were kept. These were used for starting a fire before matches were invented (see **tinder**).

tinker *"I was just eight." says Phil, "agreeable to the parish calculation, when I went with the tinker."* {Bleak House 26}
An itinerant mender of pots and pans.

tinkler *Jerk the tinkler.* {Oliver Twist 15}
Slang for bell. The word is translated by Dickens in the sentence following this quotation.

tinman *"Capital things those shower-baths!" ejaculated Wisbottle. "Excellent!" said Tomkins. "Delightful!" chimed in O'Bleary. (He had once seen one, outside a tinman's.)* {Sketches, Mr. Minns and his Cousin}
A dealer in tinware, a tinsmith.

tip *It was the Inn where friends used to put up, and where we used to go to see parents, and to have salmon and fouls, and be tipped.* {The Holly-Tree 1}
To give money to a school child.

tip-cheese ... *he forgets the long-familiar cry of 'knuckle down,' and at tip-cheese or odd and even, his hand is out.* {Pickwick Papers 34} Probably a mistaken name for the game of 'tip-cat'. The tip-cat is a piece of wood, tapered at both ends. It is struck on one end with a stick, causing it to fly up, and then hit with the stick.

tip-top sawyer *[Mr. Pyke is] fine, pleasant, gentlemanly... and a tip-top sawyer.* {Nicholas Nickleby 34} First-class, top-notch person. 'Sawyer' actually means one whose occupation is the sawing of wood, but it has the additional slang meaning of 'person'. When logs were sawed into boards by hand it was done over a pit, using a large two-man saw. The man beneath, in the pit, got sawdust in his face and had the worse job. The top sawyer was the better off and more important person.

tippet *She had furry articles for winter wear, such as tippets, boas, and muffs, which all stood up on end in a rampant manner...* {Dombey & Son 1} A garment which just covered the neck and shoulders.

tipstaff ... *Pickwick was soon afterwards confided to the custody of the tipstaff, to be taken by him to the warden for the Fleet Prison ...* {Pickwick Papers 40} A sheriff's officer, or court usher. So-called from the staff he carried, which was tipped with metal.

tiring-room ... *then converting the parlour, for the nonce, into a private tiring-room, she dressed her, with great care ...* {Dombey & Son 6} A dressing room, usually the dressing room of a theater. Possibly from the word 'attire'.

tittlebat ... *fanning his flushed face with a spelling-book, wishing himself a whale, or a tittlebat, or a fly, or anything but a boy at school ...* {Old Curiosity Shop 25} A stickleback, a small spiny-finned fish.

tittivate *Regular as clockwork--breakfast at nine--dress and tittivate a little--down to the Sir Somebody's Head--a glass of ale and the paper...*

{Sketches, The Misplaced Attachment of Mr. John Dounce}
To spruce up, to touch up one's hair, make-up, clothing, etc., so as to
improve the appearance.

toad-eater *I see little to choose, between assistant to a brutal pedagogue,
and a toad-eater to a mean and ignorant upstart, be he member or
no member.* {Nicholas Nickleby 16}
A fawning flatterer. From the attendant to a charlatan, who pretended to eat toads, which were believed to be poisonous, and then pretended that his master's nostrums had cured him.

toadies ... *they somehow conveyed to me that they were all toadies and
humbugs*... {Great Expectations 11}
A toady is a toad-eater (as in the entry above).

toad in a hole *The most enthusiastic admirer of [ham and beef] would
probably not object ... to a little innocent trifling with Irish stews, meat
pies, and toads in holes.* {The Uncommercial Traveller, The Boiled
Beef of New England}
A piece of meat, often sausage, baked in a batter and served on a bed of
gravy.

tobacco-stopper ... *a silver tobacco-stopper, in the form of a leg*...
{David Copperfield 31}
A gadget for pressing tobacco down into the bowl of the pipe.

tocsin ... *sent word to the sacristan, who kept the keys of the
church, that there might be need to ring the tocsin by-and-by.* {Tale of
Two Cities 2-23}
An alarm signal sounded by ringing bells.

toepic *It ain't my place, as a paid servant of the company, to give my
opinion on any of the company's toepics*... {Mugby Junction 1}
Apparently dialect for 'topic'.

togs *Look at his togs!--Superfine cloth, and the heavy-swell cut!* {Oliver
Twist 16}
Slang for clothes.

toilet ... *darting out of the sleeping-closet where he made his toilet* ...
{Tale of Two Cities 2-1}
The action or process of dressing.

toilette-table ... *pushed that sister away from the toilette-table at which
she sat angrily trying to cry* ... {Little Dorrit 2-14}
Dressing table.

told ... *Fagin told the amount into her hand.* {Oliver Twist 39}
Counted.

to let *There are always a good many houses to let in the street; it is a by-
street too, and its dullness is soothing.* {Pickwick Papers 32}
For rent.

tollbar *He had got through the village, and this tollbar was his last
trial* ... {Martin Chuzzlewit 31}
The barrier across a toll road where the toll must be paid.

tollman *The very tollman* ... *came out himself to take the toll and give him
a rough good morning* ... {Martin Chuzzlewit 5}
Turnpike man, the collector of the tolls on a toll road.

tompion clock *The Great Pump Room is a spacious saloon, ornamented
with Corinthian pillars, and a music gallery, and a tompion clock* ...
{Pickwick Papers 36}
A clock made by Thomas Tompion, Britain's most famous watchmaker,
who worked in the seventeenth century.

tooth-powder ... *a most searching division of tooth-powder diffusing
itself around, as under a deluded mistake that all the chinks in the
fittings was divisions in teeth.* {Somebody's Luggage 1}
A powder used like toothpaste to clean teeth. It was applied to a moistened toothbrush.

top and bottom ... *nobody ever dreamed such soup as was put upon the
table* ... *or such fish; or such side-dishes; or such a top and bottom; or
such a course of birds and sweets* ... {Martin Chuzzlewit 12}
Top and bottom can mean the halves of small rolls sliced and reheated

in an oven. It also may refer to those seated at the head and foot of the table. Since the phrase appears in a list of foods it probably refers to the rolls.

top-bar ... *prepared such a haystack of buttered toast that I could scarcely see him over it as it simmered on an iron stand hooked to the top-bar*... {Great Expectations 37}
The uppermost iron bar at the front of a fireplace.

top-boots *He wore the white riding-coat and top-boots, then in vogue*... {Tale of Two Cities 3-9}
1. A kind of boot with the top portion a different color from the rest, either because the top of the boot was turned down or in imitation of a turned down top.
D'ye know a pair of top-boots when you see 'em, Polly?--look here! {Martin Chuzzlewit 26}
2. Top-boots were so often worn by servants in livery that to 'go into top-boots' meant to take a job as a footman. Young Bailey is announcing that he has such a job.

top couple *Away they went, twenty couple at once* ... : *old top couple always turning up in the wrong place; new top couple starting off again, as soon as they got there; all top couples at last, and not a bottom one to help them out.* {A Christmas Carol 2}
The lead couple in a dance.

toper *Away with four fresh horses from the Bald-face Stag, where topers congregate about the door admiring* ... {Martin Chuzzlewit 36}
A habitual drinker, a drunkard.

top of the table *Doctor Blimber was already in his place in the dining-room, at the top of the table* ... {Dombey & Son 12}
Head of the table.

top-sawyer *Wasn't he always a top-sawyer among you all! Is there one of you that could touch him or come near him on any scent!* {Oliver Twist 43}
(See **tip-top-sawyer**)

tops ... *he had a very large pair of boots, originally made for tops, which might have been once worn by some stout farmer, but were now too patched and tattered for a beggar.* {Nicholas Nickleby 7}
Short for top boots.

toque ... *and out came an old lady in a large toque, and an old gentleman in a blue coat* ... {Sketches, The Bloomsbury Christening}
A bonnet with a very small, turned-up brim.

tosspot ... *to be looked upon as a common pipe-smoker, beer-bibber, spirit-guzzler, and tosspot!* {Barnaby Rudge 13}
Someone who tosses off his pot of liquor, a heavy drinker, a drunkard.

toucher *We just twist up Chancery Lane, and cut along Holborn, and there we are in four minutes' time, as near as a toucher.* {Bleak House 4}
'As near as a toucher' means 'very nearly'.

touch-hole ... *say that the draught from the touch-hole of a cannon of such a calibre bears such a proportion in the nicest fraction to the draught from the muzzle* ... {The Uncommercial Traveller, Mr. Barlow}
A vent in a cannon, leading to the powder charge, through which the charge was ignited.

touchwood ... *your mother, who was a prudent woman as dry as a chip, just dwindled away like touchwood after you and Judy were born* ... {Bleak House 21}
Wood which has undergone dry rot, becoming friable and powdery.

tout, touter ... *nor did it mark him out as the prey of ring-droppers, pea and thimble riggers, duffers, touters, or any of those bloodless sharpers* ... {Martin Chuzzlewit 37}
A person who tries to get customers for a business, lawyer, hotel, or in this case for a con game of some sort.

touzled ... *and Toby himself all aslant* ... *would be so banged and buffeted, and touzled, and worried, and hustled, and lifted off his feet* ... {The Chimes 1}
Disarranged, disheveled.

tow ... *they fired the pile with lighted matches and with blazing tow, and then stood by, awaiting the result.* {Barnaby Rudge 64}
Flax fibers. Like straw, they burn very easily.

trace *"Would have been here before," said the hostler, "but they broke a trace."* {Pickwick Papers 9}
Part of the harness of a horse drawing a vehicle.

traduce ... *when he gave me the picture of your lovely face so carelessly traduced by him* ... {Edwin Drood 19}
Translated, rendered. Here in the sense of translation from the real face into the portrait.

train ... *the train was laid, the mine was preparing, the sapper and miner was at work.* {Pickwick Papers 34}
1. The trail of gunpowder or other material used as a fuse to ignite the explosive charge of a mine.
I only want to have everything in train, and to know that it is in train by looking after it myself. {Bleak House 57}
2. In proper order or sequence, also 'underway'.

trained down *Certainly, it has trained you down, Mr. Wegg* ... {Our Mutual Friend 4-14}
Caused to lose weight. The implication is of weight lost during athletic training.

train oil *Mr. Chadband is a very large yellow man with a fat smile and a general appearance of having a good deal of train oil in his system.* {Bleak House 19}
Oil obtained from the blubber of whales. From the word 'train', which used to mean oil which had been extracted or exuded.

training *"It's all in training, sir," said Sam. "What's in training, Sam?" inquired Mr. Pickwick. "I have found 'em out, sir," said Sam* {Pickwick Papers 23}
Underway. Sam means to say 'in train'.

tramper . . . *passing numerous groups of gipsies and trampers on the road.* {Old Curiosity Shop 19}
Tramp, vagabond.

tram-road *How the wheels clank and rattle, and the tram-road shakes, as the train rushes on!* {Martin Chuzzlewit 21}
The tracks on which the railroad cars run.

transport . . . *a secret that might transport her* . . . {Oliver Twist 38}
1. To be sent out of the country into exile as punishment for a crime.
This man was a returned transport, and his name was Kegs. {Oliver Twist 50}
2. A person who was transported, sentenced to exile.
The person . . . received his twopence with anything but transport, tosses the money into the air, catches it over-handed, and retires. {Bleak House 26}
3. A strong feeling of pleasure.

transportation *Not even the unlooked-for commutation of his sentence to transportation for fourteen years softened for an instant the sullen hardihood of his demeanor.* {Pickwick Papers 6}
. . . *he was tried and ordered to be transported.* {David Copperfield 48}
Sentencing to exile.

trap *Why, the traps have got him, and that's all about it* . . . {Oliver Twist 13}
1. Slang for policeman.
. . . *Nadgett suddenly appeared before Mr. Montague's house in Pall Mall--he always made his appearance as if he had that moment come up a trap* . . . {Martin Chuzzlewit 38}
2. Trapdoor.
"Cuttle," said the Commander, getting off the chest, and opening the lid, "are these your traps?" {Dombey & Son 39}
3. Short for trappings. Personal effects, clothes, portable furniture, and the like.
. . . *had tried to sit people agin the mas'r swips, and take the shine out o' their bis'nes, and the bread out o' the traps o' their preshus kids* . . . {Sketches, The First of May}
4. Slang for mouth.
"What has been doing in the city to-day?" "Trap, bat, and ball, my

dear," said Mr. Orange; "and it knocks a man up." {Reprinted Pieces, Holiday Romance 4}
5. A device used in the game of trapball. It consists of a flat stick on a low pivot placed on the ground, with a ball resting on one end. The opposite end is hit with a bat causing the ball to fly up so that it can then be struck with the bat.

traveling post ... *I was unconsciously riding fast just now, in compliment I suppose to the pace of my thoughts, which were traveling post.* {Barnaby Rudge 14}
Traveling fast, like the King's messengers riding post horses.

traveller for a house *It's eighty years ago since the circumstance happened to a traveller for that house, but he was a particular friend of my uncle's* ... {Pickwick Papers 14}
Traveling salesman for a company.

travelling-desk *When he had finished his writing and had dried it on the blotting-paper in his travelling-desk; he looked up* ... {Martin Chuzzlewit 44}
A box, usually one with a sloping top and small enough to hold on the lap, containing writing materials and used as a writing surface.

treacle *They have brimstone and treacle, partly because if they hadn't something or other in the way of medicine they'd always be ailing and giving a world of trouble, and partly because it spoils their appetites and comes cheaper than breakfast and dinner.* {Nicholas Nickleby 8}
Molasses. Brimstone and treacle is sulfur and molasses.

treat *Chapter XXIV treats of a very poor subject* ... {Oliver Twist 24}
Deal with.

trebly *But it really is doubly and trebly hard to have crowds and multitudes of people turning up after him* ... {Tale of Two Cities 2-6}
Triply, tripled.

trench ... *he could contrive to exist, without trenching upon the hospitality of Newman Noggs* ... {Nicholas Nickleby 16}
To encroach or infringe upon.

trencherman ... *I agreed to ship myself as an able trencherman on board the Temeraire.* {The Uncommercial Traveller, A Little Dinner in an Hour}
A hearty eater, from 'trencher', a flat board on which food was served before pottery became easily available.

trepanned ... *Mr. Inspector... having been trepanned into an industrious hunt on a false scent.* {Our Mutual Friend 4-16}
Trapped or decoyed.

tressel ... *the homely alter where they knelt..., the plain black tressels that bore their weight on their last visit to the cool old shady church.* {Old Curiosity Shop 17}
Trestle. Here the word refers to the sawhorse-like structures on which a coffin was placed.

trifle *When the salt-cellar, and the fowl's breast, and the trifle, and the lobster salad were all exhausted* ... {Sketches, Some Particulars Concerning a Lion}
A dessert made, in the seventeenth century, of cream boiled with sugar, mace, and cinnamon. Currently, it is made of sponge cake covered with whipped cream, custard, and fruit.

trim the light ... *drawing a small table towards his bedside, trimmed the light, put on his spectacles, and composed himself to read.* {Pickwick Papers 11}
Trim the wick of a candle.

triple-bob-major ... *Mr. Pecksniff was a special hand at a triple-bob-major.* {Martin Chuzzlewit 30}
A bell ringing change, a particular sequence in which bells are rung. Various sequences are given special names.

trod with stir enough ... *those two... trod with stir enough, and carried their divine rights with a high hand.* {Tale of Two Cities 1-1}
Went about with commotion and tumult.

troll *[The kettle] trolled its song with that strong energy of cheerfulness, that its iron body jumped and stirred upon the fire* ... {Cricket on

the Hearth 1}
To sing in a full, rolling voice.

trotter-case ... *he applied himself to a process which Mr. Dawkins desig-nated as 'japanning his trotter-cases'.* {Oliver Twist 18}
Slang for boot.

Trotters *[Says Toby smelling the dinner basket] "... It's very nice. It improves every moment. It's too decided for Trotters. An't it?"* {The Chimes 1}
Cooked pig's feet or sheep's feet.

truckle-bed ... *there was a small copper fixed in one corner, a chair or two, a form and table, a glimmering fire, and a truckle-bed, covered with a ragged patchwork rug.* {Barnaby Rudge 8}
A low bed which moves on truckles, or castors, and is kept under a higher bed, being rolled out for use. A trundle bed.

truck ... *to make their way, as they best could, among carts, baskets, barrows, trucks, casks, bulks, and benches* ... {Barnaby Rudge 60}
A wheeled vehicle for carrying heavy weights.

truckling ... *a servile, false, and truckling knave* ... {Barnaby Rudge 43}
Servile, submissive.

trump ... *he is a thoroughgoing, downright, plain-spoken, old trump, sir* ... {Dombey & Son 10}
A term of commendation, a fine person.

trumpery *You may talk of your Lord Mayors ... your sheriffs, your common councilmen, your trumpery* ... {Martin Chuzzlewit 19}
Trickery, deceit.

truncheon ... *dealing out smart and tingling blows with their trun-cheons, after the manner of the ingenious actor Mr. Punch* ... {Nicho-las Nickleby 2}
A short, thick club.

trunks ... *Mr. Snodgrass in blue satin trunks and cloak, white silk tights and shoes, and Grecian helmet* ... {Pickwick Papers 15}
Short trousers ending on the thighs, usually made of thin material and worn over tights.

truss *[He] was lying at full length upon a truss of straw, high and dry at the top of the van, with the tilt a little open in front for the convenience of talking to his new friend* ... {Martin Chuzzlewit 13}
A bundle of straw containing about 36 pounds.

try *"I have a short narrative on my lips," rejoined his friend, "and will try you with it. It is very brief."* {Old Curiosity Shop 69}
... *therefore they try me as they do* ... {Barnaby Rudge 7}
1. To strain endurance or patience. It also may have the sense of 'test'.
I--don't know what comes over me. I--try against it. {Our Mutual Friend 1-16}
2. Attempt to do something, struggle to do something.
the night wind ... trying with its unseen hand the windows and the doors ... {The Chimes 1}
3. To find out if a window or door is fastened by attempting to open it.
... *pointing to where the earth by the watercourses and along the valleys was turned up, for miles, in trying for metal.* {Message From the Sea 3}
4. To search a place in order to find something. Here it means searching for metals which can be mined.

tub *Dodger, take off the sausages; and draw a tub near the fire for Oliver.* {Oliver Twist 8}
A low wooden vessel made like a half barrel, here turned over and used as a crude seat.

tucker *Whereat Scrooge's niece's sister--the plump one with the lace tucker: not the one with the roses--blushed.* {A Christmas Carol 3}
A lace frill worn around the neck.

tumbler *The wheeling and circling flights of runts, fantails, tumblers, and pouters* ... {Barnaby Rudge 1}
A kind of pigeon that characteristically turns over and over in its flight.

tumbril *My friend, I don't care a pinch of snuff for the whole Royal Artillery establishment--officers, men, tumbrils, waggons, horses, guns, and ammunition.* {Bleak House 34}
A two-wheeled covered cart for carrying ammunition.

Turkey-carpet *A thick and dingy Turkey-carpet muffles the floor where he sits* ... {Bleak House 10}
Turkish carpet, Turkish rug.

Turkish frame of mind *... abandoning myself to the narrow streets in a Turkish frame of mind, relied on predestination to bring me somehow or other to the place I wanted* ... {The Uncommercial Traveller, Wapping Workhouse}
Submitting to predestination. The Crimean War made the British very aware of Islamic ideas, and they were especially impressed by Islamic fatalism.

Turkish trousers *He was dressed in a gorgeous morning gown, with a waistcoat and Turkish trousers of the same pattern* ... {Nicholas Nickleby 10}
Trousers 'a la Turque', patterned after those supposedly worn in Turkey. They were very wide in the leg and made a brief fashion appearance about 1800.

turncock *... he hopes the heart of the turncock as cut the water off'll be softened and turned in the right vay* ... {Pickwick Papers 27}
The official from the waterworks responsible for turning on or shutting off the water supply to individual homes and buildings.

turner *... one Mr. Kenwigs, a turner in ivory, who was looked upon as a person of some consideration* ... {Nicholas Nickleby 12}
Someone who makes things on a lathe from wood and other materials. The process is called 'turning'.

turnkey *... held by Defarge's arm as he held by the turnkey's.* {Tale of Two Cities 2-21}
A jailer or jail guard. Originally, someone who had charge of the keys and locked and unlocked the doors by turning a key in the lock.

turn-out *"... it's a neat turn-out," replied Ben Allen, with something of pride in his tone. "They're not used to see this sort of thing every day, I dare say."* {Pickwick Papers 50}
An equipage, including horses, carriage, and footmen.

turnpike *"You had better lead him till we come to a turnpike," replied Mr. Pickwick from the chaise.* {Pickwick Papers 5}
A tollgate. Originally it was a pair of crossed boards rotating on a vertical post, a turnstile. Also means the toll road itself.

turnpike house *... an old man in his shirt and trousers emerged from the turnpike house and opened the gate.* {Pickwick Papers 9}
The building in which the turnpike-keeper lived.

turnpike-keeper, turnpike-man *"What do you mean by a 'pike-keeper'?" inquired Mr. Peter Magnus. "The old 'un means a turnpike-keeper, gen'lm'n," observed Mr. Samuel Weller in explanation.* {Pickwick Papers 22}
The person who collected tolls and opened the turnpike gate.

turnspit *A pack of idle dogs ... only fit to be turnspits.* {Dombey & Son 11}
A dog who ran inside a tread-wheel to turn the roasting spit.

turnstile *I left 'em at the turnstile to run forward and tell you they were coming...* {Martin Chuzzlewit 20}
A kind of gate having four arms turning horizontally and permitting only one person at a time to pass.

turn-up *He was lying on an old bedstead, which turned up during the day.* {Pickwick Papers 3}
It was not a turn-up bedstead, nor yet a French bedstead, nor yet a four-post bedstead... {Martin Chuzzlewit 49}
1. A bed that folds up to take less room.
... and what with having turn-ups with the tinker as I got older, almost whenever he was too far gone in drink--which was almost always--... {Bleak House 26}
2. Fist fights.

turpentining ... *the lady of the house was busily engaged in turpentining the disjointed fragments of a tent-bedstead* ... {Nicholas Nickleby 46}
Turpentine was used to remove the old wax on furniture before new wax was applied.

turret *They were standing near the foot of the turret, where the alarm bell hung.* {Barnaby Rudge 56}
A small tower, often starting above the bottom of a building and projecting from its wall.

turret-chamber, turret-room *From one solitary turret-chamber, however, there shone a ray of light* ... {Barnaby Rudge 34}
Mr. Tulkinghorn arrives in his turret-room a little breathed by the journey up, though leisurely performed. {Bleak House 41}
A room in a turret.

turret-door *Hugh and his friends kept together at the turret-door where Mr. Haredale had last admitted him and old John Willet* ... {Barnaby Rudge 55}
The door leading to the inside of the turret.

turtles *Divide the lively turtles in the bills of mortality, by the number of gentlefolks able to buy 'em; and whose share does he take but his own!* {The Chimes 2}
Mr. Filer attempted to prove that by eating tripe, a cheap food, he was depriving orphans and widows of food. Trotty is noting that, in accord with that reasoning, the eaters of expensive turtles do not so deprive anyone. The bills of mortality were statistics of births and deaths in the London parishes.

tutor's assistant ... *one [of the tables] bore some preparations for supper; while, on the other, a tutor's assistant, a Murray's grammar, half a dozen cards of terms, and a worn letter directed to Wackford Squeers, Esquire, were arranged in picturesque confusion.* {Nicholas Nickleby 7}
A book used by a teacher. It probably contained such things as answers to arithmetic problems.

twaddler ... *you will perhaps be somewhat repaid by a laugh at the style of this ungrammatical twaddler.* {Pickwick Papers 51}
One who talks or writes twaddle, senseless, silly, or trashy material.

twelfth-cake ... *juicy oranges, luscious pears, immense twelfth-cakes, and seething bowls of punch* ... {A Christmas Carol 3}
A large frosted cake with a bean or coin baked in it that was used at Twelfth-night celebrations. The person who received the bean or coin in a piece of the cake was named king or queen of the feast.

twelvemo ... *a work purporting to be "Sketches of Young Ladies;" written by Quiz, illustrated by Phiz, and published in one volume, square twelvemo.* {Sketches, To the Young Ladies}
A sheet of paper folded to produce twelve leaves. The Latin word *duodecimo* was abbreviated in English as '12mo', which was then pronounced 'twelve-mo'.

twelvemonth ... *he might have sat there for a twelvemonth* ... {Pickwick Papers 39}
A year.

twig, in twig *You'll be tackling somebody presently. You're in twig tonight, I see.* {Barnaby Rudge 11}
In good twig, in a fine state, in good fettle.

two for his heels *The Marchioness dealt, turned up a knave, and omitted to take the usual advantage; upon which Mr. Swiveller called out as loud as he could--"Two for his heels!"* {Old Curiosity Shop 64}
'His heels' refers to the knave, or jack. In cribbage the dealer gets two points for turning up a jack. Swiveller is saying 'two points for the jack'.

two-pair ... *whether a splendid French-polished mahogany bedstead should be erected for herself in the two-pair back of the house in Cadogan Place, or in the three-pair front* ... {Nicholas Nickleby 21}
An apartment up two flights of steps, or in Great Britain, on the second floor.

twopenny post ... *I will put a note in the twopenny post*... {Nicholas Nickleby 34}
Ordinary postage in London from 1801 to 1839 was two pence. There were six daily deliveries and collections. Dinner invitations for the same day could be sent in the morning, and a reply received in plenty of time to prepare for the guests.

Tyburn tree ... *you shall hear of him at Tyburn tree if we have luck.* {Barnaby Rudge 17}
The gallows at Bayswater and Edgware roads, at the northeast corner of Hyde Park, in London. The word 'Tyburn' by itself also often means the gallows.

umbragious ... *and the gnarled and warted elms and the umbragious oaks stand deep in the fern and leaves of a hundred years* ... {Bleak House 28}
Umbrageous, casting abundant shade.

unbear *Unbear him half a moment to freshen him up, and I'll be back.* {Bleak House 56}
To free a horse from the bearing rein.

unbraced ... *his knee-smalls unbraced* ... {David Copperfield 16}
Unfastened, loosened. Probably with suspenders removed.

uncle *Do not be angry. I have parted with [your gravy spoon]--to my uncle.* {Martin Chuzzlewit 1}
Slang for pawnbroker.

under the mahogany *I had hoped... to have seen you three gentlemen one day or another with your legs under the mahogany in my humble parlor...* {Old Curiosity Shop 66}
Sitting at a table, from the table top being made of mahogany.

under-jaw *At this the nearest stone face seemed to stare amazed, and, with opened mouth and dropped under-jaw, looked awe stricken ...* {Tale of Two Cities 2-9}
The lower jaw, the mandible. In the United States the word would be 'jaw' alone.

undress ... *a groom in undress was idling about ...* {Pickwick Papers 39}
Ordinary clothing, not formal livery. It does not mean he was in his underwear.

Union House ... *some worn-out relative or friend who had been charitably clutched off to a great blank barren Union House, as far from old home as the County Jail* ... {Our Mutual Friend 3-8}
A poorhouse, or workhouse. The union is that of several parishes combined to support one poorhouse.

unstamped advertisement *So he stopped the unstamped advertisement--an animated sandwich composed of a boy between two boards* ... {Sketches, The Dancing Academy}
Official and public advertisements were taxed until 1833 and were stamped to show the tax had been paid. Sandwich boards were not in the taxable category.

Upas tree ... *as if a Upas tree had been made a capture of* ... {Little Dorrit 2-27}
A fabled tree so poisonous that nothing could live for miles around it.

upon the morrow ... *Mr. Quinion was to go upon the morrow.* {David Copperfield 10}
In the morning.

Up X *She goes off in a sidin' till the Up X passes* ... {Mugby Junction 1}
The up express train, the train coming up to town or to London.

uses me to it *It is a sensation not experienced by many mortals....* *Nothing uses me to it.* {Our Mutual Friend 2-13}
The sense here is 'nothing gets me used to it'.

usher *Now, a proud usher in a Yorkshire school was such a very extraordinary and unaccountable thing to hear of,--any usher at all being a novelty* ... {Nicholas Nickleby 9}
An assistant to a headmaster or teacher.

usquebaugh ... *what does my noble captain drink--is it brandy, rum, usquebaugh? Is it soaked gunpowder, or blazing oil?* {Barnaby Rudge 8}
The Gaelic word for whiskey, from which the English word is derived.

vacancy ... *his favourite action of stooping a little, to look across the table out of window at vacancy, under the window-blind* ... {Tom Tiddler's Ground 1}
To be at vacancy is to be unoccupied with work or business.

vandyked corners ... *and placing my finger upon this blue wafer with the vandyked corners* ... {Old Curiosity Shop 14}
Wafer corners embossed with a lace pattern like the collars in Van Dyke portraits (see **wafer**).

vane *When at intervals the window trembled, the rusty vane upon the turret-top complained, the clock beneath it recorded another quarter of an hour was gone* ... {The Haunted Man 1}
Weather vane, wind vane.

vaunt *This was not a mere empty vaunt, but a deliberate avowal of his real sentiments* ... {Old Curiosity Shop 48}
Boast, brag.

vegetable-marrow *Cucumbers and vegetable-marrows flying at the heads of the family as they walk in their own garden* ... {Nicholas Nickleby 37}
A kind of gourd used as a table vegetable.

vellum ... *the spruce serjeant who hurried past with a cane in his hand, and under his arm a clasped book with a vellum cover* ... {Barnaby Rudge 58}
A fine, superior quality of parchment.

velvet shorts ... *the upper portion of his legs encased in the velvet shorts, and the lower part thereof swathed in ... complicated bandages* ... {Pickwick Papers 15}

Knee breeches made of velvet cloth. Knee breeches are trousers ending just below the kneecap. Dickens uses the word 'trunks' when he means short trousers ending on the thigh.

velveteen *Here we found a gentleman with one eye, in a velveteen suit and knee breeches* . . . {Great Expectations 151}
A fabric looking like velvet, but made from cotton instead of silk.

vendible *You* . . . *were bought and sold like any other vendible.* {David Copperfield 50}
Any object that can be bought or sold.

vent-peg . . . *pulling out the vent-peg of the table-beer, and trying to peep down into the barrel through the hole.* {The Chimes 4}
A plug, usually wooden, to fill the air vent of a barrel or keg of liquid.

verger . . . *a very earthy old verger insisting on locking up the Cathedral forthwith.* {Martin Chuzzlewit 5}
A person whose job is to care for the interior of a church.

vestry-boards *As to corporations, parishes, vestry-boards, and similar gatherings of jolter-headed clods who assemble to exchange such speeches that, by heaven, they ought to be worked in quicksilver mines for the short remainder of their miserable existences* . . . {Bleak House 13}
The council of management for the temporal business of a church.

vestryman *Among our number was a vestryman,--the densest idiot I have ever seen* . . . {Doctor Marigold 3}
A member of the board managing a parish church.

vestry-room . . . *the clergyman had not arrived; and the clerk, who was sitting by the vestry-room fire, seemed to think it by no means improbable that it might be an hour or so, before he came.* {Oliver Twist 5}
A room in a church, originally the place that robes, vessels, and records were kept, but often used as a meeting room.

vetturino carriage *How the bottle had been got there, did not appear; but the difficulty of getting it into the ramshackle vetturino carriage in*

which I was departing was so great, and it took up so much room when it was got in, that I elected to sit outside. {The Uncommercial Traveller, The Italian Prisoner}
An Italian four-wheeled carriage for hire.

viands *Yet human fellowship infused some nourishment into the flinty viands, and struck some sparks of cheerfulness out of them.* {Tale of Two Cities 2-22}
Articles of food.

vice *Not far off is the strong, rough, primitive table with a vice upon it at which he has been working.* {Bleak House 21}
1. A vise, a tool for holding materials tightly.
... Mr. Crummles was placed upon the chairman's right, the Phenomenon and the Masters Crummles sustained the vice. {Nicholas Nickleby 48}
2. Vice-chairman, here referring to Mr. Crummles.

victualler *... veritable licensed victuallers ...* {Barnaby Rudge 13}
Someone who has a license to sell food and, especially, drink. A publican or tavern keeper.

vingt-et-un *... the first instalment of punch was brought in, in a white jug; and the succeeding three hours were devoted to* vingt-et-un *at sixpence a dozen ...* {Pickwick Papers 32}
French for 'twenty-one', the card game, also called blackjack.

vintner, free vintner *Her affectionate forethought likewise apprenticed me to the Vintners' Company, and made me in time a Free Vintner ...* {No Thoroughfare, Act I}
A wine merchant invested with the privileges and franchises of a chartered company or guild.

violoncello *... Mr. Brown, who had kindly undertaken, at a few hours notice, to bring his violoncello, would, no doubt, manage extremely well.* {Sketches, Mrs. Joseph Porter}
Also spelled v-i-o-l-i-n-c-e-l-l-o. A bass violin, the instrument now called a cello.

volatile *What a rattle I am! Mr. Copperfield, ain't I volatile?* {David Copperfield 22}
Readily changeable in interests or mood.

votaries ... *avoid the cloud which takes its rise among the pleasures of the world, and cheats the senses of the votaries. The veil, daughters, the veil!* {Nicholas Nickleby 6}
Persons devoted or bound to a particular religion, a devout worshiper.

vurkis ... *he believed he'd been born in the vurkis, but he'd never know'd his father* ... {Sketches, The First of May}
Dialect for workhouse.

wafer *The mantelshelf was ornamented with a wooden inkstand, containing one stump of a pen and half a wafer* ... {Pickwick Papers 14}
Flour and water baked in a thin round form. It was adhesive when moistened, and was used to seal folded letters and documents in the absence of envelopes, and to stick notices and the like on walls.

wafer-box ... *Wilkins Flasher, Esquire, was balancing himself on two legs of an office stool, spearing a wafer-box with a penknife* ... {Pickwick Papers 55}
The box in which wafers were kept (see **wafer**).

wafered ... *and put* ... *[the letter]* ... *into his pocket, wafered and ready for the general post.* {Pickwick Papers 33}
1. Sealed with a wafer.
I noticed the scantiest necessaries in the way of furniture; a few old prints from books, of Chancellors and barristers, wafered against the wall ... {Bleak House 5}
2. Pasted to a wall or surface by means of a wafer.

Wagerbut *A little less on you, and you'd a' most ha' been a Wagerbut* ... {Our Mutual Friend 4-1}
A wager boat. A light racing rowboat.

waggoner *By Fagin's direction, he immediately substituted for his own attire, a waggoner's frock, velveteen breeches, and leather leggings* ... {Oliver Twist 43}
Driver of a wagon.

wainscot *The parlour was wainscoted, and communicated to strangers a magnetic and instinctive consciousness of rats and mice.* {Martin Chuzzlewit 8}
Wooden panel work on the walls of apartments.

waistcoat, waistcoat strings *Gorgeous are Mr. Dombey's new blue coat, fawn-coloured pantaloons, and lilac waistcoat . . .* {Dombey & Son 31}
. . . the head waiter (who wore powder, and knee-smalls, and was usually a grave man) got to be a bright scarlet in the face, and broke his waistcoat-strings, audibly. {Martin Chuzzlewit 53}
A kind of long vest, worn under a coat and sometimes tied together in back with strings or bands.

waits (see **Christmas Waits**)

waiter *. . . a heterogeneous litter of pastrycook's trays, lamps, waiters full of glasses, and piles of rout seats which were strewn about the hall . . .* {Nicholas Nickleby 17}
A salver, or small tray.

wait on *The proprietor, knowing that Miss Kenwigs had two sisters . . . good for sixpence a-piece, once a month at least, . . . waited on the young lady himself.* {Nicholas Nickleby 52}
1. To attend to the needs of someone, as a servant or shop attendant. *How many disconsolate fathers and substantial tradesman had waited on the locksmith for the same purpose . . .* {Barnaby Rudge 41}
2. To pay a respectful visit.

walk *"Pray, does Mr. Henry Gowan paint--ha--portraits?"* Mr. Sparkler opined that he painted anything, if he could get the job. "He has no particular walk?"* {Little Dorrit 2-6}
A special line of work, a specialty.

walking-match *I know I've been going wrong, sir, ever since I took to bird-catching and walking-matching.* {Dombey & Son 22}
A walking race.

walk-out *. . . on fine Sundays, he often walked-out, before dinner, with the Doctor and Lucie . . .* {Tale of Two Cities 2-6}
To take a walk, although it also has the connotation of courting.

wall, go to the wall, give the wall *. . . even Tellson's shall go to the wall . . . before him.* {Tale of Two Cities 2-18}
1. To fail in business, become bankrupt.

... the chance passengers who were not so decorated, appeared timidly anxious to escape observation or attack, and gave them the wall as if they would conciliate them. {Barnaby Rudge 48}
2. Allowed them to walk close to the house walls and away from the road, which was usually dirty and had water or sewage in the gutters.

wall-chalking *Lady Dedlock, the wall-chalking and the street-crying would come on directly*... {Bleak House 41}
Scrawling things on walls, often crude advertisements. Here it probably refers to graffiti spreading scandal.

wall-eyed *... a little, pale, wall-eyed, woebegone inn like a large dust-binn of two compartments and a sifter.* {Bleak House 39}
Having a squint, the eyes aimed in different directions. It can also sometimes mean eyes of different colors or one eye streaked with a different color.

wall-fruit *... there was to be no wall-fruit this year.* {Little Dorrit 2-12}
Fruit of trees grown against a wall.

wallet *The old man had forgotten a kind of wallet which contained the light burden he had to carry*... {Old Curiosity Shop 12}
A bag or kind of knapsack.

wallflower *... drinking some coffee from an old china cup--it was then about mid-day--and looking at a collection of wallflowers in the balcony.* {Bleak House 43}
A kind of flowering plant that, in the wild form, will grow against a wall.

Wallsend *... but we will take him by twilight, enlivened with a glow of Wallsend.* {Our Mutual Friend 10-12}
A kind of coal, originally obtained at the town of Wallsend. The town was built at the end of the Roman wall, hence its name.

walnut ketchup *... ask him if he would step up and partake of a lamb chop and walnut ketchup*... {Hard Times 2-11}
Ketchup, used as a relish, was made from a variety of foods including mushrooms and walnuts.

want *I wanted the resolution to go downstairs.* {Great Expectations 19}
It wanted a quarter to eight when they reached Cadogan Place. {Nicholas Nickleby 33}
1. To lack or need.
Do you mean to come to want in your old age, that you take to wasting now? {Martin Chuzzlewit 18}
2. Poverty.

ward, of a key *"Oh! I knew that, did I?" says Mr. Tulkinghorn, examining the wards of the key.* {Bleak House 42}
The slots cut into the bit, the flat part of old-fashioned keys.

warded *The garment hung so loosely on the figure, that its capacious breast was bare, as if disdaining to be warded or concealed by any artifice.* {A Christmas Carol 3}
Protected, guarded.

warder *Two dismally absurd persons . . . were posted at the front door . . . and as I came up, one of the two warders (the post boy) knocked at the door . . .* {Great Expectations 35}
Guard or watchman.

wardrobe *This occupation was, to take down from the shelves of a worm-eaten wardrobe, a quantity of frowsy garments . . .* {Nicholas Nickleby 51}
A cupboard in which clothing is kept.

warm-baths *I come from the warm-baths, sir, round in the neighboring street.* {Little Dorrit 2-25}
A public bathhouse.

warming-pan *And then follows this very remarkable expression. 'Don't trouble yourself about the warming-pan.'* {Pickwick Papers 34}
A covered pan with a long handle. Hot coals were placed in it and it was put into a bed to warm the sheets.

warrant *Mrs. Micawber had not spoken of their going away without warrant.* {David Copperfield 12}
Authorization freeing someone from legal responsibility.

warrant of distress *"It is, mum, " says Fixem again; "this is my warrant of distress, mum, " says he, handing it over polite as if it was a newspaper . . .* {Sketches, The Broker's Man}
The legal document authorizing the seizure of someone's property to force the payment of a debt.

Warren's blackin' *Poetry's unnat'ral; no man ever talked poetry 'cept a beadle on boxin' day, or Warren's blackin', or Rowland's oil . . .* {Pickwick Papers 33}
A brand of boot blacking, boot polish. The reference here is to rhyming advertisements, jingles, often used by Warren's to promote their shoe polish.

wash-hand-stand *[He] locked the door, piled a wash-hand-stand, chest of drawers, and table against it, and packed up a few necessaries ready for flight with the first ray of morning.* {Pickwick Papers 36}
A small table holding the basin, ewer of water, soap, etc., needed for washing hands.

wash-hand-stand jug *. . . Mr. Micawber had prepared, in a wash-hand-stand jug, what he called "a Brew" of the agreeable beverage for which he was famous.* {David Copperfield 36}
The water ewer on a wash-hand-stand.

wash-house *. . . the two young Cratchits hustled Tiny Tim, and bore him off into the wash-house, that he might hear the pudding singing in the copper.* {A Christmas Carol 3}
The outbuilding in which clothing was washed, the laundry.

wash-leather *[A silver teapot which] had been kept from year's end to year's end wrapped up in wash-leather on a certain top shelf . . .* {Nicholas Nickleby 43}
A soft leather, called chamois in the United States.

wash'us *Charley and I made our lucky up the wash'us chimney.* {Oliver Twist 50}
Dialect for wash house.

wassail ... *they sat down by the huge fire of blazing logs to a substantial supper and a mighty bowl of wassail* ... {Pickwick Papers 28}
Liquor, usually spiced ale, with which healths, or toasts, were drunk at Christmas.

watch *Then there was the watch with staff and lantern crying the hour* ... {Barnaby Rudge 16}
The night watchman.

watch and ward *[He] signified his pleasure that [the jury] should retire under watch and ward, and retired himself.* {Tale of Two Cities 2-3}
An emphatic way of saying that they should be watched carefully.

watch-box ... *bearing about the same relative proportion to the size of the room as a lady's pocket handkerchief might to the floor of a watch-box.* {Pickwick Papers 14}
A sort of sentry box, with a seat and half door.

watch-guard ... *a pale youth with a plated watch-guard.* {Pickwick Papers 32}
A chain or ribbon used to secure a watch when it is being worn.

watch-lining *An old silk watch-lining, worked with beads.* {Little Dorrit 1-30}
A cloth or paper placed between the inner and outer case of an old-fashioned two-case pocket watch. It was usually decorated. It was also called a 'watch-paper'.

watchman *"Now, Sammy," said Mr. Weller, taking off his great coat with much deliberation, "just you step out and fetch in a watchman."* {Pickwick Papers 33}
Men who patrolled the streets, especially after sunset. Before the London police force was organized they were often old, decrepit men who frequently slept in their watchmen's boxes and were of little value in controlling crime.

watchman's box ... *and in an ecstasy of unrequited love, taken to wrench off door-knockers, and invert the boxes of rheumatic watchmen!* {Barnaby Rudge 41}

A watch-box, a sort of sentry box, with a seat and half door. Knocking them over was a common prank.

watchman's rattle ... *with a face carved out of very hard material, that had just as much play of expression as a watchman's rattle* {Our Mutual Friend 1-5}
A noisemaker carried by the watchman to sound an alarm. It consists of a short stick on top of which a small box rotates. When the stick is swung, the box rotates and makes a loud ratcheting sound.

watch-pocket over his head *The possibility of going to sleep unless it were ticking gently beneath his pillow or in the watch-pocket over his head had never entered Mr. Pickwick's brain.* {Pickwick Papers 22}
A pocket affixed to the head of a bed to hold the sleeper's watch during the night.

water, go up the water ... *who had lodgings of his own in town; who had a free admission to Covent Garden theatre; who always dressed according to the fashions of the months; who went up the water twice a week in the season ...* {Sketches, Horatio Sparkins}
To go up the water was to take a boat trip up the Thames river. The word 'water' sometimes referred to the Thames river.

water-butt *You're really worse than the dripping of a hundred water-butts outside the window ...* {Barnaby Rudge 51}
A small keg or barrel used for water, usually drinking water.

water-cart *"Wonders'ull never cease," added Sam, speaking to himself. "I'm wery much mistaken if that 'ere Jingle worn't a-doin' somethin' in the water-cart way!"* {Pickwick Papers 45}
An allusion to crying tears, from the water cart used to sprinkle water on the dusty streets.

watering-place *There is a good deal of water about Mudfog, and yet it is not exactly the sort of town for a watering-place, either.* {Sketches, The Public Life of Mr. Tulrumble}
A health resort with mineral springs for drinking or the ocean for bathing. Some of these spas were considered very fashionable and were visited more for social reasons than health.

water-line ... *whenever the light struck aslant, afar off, upon a cloud or sail or green hillside or water-line, it was just the same* ... {Great Expectations 15}
The outline of a coast seen from a distance.

water-meadow *'Water-meadows, or such like,' she had sometimes murmured* ... *when she had raised her head and taken any note of the real objects about her.* {Our Mutual Friend 3-8}
A meadow periodically overflowed by a stream.

waterman ... *with a brass label and a number round his neck, [he] looked as if he were catalogued in some collection of rarities. This was the waterman. "Here you are, sir. Now, then, fust cab!"* {Pickwick Papers 2}
1. At each cab stand there was a man who watered the horses and also saw that the cabs were hired in rotation.
Mealy's father was a waterman ... {David Copperfield 11}
2. A Thames waterman was the operator of a small boat that acted as a water taxi. It is not clear from the text which of these two meanings is intended in the second quotation.

water-mill ... *the wheels sent the road drift flying about our heads like spray from a water-mill.* {Bleak House 6}
Water wheel, the large paddle wheel driven by flowing water and used to power machinery.

water-party *If Mr. Hardy should call, say I've gone to Mrs. Taunton's about that water-party.* {Sketches, The Steam Excursion}
A social gathering on a boat on the Thames river.

water-plug *The water-plug being left in solitude, its overflowings sullenly congealed, and turned to misanthropic ice.* {A Christmas Carol 1}
The public water pipe in the square. The plug was the valve that turned the water on and off. The construction remains in the word 'fireplug'.

water-rate *Here was a collector of water-rates without his book, without his pen and ink, without his double knock* ... {Nicholas Nickleby 14}
A tax levied for the supply of water.

wax-chandler ... *Miss Snevellici was happily married to an affluent young wax-chandler who had supplied the theater with candles* ... {Nicholas Nickleby 48}
A maker or seller of wax candles.

wax doll *My father had once been a favorite of hers, I believe; but she was mortally affronted by his marriage on the ground that my mother was a 'wax-doll'* ... {David Copperfield 1}
A doll with head and chest made of molded wax. The implication is that she was pretty but useless.

wax-end ... *adjusting the wax-end which was twisted round the bottom of his cane, for purposes of parochial flagellation.* {Oliver Twist 7}
Shoemaker's thread, coated with cobbler's wax.

wax-light ... *Mr. Bucket with a wax-light in his hand, holding it above his head* ... {Bleak House 56}
A wax candle.

wax-work ... *the wax-work that had travelled into our neighborhood* ... {David Copperfield 2}
A wax museum, an exhibition of wax replicas of famous people.

way *Way! This monosyllable was addressed to the horse, who didn't mind it at all.* {Cricket on the Hearth 2}
A call to a horse to stop, like whoa.

way, in the way *See after your friend, and be in the way to-morrow at one, do you hear?* ... {Pickwick Papers 47}
To be in the way is to be within reach, nearby.

way-bill, waybill ... *when the coachman and guard were comparing notes for the last time before starting on the subject of the way-bill* ... {Nicholas Nickleby 5}
A document listing passengers and goods carried by a coach.

wayward ... *she was rather what might be called wayward* ... {David Copperfield 21}
Wrong-headed, disobedient, refractory.

wayworn *Suppose some of the boys had seen me coming through Canterbury, wayworn and ragged, and should find me out?* {David Copperfield 16}
Worn out by traveling.

weales *I'm covered with weales and I smart so!* {Our Mutual Friend 4-8}
Wheals. The red, elevated marks on the skin produced by a blow from, for example, a whip.

weasen *... a short thin weasen blear-eyed old woman, palsy-stricken, and hideously ugly ...* {Nicholas Nickleby 51}
(See **weazen**)

weathercock *... the Town Hall, with a clock tower and a weathercock.* {Old Curiosity Shop 28}
A wind vane. It often had the figure of a rooster on it.

weather-glass *All the weather-glasses in the shop are in low spirits, and the rain already shines upon the cocked hat of the Wooden Midshipman.* {Dombey & Son 4}
A barometer made of a glass tube closed at one end and containing a liquid, the open end being placed in a container of the same liquid.

weazen *He is a town made article, of small stature and weazen features, but may be perceived from a considerable distance by means of his very tall hat.* {Bleak House 20}
Wizened, shrunken, shriveled.

weeds *It was ... part of Mrs. Heep's humility that she still wore weeds.* {David Copperfield 17}
... my mother's mourning weeds ... {David Copperfield 1}
Usually means the black clothing worn for mourning, but sometimes just means clothing.

ween *Of right choice foods are his meals, I ween ...* {Pickwick Papers 6}
To think or believe.

weigh, under weigh ... *[the ship]* Tartar Frigate *under weigh as on the plates* ... {Dombey & Son 4}
Under way, moving.

well ... *the banking-houses, with their secrets of strong rooms and wells, the keys of which were in a very few secret pockets* ... {Little Dorrit 2-10}
1. A deep, dark place.
Climbing to a high chamber in a well of houses, he threw himself down in his clothes ... {Tale of Two Cities 2-5}
2. A narrow shaft formed by the walls of houses, for air and light.

Wellington boots ... *his short black trousers drawn up so high in the legs by the exertion of seating himself, that they scarcely reached below the tops of his Wellington boots.* {Nicholas Nickleby 34}
The name applied to several kinds of boot, supposedly introduced by the Duke of Wellington. Usually refers to a boot reaching just below the knee and worn under the trousers.

Welsh wig *To say nothing of his Welsh wig, which was as plain and stubborn a Welsh wig as ever was worn* ... {Dombey & Son 4}
Not a wig at all, but a worsted cap.

wen ... *we had a footboy once, who had not only a wart, but a wen also, and a very large wen too, and he demanded to have his wages raised in consequence, because he found it came very expensive.* {Nicholas Nickleby 45}
A rounded cyst in the skin, now called a sebaceous or epidermal cyst.

wet the other eye *Moisten your clay, wet the other eye, drink, man!* {Old Curiosity Shop 62}
Take another drink, drink one glass after another.

whalebone ... *a faded green umbrella with plenty of whalebone sticking through the bottom* ... {Pickwick Papers 27}
A stiff but flexible horn-like material obtained from the baleen of a whale. Most often used for stiffening cloth, as in corset stays and umbrella ribs.

wharfinger *Mr. Winkle is a wharfinger, sir, at the canal, sir.* {Pickwick Papers 50}
The owner of a wharf.

what time *What time Mrs. Veneering, carrying baby dressed as a bridesmaid, flits about among the company . . .* {Our Mutual Friend 1-10}
While; during the time that something is happening.

wheat *Patches of poor rye where corn should have been, patches of poor peas and beans, patches of most coarse vegetable substitutes for wheat.* {Tale of Two Cities 2-8}
Although the British use the word corn for wheat, and sometimes for other grains, the word 'wheat' is the same as in the United States.

wheeler *The boy on the wheeler touched his hat, and setting spurs to his horse, to the end that they might go in brilliantly, all four broke into a smart canter . . .* {Old Curiosity Shop 47}
The wheel horse, the one harnessed just in front of the wheels.

wheelwright *. . . talking and drinking and shaking hands at every bar and tap, friendly with every waggoner, wheelwright, blacksmith, and toll-taker, yet never seeming to lose time . . .* {Bleak House 57}
One who makes wheels and wheeled vehicles.

wherry *It was flood tide when Daniel Quilp sat himself down in the wherry to cross to the opposite shore.* {Old Curiosity Shop 5}
A shallow, light boat often used on the rivers.

whet *. . . Jerry stood: aiming at the prisoner the beery breath of a whet he had taken . . .* {Tale of Two Cities 2-2}
A small drink.

whether or no *I don't know why you should be sorry . . . but I am engaged to Mr. Turveydrop, whether or no, and he is very fond of me.* {Bleak House 14}
Whether or not.

whip   ... *you're a wery good whip and can do what you like with your horses, we know.* {Pickwick Papers 13}
A coachman, a driver of a coach.

whip-lash   *From this ledger he drew forth a couple of whip-lashes, three or four small buckles, a little sample-bag of corn, and finally a small roll of very dirty bank-notes* ... {Pickwick Papers 43}
The thin end of a whip.

whipster   *I recollected it well when I first saw this whipster; but I remember it better now.* {Nicholas Nickleby 34}
An insignificant or contemptible person.

whist   *Two card-tables were made up in the adjoining card-room, and two pair of old ladies and a corresponding number of stout gentlemen were executing whist therein.* {Pickwick Papers 2}
A card game similar to bridge.

whitebait   ... *they had become of one hue by being cooked in batter among the whitebait.* {Our Mutual Friend 4-4}
A small edible fish, so called because of its color and that it was often used as bait.

white-livered   *Five of 'em strung up in a row; and none left to play booty, or turn white-livered!* {Oliver Twist 9}
Slang for coward.

whitening   *It was a stiff leather purse, with a snap, and had three bright shillings in it, which Peggoty had evidently polished up with whitening, for my greater delight.* {David Copperfield 5}
Bleach or whitewash.

White sand and grey sand   *I've been singing. I've been taking a part in White sand and grey sand.* {Little Dorrit 1-32}
A traditional song, a three-part round.

whitesmith   ... *one man's a blacksmith, and one's a whitesmith, and one's a goldsmith, and one's a coppersmith.* {Great Expectations 27}

A person who works with tin, a tinsmith. Also, a person who polishes and finishes metal objects.

whitey-brown ... *a whitey-brown parcel--flat and three-cornered--containing sundry small adornments which were to be put on upstairs* ... {Nicholas Nickleby 9}
A coarse paper of light-brown color.

wicker bottle ... *a morose and lonely man, who consorted with nobody but himself and an old wicker bottle, which fitted into his large deep waistcoat pocket* ... {Pickwick Papers 29}
A bottle encased in a wicker cover.

wicket ... *startled by the apparition of Mr. Bumble, the beadle, striving to undo the wicket of the garden-gate* ... {Oliver Twist 2}
1. A small door or gate built into a larger gate.
... *every little indentation made in the fresh grass by bat or wicket, ball or player's foot, sheds out its perfume on the night.* {Martin Chuzzlewit 36}
2. The five sticks of wood at which the bowler in a cricket game throws the ball.

wicket-gate *The sun was setting when they reached the wicket-gate at which the path began* ... {Old Curiosity Shop 16}
A small gate into a field or enclosure.

widow's mite ... *Mr. Gusher spoke for and hour and a half on the subject to a meeting, including two charity schools of small boys and girls, who were specially reminded of the widow's mite, and requested to come forward with halfpence and be acceptable sacrifices* ... {Bleak House 15}
A small contribution. From the fact that a widow could ill afford to make a large one.

wight *And woe to Boythorn or other daring wight who shall presumptuously contest an inch with him!* {Bleak House 16}
A person.

wiglomeration ... *if I could get out of the mountains of wiglomeration on which my unfortunate name has been so long bestowed (which I can't) or could level them by the extinction of my own original right..., I would do it this hour.* {Bleak House 35}
A made-up word combining lawyer's 'wig' with 'conglomeration'.

wind is low ... *and always goes better when the wind's low with people, than when it's high* ... {Oliver Twist 8}
Slang for money is short.

winding-sheet *"There's a blessed-looking candle!" says Tony, pointing to the heavily burning taper on his table with a great cabbage head and a long winding-sheet.* {Bleak House 32}
Solidified candle drippings, superstitiously believed to be omens of death.

window-board ...*the fruit-pie maker displayed on his well-scrubbed window-board large white compositions of flour and dripping, ornamented with pink stains, giving rich promise of fruit within* ... {Sketches, Scotland-yard}
The wooden ledge at the base of the outside of the shop window. It was used to display the goods for sale inside.

window tax *The amount of money he annually diverts from wholesome and useful purposes in the United Kingdom, would be a set-off against the Window Tax.* {Reprinted Pieces, The Begging-letter Writer}
There was a tax on windows, designed to fall most heavily on owners of mansions. Because many windows were then bricked up and new construction had as few windows as possible, British homes became dark and stuffy.

Windsor arm-chair ... *sitting* ... *in a clean cap and a Windsor arm-chair* ... {Somebody's Luggage 1}
A wooden chair with a back made of upright rods and a crosspiece.

Windsor soap *[We] came into a peculiar atmosphere of bilge-water and Windsor soap* ... {The Uncommercial Traveller, Aboard Ship}
A scented brown soap.

wine-coopering ... *he was not brought up to the law, but to the wine-coopering.* {Great Expectations 5}
The making of wine barrels. A cooper is a barrel maker.

wine-lees ... *one tall joker... scrawled upon a wall with his finger dipped in muddy wine-lees* ... {Tale of Two Cities 1-5}
The sediment precipitated from wine.

wine-vaults ... *would you have any objections to mention why, being in general so delicately circumspect in your conduct, you come into a wine-vaults before breakfast?* {Bleak House 33}
A pretentious name for a public house, a pub or tavern.

wings ... *the large dining-room... presented a strange jumble of flats, flies, wings, lamps, bridges, clouds, thunder and lightening... and various other messes in theatrical slang included under the comprehensive name of "properties."* {Sketches, Mrs. Joseph Porter}
The flat, painted scenery that stood at the sides of the stage. It later came to mean the space at the sides of the stage.

winkle ... *the oyster in his pearly bed, the still mite in his home of cheese, the very winkle of your country in his shelly lair* ... {Martin Chuzzlewit 21}
A pun ('very winkle') on periwinkle, an edible mollusk.

winter-pippin ... *the Doctor had a streaked face like a winter-pippin* ... {The Battle of Life 1}
A kind of winter apple. There are many varieties of apples called pippin.

wipe ... *he's a-sortin the wipes.* {Oliver Twist 8}
Slang for a pocket handkerchief.

wire blinds ... *a spacious house, resplendent in stucco and plate-glass, with wire blinds in all the windows* ... {Martin Chuzzlewit 27}
A kind of shutter or blind made of woven wire.

withal *Mr. Trundle was in high feather and spirits, but a little nervous withal.* {Pickwick Papers 28}
In addition, at the same time.

withers wrung *This was intended for Mr. Toodle's private edification, but Rob the Grinder, whose withers were not unwrung, caught the words as they were spoken.* {Dombey & Son 38}
To wring is to inflict pain by pressure or twisting. The withers is that part of a horse's back between the shoulder blades. In the example here the implication is that Rob the Grinder had already been caused some discomfort.

withy, withies *... the women cutting the vines, creepers, and withies for the lashings.* {English Prisoners 2}
A flexible branch of willow.

witler *Mr. Chickweed, licensed witler ...* {Oliver Twist 31}
Dialect for 'victualer', one who is licensed to sell food.

woman *Professor Woodensconce has just called 'woman,' but the coin having lodged in a beam, is a long time coming down again.* {Sketches, Full Report of the Second Meeting of the Mudfog Association}
The side of the coin bearing the figure of Britannia, the female representation of Great Britain.

wont *... the fire burnt clear and high, and the crickets in the hearth-stone chirped with a more than wonted satisfaction.* {Barnaby Rudge 11}
Habitual, customary, usual.

wood-sawyer *The wood-sawyer, who was a little man with a redundancy of gesture ...* {Tale of Two Cities 3-5}
One who saws wood as an occupation.

wooden measure (see **Grenadier wooden measure**)

wool-packs *... a few boys in smock-frocks were lying asleep on heavy packages, wool-packs, and other articles that were scattered about ...* {Pickwick Papers 10}
A large bag in which wool is packed for shipping or sale.

woolsack *Mr. Micawber saw himself, in his judicial mind's eye, on the woolsack.* {David Copperfield 36}
The seat of the Lord Chancellor in the House of Lords is made of a large sack of wool.

worked *. . . to say nothing of the blue sash which floated down her back, or the worked apron, or the long gloves, or the green gauze scarf . . .* {Nicholas Nickleby 9}
Ornamented with needlework, embroidered.

workhouse *"And the Union workhouses?" demanded Scrooge. "Are they still in operation?"* {A Christmas Carol 1}
A place in which paupers were housed and the able-bodied among them required to work. The Union workhouse was supported by the united funds of several parishes.

works *. . . and went past gas-works, rope-walks, boat-builder's yards . . .* {David Copperfield 3}
1. Factories, industrial work places.
. . . and outshouted the mob again, as if lungs were cast-iron with steel works. {Pickwick Papers 13}
2. Mechanical parts, e.g., the works of a watch.

worrit *"God bless my soul, I believe people turn Catholics a'purpose to vex and worrit me," cried the Lord Mayor . . .* {Barnaby Rudge 61}
Worry or distress.

worry *. . . Mr. Guppy takes him in hand as a witness, patting him into this shape, that shape, and the other shape like a butterman dealing with so much butter, and worrying him according to the best models.* {Bleak House 19}
1. To vex, distress, or persecute.
Hissing and worrying the animal till he was nearly mad . . . {Old Curiosity Shop 21}
2. To irritate an animal by pretending to attack it.

worsted *. . . clapping his worsted gloves in rapture!* {David Copperfield 17}
A fine wool used in knitted goods.

wrapt ... *your eyes fast closed, and your senses wrapt in perfect uncon-sciousness.* {Oliver Twist 9}
Wrapped, enfolded, sunk in.

wristbands *As Sam Weller said this he tucked up his wristbands ... to intimate his readiness to set to work immediately.* {Pickwick Papers 39}
The portions of a shirt covering the wrists, the cuffs, and usually made of fancy material or lace.

writing-master ... *the writing-master touched them up afterwards with a magnifying glass and a silver pen ...* {Nicholas Nickleby 26}
A teacher of penmanship.

yard *When mariners at sea, outlying upon the icy yards, were tossed and swung above the howling ocean dreadfully.* {The Haunted Man 1}
The horizontal pole, attached to the mast, from which the square sail of a ship was suspended. Sailors were forced, in all kinds of weather, to climb on the yards to work the sails.

yard-measure *... the little bit of wax-candle she kept for her thread ... the little house with a thatched roof, where the yard-measure lived ... her work-box with a sliding lid ...* {David Copperfield 2}
A tape measure. In this quotation it was one kept in a box shaped like a little house.

yellow-boys *The delight of picking up the money--the bright, shining yellow-boys--and sweeping 'em into ones pocket!* {Old Curiosity Shop 42}
A gold coin, a guinea or sovereign.

yellow jack *... his elder brother died of yellow jack in the West Indies.* {Dombey & Son 10}
Slang for yellow fever, a frequently fatal tropical disease spread by mosquitos.

yellow-soap *The morning arrived: the children were yellow-soaped und flunnelled, and towelled, till their face shone again ...* {Sketches, The Ladies' Societies}
Made from tallow, rosin, and alkali, yellow-soap was a coarse soap used mainly for laundry. To be yellow-soaped was to be scrubbed with tha material.

yeoman *At the Queen's palace, a double guard, the yeoman on duty, the groom-porters, and all other attendants, were stationed in the pas-*

sages and on the staircases . . . {Barnaby Rudge 67}
The Yeoman of the Guard was a royal bodyguard.

Yoicks *Or if Yoicks would be in better keeping, consider that I said Yoicks.* {Our Mutual Friend 3-10}
A call used in fox hunting, supposed to urge on a pack of dogs.

yore . . . *as they are known to have done in days of yore.* {Martin Chuzzlewit 3}
Time long past.

yokel . . . *this wasn't done by a yokel* . . . {Oliver Twist 31}
Slang for someone from the country, a hick.

younker *Sit down by the fire, younker, and rest yourself* . . . {Oliver Twist 22}
Young person, child.

zest *Such zests as his particular little phial of cayenne pepper* . . . {Little Dorrit 1-8}
Something that imparts a relish or piquancy, improving the flavor of a food.

zone . . . *what a beautiful necklace. Ah! How it glitters! Ear-rings, too, and bracelets, and a zone for your waist.* {Martin Chuzzlewit 53}
A girdle or belt.